Caroline Moorehead's books include biographies of Freya Stark and Bertrand Russell. She has worked for *The Times* and the *Independent,* is a regular book reviewer and writes and makes television films about human rights.

THE LOST
TREASURES
OF TROY

Caroline Moorehead

PHOENIX GIANTS

To Teddy

A PHOENIX GIANT PAPERBACK
First published in Great Britain in 1994
by Weidenfeld & Nicolson

This edition published in 1995 by Phoenix,
a division of Orion Books Ltd,
Orion House, 5 Upper Saint Martin's Lane,
London WC2H 9EA

A CIP record for this book is available
from the British Library

ISBN 1 85799 340 3

Printed and bound in Great Britain by
Butler & Tanner Ltd, Frome and London

Homer wrote a romance; for nobody can believe that Troy and
Agamemnon had any more existence than the golden apples of the
Hesperides. He had no intention to write a history, but only to amuse
us.

Pascal

MICYLLOS: Well, tell us about Troy first.
           Was it all just as Homer says?
COCKEREL: What would he know about it?
           When all that happened, he was a camel in Bactria.

Lucian: *The Dream of the Cockerel*

I have proved that in a remote antiquity there was in the plain of Troy
a large city, destroyed of old by a fearful catastrophe, which had on the
hill of Hissarlik only its acropolis, with its temples and a few other large
edifices, whilst its lower city extended in an easterly, southerly, and
westerly direction ... and that this city answers perfectly to the Homeric
description of the site of sacred Ilios ...

Heinrich Schliemann

CONTENTS

PART THREE: BERLIN AND AFTER

ILLUSTRATIONS

Sources

Sources have been credited where known

[1] Illustrated London News
[2] Alex L. Mélas
[3] Mrs Gray Johnson Poole
[4] Hulton-Deutsch
[5] ARTnews

Map in the text

The Eastern Mediterranean, showing
Mycenae and Troy   page 68

ACKNOWLEDGEMENTS

This book would not have been possible without the discovery by two Russian art historians, Konstantin Akinsha and Grigorii Kozlov, of documents relating to Schliemann's treasure in the Moscow state archives. Their persistence, and the story they have put together about the looting of art treasures during the Second World War, has opened the entire subject of the return of looted art, and negotiations are now under way all over Europe for some settlement for the thefts that took place between 1939 and 1945. Their own account of their discoveries is to appear shortly.

Nor would the book have been possible without the help and advice of a number of British archaeologists – Donald Easton, Oliver Dickinson and Ken Wardle – who talked to me at length about Troy, Homer, Mycenae and nineteenth-century archaeology, and spent much time correcting my mistakes – those that remain are, of course, entirely mine. I am most grateful to them, as well as to Klaus Goldmann, current director of the Pre-and-Early History Museum in Berlin who is leading the search for art objects looted from his museum during the last war.

I am indebted to the Librarian and staff of the Gennadius Library in Athens, where Schliemann's papers are kept, of the British Library and its Manuscripts Department, of the London Library, the Public Records Office and the Library of the Imperial War Museum.

I would also like to thank Francesca Beddy, Jane Birkett, Boris Brodsky, Andrei Chegodaev, Charles Elliott, John Erickson, Alexander Georgievitch Halturnin, Robert Haupt, Teddy Hodgkin, Sinclair Hood, Geoffrey Hosking, Michael J. Kurtz, Catherine Lightfoot, Alexander Morozov, Julia Neronova, Alexei Rastorguyev, Sir Frank Roberts, Harry

Shukman, Ann Tusa, Mechthilde Unverzacht, Saveli Yamschikov, as well as my husband, Jeremy Swift, my publisher Ion Trewin, and my agent Anthony Sheil. I also wish to thank Douglas Matthews for his index.

Caroline Moorehead
July 1994

FOREWORD

For classical scholars of the eighteenth and nineteenth centuries, the story of the siege of Troy, told by Homer in the *Iliad*, was one of the great puzzles of antiquity. The archaeologist who solved it was guaranteed a place in history. In an age when every educated person read the classics, and the names of Agamemnon, Helen and Priam were as familiar as those of Gideon or Abraham, to locate the besieged city was as exciting a challenge as discovering the Ark on Mount Ararat.

What made it all so difficult was that there was no proof that the Trojan Wars had been anything other than legends of long-lost epic heroes, sung by bards, and handed down from generation to generation in memory of earlier, more glorious times. There were even doubts about Homer himself, and when and where he might have lived.

So historians and classicists argued, and speculated, and rode up and down the Troad, the land of Troy described by the Greek historian Strabo as lying on the north-west shores of the subcontinent of Asia Minor, stretching south from the Dardanelles. 'The *Iliad*,' wrote Alexander Kinglake, who visited the area in 1844, trying to reconstruct the war between Trojans and Achaeans, 'line by line, I clasped to my brain with reverence as well as love ... the rapturous, and earnest reading of my childhood which made me bend forward so longingly to the plains of Troy.' There were many others like him; but no remains to provide any evidence.

In the absence of proof, faith was all that was left. And no one had more faith in Homer than a grocer's apprentice called Heinrich Schliemann, from the sandy plains of northern Germany. Where ortho-dox scholars floundered, Schliemann was a dreamer who forced his dream to come true, a lonely, driven, restless man who was both ruthless and anxious, single-minded and generous, and who was capable of great courage. The story of his odd life, and his quest for Troy and the great palaces of the Mycenaean age is one of the most dramatic tales of nineteenth-century archaeology.

But the story of the gold of Troy does not end with Schliemann's death in 1890. It continues in Berlin, during both world wars and in the early summer months of 1945. It takes up again in the Soviet Union, under Stalin. And it is still unfolding today, in Yeltsin's Russia. A new puzzle, almost as strange and challenging as the one that faced nineteenth-century archaeologists is, at the time of writing, on the verge of being solved.

PART ONE

THE MAKING OF
AN ARCHAEOLOGIST

1

PANDORA AND
HER BOX

A ll through the 1950s and 1960s, strange stories were told in secret among the art historians and curators of the museums in the Soviet Union. Some said they had seen lost Impressionist paintings hanging unlabelled on the walls of their directors' offices. Others spoke of glimpsing engravings, stacked in basement vaults. Others still whispered of bolted storerooms, to which only the most senior curators had access. There was talk of fragments of catalogues, of confusing lists, of unpublished memoirs, of heavy sealed crates full of pottery, gold, silver and jewellery, of boxes of papers and documents. But the talk was always furtive, among friends, behind closed doors, far from the museum offices. Such matters, during Stalin's lifetime and long after, were secrets of state.

With *perestroika* in the early eighties, the rumours grew bolder. Were there really hidden paintings by Degas, Delacroix, Manet and Monet? Engravings by Dürer? Drawings by Palladio? If there were, how did they get to the Soviet Union? Why was no one prepared to talk about them?

And was it really possible that the best-kept secret of them all, the whereabouts of Priam's treasure from the city of Troy – the nine thousand or so pieces of gold, silver and bronze, and the diadem said to have been worn by Helen, whose beauty sparked off the ten-year siege – was actually hidden away in some cellar in Moscow? Could it be true that Schliemann's unique archaeological find, donated to his native Germany in 1880, was not, as had always been assumed, lost? That it had not, after all, been destroyed in the Allied bombing of Berlin, or melted in the fires that engulfed the city as the Russians moved in, sending, as one story had it, rivers of gold and silver flowing down the museum's stairs ? That Priam's gold was not lost at all – but stolen ?

Konstantin Akinsha and Grigorii Kozlov met at the University of Moscow in the late 1970s. They were both students of art history, and they soon discovered that they shared a common fascination with private collections and archives, a subject largely taboo during the Stalinist years. They met elderly collectors who told them tales about the war which they found hard to believe, but when they were alone they often spoke of the way so much art had gone missing in the chaos of post-war Europe. The rumours, they agreed, were beginning to have a peculiarly consistent pattern. In the corridors of the Pushkin Museum in Moscow where, in 1987, Grigorii Kozlov had himself transferred from the Ministry of Culture to work in the new section on Private Collections, he heard talk of basement rooms for which no one was ever lent a key.

In the muddled excitement of *perestroika*, rumours of this kind flourished. As bold questioning, long punished and repressed, became the tone of this new age, so Akinsha and Kozlov found themselves in possession of a story that soon assumed unbelievable dimensions, a story involving the planned and systematic looting of art, during World War II, by Russian 'trophy brigades' from the countries which they occupied. Victorious armies have always looted, but the thefts of the Nazis – who had proved the greatest pillagers of all – had to a very large extent been uncovered and the treasures returned to the museums and private individuals they had been stolen from. Here was something very different : a vast, unknown haul, kept secret for nearly half a century. There was talk not of thousands of objects, nor even of tens of thousands, but of thefts runing into several million separate items. What was awesome was not the nature of these thefts, but the scale and purposefulness with which they had been carried out.

In the winter of 1990, Akinsha, then working as a curator for the Museum of Western and Oriental Art in Kiev, was contacted by an editor at *Art News*, an American art magazine which had long been interested in the subject of war loot. Akinsha undertook to push ahead with what had been, until then, somewhat casual research and out of this, in April 1991, came a first article ; its title was 'Spoils of War'. The story Akinsha told, backed by substantial research, was little short of fantastic : thousands of masterpieces of Western painting, from a Velásquez portrait to Cézanne's view of Mont-Sainte-Victoire, from an

El Greco *Saint Bernard* to *A Walk* by Degas, drawings, books, rare manuscripts, Aubusson carpets, prehistoric pottery, bronze cups, gems, silver candelabra, Roman sculpture – all hidden in secret locations scattered around the Soviet Union. Here, it seemed, lay the missing treasures of Soviet-occupied Europe.

Akinsha and Kozlov had decided to keep quiet about where, precisely, the treasures were being kept. New to the ways of the Western world, they regarded their discoveries as something that the Soviet authorities, in the growing mood of freedom, would welcome and encourage. They were quite wrong. Their revelations were indeed sensational, but made them extremely unpopular. Even before the article in *Art News* was published, details of what it contained had been leaked. News agencies and newspapers throughout the world, from New York to Tokyo, Sidney to London, Bonn to Madrid, picked up the story and gave it their front pages. Masterpieces belonging not to the Soviet Union, but to the whole world, had been stolen and kept secret for almost fifty years, and even the new leaders who had professed *glasnost* had not admitted having them – here, indeed, was what Akinsha was soon calling the 'last secret of the Cold War'. No one in the Kremlin was pleased. Kozlov, accused by the Pushkin Museum of being a 'traitor', was sacked.

In order to punish Prometheus for stealing fire and bestowing it on mortals, Zeus is said to have fashioned Pandora – the first woman – out of earth, presented her with the choicest gifts of the gods and given her a jar which, when opened, released all manner of evils. What box had Akinsha and Kozlov now opened? Their article launched the greatest treasure hunt the world has ever known. It has come to involve six countries, hundreds of art historians, curators, librarians and archivists, dozens of international lawyers, and, increasingly, politicians and governments. For Akinsha and Kozlov, it was the start of a new life as art detectives, prompted first by the scandal sparked off by their disclosures in *Art News*, and then by further finds of documents in five different archives in Moscow, all – astonishingly – open to the public. The absurd thing is that this well-guarded state secret, the existence and location of war loot brought back to the USSR in 1945, was in fact no secret at all: it had been freely available to researchers in papers filed in the mid-1940s, when the trophy art was regarded as legitimate booty, a fair repayment for the destruction by the Nazis of some of the USSR's most important picture collections, monasteries, palaces and churches. But no one had previously thought to look.

What many of these papers consisted of were lists – transport lists made out by the 'trophy brigades' which had been sent to Berlin to coordinate the shipping of the treasures back to the USSR, museum lists compiled by the German curators as they packed up their treasures for safekeeping at the beginning of the war, reception lists by Russian art experts drawn up as they unpacked the loot and decided where it should be stored. Most remarkable of all, there were even lists put together in the 1950s, when a political decision was taken to return to East Germany art looted when the GDR was still in the Soviet zone of occupation. (Surprisingly little notice, in the West, was taken of the returned treasures: once they had been despatched – over one-and-a-half million art objects – silence fell again.) These lists proved extremely, embarrassingly, revealing, for they set out, object by object, what was held and where, and where it came from: like the 490 Old Master drawings from the Franz Koenigs collection in Rotterdam, hidden in the vaults of the Pushkin Museum in Moscow; or the forty-four drawings by Goya and Daumier, and Goya's *The Disasters of War*, from the German Gerstenberg collection, concealed in the basement of the Hermitage museum in Leningrad – and the Schliemann gold.

For many months after the Akinsha and Kozlov revelations, the Soviet authorities hesitated. To admit to holding further looted art could only lead to vast claims of ownership and restitution. To say nothing was to look ever more foolish, as month after month the two young art historians uncovered increasingly precise and incriminating information. Soon, there were very few people interested in art anywhere in the world who did not know that the previously respected curators and directors of the major Soviet galleries and museums had, in fact, been lying when they declared that they knew nothing and that their basements and vaults contained no secret treasures. Still the Ministry of Culture dithered. It was not until the autumn of 1991 that a formal public acknowledgement was at last made about the secret depositories. Soon afterwards Akinsha and Kozlov, following a series of leads, uncovered over three hundred Old Master drawings belonging to the Kunsthalle in Bremen, stolen from a cellar during the war by a former Red Army officer called Viktor Baldin, then taken back by him and hidden when he became curator of a small Moscow museum. As a first gesture, the Soviets reluctantly returned them to Bremen.

For a while, it looked as if this might have unlocked the door to the Soviet depositories. A Soviet–German General Relations Treaty, signed by Chancellor Helmut Kohl and President Gorbachev in November 1990, agreed to the reciprocal return, without compensation, of 'art treasures illegally taken away'. The Soviets and the Germans subsequently undertook to form a joint commission to deal with the whole subject of wartime plunder, and diplomats, cultural officials and art experts began to catalogue the missing art. The Soviets also agreed to cooperate with the Dutch government in 'locating' the 490 Old Master drawings from the Koenigs collection, sold to the Nazis in 1941 and taken by the Soviet forces in 1945.

These moves have recently been somewhat checked by political events in the former Soviet Union, where the crumbling of the Communist system has put paid to any hope of a speedy agreement on art restitutions. President Yeltsin has stated that the embarrassingly named 'trophies' are indeed to be returned, but only on a mutual basis, piece by piece, in exchange for objects of 'equivalent artistic value' stolen from the USSR by the Germans: a truly confusing challenge, for questions of artistic equivalence are not easily settled and, in any case, the Red Army looted far less destructively than the Germans, who demonstrated their contempt for all things Slav by wholesale vandalism and destruction in the USSR.

How soon the rest of the missing art works will be retrieved from the secret depositories, identified, catalogued and returned to their owners – many of whom are no longer alive – no one can say, though it now seems likely that more than half a million looted pictures, sculptures and archives of various kinds, worth many billions of dollars, are still in the former Soviet Union. The Soviets have taken to calling their fifty-year concealment 'temporary keeping'.

Nor is it known how the art objects have fared during this period, for while the boxes of treasures and pictures that are in the vaults of the major museums are thought to have been well preserved, those that ended up in monastery cellars and outbuildings may have rotted or been stolen. Thousands of pictures have come to light in the fourteenth-century monastery of Zagorsk, 70 kilometres north of Moscow, place of pilgrimage for successive generations of Tsars, where they were hidden in the Utichya Tower, a five-tiered blue-and-white baroque bell-tower, built in the mid-eighteenth century and strongly suspected to be very damp. Other paintings and art objects may well never be seen again. In 1983 the Museum of Military Medicine in Leningrad was closed for restoration and its collection moved into huts in the courtyard. When, in 1991, these were finally opened, many of the 23,550 trophy objects which had been stored there were found to have vanished. Since then, some of these have turned up in art auctions in the West.

As predicted, the discovery of the museum lists has led to a baffling outbreak of claims, not only from museums and private collectors throughout Holland, France, Hungary and Poland, but from the newly independent Soviet states who are now asking that the art taken from their museums for the greater glory of Leningrad and Moscow be returned to them. While no one is yet sure quite where this may lead, the Ukraine is said to be talking in terms of three million objects, among them early finds excavated in the area of the Black Sea in the late nineteenth century, as well as the ceremonial staff of their national hero, Mazepa, who led the struggle for Ukrainian independence against Peter the Great. The Russian Orthodox Church is also pressing claims : its new Patriarch, Alexei II, is calling for the return of all church buildings, books and treasures confiscated by the state after the revolution of 1917. He is supported by the Union of Russian People, a revived ultra-nationalist anti-Semitic group, famous in the old days for its pogroms, and which is now arguing that icons and churches were designed for prayer and not as museum exhibits and public lavatories.

Within the Russian art world, and among the men and women sitting on the commission set up to debate the future of trophy art, the mood is mixed. Art critics favour straightforward restitution. Historians tend to support the idea of financial atonement of some kind. Museum directors, who have spent their entire careers denying all knowledge of the trophy art in their basements, are understandably leaning towards obfuscation. Meanwhile the voice of patriotism and nationalism gripping the country has found expression in the attitude of those who argue that everything taken by the Red Army should be regarded as compensation for the havoc wrought on the Soviet Union by the Nazis and that nothing at all should be returned.

No secret about the trophy art was better kept than that of the gold from Troy. And no collection has been more repeatedly denied, or more reluctantly acknowledged. Not until August 1993, despite clear evidence from Akinsha and Kozlov long before, did the Minister of Culture, Evgeny Sidorov, finally admit to having seen for himself the Trojan treasures. He has since discussed sending them on a travelling exhibition around Europe – though not to Germany, the country with the strongest claim to them. In words widely regarded as provocative, he has spoken of the need to return this 'unique collection to the cultural circulation of humanity'. For there is something about King Priam's gold that sets it apart from other collections and other trophy art. It is not just its value, put at over one billion dollars; nor its historical importance as one of the finds that sparked off the entire modern study of prehistory. Rather, it is to do with the strange property of gold, the magic it exercises over the imagination and the cupidity of men.

Schliemann's gift to the German nation, made over a century ago, has become a symbol for both looters and looted. For Schliemann himself, the treasure was the first step in his life's ambition to prove Homer not simply a poet but a reliable historian of the Trojan War. For the Russians, it is the visible sign that great damage was done to their country by the Germans during the Second World War and that a price has to be paid for it. For the Germans, it is the lost jewel in the crown of their famed prehistoric collections, as well as the key to the future of all their stolen art treasures: if Schliemann's gold comes home to them, the rest will follow.

Schliemann's remarkable life, and his driven and unhappy nature, are essential ingredients in the long treasure hunt for Troy and its riches. It is with his early years and his personal quest for the lost city that the story must properly continue.

2

A MECKLENBURG CHILDHOOD

Heinrich Schliemann, one of the acknowledged fathers of modern archaeology, was a strange man. Few dispute the fact that his achievements led to a new chapter in the exploration of the ancient world; that, almost single-handedly, he opened the early pre-Hellenic civilizations to students of antiquity. Yet archaeologists are still quarrelling, a hundred years after his death, as to whether or not his personality was so flawed that all his work needs to be reappraised. Schliemann told lies, certainly; he fabricated events; he introduced characters into places where they had never been; he rounded and perfected his reminiscences. But whether he did so more than many other driven and self-made men of his day, whether his embellishments actually distorted his contribution to archaeology, seems improbable.

Schliemann was, for his entire life, an obsessive hoarder of papers. He kept letters, postcards, appointment slips, bills, drafts, diplomas, testimonials, visiting cards, newspaper cuttings, deeds, ledgers and exercise books in which he practised foreign vocabularies. He wrote and received in all some 60,000 letters, and copied out many of his own, in a regular, sloping hand, filling page after page, top to bottom, margin to margin. In one year alone his correspondence ran to over 1800 letters. Deciphering his handwriting, after more than a century, is not made easier by his use of tissue copy paper which absorbed and spread the ink, or by the fact that, being exceedingly frugal, he often used the same copy paper for two separate letters.

He kept diaries, eighteen of which survive, only when travelling or excavating, writing them up in ten different languages, switching from one to another – Arabic to Greek, say, then back to German – as he moved around the world; whenever he could, he wrote his journal in the language of the country in which he found himself. These diaries are methodical and neat, and say much about his character and his taste, at times excessive, for precision and accuracy; wherever he was, he recorded, often in tedious detail, measurements, statistics, temperatures and plans. Schliemann also wrote twelve books – some of which contain autobiographical fragments – and at least two brief memoirs, the first written as part of a travel diary in America in the 1860s, the second as he approached his sixtieth birthday.

Not surprising, then, to find that most biographies of Schliemann have tended to reproduce his own version of his life, or that contemporary critics have objected that the 'mendacity of Schliemann is exceeded only by the gullibility of his biographers'. Vilified, when at the peak of his fame in the 1870s, by fellow archaeologists who denounced his claims as preposterous, in the 1990s Schliemann is again under attack, some of it out of all proportion to the allegations made against him; he is regarded as a man who was ill, in the way that alcoholics, child molesters or dope fiends are ill, in that 'he did not know the difference between right and wrong'. He has been likened to Ibsen's Peer Gynt, a self-made man and a pathological liar.

Many of the attacks on him are about the way he played around with the truth when presenting his archaeological finds, and about the manner in which he rewrote his childhood. In his own memoirs, Schliemann tends to dwell on the fact that by the age of eight, he was already planning not just to be an archaeologist, but to excavate Troy; yet even a cursory study of his papers makes clear that archaeology only entered his life in 1868, when he was already in his mid-forties. Though Schliemann was not a humorous man, an episode recalled by his second wife, Sophia, after his death, gives an endearing, if not altogether reassuring, picture of his attitude towards the truth.

The Anglo-German philologist and orientalist Max Müller had been helping Schliemann arrange the treasures from Troy in the South Kensington Museum in London, where he had decided to put them on temporary display. Referring to her husband, Sophia wrote that this was 'an arduous task, for, as is well known, though he had the scent of a truffle dog for hidden treasures, he had little or no correct archaeological knowledge. ... One day when Müller was busy over a case of the lowest stratum [the excavations at Troy had at that point revealed five strata, corresponding to different dates of occupation] he found a piece of pottery from the highest. "Que voulez-vous", said Schliemann, "it has tumbled down !" Not long after, in a box of the highest stratum, appeared a piece of the pottery from the lowest. "Que voulez-vous," said the imperturbable Doctor, "it has tumbled up !'"

Too much time has now elapsed for it to be likely that any fresh information will emerge about Schliemann's childhood and youth. In any case, his own account of his early years makes a beguiling and entertaining tale, though it is in his letters rather than in these carefully crafted passages that the full strength of his character emerges : ferociously determined and energetic, obstinate, full of insights and imagination, tending towards the boastful, intensely vulnerable to criticism, and haunted by an unappeasable sense of failure. Schliemann is not the only man to have returned in later life to a re-examination of childhood influences, perceived the germ of an obsession, and tried to capture the meaning of life by recasting it as the pursuit of a dream.

In Schliemann's own words, he was born with a 'natural disposition for the mysterious and the marvellous'. History, tales of ancient feuds and heroic exploits, enchanted him. If we are to believe him, his early companions were the characters of myth and legend first glimpsed in his father's Christmas present of Georg Ludwig Jerrer's *Universal History*, and none more so than Aeneas, fleeing from burning Troy with his father Anchises on his back, holding his son Ascanius by the hand. That was 1829, shortly before Schliemann's eighth birthday. Father and son disagreed, so Schliemann later claimed, over the question of whether or not Jerrer had seen for himself the city of Troy in flames, so vivid and convincing were his words and illustrations, but they were united in the decision that 'I should one day excavate Troy'. Jerrer's book exists, as does his picture of Troy, with imposing fortifications and the Scaean gates lit up by the fire. Whether Schliemann received the book that Christmas Day, or whether it was many years later (a handwriting expert, called in by Schliemann's adversaries, has certified that the writing on the flyleaf is that of an adult) is certainly now lost in time.

Johann Ludwig Heinrich Julius Schliemann was born, the fifth of nine children, on 6 January 1822 in the village of Neu-Buckow, on the flat, sandy plains of north-east Germany, near the town of Mecklenburg, not far from the border with Poland. It was a landscape of lakes and beech forests, dotted with peaceful and rather pretty villages, large estates and manor houses ; the province was renowned for its excellent potatoes and fat cattle. Serfdom had been formally abolished only two years before.

Schliemann's ancestors, on both sides of the family, were Protestant clergymen, and in 1823 his father Ernst had been elected pastor of the village of Ankershagen. It was here, in the cemetery behind the rectory, among the graves and the ruins of a medieval castle that Heinrich – who had been christened, as was the custom, with the name of an elder brother who had died just ten weeks earlier – first enjoyed imaginative encounters with the past; or, at least, this is what he later maintained. Ankershagen's castle, which still contained secret passages and an underground road, was said to be haunted by 'fearful spectres', while fabulous riches were thought to lie in the grounds of its round tower; nearby, a burial mound held the remains of the dead child of a knight, buried in a golden cradle. Best of all, there was a peculiar local story about the left leg of a robber baron, a malefactor who, enraged by the betrayal of a cowherd, had fried him alive in a large iron pan. As the man frizzled to death, the baron had given him a parting kick with his left foot. Faced with a punitive raid by the outraged Duke of Mecklenburg, who gathered his men together and laid siege to the castle, the robber baron committed suicide. Ankershagen's children relished the gory details: right up until the turn of the century, so both sexton and sacristan swore, this left leg, clothed in a black silk stocking, kept sprouting from its grave – for had not they themselves as boys often chopped off the bone and used it to knock down pears?

Ernst Schliemann had abandoned a career as a schoolmaster to take up theology at the advanced age of twenty-six. Photographs show a round-faced, mutton-chopped, genial figure, with eyes set far apart and a soft and contented mouth. His years as a teacher had left him with a taste for early history and story-telling. Grimms' fairy-tales were read aloud around the fire. By day, during long excursions on foot, for Ernst Schliemann was a keen walker, he talked to his children about Herculaneum and Pompeii, and even, Schliemann recalled, about Homer and his epic poems, for though he knew no Greek, he had absorbed some of the *Iliad* and the *Odyssey* through reading Goethe and Schiller. Though Heinrich was later to take a firm and moral line towards his father, the pastor was an interesting man, by turn tight-fisted and generous, garrulous and morose, explosive and loving. He enjoyed practical jokes.

Less is known of Heinrich's mother, Luise Therese Sophie, thirteen years younger than her husband, well-educated and musical, given to much playing of the piano and the wearing of lace cuffs, which neighbours attributed to a desire to give herself airs. It was from her that Schliemann was to say that he had inherited his sensitivity and philosophical curiosity. Sophie was only thirty-nine when she died, three weeks after giving birth to her ninth child. Some distant flavour of her personality, a touch of wryness and bitter humour, comes through the last letter she wrote to her eighteen-year-old daughter, Louise. 'If God helps me happily to survive my time of suffering, and my life afterwards becomes such that I once again find joy and happiness among men, I promise you to wear my pretty cap very often. I must now conclude, as I am in the middle of killing the pigs . . .'

Sophie Schliemann had every reason to feel bitter. While she was carrying and giving birth to nine children in a little under twenty years, Ernst had been having an affair with their maid, Sophie Schwarz, to whom he gave 'dresses of the heaviest satin and shawls of velvet and silk'. His parishioners refrained from public condemnation while Sophie was alive; but on her death they ostracized the pastor and his children, and Heinrich was soon sent to stay with his uncle Friedrich, also a clergyman, in the nearby village of Kalkhorst. For a while, it seemed as if Ernst was to be defrocked, though less for moral turpitude than suspected misappropriation of church funds.

The loss of mother and home were clearly devastating to the nine-year-old Heinrich, but not, apparently, one 'thousandth part' as much as the loss of the companionship of a girl called Minna Meincke, a blue-eyed, yellow-haired child who looked like a Dutch doll and whose farmer parents now joined in the village hostility. For Heinrich had fallen in love. Unlike the other village children, he was to claim, Minna shared his obsession with the past. While their comrades took dancing lessons, Heinrich and Minna, agreeing that neither 'derived any profit' from them, roamed the churchyard and conducted their own 'important archaeological investigation'. They planned to marry and dig for treasure, and Heinrich could never understand why his penniless father did not look for the gold under the tower himself. 'We could imagine,' wrote Schliemann over half a century later, 'nothing pleasanter than to spend all our lives digging for the relics of the past.' In between forays down the secret tunnels of the ruined castle, they listened to the stories of the one-eyed village tailor, a man called Wollert, who had put a tag around the leg of a stork one spring and received a poem back when the stork returned the following year.

One of Schliemann's later and most enduring myths was that he had lacked all childhood education. In fact, the uncle in Kalkhorst was a man of considerable learning, and by the age of eleven Heinrich was already able to present his father with an essay on the exploits of Odysseus and Agamemnon, written in Latin. He was now sent to study at the Carolinum Gymnasium, which prepared boys for university, in Neustrelitz, a new, neo-classical town constructed by the orders of the local ducal family after a fire had destroyed their palace at Altstrelitz. It was here, in the pension in which he boarded, that Schliemann heard talk of the wonders of St Petersburg and the openings Russia provided for ambitious young Germans. Funds to keep him at the Gymnasium, however, dried up three months later, when Ernst was suspended from his parsonage and decided to resign from the Church, foolishly accepting a lump sum instead of a pension, which 'lacking in self-control and therefore without success', he soon squandered. Ernst's fecklessness was to be a lifelong irritant to the prudent Heinrich, who was now moved to the local Realschüle, which was free and emphasized 'useful studies' in business, and where he claimed to have learned very little before he was obliged, at the age of fourteen, to start earning his own living.

Before leaving Ankershagen to take up an apprenticeship with a grocer in Fürstenberg, after Easter 1836, Heinrich caught one more glimpse of his 'bride'. Minna was by now a young woman and dressed in black, which seemed to Heinrich to 'enhance her fascinating beauty'. On seeing each other again after five years, both burst into tears and neither could speak. The sight of Minna, however, filled Heinrich with 'a boundless energy' and he left for his new life determined, as he was later to insist, to progress in the world and prove himself worthy of her love. His one fear was that she would find and marry another in his absence.

Ernst Holtz, the grocer who took Heinrich on, was not a harsh man, but his shop near the church was modest and life as an apprentice was both dull and exhausting. Fürstenberg, built on the banks of the River Havel, was an agreeable place, famous for its butter market, which was held nine times a year and drew merchants from all over Mecklenburg. From five o'clock every morning in some versions of his memoirs, Schliemann says four – until eleven o'clock at night, Heinrich swept, sold milk, sugar, herrings, butter, oil and candles, ground potatoes for the whisky still, and packed parcels. When he had a few hours off, he went to listen to the tales of the sailors who had put in to Fürstenberg on their ships. Intellectual tedium was relieved only by the visits of a young customer, a 'drunken miller' called Hermann Niederhoffer, who had been expelled from the Gymnasium for bad conduct, but not before he had mastered enough Greek to be able to recite from memory long

passages of Homeric verse. The young Schliemann was apparently captivated; spending his pitiful salary on glasses of whisky for Niederhoffer,
he begged him to recite whatever he could remember. Though he understood not a syllable, the 'rhythmic cadences' and the 'melodious sound
of the words' made a deep impression on him. 'From that moment,' he
was to write, in pious solemnity, 'I never ceased to pray to God that by
His grace I might yet have the happiness of learning Greek'.

That moment was not now far off. Schliemann might indeed have
spent the next fifty years serving oil and coffee, but ill-health intervened.
It was an extremely lucky break. This 'hapless and humble position' was
abandoned when one day, five and a half years after reaching Fürstenberg, he tore a blood vessel while carrying a cask of chicory. He spat
blood. No longer able to do heavy work, he was dismissed. His release
came just in time for by now, he later told a friend, he 'could barely read
and write my mother tongue'.

Casting around, he met up with an old schoolfriend who was planning
to sail for New York with his father, on board the packet boat *Howard*.
Emigration seemed an excellent idea to Schliemann, not least because
his father, married for the second time to a Sophie Behnke, the daughter
of a weaver, was creating further scandal by the violence of his behaviour
towards his new wife; Sophie had already borne him two more sons and
was being forced to take refuge in a lodging house, lest she be beaten to
death by the irascible Ernst. Permission to leave for America was,
however, refused and Heinrich settled down reluctantly in Rostock to
master 'double book-keeping' by the notoriously difficult Schwanbeck
system. 'To the surprise of instructors and fellow students alike', his
skills proved such that he covered the course in three months, barely a
quarter of the time it took the other pupils. The legend was beginning
to take shape. Something of Schliemann's later prodigious will and
intellectual energy was now emerging. Revolted by his father's continuing domestic chaos and sensual needs, he set out to seek his fortune
in Hamburg, pausing briefly in Wismar to become infatuated with a
cousin, another Sophie, who had 'ravishing shining eyes' and 'beauteous
cheeks'. He was not to set foot in Ankershagen again for more than
fifteen years.

'Oh Hamburg! Hamburg!' Schliemann was later to write of his initial
pleasure and astonishment on reaching the city. It was 13 September
1841. Hamburg, one of the great pillars of the Hanseatic League, was at

a peak of prosperity and activity. Travellers far more worldly than Schliemann compared it favourably with Paris and London for its magnificence and its promise of adventure. 'The Hamburgers are greedy of amusement,' wrote a cautious Englishman, who visited the city not long before Schliemann's arrival.

Waking on his first morning to see the five tallest towers spread out before his window, the young man was 'overcome by sublime, indescribable emotions ... Contemplating Hamburg, I turned into a dreamer.' Because most of what is known about his stay comes from the long letters written to his sisters Wilhelmine and Dorothea, and thus not with the judiciousness of hindsight which suffuses his autobiographical writings but fresh with his impressions, there is less problem in believing what he says. Though his tendency to self-dramatization can be annoying, these letters give a very vivid indication of what were to become the most important themes of Schliemann's life: love of travel, the ferocious will to survive and succeed, religious scepticism, and an unshakable belief in the necessity of mastering as many foreign languages as possible.

Hamburg was not simply lively and fashionable; it was also an important commercial centre, with an Exchange, a number of vast markets, and offices for hundreds of international firms. The city seldom slept. Over a hundred newspapers, published in thirteen languages, were to be found in the halls where the merchants gathered, which gives some idea of the cosmopolitan feel of the place. The port was packed tight with sailing ships, bringing and carrying away merchandise. Hamburg was noisy, smelly and vastly exciting.

First, Schliemann had to find work. His determination to prosper quickly paid off for he was soon taken on by the firm of S.H.Lindemann, a grocery business with premises near the fish market of Altona. Once again he was saved from drudgery by fortuitous ill-health, for the heavy work, all of it carried out in the dark inner storeroom, threatened to reopen his torn blood vessel. Quickly dispirited by a failure to find a less menial occupation, he wrote to an uncle for a loan and was disgusted by the 'impertinent and nasty' letter that came back, making him swear never again to ask a relation for help, though this humiliating experience was to do little to temper his own self-righteousness when he later received similar calls for help.

So he was delighted when a shipbroker by the name of J.F.Wendt – either a former pupil of his father's, or a family friend of his mother's, depending on the different versions of his life – provided him with an opportunity to emigrate to the New World. A business firm in Colombia was looking for hale young men, and Schliemann hastened to present himself, refusing to be deterred either by the 2000-mile sea voyage or by the yellow fever which had killed off so many earlier recruits. Despite his apparent lack of early education, he was able to pass the test set for applicants – business letters written in German, French and English. He sold his silver watch for three dollars, by now all that was left of a very meagre inheritance, bought three shirts, a pair of trousers, a coat, a seagrass mattress and two woollen blankets and went to find the captain of the *Dorothea*, a brand-new, three-masted vessel, fitted with a copper bottom for faster sailing. What impressed Schliemann most was the mahogany in which floors, walls and furniture of the fine new ship had all been built, a vast improvement on the more spartan sailing packets of the day, where passengers, crammed into dark berths, their days spent huddled in a single saloon, were meant to provide their own furniture. Some even took goats and sheep on the journey.

The account of the *Dorothea*'s maiden voyage is one of Schliemann's most graphic pieces of writing. Gales postponed departure for several days but at last, at four o'clock on the morning of 28 November 1841, the sailing ship set forth to the sound of cannons, fired from the harbour walls to wish the *Dorothea* luck. For the first few days, all went well. So brisk were the winds, so finely tuned the ship, that it 'flew faster and faster'. Confined to his cabin with a bucket, Schliemann retched and heaved.

On the ninth day, just over a hundred miles out of Cuxhaven, the gale still blowing, he felt well enough to munch some hard ship's biscuits and study a little Spanish, having lashed a comfortable armchair to the side of his cabin. He could see dolphins from his porthole, playing with the white crests.

On 11 December a hurricane struck. Waves, 'swollen to mountains', tossed the *Dorothea* in all directions like a shuttlecock. One by one, gusts of wind shredded the sails. Though his fellow passengers kept to their cabins, 'jittery' with panic, though the ship's cat and dog both 'whimpered' with terror, and the cabin boy wept when he brought tea and biscuits, Schliemann himself 'roared with laughter', went to bed, and dreamt of the beautiful Colombian plains that awaited him. Never, he told his sisters, 'had I slept so gently and peacefully'.

Not, however, for long. At midnight he was woken by the captain, shouting out that the *Dorothea* was going down. With the water now pouring through his shattered porthole, Schliemann was unable to dress and so scrambled 'almost naked' (in shirt and underwear) up to the deck, where he was immediately caught up and tossed from side to side by an enormous wave. Miraculously still on board, he clung on to a rope and waited, watching the snowflakes fall as the crew struggled to lower the lifeboats. Having felt momentary terror, he had now 'fortunately ... completely recovered my self-control'. The lifeboats were torn apart by the waves and quickly vanished. Schliemann commended his soul to God, bequeathed his body to the sharks and pondered on the sweetness of life. He felt, not fearful, but 'foolhardy'. This is Schliemann at his most boastful. As the ship's bell rang 'dolefully without end, as if pulled by an invisible hand', as the other passengers called for St Mary and all the saints, and as the crew blasphemed and bemoaned the fate of their families, the stalwart young man kept his nerve.

Minutes passed. The *Dorothea*, now taking water rapidly, began to sink below the waves. Making one last effort to reach the rigging, Schliemann lost his foothold and plunged into the water, catching hold of the edge of an empty wooden barrel as he fell. The *Dorothea* disappeared.

At dawn, Schliemann recovered consciousness and found himself on a sandbank, from where he was rescued and taken to an inn in the village of Eislandshuis on the Dutch island of Texel. He was in great pain, his feet, face and body gashed and swollen, and two of his front teeth had snapped off. A few days later, refusing offers by the *Dorothea*'s owners to return him to Hamburg or Mecklenburg, he felt strong enough to make his way to Amsterdam, where he hoped to find work, though he did at some point wonder if he should not consider Japan, 'for my instinct tells me I am not meant to stop in Europe'. He was now totally destitute, and somewhat comically clad in a torn jacket and an old pair of clogs.

Once again Mr Wendt, and the local German Consul, came to Schliemann's aid, the one raising a subscription among merchant friends for the unfortunate young man, the other writing out a certificate for admittance to the hospital where, in atrocious pain, the roots of his jagged front teeth were extracted without anaesthetic. He felt happy to be alive. Of the entire ship's complement, apart from the captain and one member of the crew, all had gone down with the *Dorothea*. What was more, he felt healthy ... 'indeed, I felt reborn'. So healthy in fact that he was able to shed the 'two underdrawers, a cat's fur, and two woollen undershirts' – though just where he had worn the cat's fur is not clear. 'Fate', he noted with satisfaction, 'seemed to have planned for my blessing and advantage'.

Amsterdam, though extremely expensive, was as delightful to Schliemann as Hamburg. Too poor to attend the nightly plays, concerts, dances and masked balls that were the pride of the city, he roamed the streets admiring the newly installed gas-lighting and stood for hours watching the steam railway carriages leave from Amsterdam for Haarlem. Scientific inventions, progress in all its forms, were to fascinate him throughtout his life. 'Everything', he told his sisters, was 'truly metropolitan'. He described to them the wonders of the windows of the hairdressers he passed, where dolls with 'beautiful coiffures' modelled different styles as they revolved mechanically around each other. Like Hamburg, Amsterdam breathed a heady air of adventure, foreignness and infinite possibility. It was not long before Schliemann found work, with the recommendation of the Prussian Consul-General, as a clerk.

The moment had come to review his future. Though possessed once again of the 'boundless courage' which he hoped would soon allow him to ask for Minna's hand, he was forced to conclude that unless some better-paid work came his way, it would be many years before he would be in a position to do so. Moreover, he felt he deserved better than a 'wretched garret without a fire', where he shivered in winter and scorched in summer, forced to survive much of the time on rye-meal porridge and dry black bread. 'Unremitting work' was his only way out: he resolved to set aside half his annual salary of £22 towards further education.

Most important, he calculated, was the need for a neat hand, and this he acquired by taking a course of lessons from a famous Belgian calligrapher, a man called Magnée. Foreign languages came next. Schliemann was clearly a natural linguist, and neither endless repetition nor grindingly hard work daunted him. He now set about inventing his own method for learning foreign languages, which he was to perfect as the years went by. The resolve with which he improved his faltering English and French was impressive. His system involved a great deal of reading aloud, without translation at hand, and a daily lesson in which he rehearsed, again out loud, essays that he had written and which had been corrected the day before by his teacher. To perfect his English accent, he attended two services on Sundays at the English church, during which he repeated, under his breath, word by word, the sermon. Wherever he went, he practised, never going 'on my errands, even in the rain, without having my book in my hand and learning something by heart.' The key, he soon decided, was memory. Being a poor sleeper, and in any case 'over-excited' by the turmoil in his mind, he spent much of every night working his memory, repeating over and over again all that he had learned the previous day.

Committing to memory twenty pages a day, first of Goldsmith's *Vicar of Wakefield*, then Walter Scott's *Ivanhoe*, Schliemann took six months to acquire a 'thorough knowledge of the English language'. Then came French, this time memorizing Fénelon's *Aventures de Télémaque*, and Bernardin de Saint-Pierre's *Paul et Virginie*. After that, he allowed himself just six weeks each to master Dutch, Spanish, Italian and Portuguese. His claims would appear boastful, were it not clear, from his very earliest correspondence, that his gift for languages was indeed exceptional. He was to make use of it all his life, eventually mastering twenty-two languages, of which he wrote ten fluently, spending many odd hours when not otherwise employed revising, reading, adding to his vocabulary. His enormous ledger-like exercise books, with their marbled endpapers, filled page after page with his neatly written lists of foreign words, bear witness both to his talents and to his astonishing doggedness.

Schliemann was now twenty-two, a somewhat priggish young man to judge by the tone of his letters, and rather too pleased with himself. There was very little self-mockery in him. The speed with which he was visibly climbing the ladder of life was, he declared, due to nothing but temperance, self-denial and hard work, though he could not quite rid himself of a rather touching and naïve desire to impress. Describing his exploits to his sisters, he included in one letter a consular document which would enable them, he said, to see for themselves 'that I have not been lying to you'.

What was more, his health was so far improved that the weakness in his chest, and his tendency to spit blood – which he never, curiously, seems to have suspected might be tubercular – had vanished and was not to return. He had become a passionate advocate of sea-bathing, and would remain one for the rest of his life, whatever the temperature of the water or the state of the weather, saying that it was the panacea for all ills.

The one drawback was that his present employers, the firm of F.C.Quien, were being slow to recognize his talents or to promote him. He was tired of stamping bills of exchange and running errands. Through the intervention, once again, of various benefactors, he was taken on, in March 1844, as a bookkeeper by the Amsterdam branch of B.H.Schröder & Co., founded in 1818 and already, as Schröders, one of Europe's leading merchant banks, at a salary of £48 a year. Quickly perceiving that much of their most valuable trade lay with Russia, and that no other employee spoke the language, Schliemann hastened to add Russian to his collection, only momentarily disheartened by not being able to find a single native Russian speaker in Amsterdam. Discovering that he worked better with an audience, he fell back on the services of a 'poor Jew' who, for four francs a week, came 'every evening for two hours to listen to my Russian recitation, of which he did not understand a syllable'. Nor, indeed, did the other tenants in his building, who soon prevailed upon the landlord to evict him. He moved to a more tolerant establishment, or possibly one with thicker floorboards, and continued by night to pace and recite out loud, sometimes from a volume of Pushkin's poems, given him by a visiting Russian; by day, when not working, he read foreign newspapers and tried to learn and understand the politics of the day. To judge both from his letters and from his later reminiscences, Schliemann at this time had few friends; none are ever mentioned, despite an often extraordinarily literal and detailed recitation of his daily routine. Friendlessness, a sense of being alone, is one of Schliemann's most enduring characteristics; even at the height of his fame and popularity, friends were to play a surprisingly small part in his life.

Schröder, unlike his former employers, were quick to spot the excellent potential in their new bookkeeper. They liked the way he was able to converse so readily with their many foreign agents in their own languages, and the ease with which he endeared himself to them; they noted, too, how very little time it had taken him to distinguish Javan from Haiwaian and Jamaican sugar. Within two years, Schliemann had fifteen clerks working under him and considerable personal responsibility. Feeling understandably proud, and wishing his family to reflect his growing status in the world, he sent money home and ordered that two casks of Bordeaux wine and a box of cigars be delivered to his father.

Now, at last, the moment had come when Schliemann felt able to ask for Minna's hand. Whether or not there is any truth in the story of his romantic attachment and the grief it was to cause him matters little, for it makes a romantic tale. He began by writing to a mutual friend, asking him to make the first enquiries. A month later came the 'heart-rending answer': Minna was already married, to a farmer called Friedrich Richers, twenty years her senior. Worse, the marriage had only just taken place. Schliemann allowed himself a rare flight of poetic fancy. 'It had indeed happened to Minna and me,' he was to observe, 'as it often happens to us in our sleep, when we dream that we are pursuing somebody and could never catch him, because as often as we reach him he escapes us again.' Lamenting that he would never recover from the disappointment, Schliemann now took up Schröder's offer to become their agent in St Petersburg.

3

A MAN OF SUBSTANCE

What drew Schliemann to Russia was indigo, the dark blue natural dye imported from Java and India, in which Schröder & Co. had cornered the market. Soon he was also dealing in Rhine wines, saltpetre, sugar, tea and coffee.

He reached St Petersburg on 30 January 1846, three weeks after his twenty-fourth birthday. Tsar Nicholas I was on the throne. Though Russia was on the eve of social turmoil, the city seemed to him both agreeably prosperous and architecturally imposing, with 'its beautiful and clean houses, the fine streets and delightful climate', though it is hard to see how a city which suffered from frequent flooding in spring and autumn, and deep snow and arctic winds in winter, could be said to possess delightful weather. Or, indeed, how a society renowned for its habit of spitting in antechambers, halls and corridors could be regarded as clean, though it was true that the government buildings had fine façades and that the vistas of the Imperial palaces were spectacular.

Being the middle of winter, the canals and the River Neva were frozen. In the afternoon, fashionable society ladies promenaded up and down the Nevsky Prospekt in their horse-drawn sleighs. While other travellers to St Petersburg complained of the inadequate oil street-lighting, and the 'miserable' dwellings concealed behind the classical façades, Schliemann quickly took to the vigorous feel of the city. As an admirer of Hamburg's entrepreneurial spirit, he felt at home in the cosmopolitain crowds, and there were few cities in the mid-1840s to rival St Petersburg for its large numbers of foreigners, from all parts of Europe and Asia, who owned and ran most of the best shops in the smarter districts.

On 7 February, barely a week later, he set out for Moscow. Though tracks were being laid for a railway system, the 400-mile journey was still by open sleigh in winter, forty-six hours in temperatures that seldom rose above 72 degrees of frost. He reached Moscow to find the city in the midst of an ambitious building programme, started in the wake of the fire of 1812, with the richer merchants putting up houses for themselves modelled on the palaces of the aristocracy. Like St Petersburg, Moscow was a city of exaggerated contrasts, splendid on the surface and pitifully poor beneath, rich brick and stucco mansions alongside wooden hovels. For all the improvements, the roads were still cobbled and uneven, and it was not unusual, when the snows melted, to see horses sunk up to their bellies in oozing black mud. Few houses possessed their own wells, so water was drawn from stone basins in the streets. In winter there was at least little smell, but in the spring a terrible stench rose from putrefying meat and fish, preserved frozen all winter long, and kites and buzzards descended to scavenge.

None of this was apparent to Schliemann on his first winter visit, and in any case he was far more concerned with the mercantile possibilities Moscow had to offer. Like St Petersburg, Russia's second city had become a lively centre for trade, its merchants said to be of a more cheerful disposition than their German and British counterparts, more prone to mix business and pleasure, negotiate deals while gossiping, laughing, praying or drinking tea. There was something about the conviviality of the place that pleased him and he was soon on excellent terms with the leading traders. That first year, he made the two-day journey from St Petersburg to Moscow four times.

By the late spring of 1846, business was going exceptionally well. Schröder & Co. had forty-one clients in St Petersburg and twenty-two in Moscow. Employed by Schröder as their Russian agent, Schliemann was soon taken on by other firms, for whom he also dealt and traded, taking immense care to keep the various business transactions both separate and secret. He was already showing considerable canniness, and his personal savings increased at a steady rate. Though Schröder & Co. admired their new agent's enormous energy, they sometimes found his impatience and unmistakable desire for total independence irksome, particularly when he dabbled in merchandise he as yet knew far too little about, and lost openings through ignorance and over-eagerness. In June, one of the senior managers in Amsterdam wrote testily that 'our worst fears have unfortunately come true ... Never tell us what we should do ... You have an opinion of your influence and power which we by no means share ...' Soon afterwards came a further and harsher rebuke : 'You lack all knowledge of men and the world, prattle too much, have too high expectations, and are infatuated with brainless chimeras ...' But when Schliemann's bumptiousness gave way to despair, they were equally quick to bolster his self-assurance. 'The world will not come to an end,' they wrote encouragingly. 'Besides, we shall not let you down ...'

They had much to be pleased with. Schliemann, the little-educated country boy from the sandy plains of north-east Germany, had natural style. The Russian merchants, observing his growing assurance and great ambition, appreciated his panache and soon came to trust his judgement, feeling all the more easy in his company since he took such pains to speak their language so fluently. One after another, the leading traders, men like Peter Alexev who was rumoured to be worth a hundred million roubles, befriended him. It was not long before a prominent sugar and timber merchant called Ponomarev, a man many years his senior, was using him to conduct deals in which each took half of the profit. By the beginning of 1847, barely a year after his arrival in Russia, Schliemann was registered as a Merchant of the First Guild, which meant not only that he could now obtain credit of up to 57,000 silver roubles, but that he had been accepted as a trader of stature. He now felt confident enough to ask Schröder & Co. for a larger cut, arguing that St Petersburg was the most expensive city in the world. His percentage was duly raised from 0.5 per cent to 1.0 per cent; the tone of his letters suggests that he was beginning to see his employers more as colleagues and partners than as people with authority over him. Throughout the commodity market, Schliemann was coming to be regarded as a man of substance.

Schliemann, today, is remembered solely for his archaeological finds. But he was also an enterprising and apparently fearless traveller, making journeys, by sailing ship and paddle-steamer, horse-drawn coach and sleigh, that even now would daunt most people. His diaries from the mid-1840s onwards often read like the pages of one of the celebrated John Murray guidebooks, though his extraordinary attention to detail – how the interior of a railway carriage is laid out, for instance – and meditative asides – the difficulties of setting up a railway network in Russia – give them a particular flavour of their own. As he prepared for his first real trip abroad, he started the first of what would be a remarkable series of travel diaries; this one would, he noted, be useful both for 'entertainment for my Muscovite friends and gratification to myself in reading at a future period . . .' It is hard, sometimes, to remember that in 1846 Schliemann was not yet twenty-five. He could be very pompous.

In 1841 Schliemann had been obliged to abandon plans for emigration after the sinking of the *Dorothea* off the shores of Holland. In a little under five years, his life had altered beyond recognition. He was now a different person, with money, letters of credit, introductions and growing confidence in his own abilities. Not surprising, perhaps, given the two languages he had decided to master first, that his strongest desire was to visit England and France, though on the way there and back he took in Holland, Belgium and Germany. He left St Petersburg on 1 October 1846 and was away two-and-a-half months. It was on this first business trip that he set the tone and style of his future journeys: energetic sightseeing, no pauses for rest, grandeur tempered by frugality – the best hotels but the cheapest rooms. Theatre, music, opera all bored him; progress, new technology, the revolution of the industrial world were what drew him.

England in the mid-nineteenth century was a country guaranteed to please and impress him. Schliemann was, and remained all his life, fascinated by all forms of travel, and especially by speed. Impatient at the slowness of the mail coaches, he dreamed of the day when letters and goods would move at what he considered a satisfactory pace. He reached an England in the grip of train fever, the entire country undergoing total transformation as railway companies scrambled to buy up land, and as houses and whole districts were destroyed to make way for the railway lines, stations, marshalling yards, ticket offices and coal bunkers. Euston and Paddington stations were both open, other major terminals were under construction and three hundred smaller stations were already operating within five miles of Charing Cross. Clapham, and even Dorking, were now within easy reach, while Brighton, once a distant spa, was being described as a 'marine suburb' of London.

What interested Schliemann, however, was not the social history brought to light wherever the railway lines penetrated – the poverty and squalor of early Victorian England described by Dickens – but their immense mercantile openings. Twenty years earlier, the prospect of hurtling through the countryside at a terrifying 18 miles an hour had been greeted with scorn and horror, but by the mid-1840s Queen Victoria had made her maiden voyage – from Slough to Paddington – at 44 miles an hour, and professed herself perfectly calm (though Prince Albert had found it a bit dangerous). The *Great Britain* steam engine was already running at speeds of up to a mile a minute. The implications, for trade, were limitless. During the year of Schliemann's visit, two-and-a-half million tons of coal travelled by train from the north Midland fields alone.

What was more, lines were now being proposed to run below the ground, despite protests that digging holes for trains was contrary to the laws of God, and despite the Duke of Wellington's gloomy warning that there would be nothing to stop a French army from arriving secretly in London by train without anyone knowing that it had even crossed the Channel. Dickens, in *Dombey and Son*, published soon after Schliemann's first visit to England, gives one of the best onomatopoeic pictures of the tremendous excitement of the new rail travel: 'Through the hollow, on the height, by the heath, by the orchard, by the park, by the garden, over the canal, across the river, where the sheep are feeding, where the mill is going, where the barge is floating, where the dead are lying, where the factory is smoking … Louder and louder yet, it shrieks and cries and it comes tearing on.'

Schliemann took lodgings in a coffee house overlooking St Paul's, admired the dazzling new gas-lighting and the electric telegraph system, called at Schröders' offices at 145 Leadenhall Street, marvelled at the energy of London – omnibuses, hansoms, vans, carts, gigs, phaetons, landaus, broughams, dogcarts and donkey-carts jostling for space with herds of animals on their way to market, and tens of thousands of pedestrians and riders – and took refuge in the British Museum. His immediate interest in what he found there, and in particular the Egyptian collection, pride of the rapidly expanding Department of Antiquities, was clearly neither feigned nor later embroidered on, for he took detailed notes, with his usual precision, of the sarcophagi and mummies, prominently arranged along one of the main galleries. Wandering through the collections of stuffed birds, fish and animals, he paused among the Greek and Roman sculptures, pondering later in his diary on the fact that it seemed clear that as countries bettered themselves, so they made extraordinarily rapid progress.

From London Schliemann went to Liverpool and Manchester, greatly enjoying a visit to a yard in which steam engines were being built. Manchester, however, provoked a burst of moralizing. Never had he seen 'more dissoluteness, temptation and seduction'. Almost everyone he set eyes on seemed to bear the marks of 'self-abuse and consequently thereupon loss of physical powers'.

This theme accompanied him across the Channel to France. 'There is too much freedom here,' he noted sternly. The Parisians were 'too seldom married, preferring instead the most immoral of lives'. He was appalled by the conversations in his lodging house, 'so indecent' that it was embarrassing for a foreigner even to listen. Pages of descriptions of Paris and its inhabitants were interspersed with renewed attacks on French morality and *mœurs*. 'From the age of 13 onwards,' he stated, 'no one thinks of anything other than finding the easiest way to satisfy as frequently as possible his cupidity, his most bestial instincts.' Twenty-year-old Parisians struck him as 'looking as if 30', while the few who reached forty were 'old men, languishing under the weight of the terrible consequences of the vicious and debauched life of their youth'. One evening he attended a performance by Houdin, the celebrated magician, describing his innocent tricks with relief. If Schliemann could be excessively stuffy, and somewhat lacking in humour, he was also turning into an impressive reporter.

On his way home to Russia, Schliemann's steamer passed along the shores of Mecklenburg. He did not stop off to visit his family, declaring later that it had been with 'the utmost indifference that I gazed upon my native country', and contrasting the German taste for 'noisy pastimes' unfavourably with the family-loving Muscovites. Though he was increasingly assuming the role of guardian and benefactor to his father and brothers and sisters, Schliemann evidently preferred to keep them at a physical distance. He sent money, he took out a subscription for his father to a Hamburg newspaper, and he was always ready to give his views on his younger brothers' futures – hard work and foreign languages – but he does not appear to have wished to see them. He was, all his life, capable of great generosity, but he recoiled in fury whenever he was asked directly for money. Perhaps prudently, Dorothea and Wilhelmine were careful to address him as 'our saviour and helper'. In his letters home, Schliemann was crowing, bossy and sentimental. Sometimes one gets the feeling that he was trying out on his relations a mythical picture of himself. 'I am far less happy,' he wrote sanctimoniously one day to his father, 'than I was when, from behind the shop counter at Fürstenberg, I used to chat with the fishman about the dog with the long tail.'

Though he did bring his fifteen-year-old brother, Paul, to help in his St Petersburg office in 1846, running errands and copying letters, he was adamant that Louis, who had followed his path to Amsterdam, should stay where he was, and he encouraged him to do so by asking him to provide regular news of the Amsterdam business world. Louis, who seems to have inherited Schliemann's volatile character, but was more given to histrionics, threatened to commit suicide if not allowed to visit Russia. Schliemann was immovable on the subject, and instructed his younger brother to take charge of his wardrobe, which he seems to have considered better purchased in Holland than Russia. In dress, as in all things, Schliemann was turning out to be neat, precise to the point of obsessiveness, exigent and thrifty. Discussing an order for thirty-nine shirts, he told Louis that they should be washed and starched before despatch to St Petersburg, adding: 'Of course, I do not expect to pay for laundering.'

It was Louis who was responsible for the next chapter in Schliemann's life. Dispirited by his older brother's intransigence, Louis took off, in June 1948, for the New World, settled briefly in New York as a teacher of French, dabbled in business ventures, then suddenly dropped everything to join in the Californian gold rush. From the West Coast, he sent excited letters home: 'Gold is all over the country, and even in the mountains around San Francisco . . .' News came that he had opened an inn and that the money was pouring in. Did Schliemann feel a touch of envy ? He was to say that he had long been thinking about travelling to America himself when a letter arrived announcing Louis's death from typhus in Sacramento, at the age of twenty-seven.

The commodity markets were flourishing and Schliemann was restless and curious. Declaring that he was intending to investigate what had happened to Louis's fortune, in order to bring back what he could salvage for his sisters, he made plans to sail for New York, the first leg of the trek to California. On 10 December 1850, he gave a last farewell dinner for his merchant friends in St Petersburg. It was an exceptionally cold winter, and the Neva had been frozen over since October. They accompanied him, in icy winds, to the central post office, from where the sleighs set out for the long journey to Germany.

Schliemann was to devote just six and a half lines in his autobiography to his first American trip, though he was away for two exceptionally adventurous years. What was more, these few lines contain two untruths – the exact reason for his visit, and the claim that he became an American citizen on 4 July 1850, when in fact not only did he not reach America until 1851, but he did not obtain citizenship until March 1869 – neither of very great importance, but enough to fuel the doubts about his fundamental honesty. He did, on the other hand, keep a detailed diary, eighty pages long, most of it in English. It is Schliemann at his best, fluent, inquisitive, with a keen eye for the telling detail.

He set out from St Petersburg in the company of three Englishmen, 'that is to say, most polite, amiable and interesting persons', was agreeably surprised by the neat villages and cultivated fields of Prussia after the 'snowy deserts' of Russia, conducted some business in Rotterdam and arrived in London in an exuberant mood. It was Christmas Eve. He went to the Bank of England, arranged for the sale of some gold, then went off to admire the splendours of the Crystal Palace, Paxton's immense iron-and-glass building being erected in Hyde Park for the Great Exhibition of 1851. The first column in what was to be a nearly 2000-foot-long building had gone up in September, and Schliemann was in time to see the last of the ribs of the transept winched into place, using only the men from the two-thousand-strong workforce and horses. He called it a 'stupendous masterpiece of modern art', noting that it would make the people of the world 'more amalgamated', and set off to inspect the new hippopotamus in the London Zoo, a present from the Pasha of Egypt. On Christmas Day he attended a service in Westminster Abbey. A small lie crept into the diary. Schliemann claimed to have seen the celebrated tragedian William Macready's last performance – on a day when Macready was in fact with his family in Sherborne and was not, in any case, due to retire for another two months.

There was a jinx on the ships on which Schliemann travelled: the *Atlantic*, which he now boarded for his crossing to New York, was soon put out of service, losing both engines and the main shaft in 'mountain high waves' and westerly gales. Sails were raised, which, he noted, looked just like handkerchiefs, the wind was good, and the *Atlantic* crept back to Ireland in sixteen days. The delay gave him time to enjoy the luxury provided by this flagship of the Collins line. Barely a year old, the *Atlantic* had a vast turbine and enormous paddles, steam acting as an auxiliary to the sails. The era of the steam floating palaces was dawning – the *Atlantic's* breakdown was not unusual at a time when the race to break the record to New York drove ships to greater speeds than they could easily handle – and the interior decoration of the ship rivalled that of Europe's grandest hotels. The woodwork was in white holly, satinwood and rosewood; the pillars had mirrors inlaid with seashells, and panels painted with allegorical figures, representing the myths and legends of the ancient world, in bronze and burnished gold. Schliemann, with his delight in the industrial revolution, now had the leisure to inspect the steam-heated apartments – the *Atlantic* was the first ship to use steam heat – and the bathrooms, as well as the ice-rooms packed for the crossing with forty tons of ice. He was to spend many months in the years to come on these paddle-steamers, though few had the luxury of the *Atlantic*. From Ireland, Schliemann made his way back to London, crossed to the Continent for another bout of business, then returned to set sail for America once again, this time from Liverpool, on 1 February 1851.

The crossing to Jersey City took just over two weeks; ('ten days was the number the steamers aimed for'). Schliemann took a room in the Astor House on Broadway in New York, the 'grandest and most gigantic Hotel I ever saw' and, in the 1850s, still the most fashionable of the New York hotels. It contained a barber's shop, and it was possible to have a shirt laundered while taking a bath. Diary in hand, he set about recording everything around him. Full board cost him $2.50 a day, not including wine. However the food was excellent, and breakfast, of ham and eggs, buckwheat cakes, fried hominy and chocolate, delicious; at 11 p.m., before going to bed, he had a supper of cold turkey and ham. He observed that the Astor House took no foreign newspapers, regarding them as 'unpatriotic', that New York, despite its colossal and elegant buildings, could not compare architecturally with European capitals, and that the New Yorkers were too busy to go very often to the theatre. Everywhere he went he ate a great many oysters.

Schliemann was not the only traveller to New York in the middle of the nineteenth century to marvel at the crowds, the liveried black coachmen, the intense social life and the bustling hotels. The city was at a moment of expansion, with growing numbers of foreign tourists pouring across from Europe as transatlantic travel improved and the steamer replaced the far slower sailing packet. It was a city of extremes. While the splendid, granite-faced Astor House was all marble and silks inside, with visitors competing fiercely for unreserved places in the dining rooms – themselves a novelty to Schliemann who was accustomed to European inns, where travellers were served in their rooms – New York possessed many miles of slums, inhabited mainly by Irish immigrants and freed slaves, and pigs which scavenged freely in the streets. Opposite the Astor House stood Barnum's Museum, which contained a live 25-foot-long boa constrictor, a giraffe, also alive, wax figures of Wellington, Nelson and Napoleon, and the club said to have been used to kill Captain Cook. 'Ice-saloons' were very popular. Like other visitors of the time, Schliemann cannot have failed to have been disgusted by what Dickens called the most 'revolting custom' he encountered: the universal habit of spitting – at home, in the theatre, in shops, on carpets, and during meals – which made him feel that the whole of America was 'covered in spit'.

Invited to a ball given in the Astor House by the Light-Guard, he noted that 'Yankee' ladies faded fast, and though 'beautiful and symmetrical' at sixteen and eighteen, they were worn out and old by the age of twenty-two. He also found them frivolous. Another European visitor to America at this time, the Nobel Prize-winning author of *Quo Vadis*, Henryk Sienkiewicz, equally remarked that American women led 'a life of external superficiality like so many frolicsome kittens'. Schliemann decided that American men were 'thin and weak' compared to English ones, but, if properly approached, 'very frank and communicative'.

In Washington came what has been dismissed as another lie;* but here Schliemann's detractors are on weak ground. In his American diary, Schliemann described an audience with President Fillmore, at seven o'clock one evening, lasting an hour and a half. The President was 'very plain and friendly looking'; his wife 'noble' and also friendly; his seventeen-year-old daughter 'rather green' (perhaps pale ?). There is no record of what was said. At eight-thirty, the doors were opened for a 'levee' and some eight hundred people entered; Schliemann stayed until eleven o'clock. Considerable doubt has been cast on whether it was possible that the President of the United States would devote ninety minutes to an unknown young German businessman, but many other European travellers to Washington in the middle of the last century left accounts of personal audiences with the President, recording their amazement at the informality of the White House, and the ease with which a foreigner could drop in with no more introduction than a personal calling card.

Early in January 1851, six months after Millard Fillmore became President, the journalist and lawyer Benjamin Brown French came to the White House and joined 'as dense a crowd as it has been my fortune to get into for many a day ... we at length had the pleasure of reaching the *presence* and shaking by the hand our excellent Chief Magistrate, Mr Fillmore, and paying our respects to the Presidentess and her daughter'. In 1854, three years after Schliemann's visit, a British publisher called William Chambers wrote of his astonishment when President Pierce was called out of a cabinet meeting simply to shake hands with

---

* W.Calder III, 'Schliemann on Schliemann : A Study in the Use of Sources', *Greek, Roman and Byzantine Studies*, vol. 13, 1972.

him. Dickens, when he was in Washington in 1842, compared the White
House to an English club. A friend took him to call on the President.
They rang the front-door bell several times and, when no one answered,
pushed the door open and joined other visitors strolling or lolling about.
After a while, Dickens was ushered into a small room, where the President greeted him warmly. Both Chambers and Dickens attended a 'levee',
recording that the doors were kept open to all comers, that sometimes
as many as three thousand people turned up, that there were no police
or guards, and that the President wandered casually around, shaking the
hand of anyone who approached. Even Trollope, who spent nine months
in America in 1861, remarked that there were times when anyone could
walk into the President's house without introduction or invitation. It
seems highly likely that Schliemann's account was basically accurate.

Schliemann spent several days sightseeing around Washington, a city
universally disliked for its vast open spaces, half-finished buildings and
air of desolation, its immense avenues leading nowhere and whole areas
'wild, trackless, unbridged, uninhabited', where less than 60,000 people
rattled about in a place designed for over a million. A Scot named Baxter
called it 'a perfect pigsty'. Trollope, searching for something nice to say,
admitted that at least the 'design is grand'. Schliemann then went back
to New York, admiring the ambitious new railway-building programme,
and embarked by steamer for Chagres in Panama, the first step in what
was then a very long and perilous trek west, noting forlornly that the
lavatories on board were dirty, that there were no ham and eggs, choc-
olate, ice or fresh meat, and that the ship's servants were reluctant to
indulge his habit of taking baths in saltwater. As he neared Panama, he
switched over to Spanish in his diary.

From Chagres, the most miserable place he had ever seen, he rode on
a mule over the Cordilleras Andes, overcome by this 'immense Eden',
with its monkeys and brightly coloured parrots, in which all nature
'seemed to ring the praise of the Almighty', reaching Panama to slake
his thirst on the only safe drink, a mixture of brandy and water. On the
last leg of the journey to California, on another steamer putting in to
Mexico, he found time to remark that the Mexicans were 'false, ignorant,
arrogant'. The journey from New York had taken a month. Schliemann
very seldom complained about physical discomfort in his diary. Whatever moved was described and appraised; whatever stayed still, measured
and evaluated. He was interested in everything: longitude and latitute,
investments, costs, inventions of every kind, the freeing of black slaves,
the dimensions and designs of railway carriages, church services, clothes,

manners, habits. But his health makes few appearances.

On Wednesday 2 April Schliemann's steamer reached San Francisco. Some eight hundred ships, of every size and type, and from every country in the world, were anchored in the bay so densely that though they appeared 'grand and beautiful' it was impossible to see the city beyond their masts. A number of them were in fact permanently anchored, abandoned by their crews who had deserted to the gold mines, and were being used as shops and boarding houses. The Union Hotel, the best in San Francisco, agreed to rent him a room, but both size and price horrified him: a space six feet by five, at $7 a day. He was lucky to get one at any price. Another European traveller complained bitterly about having to share an attic full of hay with 'two judges, five ex-governors, three lawyers, three doctors and a few blacksmiths, tinkers and tailors'.

Schliemann had chosen to visit California at an extraordinary moment. For the previous two years, ever since a trader called John Sutter had found gold on his land, 'California fever', a great primitive rush for gold, had swept tens of thousands of Americans, Europeans, Latin Americans and even Chinese into a wild and forbidding country that, but for the call of wealth, would have been left to the Indians and the pioneers. The journey alone was a severe test of endurance. With veteran miners from places like Wales and Germany came the young, the destitute, the profiteers, the adventurous, not all to dig for gold, but many to provide services for the diggers – merchants, stagecoach owners, skilled craftsmen, lawyers, prostitutes, gamblers, saloon keepers, quack doctors and journalists. Most of them were men, and the atmosphere of the new gold towns was rough and tense, from the despair of those who found nothing and the excitement of those who struck lucky. In a single year, 25,000 Chinese passed through the port of San Francisco alone. In 1848, the total population of California was 14,000 people (not counting the Indians); it was to reach 250,000 by the end of 1852. Not all, of course, prospered. But over $200 million in gold dust is said to have been brought out of the ground in the five years of California's gold rush.

Schliemann decided to make Sacramento his base. One of the three main towns supplying the miners, Sacramento was barely two years old, a place of wooden houses and canvas shelters laid out on a grid, like a suburb of snow-white tents, the streets still unpaved and often piled high with goods, with excellent sport provided by rabbits, coyotes and quails in the nearby meadows (though not, as a French doctor called

Garnier maintained, tigers). Schliemann compared it to 'an immense garden covered with beautiful trees'. Despite a plague of rats, he preferred its weather – hot days and cold nights – to the gales of San Francisco. He tracked down his brother's grave, ordered a tombstone, established that Louis had been cheated of a fortune of $30,000 by his partners, and that he had died not of typhus but of mercury-poisoning from the drugs administered to cure it. He then set out to explore his surroundings. Being accustomed to incessant hard work, and finding no congenial company, he was soon profoundly bored with his idle life, and complained about the heat which descended over the country in late spring, made worse in his case by the fact that he was 'very full-blooded'. 'In no country of the world,' he wrote to his family, 'have I found so much selfishness and such immense love of money as in this Eldorado'. Money, he said, brought out in the Americans 'indescribable . . . boundless energy'.

Was Schliemann in San Francisco during the great fire of 4 June 1851, as he maintained, or did he falsify his dates ? While it now seems likely that he was in Sacramento on the night of the fire, and that his account was written from hearsay and newspaper reports, it remains an admirable piece of reporting. According to his probably doctored diary, he was awoken by calls of 'fire' to see first one, then another, of the surrounding wooden houses catch alight, and collapse inwards like houses made of cards. For a while, it seemed as if people in the sturdier brick-and-iron buildings might survive, but as the heat expanded the locks and hinges, so the doors jammed, trapping them inside: 'Sometimes by burning their hands and arms people succeeded to open the doors and get out, but finding themselves surrounded by an ocean of flames they made but a few paces, staggered and fell, rose again and fell in order not to rise any more.'

Schliemann himself claimed to have escaped by climbing to the top of the nearby Telegraph Hill, which gave him a 'frightful but sublime view, in fact the grandest spectacle I ever enjoyed', as the fire swept down Washington, Kearny, Montgomery and California streets. 'The roaring of the storm, the crack of the gunpowder, the crackling of the falling stone walls, the cries of the people and the wonderful spectacle of an immense city, burning in a dark night all joined to make this catastrophe awful in the extreme.' A rumour that the fire had been started by French incendiaries led to at least one Frenchman being thrown onto the flames.

Next morning he wandered among the 'smouldering ashes and ruins', astonished to find the Americans laughing and joking as they prepared to start building the city once again – repeated fires were to give the phoenix a place on San Francisco's official seal – though the Germans, French and English were sitting 'half in despair ... and weeping on the ashes of their destroyed property'. There was a resilience and determination in the American spirit that Schliemann was coming to admire. With its great natural resources, and its wind of democracy, the New World was infinitely appealing.

On 31 July Schliemann wrote in his diary : 'My position in the world has undergone a most memorable change to my advantage.' He had found a niche in the gold rush. Observing that vast sums of money were circulating in Sacramento, he opened a banking house in a stone-and-iron building on the corner of Front and South Streets to deal in gold dust, soon buying as much as 150 lb in a day, which was then transported, in return for coin, to Rothschilds in London, via their agent Davidson in San Francisco. From now on, Schliemann did what he enjoyed most : he worked from five in the morning until ten at night, every day, including Sundays and Christmas Day, using eight different languages, arming himself and his two clerks with Colt revolving pistols against thieves with slingshots. Between 19 October 1851 and 5 April 1852 he sold $1,350,000 worth of gold dust to Davidson.

As the months went by, he grew increasingly rich, but also increasingly disenchanted. Having initially admired the speed and energy with which the 'Californian Yankees' pursued their lives, he now complained that 'all is based here on swindling ... abominable falsehood, fraud and humbug'. To his sisters, he wrote that he would recommend a year in California to any young, hard-working, ambitious man under thirty who was intent on making his fortune ; anyone else should on no account think of joining the gold rush. In the great heat and humidity, diseases spread rapidly, and Schliemann interspersed the daily chronicles of his business deals with sentimental longings for 'my beloved Russia, my charming St Petersburg', with its 'wise and most glorious Emperor Nicholas', though some of these asides were probably edited in after his return to Europe. Although he regarded the Chinese he dealt with as 'harmless, honest and industrious', he found the 'New Granadians' and Mexicans lazy and false, the Kanakas from the Sandwich Islands robbers and marauders, and the Californian Indians 'the most disgusting people I ever saw ... very little above the beasts, of which they have the habits ... extremely dirty' living like 'ants in heaps of earth in which they literally roast, the fire being kindled in the midst of the earthen hut ... All of them are attacked by venerial sickness.' So clean and fastidious himself, Schliemann was repelled by all the dirt. Even the tiger-hunting Dr Garnier found the Indian repulsive and degenerate: 'everything about him seems languid,' he wrote in his diary, 'even his heart-beats are listless and less frequent than those of Europeans.'

After several bouts of fever, which covered Schliemann's body with yellow spots and left him vomiting and raving – he was prone to say that he resisted illness so successfully because of personal hygiene and moderation in eating and drinking – and floods which roared down from the mountains, turning the streets into waterways, the waves hurtling pedestrians into the mud, Schliemann decided that he had had enough. Even at this stage, there is a grudging admiration for the American entrepreneurial nature, and he noted, not entirely without approval, that during the flood several people 'are said to have made a hundred dollars in a single day by conveying people across the streets'.

In his diary he chose to gloss over the reasons for his abrupt departure, which seems to have been due to excessive greed on his part rather than to illness. Davidson, the agent in San Francisco, appears to have got wind of some shady deals – was Schliemann weighing the gold dust short, and making separate deals on the side, despite their agreement? – and threatened to break off their contract. Since this was crucial to Schliemann's business, he sold up the bank, and embarked on the *Golden Gate* for Panama with his last consignment of gold dust. 'Nothing', he noted, 'exceeds my joy and exultation in finding myself away from California, which seemed destined to become my grave'.

His relief was premature. Panama, with Nicaragua one of the two main gateways back to the East, was full of thieves, eager to rob the returning miners of their gold. The Andes, in the torrential rains that arrived in December and January, became extremely hazardous. After a miserable journey, Schliemann reached the Atlantic coast to find that the steamer for New York had left that same morning. Though the Californian gold rush was to act as a spur to the development of passenger ships along the coasts of the United States, leading not just to more ships being built but to far greater comfort for passengers – ice-rooms, ventilators, upholstery in every shade of velvet and damask – the delays between sailings could still be interminable. What followed was the stuff of nightmares. The rain poured down. There being nowhere to stay, Schliemann camped under some trees, lying on his trunks to stop them being stolen. There was nothing to eat. Together with other stranded passengers, he managed to kill an enormous lizard, which he then ate raw 'with the same voracious appetite as if it had been a roasted turkey'.

By the end of the month, over 2500 desperate people had gathered in Panama to wait for a ship. To avoid starvation, they foraged for monkeys, lizards, turtles and even crocodiles, and ate them raw, because there was nothing to make a fire with. Isthumus-fever, diarrhoea, dysentery, the ague, not to mention scorpions and rattlesnakes, carried off dozens of people every day, and their decomposing, putrefying bodies filled the air with 'fetid odours and poisonous miasma'. Mosquitoes tormented the survivors, who wallowed in the mud to avoid being bitten. 'We became so familiarized with death,' Schliemann was to write, 'that we laughed and amused ourselves at the convulsions of the dying ... crimes were perpetrated among us; crimes so terrible! that now at a later date I cannot think of it without cold and trembling horror.' Murder? Cannibalism? Schliemann was never to explain.

After fourteen days, a cannon-shot was heard signalling the arrival of the *Sierra Madre*. Schliemann splashed out on a stateroom with two beds to himself (at a cost of $130), gave his wet and filthy clothes to the steward, took some wine and beef tea and collapsed into bed. He felt extremely lucky to be alive. A minor sore on his leg which had begun to fester, had 'enlarged daily and the flesh fell off for a considerable distance and the bare bone was visible'. The ship's surgeon disinfected and dressed the wound.

Six-and-a-half days later, the *Sierra Madre* docked on the American East Coast. Schliemann was exhausted but jubilant. 'Full of enthusiasm, I cried out: Oh New York! New York!' It was like the day he first saw Hamburg, as an ambitious young man of nineteen, all over again. But this time he was very rich.

4

CLEVER, CRAFTY
AND COMPETENT

Schliemann was a man who yearned to be in the places he had just left, forgetting the miserable times, remembering only the good ones. While in California he had longed for the old world, and particularly for St Petersburg, 'where all my hopes, all my desires are concentrated', and for whose inhabitants he claimed he felt 'liking and love' a thousand times more powerful than anything he felt for other people. Even before docking in Liverpool, he was writing to Wilhelmine and Dorothea that his passion for New York was such 'that I desire nothing better than staying on; and as soon as I complete my European voyage I have the intention to settle there.'

He reached St Petersburg in August 1852, pausing in London to cash in the gold dust and have his wound treated by a doctor in Chiswick, who ordered him to stay absolutely still in his hotel room, with his leg kept permanently horizontal. Driven 'nearly to despair' by loneliness and boredom, he followed the doctor's advice for barely a week then departed for Mecklenburg and Ankershagen. It was many years since he had last seen his family. It must have been a sweet homecoming, for he was now, as he was quick to report to his father, widely considered 'the most clever, crafty and competent merchant'. The brief stay in his childhood village passed in a mood of heightened emotion and sentimentality. 'It is impossible for me to describe the impressions produced upon me by the sight of the places where I spent the happy years of my childhood,' he wrote later, with cloying tenderness, conveniently quite forgetting the painful social ostracism and consequent parting from Minna. For a few hours at least, he seemed to toy with the idea of buying an estate, selling up his Russian business and becoming a landlord farmer instead. However, the appeal of Mecklenburg's sandy plains did not last and he was soon noting that 'I shall make St Petersburg my home for the remainder of my life and never think of leaving it again'.

If one believes Schliemann, there were seldom significant lengths of time when he was not in love. The diaries of his travels contain several references, some admiring, some disparaging, to the different types of women produced by different cultures and societies. After his boyhood passion for Minna Meincke, and his brief flirtation with his cousin Sophie of the 'beauteous cheeks', he had been introduced while in Moscow to the niece of a friend called Zhivago, a girl whom he described as 'an angel of virtue and beauty'. Ekaterina was sixteen. As his capital and his standing grew, so Schliemann became an ever more desirable catch and his Russian merchant associates lost no time in presenting their unmarried daughters to him. Though Ekaterina's family evidently favoured the match, Schliemann himself hesitated, trying and failing to persuade his sisters to join him in St Petersburg to help him decide on a suitable wife. An entry in the diary of his first European trip suggests that he was wary of Russian women, lamenting 'the singular and little encouraging deportment of our Muscovite ladies towards strangers' and the way they seemed to feel towards them nothing but 'antipathy and hatred'. He did, however, concede that Russian girls made fine linguists and pleasing pianists.

Ekaterina was soon replaced by another Sophie, 'the most adorable creature it is possible to imagine'. Sophie spoke three European languages; she was 'very thrifty' and so, Schliemann told his family, 'we shall grow rich'. It was not to be. By the end of the year, Sophie had fallen for a military officer. Branding her 'too young and giddy', Schliemann decided to switch his suit to a 'beautiful and very clever Russian girl' who had, unfortunately, no dowry. She, too, vanished.

In the summer of 1850, before leaving for America, Schliemann had been introduced to the niece of another business acquaintance, Ekaterina Petrovna Lyshina, a somewhat haughty young woman of twenty-six with a pale, oval face and dark eyes. In October 1852, back in St Petersburg no more than a few months, Schliemann wrote to his family: 'By the time you receive this letter I shall, please God, already have been married for five days.' His bride was Ekaterina who, having refused an earlier proposal, now consented to the marriage, largely, it seems, because of his new-found fortune. The wedding took place in a Russian Orthodox church. Ekaterina was neither beautiful nor very nice but she came from a desirable family, her father being a successful St Petersburg merchant and her brother tutor to one of the princes. Ekaterina, he reported, was a 'very good, simple, clever and sensible girl'. Their marriage, from the start, was doomed.

At the age of thirty, Schliemann was self-centred, volatile and highly exacting, a man who took pride, as he put it, in his 'fiery nature' and his ability to 'feel very deeply'. He was certainly both eccentric and autocratic. He was soon accusing Ekaterina of wastefulness; she, in return, complained bitterly that he was very parsimonious. They had not been married for long before he was writing her reproachful letters: 'Alas, how far removed from my happy anticipations are the terrible realities of life at present! You do not love me ... and are completely indifferent to all that concerns me.' He was right. Ekaterina shows no signs of having loved or even liked him; one of the few traits of her character that comes down across the years is profound selfishness. To his sisters, Schliemann moaned: 'Intense desire, hopeless passion, can drive us to despair and madness.' After the birth of a first child in 1855, a boy called Sergei for whom Schliemann felt immense love, Ekaterina became very reluctant to share his bed. He was to say that their two other children, both girls – Natalia, born in 1858, and Nadezhda three years later – had to be 'stolen' from his wife. Ekaterina had by now come to hate nearly everything about him, even the great pleasure he took in his foreign languages.

To get away from the misery at home, Schliemann worked harder than ever. Having doubled his already considerable fortune in California, he now set up his own wholesale indigo firm in Moscow. Within months, he had cargo ships arriving at the Russian ports every day, dozens of freight wagons transporting his goods from Königsberg to Memel, and a cash turnover of a million silver roubles a month. Complaining that he was obliged to work too hard, he found it impossible to leave even the most menial of tasks to the clerks he employed, continuing to write all business letters himself. He was always in a hurry, always on the move, often at odds with his employees, quick to boast of his profits and the skill with which he conducted transactions. Soon his capital had doubled again, then tripled. When he learned that the Tsar was about to issue a new Code of Laws, he hastened to buy up all the fine-quality paper he could lay his hands on, knowing that the Code would be bound to be printed in vast quantities on good paper. It was soon being said that Schliemann controlled a third of all indigo imported into Russia.

But it was the war in Crimea that turned him from a wealthy into an exceedingly rich man. Schliemann treated wars as he treated all commercial operations : as opportunities to make money. Neither in the Crimea, not later, in the American Civil War, was he much interested in the causes or morality of the fighting and those who profited from it. War meant a need for supplies, and if providing them entailed running blockades and profiteering, then it simply had to be done. Schliemann was turning out to be capable of remarkable single-mindedness ; combined wiith an apparent indifference both to politics and to many of the social issues of the day, it sometimes makes him appear curiously timeless. He sits very lightly in the history of his times.

One of the prizes at stake in the Turkish–Russian conflict was control of the Hellespont. Britain supported the Turkish position and imposed a blockade on Russian ports, including that of St Petersburg. To break it, Schliemann and a number of Russian merchants ordered large shipments of war material to be delivered to Memel, the neutral Prussian port, with the intention of transporting it to Russia overland. Schliemann invested almost his entire savings in this deal.

On the evening of 3 October 1854, Schliemann reached Königsberg on his way to Memel to take consignment of his delivery. Looking out of his hotel window, he was taken aback to see an inscription carved over the gates of a tower nearby. 'Fortune's face changes with the phases of the moon', it read. 'Waxing and waning, it does not know how to stay still.' The words seemed to him to have an ominous ring.

On the final lap of his journey to Memel, he was told that the entire city had gone up in flames, consuming every warehouse. He arrived to find 'an immense graveyard on which blackened walls and chimneys stood out like tombstones, mournful monuments to the fragility of human things'. After initial despair, calculating that eight-and-a-half years of work had been lost, he caught the mail coach to return to St Petersburg, trying to console himself with the thought that Schröders would probably give him credit so that he could start again. If Schliemann could appear ruthless, he was also largely without self-pity, and very impatient with those who indulged in regrets or self-recrimination. On the coach was one of the warehouse clerks. Having discovered who the morose passenger opposite him was, the young man exclaimed that Schliemann was in fact the only merchant whose goods had not been lost in the fire. Reaching Memel at a moment when all the warehouses were full, Schliemann's goods had been stored in a wooden barracks on the edge of the town, which happened to lie behind the building in which the fire had started. The wind blowing steadily from the north, it had eaten up all that lay before it, leaving the wooden barracks untouched. 'Divine accident', Schliemann noted piously, 'protected me marvellously'.

In an autobiographical fragment written for one of his books, *Ilios*, more than twenty years later, Schliemann described how he had then speedily sold his entire stock 'to great advantage', turned the money over again and again, carried out a successful deal in indigo, dyewoods and war material (saltpetre, brimstone and lead), and 'more than doubled my capital in a single year'. 'All through the war', he was to admit, 'I thought of nothing but money'.

In 1852, the year of Schliemann's marriage, Tsar Nicholas I was nearing the end of a reign which had seen the values of orthodoxy, autocracy and nationalism enhanced and the torrents of reform kept at bay. St Petersburg was a city of palaces and mansions, built on a colossal scale, its highly intricate social seasons still regulated by the Church calendar, age-old customs and the whims and intrigues of the Imperial court. Fasts were followed by fêtes and balls, the tone set by members of the Imperial family who vied with each other to hold ever more exotic and sumptuous receptions. At one ball given by the Grand Duchess Helene in the Michael Palace, 1500 boxes of the rarest plants in flower, including palms and banana trees, recreated a tropical forest, the greenery reflected in a thousand mirrors of glass and crystal. For occasions such as these, flowers could be rented rather than bought, and florists usually had two prices, a selling price and a renting price. Lady Londonderry, on a visit with her husband to the Russian court, remarked that, trying as the weather in St Petersburg could be, with its 'severe cold, the damp exhalation attendant on its marshy position, and the sudden changes of temperature . . .', its inhabitants were 'the most intelligent, agreeable, *distingués*, clever persons imaginable'. Russian ladies, whether for their daily promenades along the Nevsky Prospekt in their landaus, or for the incessant round of at-homes, dressed very richly and with great taste. Dinner parties took place at six o'clock in the afternoon. Galoshes, reminded the author of the John Murray *Guide to Russia*, should be removed on entering a house.

Every season, every feast-day, every occasion had its own soup, its own special pastry; fruit was eaten on 8 August, ice on Easter Sunday. Visitors sometimes complained that the Russians never let their bread bake for long enough, nor allowed fruit to ripen properly on the trees, and one German traveller of the time, Johann Kohr, protested strongly at the Russian habit of chopping everything up – vegetables, fruit, meat, fish – to put into pies. Spring each year was heralded by the sight of little carts, each loaded with a single enormous square block of ice, sparkling when the sun shone, set up along the banks of the Neva like so many pillars at Stonehenge, to be sold for the icehouses in anticipation of the warmer weather to come.

St Petersburg's large foreign community was dominated by the Germans; after them came the Finns, the French and the Swedes. French was the language spoken in society, though English was at least understood. This cosmopolitan air suited Schliemann, who found time to add Polish and Swedish to his range of languages. For all Ekaterina's reproaches, the Schliemanns lived in some style, in a house with two reception rooms and twelve bedrooms; they kept a carriage and horses and a good wine cellar. The boastful side of Schliemann's nature revelled in his prosperity. Remarking in a diary on the nature of his business relations, he observed that fellow merchants 'approved heartily of my ways of carrying things out, and *brûlant du desir* to forge active links with me to the advantage and pleasure of both of us'.

Not entirely captivated by the intricacies of Russian social life, and beginning to lose sympathy with the Imperial family – 'where an effete autocracy rules,' he observed sternly, 'greatness will never be attained' – Schliemann began to gather around him a group of more scholarly acquaintances. The 1850s were a marvellous moment in Russia; with Tolstoy and Turgenev both writing. And not only in Russia. In France, Flaubert had not long published *Madame Bovary* and the Goncourt brothers their *Journal*; in England, there were Trollope, Thackeray, Mrs Gaskell and Dickens; in America, Emerson and Longfellow. Schliemann was alive, if not to politics, then to the writers of the day, though he continued to portray himself with irritating false modesty as a 'mere dabbler in scholarly pursuits', whose 'scribblings all collapse like a house without foundations'. He was at home, to his intellectual friends, every Sunday. It was only on these occasions that he seemed to escape feeling 'like a toper in a bar parlour surrounded by bottles of spirits'.

Where Schliemann did take himself seriously, of course, was over foreign languages, though he insisted that this was a necessary skill, and not to be confused with actual knowledge. 'Languages,' he wrote some time later to his cousin Adolf, 'help to educate, but by themselves do not make an educated person.' Early in 1856, after his profits from the Crimean War had given him more leisure, he decided to tackle the one obvious European language that he still lacked : Greek, both ancient and modern. It was the first time he had studied, not for business or to make himself understood on his travels, but for sheer pleasure. Adopting his by now perfected technique of repetition and memorizing, he decided to treat ancient Greek as a modern language, learning only declensions and verbs, and none of the other rules of grammar. He resolved to devote every Sunday to nothing but Greek ; practice, reading the classics, then learning 'choice pieces' by heart, seemed to him the best way of avoiding the problems encountered by schoolboys, whom he observed being 'troubled and tormented' by eight years of tedious grammar, only to emerge ignorant. It is easy to overlook how very determined a person Schliemann was.

Soon, he was overwhelmed by the beauty of the sounds ; it was all far more glorious than he had ever expected. After the first six Sundays he felt sufficiently in control to compose a number of complicated sentences in ancient Greek ; these he wrote in a letter to his first classical tutor, his uncle Friedrich, the pastor in Kalkhorst, with whom he had stayed as a child. Over the next two years, he filled thirty-five notebooks with exercises. These lesson books, bound into volumes of several thousand pages each, with their painstakingly copied sentences, as full of blots and crossings-out as those of any schoolboy, are often more revealing of Schliemann's character than his diaries, in which weather, flora and social observations are recorded precisely and often with pedantry. Here, instead, are deliberations about whether or not to make Greece his next home, or whether to return instead to America, and speculations as to the honesty of various colleagues. At the end of the two years, Schliemann was able to announce that he could write 'in ancient Greek with the greatest fluency on any subject I am acquainted with'. To fix the words more firmly in his mind, he now read only from ancient Greek authors, going over their words again and again in his mind like a living language. He read both the *Iliad* and the *Odyssey* several times. 'Whenever a man finds errors in my Greek,' he boasted, 'I can immediately prove that I am right, by merely reciting passages from the classics where the sentences employed by me occur.' To his sisters in Germany, he spoke of the 'consuming passion' which now bound him to the Greek language. He was seldom to be seen any longer without a copy of Homer somewhere nearby. When his teacher arrived late for a lesson, he was scolded in Greek.

In the autumn of 1857, his business ventures were unexpectedly threatened by a sudden wind of instability that swept through the

European markets. This time, Schliemann was right to be concerned. He had bills outstanding not only in Amsterdam, but in London, Paris and Hamburg. Foreign firms were going bankrupt one after another. To survive, he was forced to take huge risks and to speculate in ways to which he was not accustomed. Though the gambles paid off, and his fortune survived intact, he was to say later that his anxiety had been such that his hair turned entirely grey, 'notwithstanding my toughness of mind'.

Once again, Schliemann had been contemplating retiring from business; once again, a temporary reversal in his fortunes made him pause. Instead, he decided to visit the Orient, and in November 1858 he set off for Jerusalem, Syria and Egypt, where he travelled as far down the Nile as the Second Cataract, picking up Arabic along the way, before making his way home via Turkey and Greece. Though his diaries of this trip – 254 pages, written in Italian, Arabic, Greek, English, French and Swedish – include a number of rather charming sketches, they say nothing about a short visit to Mecca. Emil Ludwig, Schliemann's official biographer in the 1920s, claims that this was kept secret because Mecca is to this day forbidden to non-Muslims. It is on these journeys, and in the diaries that accompany them, that Schliemann's sense of apartness comes through almost painfully. 'My occupations and inclinations being quite different to those of other people,' he observed on one occasion, 'and seeing the impossibility of contracting friendships in my actual position in life, I took the greatest care to avoid societies and other public houses calculated to offer too frequent opportunities of getting acquainted with other young people.' Behind the stilted, pompous phrases lies great loneliness.

While he was away, a merchant called Stepan Solovieff, who owed Schliemann a large sum of money, took the occasion to sue him for forgery, knowing that the extreme dilatoriness of the Russian legal system would safely stall matters for a very long time. The inevitable referral from Commercial court to the Senate ensured a delay of at least three to four years, but Schliemann decided to sit it out. He was now making an enormous amount of money at a remarkable rate, but he was beginning to shift his business interests away from Russia and towards the more promising New World, where he had started to buy Cuban and American railway bonds. Once again, war was instrumental in boosting his fortune. When the Civil War in America led to a blockade of the Southern ports, Schliemann instantly turned to dealing in cotton, then switched to tea, though throughout his years as a dealer indigo remained his 'staple commodity'. Later, he was to say that much of his success as a merchant came from the simple fact that he chose to deal with his customers personally, rather than entrust important transactions to 'clerks or servants'.

Schliemann was beginning to lose sympathy with the Russians. As he explained to a young Italian called Giulio Nicati, who wrote to him about employment: '... With your zeal you would do well anywhere in the world, but you would succeed best of all in Russia, for the simple reason that the native Russians are not qualified to carry out foreign export and import work, because they possess neither the stability of character, nor the necessary knowledge, nor the experience; and the cunning particular to them is of no help in foreign affairs.'

Were these all attributes which he saw in Ekaterina's character? Ten years of marriage had soured him, and it seems that Ekaterina's feelings towards him had turned from barely concealed dislike to loathing. She continued to find him mean; he regarded her as incurably extravagant. There were endless quarrels, many of them over very small sums of money.

Schliemann himself had not so much changed; he had grown more distinct as a character, more clear as to his views and purposes. He was no less mercurial, capable of sudden and often rather frightening swings of mood, but he now made few attempts to curb his impetuosity. He could be both genial and very chilly, as his sisters knew all too well, having suffered from his 'icy coldness'. A letter written at about this time to his father, who had evidently asked for money, is revealing. 'In placing this sum at your disposal I must however insist that in future you keep a respectable manservant and a respectable maid' (shades of the scandal that ruined his childhood?) 'while preserving a decent standard of cleanliness in your home. I expect your plates, dishes, cups, knives and forks to be shining and clean ...' And yet Schliemann was not without self-knowledge, and capable of regretful insights. 'I am, I know, mean and avaricious,' he admitted one day. 'I shall have to give up being so mercenary.' A photograph taken at the time shows a small man, with receding hair and a soft, drooping moustache, dwarfed by the enormous top hat and coat he is wearing. It has wide lapels and a collar made of fur, and it reaches down to the ground. Schliemann's rather small eyes have a watchful expression. Neither here, nor in any other photograph of him that has survived, is he smiling.

In the spring of 1864, at the age of forty-two, Schliemann finally took the decision he had so often postponed. Having at last won his case in the Appeal court, and been paid the money he was owed by Solovieff, he wound up his business and made plans for a world tour. He left no guarantee as to when he might return to St Petersburg, though he was leaving behind three young children, Nadezhda, the smallest, being only just three. It was a gesture of quite startling loneliness. Before he set out, he wrote his will, depositing it with Schröders in London, with instructions to open it only when no word had been heard from him for at least six months.

5

A GREAT NEED
TO KNOW

There are many reasons why people travel. Some, of course, find the whole experience lonely and threatening. But for those who thrive on strangeness, travel can be a marvellous way of forgetting. It can be used to acquire knowledge. It can serve to fill an awkward, empty, moment of time, or provide an opportunity to take stock and plan the future. For Schliemann, rich, restless, unhappy, with no clear plans in mind, it was a little of all these things. Travel can also be addictive, and his diaries exude an air of compulsion, a need to keep moving, to see nothing but new sights, to smell, taste, hear, observe, measure and compare new things.

In just under two years, Schliemann visited four continents and nine countries, some more than once, filling over five hundred pages of diaries with entries in nine different languages, many of them curiously passionless, except when a landscape moved him to bursts of purple poetry. He rode on an elephant in India, went to the theatre in Japan, visited graveyards in New Orleans, underwent an operation in Jakarta, saw a meat-packing plant in Chicago, and measured tree-trunks in the Yosemite valley. He wrote, in French, his first book. As a traveller, he could be both pernickety and extraordinarily tolerant of discomfort. Though on his own for virtually the entire time, with very little news of home or of his three young children, he does not seem to have been consciously lonely, at least not in the way most people are lonely. Above all, and at all times, he was filled with curiosity; and that overpowering sense of excitement and drive, the desire to learn more and see more, appears never to have faltered. His energy was phenomenal. The journey was a remarkable achievement. 'Devenu ensuite voyageur', he was to say. 'J'ai été voyageur par excellence.' Schliemann was to return to Europe a changed man.

The world tour began in Aachen on 21 May 1854. A week later Schliemann was in Tunis, looking at the ruins of Carthage, having paused briefly in Paris and Cagliari. Then came Alexandria, Port Said, where he drank several buckets of Nile water and broke out in spots, Italy again, for a cure at a spa near Bologna and a visit to the ruins of Capri, Paestum and Pompeii, and back to Paris via Marseilles. In mid-October he set out again for Würzburg, starting this diary in German, then switching to Italian. When he reached Vienna he mixed business with pleasure; taking an omnibus with a guide to the Zoo, he noted – still in Italian – that the cold was such that all the animals had to be kept locked inside, except for the bears and the wolves. His health was beginning to give him trouble. Apart from skin ailments and bouts of diarrhoea, he was experiencing the first of the agonizing earaches that were to continue to torment him, probably exacerbated by his obsessive belief in the curative properties of sea water. Even in his Hamburg days, Schliemann had been convinced that regular swimming in the sea was essential for good health. In the south of Italy, he suffered an attack of earache so painful that he consulted one of the many specialists who were to counsel him for the rest of his life. When it came to pain, Schliemann was remarkably stoical.

By 10 November, still writing his diary in excellent Italian, he was in Trieste, admiring the engineering that had gone into the mountain trains; two days later, he paused in Ancona where, at the opera, his attention was caught by a girl sitting not far away. 'Never', he recorded in his diary, 'have I seen a young girl who pleased me more'. She had a somewhat acquiline nose, strong features, and wore 'grey (beige) gloves'. With her was a distinguished-looking gentleman, whom Schliemann took to be her father. He longed to make their acquaintance, but since he was due to catch a boat that night for Egypt, he held back. The weather was good; his spirits were high. From Alexandria, he took a steamer to India, sharing a cabin with three other men, enjoying the goat for dinner and choosing to have his baths at 3.45 in the morning, and 3.15 in the afternoon. It was unpleasantly hot, and Schliemann recorded not just the daily temperature, but the longitude and the latitude. He was interested to discover that the hotter and more humid the weather, the more he longed for spices, particularly a sauce consisting of turmeric, chilli, coconut, coriander seed and garlic. Whenever the ship docked for any length of time, he hurried ashore and hired a carriage and driver to show him the sights. On board, he began to teach himself Hindi.

The sea journey took just under a month. By now, Schliemann was a keen connoisseur of ship life, a form of travel which seemed to soothe his restlessness. Ships were rapidly becoming much more comfortable, as rival companies vied with each other to provide ever more elegant staterooms, with carpets on the floor, padded built-in sofas and perhaps a rocking-chair or a wooden washstand, though passengers continued to bring their own sheep with them, and even, when the journeys were very long, to plant small vegetable gardens with lettuces and spring onions. Before leaving Europe, Schliemann had asked Schröders for a letter of credit so that he could buy indigo in India, and also so that he could 'find out how indigo grows and how it is processed'. Having initially planned to avoid business altogether, he was now pleased that he had accepted Schröders' offer to equip him with useful introductions. 'Mr Schliemann is undertaking an extensive tour of the Far East', a director of the firm had written, 'as much for his pleasure as anything, though he might find opportunity to advance the interest of his business'. The opportunity presented itself in Calcutta, where he went to an auction and acquired fifty chests of 'the finest and highest quality' indigo.

As he wandered, he continued to ponder on world trade, and what effect industrialization and wars were having on the production and distribution of various commodities. Since his last visit to America, North and South had been fighting over the Union and the emancipation of the slaves; and by the time Schliemann reached India in the winter of 1864, General Grant had begun his invasion of Virginia which, together with General Sherman's march through Georgia and South Carolina, would see the destruction of the Southern armies by the spring of 1865. Characteristically, Schliemann was less interested in the casualties of the war – the bloodiest in American history – than what freedom for four million slaves would do to the cotton trade.

Five months into his world tour, Schliemann was having fun. He stayed in India for six weeks, roaming about as his will took him, writing down, day after day, his observations: customs, costs, transport, sights, decorations, clothes, plants and the weather were all minutely chronicled, much of the time in English, with occasional lapses into Italian and Hindi. He proclaimed a trip to 'Agra, Delhi, Lucknow, Benares, etc' the most 'interesting' he had ever made – 'interesting' is Schliemann's highest term of praise. The Himalayas gave him enormous pleasure and brought out a touch of passion. The scenery was 'picturesque beyond all and every description'; looking from side to side 'I could not satisfy my eyes – the panoramas were too grand and too sublime'. He looked at them for two hours.

Schliemann decided to celebrate the Russian New Year, which fell on 13 January, with a ride on an elephant in Lucknow. It was a typical Schliemann occasion. Though elephants were normally ridden only by rajas and government commissioners, he had been promised an outing. For several hours he sat and waited. No elephant appeared. Exasperated, he ordered a buggy instead. Buggy and elephant arrived at the same time. Irritably dismissing the buggy, he climbed into the howdah on the elephant's back, took some measurements and wrote a description of it in his diary. The elephant set off, travelling at what Schliemann calculated to be three miles an hour; he recorded his annoyance at finding that the claim that an elephant moved at the speed of a galloping horse was a lie. They crossed a river, the water reaching up to the great beast's eyes, and called at a silkworm factory, where Schliemann noted that while Chinese silkworms were said to give six to seven harvests a year, those in Bengal, he was informed, produced only one, but of especially large cocoons. The elephant was praised for the good views it afforded, and for keeping going despite the efforts of a group of boys to provoke it.

In keeping with his frugal nature, for even at his richest Schliemann was prone to worry about money, he travelled second-class by train for the thousand-mile journey from Calcutta to Delhi. He minded less having to sleep on 'bare stones', in places where 'beds, blankets or towels are unknown things', than being overcharged for 'miserable' meals. When a Mr Heseltine, an innkeeper in Rajpur, demanded an exorbitant sum for a 'nasty watersoup with a little flour and a still more nasty blood-sausage with cold potatoes and a bottle of sour beer', he was extremely indignant. He was always on the lookout for deception. Concluding, on very little evidence, that the 'hindous' were 'great cheaters', he tested out his hypothesis on a young boy who had asked to be taken on as a servant, by declaring that he would employ only Christians. When the boy instantly offered to convert, Schliemann recorded with disgust that it would 'appear that the hindou faith has no deep roots'. It does not seem to have occurred to him that the boy might have been in desperate need of money.

Schliemann had high hopes of China; it was, after all, a country of great scholars. And yet of all his trips, it was perhaps the least successful. Most of the time he was miserable. He complained about the dust, the smell, the food, and above all about the little two-wheeled carts used to ferry people about, which he found so uncomfortable that he ended up perching astride the pole. Even the one person he met and liked, an expatriate English missionary-turned-interpreter in his mid-twenties called Robert Germain Thomas, who delighted him with a list of polite expressions used by the Chinese, he ended up by criticizing. He approved of the man's nine fluent languages, but noted censoriously that he could easily have bettered himself by trying harder.

The visit started badly. Schliemann took an instant loathing to his first port of call, Tientsin; on his travels he had seen many dirty cities, but none so repulsive. Reaching Peking at six o'clock on the evening of 30 April, he was appalled to learn that the city possessed no hotels. A Buddhist monastery offered him a room, but at such an exorbitant price that he haggled with the monks until the sum was halved. He hated his raised brick bed, but did find time to measure the scrolls that hung above it. There was no food to be had that night; when some yellow rice and green tea were served at five o'clock next morning, Schliemann remarked irritably that he could not possibly drink his tea without milk and sugar, and that there was no salt in the rice. The chopsticks were unmanageable.

He spent the first day wandering furiously about the streets, which had been turned into mud by heavy rain, fulminating against the debris and decay, dismissing the exquisite interiors as irrelevant and bemoaning the fact that Peking, 'now inhabited by a degenerate race, was once peopled by a great and inventive nation'. A distinct interest in the past, and particularly in ruins, was, however, emerging. While in Delhi Schliemann had copied the inscription in the throne hall of a palace, and made a detailed note about the pillar of the Katoob Minar: 'its form tapers or diminishes from the base to the summit ... This artistic arrangement adds to the apparent height of the pillar by exaggerating the perspective ...' In Peking he now set about examining columns, sculptures and bridges. On his walks around the city he came across a number of newly severed human heads, left after a recent execution, a sight he registered, without comment. In a restaurant, he was offered a swallow's nest to put in his soup; he said it tasted like fishy glue. In their own country, the Chinese, he observed, were depressingly like those he had encountered in the gold-mining towns of California – bestial, depraved and dirty, probably on account of the opium they smoked. So he raged, and so the rain continued to fall.

The real goal of his trip was the Great Wall. Within days he set out for Ku-pa-ku, on the frontier with Manchuria; the sun was at last shining and he wore an Arab turban around his head which, he remarked, excited rather more curiosity than would an orang-utang or gorilla on a Parisian boulevard. The last leg was a steep climb. Schliemann had wisely brought with him a measuring tape and so was able to record that the bricks were 25 centimetres high and 17 centimetres thick, that the Wall itself stood between 20 and 30 feet high, and that the distance between towers was approximately 300 feet. He spent the afternoon perched high above the ground, thinking about its early defenders, fighting off the Mongolian nomads from Central Asia, and when it began to grow dark, he slithered down on his stomach, a brick pinched from the Wall tied around his waist with a piece of string. He was, for the first and only time in China, jubilant. The Wall was indeed as 'grandiose' as he had hoped; in fact, it was a hundred times *more* grandiose, the greatest structure ever made by man, a monument to a past glory now so conspicuously lacking in modern China. The Wall seemed to him a 'fabulous work of a race of antediluvian giants'.

After this, there was not much to keep him. He returned to spend a few more cross days in Peking, going to the theatre and inspecting the bound feet of a young Chinese prostitute, condemning the custom as barbarous. The Empress Tsu Hsi was on the throne, the Tai'ping rebellion was not yet over in the Yangtse valley, and the numbers of dead in the other rebellions erupting throughout the country were already being counted in their millions; Schliemann's diary records no interest in these matters. Nor, more surprisingly perhaps, did he concern himself with the flourishing silk and tea trade.

Japan, on the other hand, fascinated him. Though it continued to rain much of the time, he would later write wistfully of how happy he had felt there. Taking rooms in a charming Japanese inn in the middle of a garden of camellias, he visited the Kabuki theatre, enjoyed the friend-liness of the Japanese women and admired their silk kimonos, approved of the neat, bare rooms, the wooden houses and the delicate formal gardens. He even remarked on the phlegmatic dogs, stretched out peace-fully asleep in the streets, and on the fact that Japanese cats had tails only an inch long. There was something about Japan's 'gentle decorum' that he found delightful. Even the porters who carried his luggage at Yokohama were not only polite but honest. They were also clean, and Japan's obsession with cleanliness matched his own.

Schliemann had reached Japan at a rare moment of peace between the

Mikado, the spritual Emperor, and the Shogun, the secular ruler. It was twelve years since Commander Perry had sailed up the Bay of Yedo, opening Japan to foreigners after three hundred years of isolation, and the country was on the verge of a vast economic and political explosion. Speculating very little about the country's future, Schliemann expressed distaste for the feudal system – feudal domains were not to be abolished until 1871 – and remarked critically on the presence of so many spies. Ever the detached reporter, he recorded, but made no protest about, one violent episode he came across. Delighting in festivals and local customs, he had obtained permission to watch the Shogun and his vast retinue as they left for a journey. Retracing the route taken by the procession next day, he came across three mangled corpses lying on the road, clearly trampled by the walkers. He learned that no one was allowed to cross a road on which the Shogun was journeying, and that a peasant, knowing nothing of the rule, had done so. The soldier ordered to hack the unfortunate man to pieces had refused, so that an officer had been forced to kill them both. At that moment, a senior officer riding by concluded that the officer had gone mad, and plunged his bayonet into his back. While adding no comment or judgement, Schliemann described the whole event, procession and killings, so precisely and evocatively in his diary that the entire scene unfolds before the reader: 'At first came a great many coolies carrying baggage on bamboo rods; then a battalion of soldiers, dressed in long white or blue blouses, black or dark-blue trousers tied at the ankles, blue stockings, straw sandals, and lacquered bamboo hats, a haversack on the back, and armed with bows and quivers or rifles and swords. The officers were garbed in fine yellow calico with a sky-blue or white robe falling to their knees and decorated with small white marks as a sign of nobility ... Their horses wore instead of iron shoes straw sandals ...' Even in an age of memorable travel writers, Schliemann holds his own.

One of the aspects of Japanese life that seems to have intrigued him was the custom for men and women to take their baths together, naked, in communal bathhouses. 'Oh holy simplicity,' he intoned for his Western readers, 'which does not fear the opprobrium of the rest of the world ...' This evidently led him to visit several brothels and to speculate about the lives of prostitutes and courtesans – at such length that some of Schliemann's biographers have suggested that he must surely have spent whole nights in them to acquire so much information. Whether he did or did not, Schliemann himself does not say.

On 4 July 1865, Schliemann left Yokohama on the *Queen of the Avon*, bound for San Francisco. The journey across the Pacific took fifty days; he used the time to put together a book, *La Chine et le Japon au temps présent*, written in fluent and impressive French, which was eventually published in Paris in 1867. He was now on his way home, though he decided to pause once again in America, explore California further, and visit Mexico. What is so extraordinary is that Schliemann, in over five hundred pages of diary, makes virtually no reference at any point to his children in St Petersburg. It is as if he were a single man, with no family ties. His son, Sergei, was barely eleven; his daughters eight and five. Nadezhda, the youngest, had hardly begun to speak when he had last seen her.

The ship docked at San Francisco at the end of August, and Schliemann was immediately seduced by California's solidity and 'wholesomeness' after the rigours of Asia and an absence of fourteen years. Almost uniquely qualified to compare countries, Schliemann sounded convincing when he praised 'this beautiful land' for having 'the climate of Italy, the soil of Egypt, the silver of Peru, and as energetic a population as New England'. His intention was to dig up and take home to Europe his brother Louis's remains, but when the grave believed to contain them was opened, it was found to belong to someone else, for the skull had teeth, while Louis had lost all his at an early age. Schliemann had a morbid fascination with graveyards; in his diaries are repeated references to corpses and burial sites. Of the four local cemeteries he explored in New Orleans, he wrote: 'I saw there lots of clothes or linings of coffins impregnated by the moisture that had run out of a dead corpse and covered in flies – ghastly to look at.'

Before leaving for Europe and home, there was still one more trip he wished to make, and this was to the Yosemite valley, in order to see for himself the 'tall trees'. Like the Great Wall of China, they apparently lived up to his expectations, and he was soon hard at work, measuring, estimating, recording. This diary shows Schliemann at his most boring and obsessive. Reaching the place where he planned to stay, he wrote that 'the hotel is a 2 storied frame building; directly opposite of it is the Yosemite waterfall, which is pouring down its waters 2634 feet high into the valley and forms a perpendicular fall of 1600 feet, then 434 feet long rapids, which fall under an angle of 30 degrees and then a third fall perpendicular of 600 feet ...' Despite the mosquitoes, the sight of the spectacular waterfall inspired a burst of eloquence, with much talk of 'veils', 'wavy sheets of spray' like 'white pearls, now contracting, now again extending themselves'. Some of this may have been borrowed from a local guidebook, which was no less eloquent on the subject of the falls, but there is no mistaking Schliemann's enthusiasm. Back at the hotel, he ate oyster soup, roast mutton and 'splendid potatoes', washed down with Los Angeles sherry.

Even after so long on the move, so many months of suitcases, ships, hotel rooms, and chronic discomfort, Schliemann remained as restless as ever. Once he decided to set off home, he chafed at every delay. Reaching Paris at 4.30 one morning, he paused only for two-and-a-quarter hours before leaving to catch a ferry from Calais for London. This was to be a shopping excursion for new clothes. On his first morning, he bought a pair of shoes for 18s 6d, a hat for £1.00 and ordered £50 worth of shirts – equivalent to about £2,000 today. It was raining hard, but he kept dry under the special umbrella he had brought back from Japan. Waiting for his shirts to be made up, he went off to Sydenham to see the Crystal Palace, uprooted since his last visit from its site in Hyde Park in June 1854, a sight bound to please him, both for its design and vast dimensions, and for the dazzling number and range of its exhibits – numbered at about 100,000. Schliemann made his way past the model dinosaurs in the gardens – a dinner party for twenty-one had been held inside the body of an iguanodon not long before – and along by the vast concert hall and many restaurants, with fountains spouting silver streams, to the courts, with their life-size plaster models of Abu Simbel in Nubia, and the Alhambra in Granada, complete with statues, sphinxes and obelisks. He strolled through various Egyptian temples, then tried skating with some new skates made of iron, which he did not greatly enjoy. What seems to have interested him most was a reconstruction of an archaeological site in the Dordogne, containing the bones of reindeers, chamois and horses, and some implements made from flintstone. Unlike Charles Dickens, who pronounced the exhibition to be 'too much' for a man with a 'natural horror of sights', Schliemann was captivated.

Next day, after a fitting for his shirts, and calling in at Schröder & Co. in the city, he went to the British Museum, looked at more excavated bones and skeletons, and visited the Egyptian antiquities. Though on this occasion Schliemann probably did not meet Charles Newton, excavator of Halicarnassus and Keeper of Greek and Roman Antiquities, with whom he was later to enter into a long correspondence, he did devote some time to Layard's collection from Mesopotamia, and he cannot have failed to have been aware of the new breath of interest in prehistoric antiquity blowing through the corridors of the museum.

With the 1860s had come not only a series of excavations in the Near East, often under the direction of local British Consuls, but a vast amount of newly excavated material pouring into the over-crammed storerooms in Bloomsbury, though there was still little to rival Layard's great winged bull from Assyria. Whether Schliemann had yet seen or read Layard's publications on Nineveh and Babylon, published a few years earlier, is not clear; but there was no doubting his growing interest in the past, though it was still largely without shape or focus. The collections in the museum, he noted, were 'so rich that they bedevilled the mind'.

On 18 January 1866 came a further fitting for shirts, six of which were to be in flannel, and then a visit to a furrier in Cheapside, where he bought five sealskins, at 70s each, to have made up into a fur coat. While waiting for it to be ready, Schliemann spent his days at the Zoo – a new generation of giraffes had been born since his last visit in 1851 – inspecting warehouses in the London docks, taking a Turkish bath and catching the new underground railway to Madame Tussaud's waxworks. A few business acquaintances invited him to dine; but there were no other social events. On 25 January he paid £18 to his furrier for the sealskin coat and a fur hat, and set off for St Petersburg.

It had been an extraordinary two years. Schliemann had discovered a very real taste for monuments and ruins, as well as revealing a lively sense of indignation at the neglect and decay into which so many were sinking through the short-sightedness of governments. The Great Wall, he noted during a rare burst of emotion while in China, 'protests silently against the corruption and depravity which have brought the Chinese Empire to its present state of degradation and decadence'.

His vehemence was uncharacteristic. For Schliemann, living in an age remarkable for its passionately argued causes and fierce convictions, was almost universally oblivious to politics. Even the abolition of slavery, in which he took some interest – though mainly on account of his investments – failed to engage him. It is worth noting that his second visit to London came just three months after an exceptionally brutal incident, involving a number of emancipated slaves in Jamaica, which had become a major scandal in Britain. In October many hundreds of former slaves in Morant Bay had rioted in protest at being destitute and given no land, and the Governor of Jamaica, E.J.Eyre, had sent in troops to repress the rebellion, flogging over six hundred people, some of them pregnant women, with steel-laced cats-o'-nine tails, and hanging several hundred more. In Britain, opinions split, with John Stuart Mill, Charles Darwin and Thomas Huxley among those calling for Eyre to be put

on trial for murder, while others like Dickens, Tennyson, Carlyle and
Matthew Arnold supported his actions. Eyre was eventually tried, but
acquitted, 'because', as *The Spectator* remarked, 'his error and judgement
involved only Negro blood'. Schliemann, who must have heard the
debates constantly during his London stay, makes no reference in his
diary to the incident.

During his two years of travel, Schliemann's health had not been
altogether good, and earaches continued to torment him in spite of, or
perhaps on account of, frequent saltwater bathing, syringing in soapy
water and even an operation in Jakarta when a local surgeon had cut out
some bony growths, but he was never a man to give in to physical frailty.
Though cantankerous and unforgiving at times, he had complained of
boredom only twice in all the months he had been away : once on board
a boat for several days in China, the other time while waiting to catch a
ship from Singapore to Java. What stands out is his immense curiosity,
a need to know so great that it seemed sometimes to be his main driving
force. The day was fast approaching when he was to give himself up to
it entirely.

Schliemann staged his return to settled European life in Paris, not St
Petersburg. He bought himself a flat in the Place St-Michel, overlooking
the Seine, and decided to continue the education denied him by his
earlier poverty. He enrolled as a part-time student at the Sorbonne, for
which he had to get special permission from the French Ministry of
Education. He must have been a strange figure to his fellow students :
his receding hair and wary expression making him appear somewhat
older than his forty-four years, immensely rich, of no clear nationality,
and fluent in a dozen languages, speaking one or another with apparent
indifference. Interested at this stage principally in the study of language,
he put his name down for courses in French linguistics and literature, to
which he added Arabic, Greek philosophy and literature, and Egyptian
archaeology. He took the work extremely seriously and was soon on
friendly terms with his professors.

Paris, in the closing years of the Second Empire, was an agreeable city.
Under Napoleon III and Haussmann, the slums that had once choked so
much of the centre of the city, the dark, crooked alleyways, dingy hostels,
masons' yards and ruined wasteland, had all been swept away, and the
streets widened to unheard-of proportions in order to open new cuttings
through the densely populated areas. By 1866 the main boulevards had

been completed, water and sewage services laid on, several public parks had been created and twenty-one new squares planted with trees. Paris was leafy, handsome and prosperous. Churches, schools, town halls and theatres had all been opened and Schliemann soon settled down to a pleasant existence. Between lectures on French grammar and Greek philosophy, he went to the Louvre, and made a series of visits to a dentist who agreed to make him some new teeth.

He had not altogether abandoned business and part of his day was devoted to keeping abreast of the stock markets in Paris, London and New York, making new deals over his distant American and Cuban investments and buying up property around Paris. Soon he was enmeshed in rebuilding, converting and decorating, arguing with plumbers and masons, and negotiating with irritable tenants over gas supplies. Writing to his sisters in Germany, he declared that Paris held no glories for a man accustomed to the sights of China and Japan, but that Parisian daily life, with its culture and its learning, was 'sublime'. To a banker acquaintance, he reported that he was in a 'state of utter happiness'.

Schliemann was not yet prepared to relinquish married life. He wrote to Ekaterina asking her to bring the children to join him in France, promising her a luxurious life and fine clothes. Ekaterina refused. She wanted the children brought up as Russians and as Orthodox Christians. Schliemann crumbled; subsequent letters adopted a pleading tone, but Ekaterina remained unmoved, even after Schliemann began writing directly to his son Sergei, and to his wife's relations, his letters full of outrage and injured pride. To one of her friends, he wrote that Ekaterina not only denied him her 'embraces', but portrayed him as a 'tyrant, as a despot, and a libertine', even though she had herself told him to take a mistress. Some of this despair and bitterness made its way into letters to his family in Germany. Though he continued to send them money, he could seldom refrain from niggling away at the spendthrift Ernst, writing to him in Latin, then pompously correcting the mistakes in his father's replies. Squabbles by post were usually conducted in German, Schliemann complaining to his sisters of the 'vulgar, nay, bestial' letters he received from his father.

When the Sorbonne closed for the summer, Schliemann decided to argue his case with Ekaterina in person. It was a failure. Within weeks of reaching St Petersburg he was off again, restless, in search of new sights. First to Moscow, then to the ancient town of Nizhni Novgorod; here, he boarded a boat on the Volga travelling towards the Caspian Sea, breaking his journey to spend a month at a spa in Samara, the first of the many cures that were to fill the rest of his life. This was followed by a visit to Sebastopol, to observe for himself the ravages left by the Crimean War, then a boat trip on the Danube into Central Europe. He reached Dresden, the fine baroque town in Saxony, where he already owned some property, and, having inspected a progressive new school, decided that this would be the ideal city for his family. As usual he acted over-hastily, first buying a house, and only then imploring Ekaterina to join him. The letter with his invitation was generous: his outline of their future life together included the house in Dresden as a base, a place kept on in St Petersburg so that she could spend time with her family and friends, a magnificent new house in Paris, where she would meet and receive the best minds of Europe, and independence. 'I will love you,' he wrote, 'only as the mother of my beloved children, but my love will remain platonic.' Ekaterina's answer was chilly: nothing would induce her to leave Russia. Schliemann tried threats: if she would join him, he would put at her disposal his fortune, to spend as she wished; if not, all she would receive from him would be fees for the children's education. Threats alternated with entreaties – how about going to live in America ? – but Ekaterina stayed put, and Schliemann went on sending money. At the end of the summer he returned alone to Paris, having wandered through Bavaria and Switzerland, whose pretty villages and neat houses suggested the fundamental 'bien-être' he so craved. Switzerland, like Japan, was deliciously clean. At times there is something very poignant about Schliemann, roaming disconsolately and alone around the world, able only to make more and more money.

In October 1867, Schliemann read in *The Times* that there was talk in America that certain government securities were to be redeemed in paper money, which might well send the value of gold soaring. Since a growing proportion of his capital was now tied up in America, Schliemann thought he smelled the chance of doubling his fortune. In any case, he felt he needed to see for himself precisely where the American markets were heading. It was his third visit and, travelling through the Southern states in the wake of the Civil War, he got an entirely new feel for the continent. The diaries of this trip are among the most brisk and businesslike, costs, interest rates, capital gains recorded along with schemes for making money. How, most economically, could goods be shipped from Chicago to Europe ? What would the abolition of slavery do to the process of refining sugar in Cuba ? Railways, as ever, fascinated him, not least because he had become a major investor in them.

Once again Schliemann was alert to the quirks and novelties of the country – the young boys on the trains who carried leaflets advertising the sweets and newspapers they sold – and to costs, deciding that he preferred to carry his own trunk rather than pay a porter one dollar to carry it for him. In Detroit he noted that the female servants were all Irish and 'of light morals'; in Jackson, that the penitentiaries abounded with Negroes 'famous for their stealing propensities'. The different types of soil, the cost of laying rail track, the ice consumed by travellers, the lack of curtains on hotel windows – and the difference in the size of towels from one hotel to another – were all recorded, among columns of figures and costs.

In Washington, came a meeting not only with President Lincoln's successor, Andrew Johnson, but with General Grant. As with his earlier presidential encounter, doubt has been cast on this visit. Admittedly, Schliemann's account of their conversation smacks of fantasy – can the American President really have discussed the annexation of Cuba with an unknown German millionaire? – but again there is no external evidence to contradict him. Whatever really took place, Schliemann felt reassured about the economic prospects, though he prudently sold two-thirds of his government bonds and invested the money in shares in the Illinois and Jersey Central Railroads, after sending some of it back to Paris to put into more real estate.

On this visit, Schliemann appears to have been unusually awake to the political issues of the day. Appalled by the devastation left by the Civil War, he was quick to praise the former slaves, declaring the rumours that they were lazy and stupid to be 'downright falsehoods'. 'I have seen the latter work in the plantations and on the railroads,' he wrote to the Schröders in Hamburg, 'and I can assure you that they are as willing and eager to work and as energetic and perseverant in their labour as any workmen I have yet seen and that, both morally and intellectually, they stand much higher than their former tyrants and calumniators.' When championing the underdog, Schliemann was capable of hyperbole. Having listened to some black delegates addressing a state convention, and admired their erudition, he announced, 'I could not help regretting that I was not myself a Negro to be able to speak as they did.' Apart from anything else, he liked their music.

Cuba charmed him. Inspecting his railway investments, he professed himself happy in the warm, tropical climate. He did, however, balk at the conditions in which the now freed black slaves, as well as the Chinese shipped in to replace them in the cane fields, were obliged to live, and noted that at least ten thousand Chinese had already committed suicide.

He came up with a plan to bring in 'Hindus from the Malakka coast' who, he was sure, would be able to adapt themselves better to the work, and even proposed to travel to India himself to make the arrangements. His zeal appears to have been curbed by receiving a sharp letter from an old Amsterdam friend: 'Do not go to Bombay to trade in human flesh, rather try to make those people happy to whom you are tied by the bonds of nature.' What Schliemann made of this advice is not known, but the Indian plan was dropped.

At the beginning of January 1868 Schliemann reached New York. Having warmly admired the city on his earlier trips, he now declared that, compared with Haussmann's boulevards, its streets were narrow, ill-lit and squalid. On the third, he went to hear Charles Dickens read from *A Christmas Carol* in the Steinway Hall on 14th Street. He disliked the whole occasion, criticizing the story for being nothing but a 'composition about ghosts and humbug', and commenting that Dickens looked 'well fed and preserved' for a man of about fifty. In fact Dickens was fifty-six and had a bad cold.

Schliemann's sincerity is not always easy to gauge. How strongly he really felt about his family has never been clear, but he was as capable as anyone of indulging in sentimental musings. 'My heart and thoughts,' he wrote sententiously on the Russian Christmas Eve, which fell just before his forty-sixth birthday, 'have been constantly with my little darlings, Sergei, Natalie and Nadja ... I weep bitter tears that I cannot share their joy and increase their happiness with presents ... I would give 100,000 dollars to spend the evening with them. Truly it requires much more strength and philosophy than I possess to pass this day without tears.'

PART TWO

THE SEARCH
FOR TROY

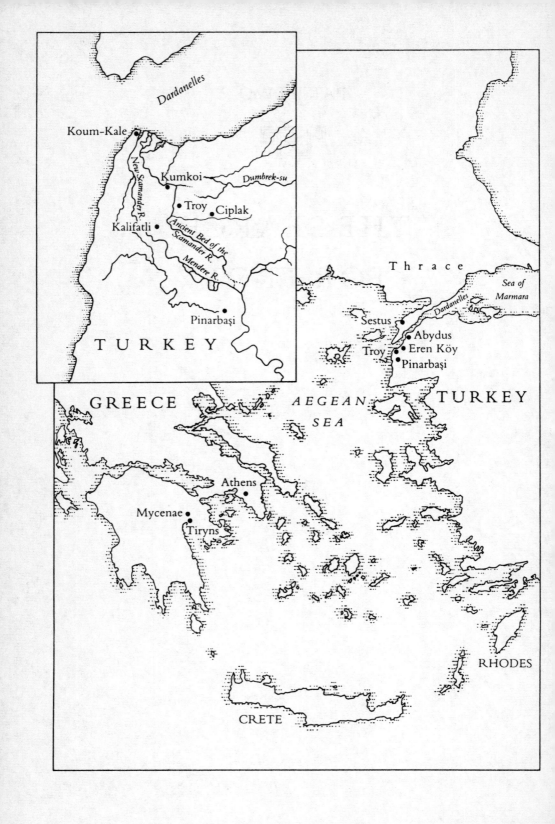

Dardanelles

Koum-Kale

New Samander R.

Kumkoi

Troy Ciplak

Dumbrek-su

Kalifatli

Ancient Bed of the
Scamander R.

Mendere R.

Pinarbaşi

T U R K E Y

T h r a c e

Sea of
Marmara

Dardanelles

Sestus

Abydus

Troy Eren Köy

Pinarbaşi

G R E E C E

A E G E A N

SEA

T U R K E Y

Athens

Mycenae

Tiryns

RHODES

CRETE

6

THE SPEECHLESS PAST

When did Schliemann really decide to search for the ruins of Troy? Not, it would seem, as a seven-year-old boy reading from Jerrer's *Universal History*, though that makes an irresistible story. In his thousands of early letters and the many volumes of diaries of those years there are virtually no references to archaeology. There are, however, signs that as the wealthy businessman roamed around the world, he grew increasingly curious about the past, about the ruins of the earlier world and the people who inhabited it. When he was in London, Schliemann never failed to visit the British Museum, wandering around the galleries with the earliest finds, musing on man's antiquity. From the 1850s on, there are also expressions of dissatisfaction with his life as a businessman, of longing to enter a more cerebral world, and fear that it might already be too late, as he wrote in a letter of December 1858, 'because I have been working too long a time as a merchant to hope that I can still achieve something in the scientific field ...' There was, too, Schliemann's growing obsession with Greece and the early Greeks. 'I must go to Greece,' he said. 'It is there that I want to live. How is it possible for any language to be so noble?'

Whatever the true date of Schliemann's official entry into the archaeological world, he brought to his new occupation a unique collection of attributes. There was no one else quite like him, and in this he was both fortunate and unlucky. He was rich enough to spend a large amount of money on his excavations; he had enough time to follow his instincts, wherever they took him, and enough mastery of all useful languages to communicate not only with workmen and government officials, but with scholars all over the world; and he was abundantly energetic. He was also immensely self-disciplined; and he was in a hurry, eager to publish his material, as others, more cautious, were not. On the other hand, the world of archaeology in the 1850s was a jealous one. Schliemann's character – boastful, impatient, provocative – was precisely of a kind most guaranteed to infuriate academics. This might not have mattered had Schliemann not been so insecure, so desperate for approval and so quick to take offence. He was a romantic and an adventurer, in a world of scholars and sceptics; a dilettante in a field of professionals; and he was not ashamed to admit to a longing to find treasure where others kept such desires to themselves. If he had a tendency to dig his sites as though they were 'fields of potatoes', he also knew instinctively what many of his more eminent colleagues did not – that the highest aim of archaeology was to answer questions, and not simply to provide a way of accumulating works of art. The remaining twenty-two years of Schliemann's life were to consist of erratic and painful swings between immense excitement and feelings of persecution.

In the most celebrated passage of his autobiographical fragment in *Ilios*, written in 1880, Schliemann described the conversation he had had with his father on Christmas Day 1829. '"Father," retorted I, "if such walls once existed, they cannot possibly have been completely destroyed: vast ruins of them must still remain, but they are hidden away beneath the dust of ages." He maintained the contrary, while I remained firm in my opinion, and at last we both agreed that I should one day excavate Troy.'

Now, at the age of forty-six, his family life at an extremely low ebb, his world tour completed, his fortune satisfactorily managed and growing, Schliemann was off, as he had once put it, to visit the 'Vaterland meines Lieblings Homers'. The siting of Homer's Troy was one of the prizes of the archaeological world. Schliemann was determined to make it his own.

His timing, of course, was vital. Schliemann's adult life – 1850 to 1890 – spanned one of the most revolutionary periods in the entire history of science, a time marked not simply by inventions like transatlantic steam travel, telegraphy and gas-lighting, but by an enormous appetite for knowledge. Mid-nineteenth-century men were not just well educated: they were intensely curious and even the amateur expected to know most things. They could quote from Homer and Horace – but they were also very eager to learn.

Schliemann came to archaeology almost at the precise moment when early Victorian fundamentalist chronology was being replaced by the idea that man had a remote past and that it was becoming possible to explore it. When John William Burgon spoke, in 1845, of Petra as a 'rose-red city half as old as time', he was talking not in poetic, but in historical, terms: for many early Victorians, time *was* six thousand years old, and it made sense to put the age of Petra at 3,000 BC. Fourteen years later, in his Bampton Lecture, George Rawlinson was still saying that Shem was probably acquainted with Methuselah who had, for 243 years, been a contemporary of Adam. As every pious early Victorian knew, Adam was the first man, made on the sixth day after the beginning of time. By the end of the 1860s, however, the notion seemed absurd. The tide of learning was running rapidly against the biblical fundamentalists.

Not that the new ideas being advanced by scholars and scientists were all in agreement with each other; on the contrary, several different sequences in development were being put forward. But one thing they did all seem to agree upon was the immense antiquity of man. The question was: how old was he? If 'time' was longer than six thousand years, then when and how did it start? And how was anyone going to find out? Even the people who were now willing to abandon Noah and his Ark and accept that the Bible did not contain answers to man's past, often agreed with Palgrave that 'we must give it up, the speechless past; whether in Europe, Asia, Africa or America; at Thebes or Palengue, on Lycian shore or Salisbury Plain; lost is lost; gone is gone for ever'

Not everyone felt as pessimistic. The early decades of the nineteenth century were marked by a series of men determined to reach back into that 'speechless' past, and to find ways of bringing 'prehistory' – times before the known written word – to light. One of the first breakthroughs had come in Denmark, a country with bogs ideal for preserving prehistoric remains, and where a museum curator called Christian Thomsen, classifying his various archaeological collections, hit on the idea of arranging them according to the materials used in the making of weapons and tools. Others before Thomsen had noted that stone preceded bronze and iron, but it was Thomsen who named them as three specific ages.

One of the next important links was to come from England, home to a number of distinguished Victorian scientists, like the geologist Sir Charles Lyell, and where, in the late 1850s, fossilized bones of lion, mammoth, reindeer and rhinoceros had been found in some small caves in Yorkshire. What made these discoveries so exciting was that beneath these fossils, buried lower down, lay flints, unquestionably shaped by man. The year 1859 is spoken of as the *annus mirabilis* of archaeology, for it was not only the year in which the presence of man on earth at a time incalculably far back in the 'speechless' past was incontrovertibly established, but the one in which Charles Darwin published his revolutionary theory about evolution in the biological world. Others before him had postulated theories about evolution, but no one so clearly, nor with such painstaking research based on years of work on both fossil and living forms. By the time Sir John Lubbock published *Prehistoric Times* six years later, public interest in the past had become such that the book became a best seller, and remained one for fifty years, going into its seventh edition in 1913. What Lubbock had done was to elaborate on the idea of a prehistoric sequence, laid down by Thomsen, modify his various ages into Paleolithic, Neolithic, Bronze and Iron, and to declare: 'A new branch of knowledge has arisen which deals in times and events far more ancient than any which have yet fallen within the province of the archaeologist ... Archaeology forms the link between geology and history.' Times that had once seemed lost could in fact be retrieved by excavation and interpretation.

The Great Exhibition held in Hyde Park in 1851 had contained no prehistory. By the end of the next decade, when Schliemann was on the threshold of his archaeological career, the idea of prehistory was so firmly established that prehistoric collections from all over Europe – flints, stone weapons, fossils – were prominently displayed at the Great Exhibition held in Paris in 1867. Prehistory was no longer regarded as a matter of guesswork, just as man's antiquity was accepted and the three- or four-age system was taken as the basis for interpreting it through excavation and stratification – the examination of different levels in the soil where one culture has been superimposed upon another. The moment was now ripe for the exploration of lost civilizations.

The middle of the nineteenth century was in all ways a remarkable moment for archaeology, not least because of the widespread sense of mission with which European archaeologists approached their labours: they excavated works of art, and brought them back to the great museums of France, Germany and England, not in the spirit of looters, but of conservationists. It was perfectly clear to them that the inhabitants of the countries in which they excavated were not just incapable of looking after their art treasures, but were in some ways unworthy of having them altogether. By the time Schliemann turned to archaeology, Lord Elgin had long since delivered his friezes, pediment and sculptures from the Parthenon in Athens to the British Museum in London, and Edward Daniel Clarke, the British don, had removed the colossal Cistophorus of Eleusis and brought it back to Cambridge. In Greece, which had been liberated from Turkish rule in 1829, a French archaeological school had been opened in Athens, later to be followed by German, British, American and Italian schools; while in Italy, Giuseppe Fiorelli was excavating at Pompeii, developing a technique of making casts of bodies by pouring plaster into the hollows left in the volcanic ash after the bodies had disintegrated.

In the next few years, as Schliemann made his first tentative steps into the ancient world, archaeology was to be dominated by excavations at sites in Egypt and Mesopotamia. But while much of the work focused on the Middle East, the Aegean was now beginning to attract ever more attention. Until now, classical scholars around the Aegean had tended to be more concerned with documents than with sites. The earliest period of Greek antiquity had been largely dismissed as legendary, nations with no written documents being thought to have no history. With his spade, Schliemann was about to show that prehistory was the perfect field for the new scientific disciplines of historical archaeology, ethnography and anthropology. The 'speechless' past was not so silent after all.

Few other literary figures have been as admired and as widely quoted as Homer, the author of the *Iliad* and the *Odyssey*, who provided a vision of a distant and legendary past, inhabited by heroic leaders and beautiful women, warriors who struggled to the death, and powerful and interfering gods. 'When reading Homer,' wrote Goethe, 'I feel as if I were in a balloon, raised far above all earthly things, posed in the intermediate space, between heaven and earth, where gods flit to and fro.'

In the *Iliad*, the only surviving early Greek epic to focus entirely on the Trojan War, the gods did indeed flit to and fro. Zeus, Athene, Hera, and Aphrodite all play at puppeteers, the warriors their puppets, though they have been given the heroic Greek virtues of honour, strength and physical courage.

According to Greek legend and Homer, Troy was a city near the Dardanelles in Asia Minor, brought to prominence and power by King Priam during a long and glorious reign. Priam had fifty sons and twelve daughters; his eldest son was Hector, 'of the glittering helmet', his second 'noble' Paris. On the mainland of Greece, when Priam was already an old man, the most powerful ruler was King Agamemnon, 'with head and eyes like Zeus the Thunderer, with a waist like the war-god's waist, and a breast like Poseidon's', whose palace was at Mycenae. These Greeks called themselves Achaeans (or sometimes Argives or Danaans) and Agamemnon's dynastic family controlled the Argolid, with fortresses at places like Tiryns and Orchomenos. Agamemnon was married to Clytemnestra, whose sister, Helen, wife of 'battle loving' Menelaus, was said to be the most beautiful woman in the world.

The *Iliad* covers just a few eventful weeks in the tenth year of the war between the Achaeans and the Trojans, a war caused by the kidnapping of Achaean Helen by Trojan Paris. Agamemnon – who is also Menelaus's brother – has called upon Achaeans from all over Greece to sail under his leadership to Troy to win Helen back, and the *Iliad* lists the catalogue of the 164 places in Greece which have sent troops to his aid. These troops, in their 'black ships', came together at Aulis, a bay in the straits between the mainland and Euboea, 'where the tides come together', before setting siege to Troy.

The *Iliad* opens as the Achaeans are camped near their ships on the edge of the plain of Troy. Achilles, the 'great runner', Prince of the Myrmidons, the greatest of all warriors, is in the middle of a bitter quarrel with Agamemnon for stealing from him a slave girl, Briseis, part of his legitimate spoils of war. Agamemnon had taken her to replace his own slave girl, Chryseis, whom he had been forced to return to her father, a priest, after he let loose a plague upon the Greeks. So bitter does Achilles feel that he has returned with his men to their tents and refuses to take part in the battle against Troy.

The Trojan and Achaean armies advance towards each other, and Hector, brother of Paris and hero of the Trojans, 'loved by the gods best of all the mortals in Ilion', proposes that his brother Paris fight it out in single combat with Menelaus, the winner to keep Helen. Paris is defeated, but is saved from death by the goddess Aphrodite. According to the agreement, his defeat should have put an end to the war, but Aphrodite wishes for a more bloody resolution to the fighting, and intervenes by having Menelaus wounded. The fighting begins again, this time the gods themselves joining in. Achilles sulks in his tent, refusing to help the other Greeks, even when Agamemnon offers to return Briseis. It is only when his friend Patroclus, who had borrowed his armour, is killed that Achilles agrees to lead his men back into battle.

The Trojan army is now forced back inside the city walls. Only Hector remains outside, awaiting Achilles, who comes sweeping across the plain. Four times the two men circle the walls of Troy, Achilles pursuing

Hector, who, abandoned by the gods, is mortally wounded and his body
dragged back by Achilles to the Achaean camp. Late at night, the aged
King Priam comes to beg for the body of his dead son. In the final scene
of the *Iliad* Achilles agrees to a truce while the Trojans burn Hector's
body, quench the fire with wine, gather the ashes into a golden casket
and bury it beneath a grave of stones. 'And so they buried Hector, tamer
of horses.' The *Iliad* ends before the death of Achilles – struck in the
heel, his only vulnerable spot, by Paris – and the fall and sack of Troy.

The tale is taken up in the *Odyssey*, which describes the long-delayed
return of Odysseus to his home, after the sack of Troy, following his
many adventures, as well as the fortunes of a number of the Achaean
heroes.

To the ancient world, the siege of Troy, the bitter fight between Achilles
and Hector, and the return of Helen to mainland Greece, were all real
events. Of all the themes of early oral poetry – wars, adventures, family
feuds or deaths – embroidered and embellished by the bards with details
selected from history as well as from the life and society they observed
around them, recited over many days and nights in chants 'singing the
famous deeds of men', none was as durable as the legend of Troy. The
Iliad and the *Odyssey* would have taken, it seems, about twenty-four
hours each to recount. There were no written records until around
the sixth century BC, but Homer's epic poems were handed down by
professional bards, with constant repetition of phrases, until it became
possible to record them for posterity, making copies by hand, first on
papyri and later on parchments. Even so, historians were prepared to
accept Homer's version with little dispute. As Herodotus, the 'father of
history', put it in the fifth century BC: 'The people of Asia, when their
women were seized, made an issue of it, whereas the Greeks, on account
of a single Lacedaemonian woman, collected a great expedition, came to
Asia and destroyed the power of Priam.' Thucydides believed the story
Homer told to be true, accepted that Mycenae was a real place, and saw
'no reason why we should not believe that the Trojan expedition was
the greatest that ever took place', though neither he nor Herodotus, of
course, had any proof.

So powerful was the legend of Troy that generations of generals and
conquerors felt drawn to make their own pilgrimage to the plain on
which the Achaeans had camped, and where a Greek colony had been
founded on the remains of the ancient city, which, somewhere around

700 BC, had been renamed by its new settlers as Ilion. For visitors to the Phrygian coast, Ilion was a place of memories. According to Herodotus, Xerxes, King of Persia, about to cross the Hellespont, climbed the citadel, sacrificed to the 'Ilian Minerva a thousand oxen and . . . poured libations to the heroes'. Later came Alexander the Great, on his way to Persia, who was said to carry the *Iliad* with him wherever he went, and who ran naked and covered in oil around the supposed tomb of Achilles, laid a wreath, and spoke of restoring the city. Julius Caesar, in pursuit of Pompey, wandered around the ruins, burned incense, prayed to the gods and, like Alexander, vowed to repair the walls. Mad Caracalla imagined himself to be Achilles, and poisoned his freedman Festus, in order to mourn his own Patroclus.

Though not even the Greeks agreed precisely where or when Homer had lived, or on the date of the great siege he chronicled, the legend of Troy became the heart of a whole literature based on the fate of the Trojans and the Achaeans; and from Greece it passed to Rome and into Latin. First Aeschylus, Sophocles and Euripides, and five centuries later Virgil, Ovid and Pliny, all wrote of Troy. The discovery of written papyri texts in Egypt, where the dry climate made papyrus last indefinitely, makes it clear that when it came to literary popularity and survival Homer and the legend of Troy were without rival. Of all the fragments found in Egypt before the Second World War nearly half were copies of the *Iliad* and the *Odyssey*.

The second great period of Trojan narrative arrived with the Middle Ages, when the legend was again accepted as true and its heroes as real people, only they were reshaped to fit the pattern of feudalism and chivalry. In Benoît de Sainte-Maure's long epic poem, the *Roman de Troie*, written somewhere around 1160, the heroes have been turned into knights, and the Trojans recast as victors instead of vanquished, while the wooden horse has been transformed into bronze. Hector became the ideal knight, the flower of chivalry, curly-haired, bearded and high-spirited, slain not in combat but by treachery. Later, a story was born that a certain Brutus had founded Britain, and that he was descended from the first founder of Troy, a story accepted by the Elizabethans and so popular that under the Tudors the *Iliad* was repeatedly translated, and Shakespeare was able to speak of 'Priam's six-gated city'. The first English travellers to set out in search of Troy did so while Shakespeare was still alive.

Interest in Homer and his poems grew stronger after the beginning of the eighteenth century, when two translations of the *Iliad* appeared within five years of each other: Anne Davier's in France in 1711, and Alexander Pope's in England in 1715. What was becoming increasingly clear to even the most sceptical of scholars was that Homer's epic poems had an intensely *real* feel to them. Though the gods played a substantial part in shaping the course of the war, both the *Iliad* and the *Odyssey* were remarkable for their descriptions of everyday life. If the details of ships, clothes, weapons and chariots all seemed so accurate, why not Homer's geography as well? And if he was so knowledgeable about the topography of the Greek islands, was it not also possible that he knew where the city of Troy actually lay?

A close reading of the poems in fact provided a number of very specific clues. Troy, Homer claimed, was a wealthy city standing on a plain near the Hellespont, visible from the heights of 'many-fountained Ida' and from the island of Samothrace. Its mighty walls, built by Apollo and Poseidon, could be scaled only where the 'wild fig-tree stood'. On an acropolis within the city had been built the 'beautiful' palace of Priam and the 'well-built' house of Hector, as well as temples to Athena and Apollo. The Scaean gates led out of the citadel towards the field of battle. On the shores of the Hellespont, at 'no great distance from the city', lay the Achaean camp, with its ships drawn up on the beach. Though Homer's sketch of the city plan was imprecise, it is clear that the Troy in his mind had wide streets and imposing buildings – among them some fifty chambers where Priam's sons lived with their wives, and twelve more, beyond a courtyard, for his daughters and their husbands. There were presumably more than two gates, since Hector ordered the Trojans to lead their men into battle through 'all the gates'.

One of the most important clues was thought to lie in the course of the 'deep-eddying' river Scamander, known to the gods as Xanthus, which ran between the Greek camp and Troy. Close to the Scaean gates were said to rise two springs: one warm, so that steam rose from it in winter; the other 'even in summer floweth forth like cold hail or snow or ice'. The Scamander was said to have a tributary, the Simois, which joined it on the left of the field of battle as seen by the Greeks. These details, together with many other references to tombs, graves, mounds and streams, were to be picked over exhaustively by scholars.

By the early eighteenth century, scholars, merchants and travellers tended to agree that Troy had not only once existed, but that it was to be found somewhere in the north-west corner of Asia Minor, buried under the Hellenistic and Roman city of Ilion or Ilium, in the plain extending from the foothills of Mount Ida in the south, bordered by a broken range of hills to the east, the Hellespont to the north, and the coast of the Aegean, possibly as far down as Cape Sigeum. Lady Mary Wortley Montagu, who visited the area in 1718, was able to conjure up in her mind the duel between Menelaus and Paris but had to conclude that 'all that is now left of Troy is the ground on which it stood'.

But where, precisely, *did* Troy lie, now that the Greek and Roman knowledge that Homer's Troy had become the Greek Ilion or the Roman Ilium was lost in time? Once the Western countries began to trade actively with the Ottoman world, a desire to solve the puzzle captured the imagination of a new generation of travellers. Robert Wood paid two visits to the Troad in 1742 and 1750, and though his detailed opinions on the site of Troy – that the city had in fact been altogether obliterated – were published only after his death, they were much discussed and inspired new visitors to the area. In the late 1780s, a French antiquarian called Jean-Baptiste Lechevalier visited Asia Minor, bearing with him not just the *Iliad* but also Robert Wood's book, carried out an extensive survey and returned to report that in his view Troy lay just above the Turkish village of Bunarbashi – now known, and subsequently referred to, as Pinarbaşi. He based his conclusions on his observations about the two springs, one hot and one cold, feeding into the Scamander. These two springs were to become a point of debate that was to divide scholars in the decades which followed. A battle, fought for the most part from armchairs, often as bitter as it was absurd. The plain of Troy had been agreed on, but the actual site remained elusive. In 1837 the German General Staff Captain, Helmuth von Moltke, who had come to train the Ottoman Army declared that Lechevalier had been right to point to Pinarbaşi, since his own military instinct also led to Pinarbaşi, the only sufficiently impregnable hill on which to construct a fortress.

Not everyone was convinced. The debate took a new turn in 1822, when the editor of *The Scotsman*, Charles Maclaren, wrote a highly technical dissertation saying that Pinarbaşi was not the right place at all and putting Troy at the mound of Hissarlik – Turkish for 'fortress' – a few miles nearer to the coast. Speculation continued. Then two British naval officers, Commander Graves and Lieutenant Spratt, were sent to survey the area by the Admiralty, and they, too, entered the Trojan debate. Troy, they said, lay not at Hissarlik at all – but at Pinarbaşi. However, they did draw up an accurate map of the whole Troad, complete with rivers, brooks, canals and marshes. As a guide to Homeric topography, their map was to prove invaluable to those who followed.

Alongside these travellers, army officers and armchair scholars now emerged a new and better informed generation of geologists and philologists, readers of Darwin and Sir Charles Lyell, men who maintained that the only way to find the site of Troy was to start digging for it. The age of archaeology had dawned. Many were classicists. One of them was William Gladstone, whose studies on Homer were published in 1858 when he was already a prominent politician. These had a widespread influence on Homeric scholarship. Gladstone, who 'let no day pass without having Homer in his hand', believed that Homer was the poet who had done the most to shape the Greek mind, and was determined to find a way of establishing just where he fitted into 'historical enquiry'. George Grote, the celebrated historian of Greece, however, held that the legend of Troy was indeed a 'legend and nothing more', for which no 'independent evidence' existed. Was Homer a poet or a historian ? Or perhaps a little of both ? The various strands were now beginning to come together.

It was at this point that a new player appeared, a man called Frank Calvert, US Vice-Consul at Çanakkale between 1859 and 1879, a passionate reader of Homer, but also an eager amateur archaeologist. Calvert was one of four brothers in a family of Anglo-Levantine bankers, consuls and merchants, long settled near the Hellespont, where they owned over 5,000 acres of land producing the main export of the Troad, valonia, for dyes and ink. They were all consuls for one country or another : Frederick, the Prussian Vice-Consul at the Dardanelles, James, the British Vice-Consul for the area, and Edmund, British Vice-Consul in Rhodes. The Calvert family were to be crucial protagonists in the discovery of Troy.

As yet, Frank was the brother most concerned with Priam's lost city. In his spare time, he combed the Troad, becoming ever more convinced that Lechevalier had been wrong, and MacLaren right, that Troy lay not at Pinarbaşi but at Hissarlik. He began to buy land from local owners, with a view to finding the time, one day, to carry out some excavations. Layard had uncovered the ruins of Nimrud. Why should he not do the same for Troy ? So certain of his position was he, in fact, that a paper written by him was read out at a meeting of the Archaeological Institute in London on 15 February 1864, in which he said that he was convinced that the walls he had observed sticking out of the mound at Hissarlik 'belong to an epoch ... posterior to that of Homeric Troy'. Priam's Troy, he declared, must therefore lie below. By the mid-1860s, Calvert was making a few preliminary excavations, and had already uncovered a temple to Minerva.

Such, then, was the state of Homeric exploration in 1870, the year Schliemann set out for Asia Minor: two possible sites for Troy, five miles apart, hotly contested; and a growing number of European classical scholars intrigued by the Homeric legend but for the most part disposed either to dismiss the *Iliad* and the *Odyssey* as a magnificent saga, very loosely based on legend, or to agree with Byron that though the city had once existed:

> The seat of sacred Troy is found no more,
> No trace of all her glories now remains.

But not Schliemann. What makes Schliemann unique is the single-mindedness of his vision. Unlike most of the other archaeologists of the day he was neither a classicist, nor a scholar, but an adventurer, with all the tenacity and energy of a successful international businessman, and 'unerring truffle dog-like instincts'. Others vacillated, believed in some bits of the *Iliad* and the *Odyssey* but not others; Schliemann believed in it all. He had no doubts. Homer, for him, was a historian. Even though he might not have actually witnessed the battle of Troy, what he wrote was not just poetry, but a description of real events. It was enough to follow Homer's words, literally, step by step, to discover where, precisely, the buried city lay.

In the spring of 1868 Schliemann set out on a journey that was to change his life. Saying that he regarded it merely as a 'pleasure trip', by a 'normal tourist' who lacked the 'knowledge necessary to scientific investigations', his plan was to start in Italy, then travel down to Greece before crossing over into Asia Minor. He was in no hurry; and, fired by his intense pleasure in his Parisian studies, he was in a mood to learn. What intrigued him was man's distant past; but first he needed some archaeological knowledge. His diary opens in Italian; as he enters the Greek-speaking world he switches to modern Greek. Like all his travel journals it is a peculiar mixture of guidebook, historical analysis, personal asides and precise, detailed information about the height, length, weight, cost and temperature of the world about him. More than the earlier diaries, it exudes pleasure and ever-mounting excitement.

Schliemann was never anything but the most assiduous of tourists. While others visited sites once, he seldom missed a second look; while some took days off, or stayed in bed, or sat sketching, Schliemann kept moving. Reaching Rome in May, he hired a servant-cum-guide – a man of seventy-three, who was soon complaining of exhaustion – and embarked on what the early Thomas Cook tourists sharing his hotel must have regarded as a most punishing schedule. Rising always at dawn or just before, he left his hotel by seven. On Monday 11 May he noted in his diary that he visited five churches, the Roman Forum, the Baths of Caracalla, the Trevi fountain, and a number of cisterns, aqueducts, towers, temples, columns and palaces. Getting from one to the other was mostly done on foot; very occasionally he took a carriage. Everywhere he made detailed notes, measuring and comparing anything that could be measured or compared. He stayed in Rome just over a month, keeping to the same rigid timetable each day, apparently never growing weary or losing his appetite for fresh sights. Both his unquenchable curiosity and his stamina were to prove invaluable in the years to come. Whether he actually enjoyed himself is not clear: the Roman diary is dry and factual, with just a few speculations about Nero or Cleopatra, and the houses they must have lived in, and one burst of sympathy for Beatrice Cenci, the Renaissance's famous victim of parental tyranny.

By 8 June, Schliemann was in Pompeii. The diary takes on a softer tone; he was captivated by the streets, theatres and canals revealed by the excavations being conducted under Giuseppe Fiorelli, which, he remarked approvingly, were being done at great speed. The paintings uncovered in the ruins filled him with wonder: '... visibly executed with great haste, but none the less with such elegance and *disinvoltura* and lightness that the brush of the artist seems to have conquered nature herself, everything is seen to come alive, nothing is forced, all is natural ...' Schliemann's interest in the past was deepening rapidly beyond that of the ordinary tourist he still professed himself to be. Before leaving southern Italy he spent a few days attending lectures at Naples University.

In July he was ready for Greece. He rented a 'bark' to take him across from Cephalonia to Ithaca. An unfavourable wind was blowing and the boat made heavy weather of the seas, putting in to harbour only at eleven that night. In the diary, Schliemann's excitement becomes almost tangible: he has at last entered 'Odysseus's kingdom'. 'Despite fatigue and hunger,' he noted, 'I was filled with tremendous joy to find myself in the fatherland of the very hero whose adventures I had read and reread with such fervent enthusiasm.' With 'ease', he leapt 'across more than one hundred generations into the most glorious epoch of Greek knighthood and poetry'. He took a room in Vathi with two elderly sisters, and rose next day at dawn to climb Mount Aëtos and inspect the ruins traditionally identified as those of Odysseus's palace. As he walked, every hill, rock, spring and olive grove conjured up in his mind some Homeric line. 'Classical antiquity', he observed, 'is alive in every farm-house on the island'.

Standing on the summit of Mount Aëtos, Schliemann had no doubts at all that what he was looking at were the walls of the 'magnificent house of Odysseus', just as the grotto he passed on Mount Neion was clearly the spot where Athene had advised Odysseus to hide the Phaeacian treasure. Even the extreme heat, 125 degrees by noon, and the dryness of the air, were unmistakably Homeric, 'well-suited for the training of excellent men'.

Next morning, having risen in the dark to swim and drink a cup of black coffee, he hired three labourers and set off back up Mount Aëtos with the idea of locating Odysseus's bedchamber which, he calculated, lay in the north-east corner of the ruined palace. Schliemann now entered the world of practical archaeology with a certain physical brutality. Wielding a pickaxe, he came up against a small vase which, when dug out, was found to contain ashes. Such was his impatience and enthusiasm that he broke it, then went on to break all but five of another twenty he brought out of the ground. Though the vases had no inscriptions, Schliemann had no hesitation in identifying them. 'It is quite possible,' he announced, 'that in my five little urns I have the ashes of Odysseus and Penelope, or' and here he introduced a rare note of caution, 'of their descendants.' Homer had enveloped and possessed him.

Schliemann, with his city clothes, excellent modern Greek and brisk and purposeful air, must have been a curious apparition to the inhabitants of Ithaca. Soon a group of people collected around him, questioning him about what he was doing. To silence them, he decided to read aloud from the *Odyssey*. 'I thought it best to read to them verses 204 to 412 ... and to translate word for word into their dialect.' Later he recorded that, having listened to the 'terrible suffering of ancient King Laertes' as told in the melodious language of Homer, 'all eyes were bathed in tears, and as I concluded the song, men, women and children came up to me and embraced me, saying: "You have given me great pleasure ! We thank you a thousand times over !" Then they bore me in triumph to their town.' This is Schliemann in triumphant mood.

The encounter with the happy peasants, a sort of operatic chorus, was followed by an altercation with four snarling dogs, but this episode too provided Schliemann with a Homeric interlude : 'As soon as the barking dogs saw Odysseus, they rushed toward him howling. Odysseus, however, wisely sat down on the ground and let his staff slip from his hands.' Schliemann did the same and although the dogs continued to bark, they refrained from 'devouring' him. When their owner arrived, a 'seventy year old man of mild mien, large intelligent eyes, and aquiline nose', Schliemann admonished him for allowing his animals to attack a stranger, but was then overjoyed to hear the farmer say that he kept them as guard dogs, just as his ancestors. Telemachus and Odysseus, had done. The owner of the dogs offered peaches and grapes. 'To show him my appreciation of his hospitality', Schliemann then read him 113 verses of the fourteenth book of the *Odyssey* 'which so charmed the old man that he kept pressing for more', well beyond the moment when 'I thought I had sufficiently paid my debt'. Refusing however to be deprived of further ecstasy, the old man became so insistent and continued to pester him until 'I had told him the main incidents from the twenty-four chapters of the *Iliad*'. What the owner of the dogs made of it all is not known.

Ithaca, with its 'sterling, amiable and virtuous people', had touched some chord in Schliemann's soul. It had also given him a first taste of practical archaeology. He had stood on sacred soil, and seen the past come to life before him. Holding Homer in one hand, he had been guided to choose a spot by some sort of intuition. His instinct had been rewarded with twenty urns, a clay goddess and a knife (though some doubts were later cast on this first haul, for Schliemann did buy some pieces from local villagers). While other archaeologists studied, contemplated, ruminated and built up methodological pictures, why should he not follow his instinct, since it seemed to work so well ? Clarity of purpose and a basic reliance on instinct were to become Schliemann's archaeological style, as the Homeric gospel gradually unfolded before him.

From Ithaca, Schliemann caught a boat to Athens, where he booked into the magnificent Hotel Grand Bretagne on Syntagma Square. It was here that he met the Austrian-born architect, Ernst Ziller, who had excavated at Pinarbaşi in 1864 and whose accounts of the site had intrigued him. 'He gave me excellent information regarding the Troad,' Schliemann noted in his diary, 'where he uncovered the walls of Pergamos.' After a few days he moved on again, this time to Corinth. Schliemann liked his initial view of a historical landscape to be as wide as possible, so his first step was to climb to the top of the ancient fortress of Acro-Corinth, 700 metres above the town. He stood looking out towards the Peloponnese.

'From this point,' he noted with satisfaction, 'you can see the most important places in Greece.'

Next day, having risen at four o'clock for his daily saltwater swim, he set off for Argos with two soldiers and a guide, riding bareback as he had been unable to find either saddle or bridle. By midday the party reached Mycenae, universally accepted as the home of King Agamemnon, but still scarcely excavated, where his companions collapsed exhausted and Schliemann rode on alone to explore. According to his later account he used the time to reread the second-century Greek historian Pausanias on the royal sepulchres he maintained had been buried at Mycenae. Wandering around, he came upon shards of pottery and fragments of tiles, and went over in his mind the possibility that Pausanias, when speaking of the graves, had in fact been misunderstood by scholars as being in the lower town. Was it possible, Schliemann wondered as he examined the site, that the king had in fact been buried within the acropolis itself, so that all the early archaeologists, who had found nothing, had in fact been looking in the wrong place ?

Hiring a boy to buy him matches in the village, Schliemann then walked down the hill and entered what he assumed to be Agamemnon's treasury, a domed chamber dug into the side of the mountain some way from the citadel. Bats, disturbed by the flickering light of the small fire he lit, circled the high ceiling, while Schliemann recited to himself Homer's description of Hermes leading the souls of the suitors down into the Underworld, and the bats fluttered above his head 'producing a whirring noise inside the divine cave'. In Tiryns, nine miles further south, where the party stopped next – the name came from that of the son of Argos, grandson of Zeus – Schliemann recalled that Pausanias, travelling this way over 1700 years earlier, had declared that the walls of the citadel were equal to the Pyramids of Egypt in magnificence. Was it possible that they were still there, buried under the debris of centuries ? Both Mycenae and Tiryns drew him; but his mind was still set on Troy. He now made plans for the long sea journey across the Aegean to Asia Minor, much as the Achaeans had done when assembling their black ships to set off in pursuit of Helen.

On 6 August, at one o'clock in the morning, Schliemann reached the Dardanelles. The plain of the Troad lay before him. What followed is not altogether clear, the next few days being one of the many times in Schliemann's life when his diaries, memoirs and the accounts of other people differ. In the autobiographical chapters he wrote later, he recorded visiting Pinarbaşi, 'almost universally considered to be the site of

Schliemann as an indigo merchant in St Petersburg.

Schliemann's father Ernst, a pastor.

Schliemann and his second wife, Sophia, on their wedding day in 1869. Schliemann was 47.

The Magazine (above) with its colossal jars, in the depths of the Temple of Athene, in June 1873. Below: The plan of Troy made by William Dörpfeld in 1890.

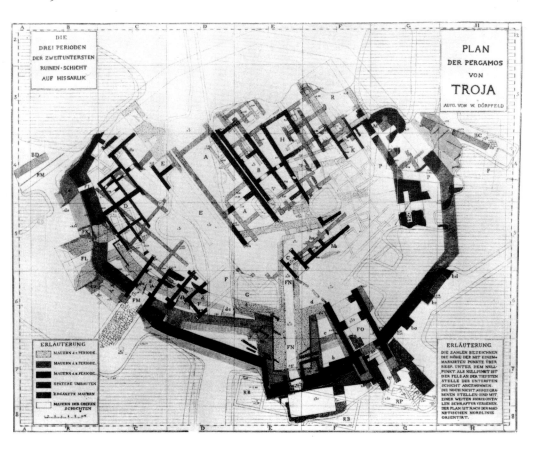

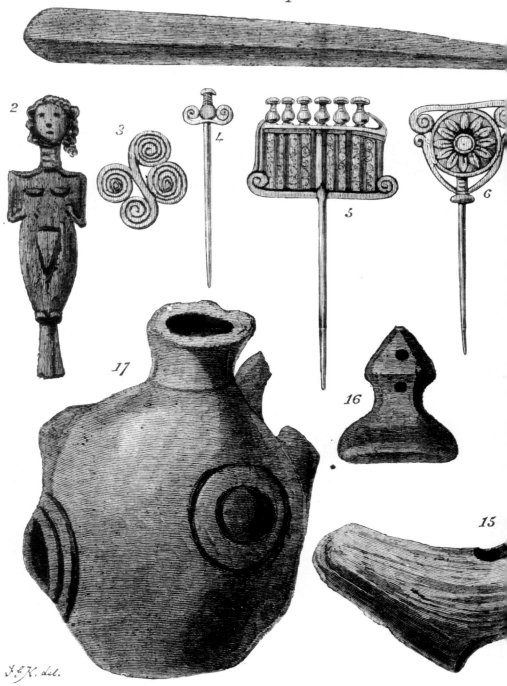

Some of Schliemann's discoveries at Troy. 1, instrument of bone; 2, idol; 3, gold ornament with tube for suspension; 4–8, gold hairpins; 9, jagger knife of steel; 10–11, ivory instruments for weaving; 12, arrow of ivory; 13, instrument

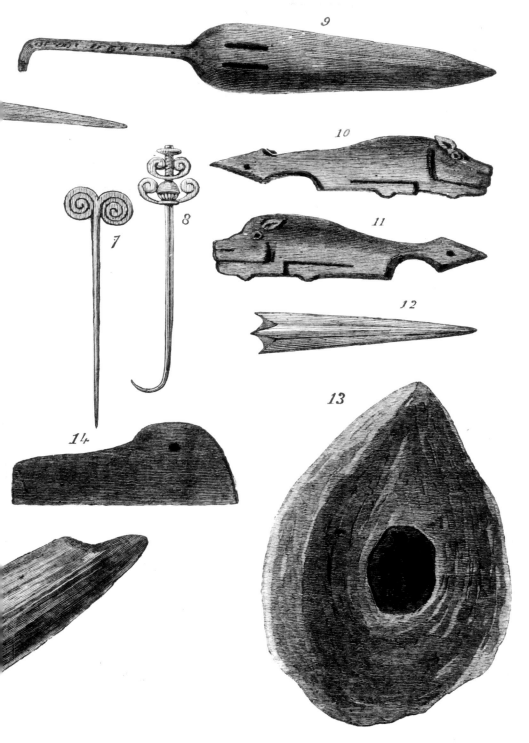

of terra cotta; 15, stick-handle of bone; 16, instrument of stone; 17, vase of terra cotta.

Troy's gold and silver, the Great Treasure, when put on display in London at the South Kensington Museum in 1877. 1–3, gold headdresses; 4–6, gold earrings; 7, silver vase with lid; 8, cup, mixture of gold and silver; 9, gold bottle, 10, gold cup, 11, silver vase (much charred); 12, silver cup; 13, gold drinking vessel, with two handles; 14, copper key of the wooden box that contained the treasure; 15, pieces of pure silver; 16, various gold ornaments; 17, selection from numerous small gold objects found among the treasure.

Schliemann's excavations
at Troy as sketched in
1877. The so-called
Scaean Gate and palace of
Priam, Hissarlik.

Schliemann in 1877.

The Great Treasure, as first displayed.

Homeric Ilium', which he described as a 'dirty village of 23 hovels', with
storks nesting on every flat roof. He approved of the storks, saying that
they were 'very useful – they eat snakes and frogs'. The bedbugs in the
room he rented were so ferocious that he quickly moved to sleep outside.
When morning came, watch in one hand, a copy of Homer in the other,
he began to re-enact the movements of the first day of battle in the
Trojan War, as described in the early books of the *Iliad*: 'from the boats
the clans came out like the countless flocks of birds – the geese, the
cranes or the long necked swans – that foregather in the Asian meadow
by the streams of Cayster, and wheel about, boldly flapping their wings
and filling the whole meadow with harsh cries ... so clan after clan
poured out from the ships and on to the plain of Scamander.'

Still according to his memoirs, Schliemann quickly calculated that if
Troy had actually been at Pinarbaşi, then the Achaeans would have had
to cover at least fifty-two miles during the first nine hours of the fighting.
He then paced up and down, traced and retraced his steps, searching for
Homer's two springs, one hot, one cold, but all he could find were
thirty-four separate streams, 'all at a uniform temperature of 17 degrees
centigrade'. What was more, he estimated that Pinarbaşi lay eight miles
from the sea, while events in the *Iliad* pointed to a far shorter distance.
And how, he asked himself, could such an insignificant hillock as Pinarbaşi possibly have been large enough for a palace such as Priam's, with
at the very least sixty-two rooms? Schliemann next recruited local men
to help him sink some thirty shafts around the mound, then, finding
'nowhere the least indication that the place had ever been settled by
men', declared that Lechevalier and his supporters had been 'blinded' by
preconceived ideas. Pinarbaşi, quite simply, could not be Troy.

Still according to his own later account, Schliemann reached Hissarlik,
the rival site for Troy, on 14 August. It is worth remembering that
prehistoric sites are very different from those of the classical period,
with their temples and theatres. The ruins of prehistory often rise no
more than a few feet above the earth, and when they lie under vast
mounds, any remains are often almost totally buried under centuries of
debris or other later settlements, with only scattered stones to indicate
ancient walls or rooms. 'The ruins,' wrote a traveller to Hissarlik named
Turner in 1816, 'consist of small stones, among which are some morsels
of marble and brick scattered over the hills, of which not one remains
upon the other.' Hissarlik, as Schliemann approached it across the plain,
was in no way spectacular; whatever might have been visible of a
prehistoric city to earlier Greek travellers had long since vanished below

the remains of the flourishing Hellenistic Roman settlement, when the top of the mound, much like cutting the top off an egg, had been flattened to make way for a vast temple to Athene, a theatre, and other buildings.

Yet here at Hissarlik, everything seemed to Schliemann, with growing excitement, to fit Homer's words – the swamp described by Odysseus to Eumaeus, the remains of a great temple, potsherds and rubble, the mountain ridge in the distance. After examining the 'entire plain of Troy' very thoroughly, Schliemann was left, he recorded in his memoirs, without doubts. 'The beautiful Hissarlik grips one with astonishment,' he announced. 'That hill seems to be destined by nature to carry a great city in its citadel.' This could only be Troy, Priam's lost city.

Reconstructing these events with the help of Schliemann's original diary, however, as well as from accounts left by other people, the truth of his first few days at Hissarlik was somewhat different, though in the end none of this was to matter greatly.

Schliemann seems to have begun by accepting Pinarbaşi as the site for Troy, and continued to do until a crucial meeting that took place on 15 August. This was his first encounter with Frank Calvert, the United States Vice-Consul in the Dardanelles. Calvert, as we know, was already convinced that Troy lay under the mound of Hissarlik, and he was very eager to find converts to his cause. A rich, enthusiastic German traveller, pursuing an archaeological dream, was an ideal supporter. Schliemann, of course, wanted to be persuaded; nothing about Pinarbaşi had impressed him. And hadn't Xerxes, Alexander the Great and Julius Caesar all identified Hissarlik, the Greek Ilion and the Roman Ilium, with Troy? Better, surely, to return to the great early conquerors than go along with the more pedestrian deliberations of contemporary scholars. For Schliemann, having talked things over with Calvert, the question now seemed settled. Hissarlik, not Pinarbaşi, was Homer's Troy. It was simply a matter of when, and how, to start excavating.

Before leaving the Troad, Schliemann had climbed to a high rock and looked out across the plain. As darkness fell, before acute hunger drove him down, 'I imagined seeing below me the fleet, camp and assemblies of the Greeks; Troy and its Pergamos fortress on the plateau of Hissarlik; troops marching to and fro and battling each other in the lowland between city and camp. For two hours the main events of the *Iliad* passed before my eyes ...'

A GOOD AND
LOVING HEART

Back in Paris, in the autumn of 1868, Schliemann settled down to write up an account of his first venture into prehistorical archaeology. It was to serve two purposes: to launch him into the rivalrous world of archaeological scholarship, and to provide him with a thesis with which to apply for a much coveted doctorate. Wisely, he devoted some time to boning up on his classical history, sensing that any weakness would quickly be exposed and ridiculed. In the process, hardly surprisingly, a somewhat more polished account of his recent travels took shape, the dates and observations slightly rearranged in such a way as to cast a better light on his earlier views as to the siting of Troy. Hissarlik, he now indicated, had always been his *real* choice. 'All I had in mind,' he wrote, with more than a touch of sanc-timoniousness, 'was the selfless goal of stamping out at the root the inane and erroneous belief that Troy had been situated on the Pinarbaşi highlands.' He found ways, too, of introducing more fulsome references to Herodotus, Strabo and Pausanias, turning them into ever present travelling companions; and he even recast his itinerary to make it seem more purposeful.

One of Schliemann's most useful strengths was an ability to absorb information at great speed; by mid-December the book was finished. To his son Sergei, now aged thirteen and still living with his mother in St Petersburg, he wrote: 'I worked day and night on my archaelogical book, for I have the hope to create for myself with this book a reputation as an author ... If it is successful, I shall continue to write books all my life, because I cannot imagine a more interesting career than that of author of serious books. Writing one is always so happy, so content ...

an author is always sought after and he is everywhere welcome; and even though I am but a novice in that *métier*, I have at least ten times more friends than I would want to have ...' Leaving aside the rosy view of the writer at work, there is something touching about the letter, as if the solitary Schliemann, whose life was singularly without friends, was trying to impress his family with his new position and standing.

Ithâque, Le Peleponnèse et Troie was published simultaneously in Paris and Leipzig early in 1869. It was not a success. The few scholars who did review it either dismissed it as lightweight, or mocked its author for his inadequately supported assertions and boastful sentimentality. With his thesis, however, Schliemann fared better. On 12 March 1869, he submitted copies of his book both in German and French, a copy of *La Chine et le Japon*, and Greek and Latin versions of a *vita*, to the University of Rostock in Mecklenburg-Schwerin, using his cousin Adolf, now a distinguished lawyer in Schwerin, as intermediary. Two classical scholars, G.L.E.Backmann and F.V.Futzsche, who were appointed his examiners, pronounced the Latin good and the French excellent, praised the 'honest, independent and noteworthy research' but said that the Greek was appalling and should never have been submitted. On 27 April 1869, Schliemann was granted his doctorate. For the rest of his life, he liked to be addressed by his title of Doktor.

When not at work on his book, Schliemann had spent the winter months determining how best to proceed with his archaeological plans. It had become clear to him that his next step must be to excavate at Hissarlik. The question was, how could a middle-aged businessman with no museum or university to back him, enter the field? Soon he was deluging Frank Calvert with questions that ranged from the practical to the absurd: 'Please inform me: what medicines I have to take with me? Must I take a servant with me? Probably it is better to have a faithful Greek who speaks Turkish? ... Have I to take a tent and iron bedstead and pillow with me from Marseilles? for all the houses in the plain of Troy are infested with vermin ... Do I require pistols, dagger and rifle? ... What sort of hat is best against scorching sun? ...'

Calvert was evidently blessed with a singularly generous nature. His answers were sensible and painstaking. Schliemann should be sure to take his own tea, since tea, like many other 'luxuries' of the kind, was not available in the Troad. As to a hat, he suggested a white muslin turban like those worn by the Turks. More important, he counselled Schliemann to wait for spring before starting to excavate, warning him that a permit or *firman* was very difficult to obtain, and that the Turkish authorities needed careful and tactful handling. With characteristic selflessness, he added : 'All my lands are at your disposal, to examine as you may think best – and if you have no permit from the Turkish government to excavate ... you can carry on your works in virtue of the one I possess ...' Calvert was to regret his generosity ; Schliemann was far too insecure to behave well towards possible rivals.

The winter of 1868 had brought an end to Schliemann's Russian marriage. Loaded with presents, he had suddenly taken off for St Petersburg where he planned to spend the Russian Christmas, only to find Ekaterina and the children away. He spent a miserable few days waiting for them, and when Ekaterina did appear, she treated him, as he put it, as if he were a 'Tartar invader'. He left St Petersburg for good, intent on getting a divorce as rapidly as possible. In Paris, he learned that proceedings were considerably faster and more efficient in the United States. The spring expedition to Hissarlik was cancelled. Writing to Calvert that the 'terrible heat, the pestilential fevers and the dryness of the soil make the works next to impossible in the summer months', he explained that he proposed to postpone his archaeological debut to the following year ; then he set off across the Atlantic once more.

There was another good reason for a fourth visit to America. Negotiations with the Greek and Turkish governments over his *firman* were going badly – possibly on account of Schliemann's bombastic behaviour and the lack of subtlety in his attempts to pull strings – and he believed that they might be smoother for an American than a German citizen. He reached New York on 27 March, and was soon recording in a new diary, begun for the trip, that wine was expensive – a bottle of Bordeaux cost $2 – and that it was a great nuisance that there were no 'pissoirs' in the streets. Once again he was agreeably struck by the energy of America. 'Nothing is made here for the outward show but all is only for practical purposes ... Of the bustle and business in the streets we are unable to make ourselves the slightest idea in the old world.' Though Americans lacked 'French politeness', they showed a good deal of '*empressement* to render service'.

Two days later, his citizenship granted, he set off by train for Indianapolis, having been told that its divorce laws were more lenient than those of New York. Unlike Charles Dickens, who complained that American railway carriages were no better than 'shabby omnibuses', Schliemann loved the railway network, which had grown vastly since his last visit. He paid $20 for a ticket, and a further $2.50 for a place in the sleeping car, where he admired the 'silver plated ornaments in great profusion', the fine carpets, mirrors, water-closets and stoves, and listened sympathetically when a Frenchwoman sitting near him told him that she had fled her drunken husband after he had beaten her for not serving meat on Good Friday. 'I lamented her sad fate, but that was all I could do for her,' Schliemann remarked in his diary.

Indianapolis, a junction for eight separate railways, was undergoing the very process of growth and prosperity Schliemann most enjoyed. Of all the states, Indiana had some of the richest mineral deposits, as well as very fertile soil. Settlers were pouring in, building themselves comfortable homes, for the most part painted white, surrounded by gardens, overlooking the prairies of wheat and maize and the forests beyond. Schliemann spent the first five days in a hotel then rented a small house, satisfactorily close to three of the main railroads, allowing him to contemplate the 'country's enormous traffic'. He bought a few simple pieces of furniture, balked at having to spend between $14 and $18 for a dozen bottles of German wine, and employed a half-Indian, half-Negro cook, whom he immediately sacked for giving his good cigars to her lovers. He was, however, impressed by the fact that she read three newspapers every day and knew a great deal about American history and politics – all the more surprising since Indiana provided no school for any children other than white. He began by rising at dawn to ride for two hours every day, but then decided that it would do him more good if he swam in the river instead. By day, he busied himself with reports on various commodity markets, became interested in polar exploration and wrote an essay on the *Arabian Nights*.

The question of a divorce might well have proved awkward, had Schliemann not been so determined. Shortly before his arrival, a particularly unpleasant divorce case had attracted widespread publicity and the Indianapolis legislature were debating a motion to toughen up their divorce laws. Schliemann hired five lawyers, and set them to work, pushing through his own case while doing all they could to contest and obstruct the proposed reforms. He had taken the wise precaution of bringing some of Ekaterina's more intransigent letters with him, though since these had been translated from Russian into English, it is possible, as his critics suggested, that they may have been doctored. 'I can merely repeat what I have told you a thousand times,' she had apparently written on 18 March 1868, '... not only I energetically refuse to live with you in a foreign country wherever it may be, but I peremptorily refuse to leave Russia even for the shortest time'; 'I would sooner die than live together with you in a foreign country' (18 April 1868); 'I herewith swear a solemn oath that I shall never pass the Russian frontier' (31 December 1868). There is undeniably something rather convenient about the forthright tone in which Ekaterina expressed these views.

To prove his commitment to the state of Indiana, he now bought a house for $1100 and shares in a local starch factory for a further $12000. Schliemann's Indiana diary is a mixture of naïvety and censoriousness. His American visits invariably began excited and ended frustrated. He was evidently impressed once again by the entrepreneurial spirit, and when he saw small boys as young as six selling newspapers, he approved of the way in which they were already earning 'their bread by useful industry'. But he took against the members of both Senate and Lower House, who seemed to him no better than schoolboys, hurling pieces of paper at each other during sessions, legs swung over the backs of their seats, chewing tobacco and spitting on the floor. Indiana, he wrote in his many letters home to Mecklenburg, was a place completely devoid of all resources for the mind. After a lifetime pursuing a difficult career in Europe, and after two-and-a-half delightful years in Paris, it was, he told his cousin Adolf, quite impossible for a man like himself, 'striving for beauty' and 'living only in metaphysics', to feel at home among such boorishness. In July, having obtained his divorce, Schliemann set off back to New York. It had cost him $1500. Whether or not he had managed to delay the passing of the new, tougher laws – they were not introduced until 1873 – is not clear, but the divorce had involved him not only in lying about his length of residence, but also in getting a witness to lie for him. This time, New York oppressed him. 'The bustle and traffic,' he observed, 'really dazzles my mind and bewilders my understanding.'

There was no immediate berth on board a ship bound for Europe, so Schliemann took the opportunity to lobby for one of his most passionately held causes, the teaching of foreign languages. The American Philological Association, the most important society for classical scholars in the United States, was holding a meeting in Poughkeepsie, not far from New York. Schliemann agreed to write a paper for it, which was read to the assembly on his behalf by Howard Crosby, the chancellor of the University of New York. In it, Schliemann urged America to take the lead in promoting a study of languages, thereby producing the same sort of miracles for philology as it had done for the 'material arts and in gigantic enterprises'.

Recalling the words of Charles V to Francis I – 'every new language one acquires is a new life' – his paper proposed that a boy leaving school at sixteen should already be fluent in English, German, French, modern Greek, ancient Greek and Latin, and have at least 20,000 foreign words in his head. The way to do this was to follow his own example and learn one language at a time, very thoroughly, taking at least fifteen lessons a week. When it came to Greek, 'in order to keep his greatest curiosity always awake', the boy should learn no fewer than a hundred verses of Homer, Sophocles, Aristophanes or Pindar per lesson. Ancient Greek, he insisted, should be taught in exactly the same way as a modern language – was he not a proof that it worked? Schliemann, himself master by now of twenty-two languages, never accepted that some people have more facility for languages than others; for him, it was all a matter of willpower and hard work, as most things were.

Schliemann ended his paper on a stern note. Americans, he declared, were always looked upon as completely useless linguists by the Europeans, incapable of learning a single foreign language, because America had such a 'miserable system' for teaching them. There is no record of what the American scholars replied.

Even before he left Indianapolis, Schliemann was already agitating for a new wife. Not any wife, but one with particular characteristics. The more he dwelt on the idea, the clearer he seemed to become about what he wanted. Schliemann's life is full of strange episodes; but few perhaps as strange as what he was now about to do.

His old friend Theokletos Vimpos, who, as a theology student in St Petersburg, had coached him in Greek, had been made Archbishop of Mantineia and Kynouria. From America, Schliemann wrote to ask him to look around for a suitable girl to become his second wife. She should, he informed the Archbishop, be 'as angelic' as Vimpos's own sister – who, alas, was already married. She should be poor, but well-educated, 'of the Greek type, with black hair and, if possible, beautiful ... But my main requirement is a good and loving heart'. And, of course, she had above all things to be enthusiastic about Homer, and the 'rebirth of my beloved Greece'. Did his friend know of anyone? An orphan perhaps? Or the daughter of some impoverished scholar, forced to earn her own living as a governess? In the envelope with the letter he enclosed two copies of his book *Ithâque* and a cheque as a 'donation to the poor'. The fact that in the eyes of the Russians he was still married, and that had he returned to Russia with a new wife he could have been arrested for bigamy and sent to Siberia, does not seem to have troubled him.

The Archbishop, as a measure of his friendship but also perhaps conscious that a satisfactory introduction might lead to a further flow of funds – he was himself in debt – hastened to scour Athens for an appropriate girl. By early May, Schliemann, who had assured his friend that as 'an old traveller and a good reader of faces' he could tell the character of any candidate from her picture, had received several photographs of possible brides. One had an Italian-sounding name, 'Polyxanna Gousti', and Schliemann instantly took against her, seeing in her features bossiness and ill-temper; she was, he judged, both 'imperious and domineering'. Another was a sixteen-year-old schoolgirl called Sophia Engastromenos, black-haired and somewhat sultry-looking, about to leave school and take exams to become a teacher. Sophia's father had fought in the Greek war of independence and, after several financial setbacks, was now a moderately successful draper in Athens. Her mother, a formidable matron of Cretan origin, known to all as Madame Victoria, was, as chance would have it, Archbishop Vimpos's favourite cousin. In order to have a more appealing photograph taken, Sophia, who had no grown-up clothes of her own, had borrowed a dress from one of her married sisters.

Schliemann was much taken with the sound and appearance of Sophia, but worried about her extreme youth. He needed a companion for his future archaeological labours, but there was something very tempting about finding a student, someone whom he could mould and teach. Had he been possessed, not just by Homer's heroes, but also by his women? Helen, over whom the Trojan War was fought, was 'fair-cheeked' and 'white-armed' and, like all Homer's women, well-behaved, amiable, correct in word and action, and so admired even by her Trojan captors that the sages, sunning themselves on the walls of Troy and seeing her approach:

> Softly spake winged words to one another: 'small blame is it that Trojans and well-greaved Achaeans should, for such a woman, long time suffer hardships; marvellously like is she to the immortal gods to look upon'.

In Homer's world, after all, marriage was a matter of arrangement and barter, the woman having no rights, her position being entirely defined by the will of men. Ekaterina had been grasping and unpleasant; French women he found immoral and threatening; would a very young and biddable Greek girl not respond to his every need?

However, he paused. Sixteen was extremely young. Though he was both 'sensuous' and 'hot-blooded', because of his 'marital difficulties', he told Vimpos, he had had 'no relations with a woman for six years'. Would a young widow 'of exemplary behaviour, who already knows what marriage means' not be better? Schliemann's tone was both apprehensive and pompous. 'Furthermore, she would be less voluptuous and sensual, while young girls believe that heaven and paradise lie in the fulfilment of their physical desire. And, I, my friend, used to be sensual and sentimental. But my character has completely changed. I live now only in the metaphysical world, and I think of nothing except scholarship ...' Try, he urged the Archbishop, 'to find me a wife with a Greek name and a soul impassioned for learning'. To another friend, he wrote: 'Thank God there are great possibilities of choice in Greece, and the girls there are as beautiful as the Pyramids of Egypt.'

The next day, Schliemann changed his mind. A new letter was drafted. 'Already I have fallen in love with Sophia Engastromenos ... so that I swear she is the only women who shall be my wife.' Naturally, he was not interested in a dowry. 'If I am physically fit, and propose marriage to Sophia in July, then I shall buy her underclothes and stockings.' Then came a very characteristic Schliemann questionnaire: What colour was her hair? Was she a good housekeeper? Would she agree to moving to Paris? He asked Vimpos to have some more photographs taken so as to be able to show them to other people. Evidently the answers were acceptable. Even though his divorce was not yet through, he wrote to his father, much as he had done twenty years before with Ekaterina, to tell him of his plans: 'Since I am enthusiastic about the Greek language I believe that I can be happy only with a Greek. I will however take her only if she has a liking for the sciences because I believe that a beautiful young girl can respect and love an old man only in the event she has enthusiasm for sciences in which he is much more advanced than she is ...'

Schliemann arrived in Athens on 4 September 1869, booked into the Hotel d'Angleterre, and went in search of his putative bride. It was the eve of St Meletios, and Sophia was decorating the local church with flowers for the coming feast-day. Hearing a friend call out 'The German has come', she hurried home, changed into her best clothes and joined her family in the formal sitting-room. Schliemann seems to have wasted no time. Speaking Greek, he tested her education. 'When', he asked her, 'did the Emperor Hadrian visit Athens?' Later, he asked her to recite some lines from Homer. He seems to have been satisfied.

The next few days were spent in yet more formal meetings, always in the presence of her family – she had six brothers and sisters – or her many cousins. One morning, Schliemann sent round a necklace made of coral with a letter. 'Can you please ask your excellent parents and write to me if it is possible to see you without all those people around? ... we need to see whether our characters go along together.' Setting out his requirements for marriage, he wrote that 'respect, love and virtue' were essential, and that she should consent to marry him, not for his wealth, but because she felt that she could learn from him. In time, he assured her, this would turn into love.

An audience, private but for the presence of her mother and father, was granted. 'Why,' he asked her, this time speaking German, of which she knew a little, 'do you want to marry me?' All might now have foundered, for her reply angered him: 'Because my parents have told me that you are a rich man.' Cross and affronted, Schliemann retired to the Hotel d'Angleterre to sulk. A chilly note was despatched: '... if you marry me, it must be so that we can excavate together, and enjoy a common enthusiasm for Homer.' He added that he planned to leave for Paris, and that if there was ever anything she needed, she would find him there. However, he lingered on long enough to receive her apologetic answer. She had not meant to offend him, she said: it was simply that she believed that he valued the truth. And, it went without saying, that was not the only reason for her wanting to marry him. Schliemann was mollified.

He was now anxious to waste no more time. The wedding took place on 23 September in the evening. St Miletios was lit by candles and the long Orthodox service was conducted by Archbishop Vimpos. Most of the guests wore brightly coloured national costume. The bride was in white, her heavy black hair parted in the middle and pulled up into a plait; she had put on Schliemann's coral necklace. Sophia was just seventeen, Schliemann forty-seven, though he looked considerably older. They had known each other nineteen days. The wedding photograph is not a joyous one; neither of them is smiling, and Schliemann peers out from above his thick black moustache a little bleakly, his expression as wary and pinched as ever. Next morning, at three o'clock, after a long wedding banquet in the Engastromenos' garden, the couple boarded a steamer for Messina and Naples. To his family, Schliemann wrote: 'Sophia ... like almost all Greek women ... has a kind of divine reverence for her husband.' He had found his Helen. Against all probability it was to be a happy marriage. 'She loves me as a Greek, with passion, and I love her no less. I speak only Greek with her, for this is the most beautiful language in the world. It is the language of the gods.'

Schliemann was clearly much charmed by his new wife, but he had meant what he said when he declared : 'I shall be her teacher my whole life long, and as she will never arrive at the point I have already reached she will always look up to me as she does now.' Long before the honey-moon was over, Sophia was hard at work. Something of her sense of inadequacy and rapidly growing exhaustion comes through the letters she wrote, almost daily, to her family in Athens. Sophia did not share her husband's gift for writing. Her letters home were long, full of conscientious but somehow lifeless descriptions of all she saw; even the feelings she expresses have an almost insincere note, the strivings of a young girl to obey and placate.

The Schliemanns travelled first up through Italy, starting with two days in Messina. Naples pleased her, not least because she was allowed time off from the museum circuit to stroll in the public gardens and drive up and down the fashionable Via Caracciolo in a carriage. Not that her education was neglected. The Palazzo Reale, the former royal palace, was made the occasion for a detailed scrutiny of white marble staircases, mosaic floors and innumerable statues. Sophia reported to her mother that Schliemann had told her that one day he would build her such a palace in Athens, looking out over the Aegean. In the National Museum, Sophia listened while Schliemann discoursed on the finds from Pompeii and Herculaneum. After a visit to Pompeii itself and to Sorrento, the couple moved north for an intensive programme in Rome, Schliemann expressing fatherly enjoyment when Sophia took pleasure in the theatre and opera, or made observations that seemed to him proof of the quick-ness of her mind. From Rome, Sophia wrote that she was finding 'things so big that they cannot enter fully into my small head'.

For the last week of the honeymoon, the cultural speed hotted up : two days each in Florence, Venice and Munich, where Schliemann bought Sophia some of the expensive underclothes he had mentioned in his letter to Archbishop Vimpos when commissioning his old tutor to find him a bride. To her family, as the days passed and one museum merged into another, Sophia wrote that she was so 'confused by the splendours that I am most certain I can never put them in place or good order'.

Paris, which they reached on 21 October, and where there was talk of settling permanently, was to be more, not less, exhausting. The city itself, turned into a vast building site by Baron Haussmann, Prefect of the Seine, was now nearly finished, as indeed was the reign of Napoleon III, whose Second Empire was crumbling. The Avenue de l'Opera, designed to run through the heart of the city, was still not completed but the anarchic growth of the capital had been checked. Wishing to avoid orthodox American city planning, with its straight streets crossing one another at right angles, Haussmann had created avenues radiating out from circuses; the wilderness of the Bois de Boulogne and the Bois de Vincennes had been tamed into ornamental parks; and the city limits had been pushed back from the barriers of 1789 to its ancient fortifications. Paris, according to its inhabitants, was now the finest city in the world – at least, that is what those with money said, for the poor had fared little better under Napoleon III, the rents having risen dramatically with the slum clearances.

Schliemann had made the Latin Quarter his home, conveniently close to the Sorbonne and his lectures. His house, at number six, Place St-Michel, was a mansion of marble, the ceiling beams and cornices decorated with mock Hellenic carvings; it looked out over the fountain of St Michael fighting the dragon, and across to the Isle de la Cité. This was one of the most agreeable parts of the city, combining Haussmann's new splendour with relics of old Paris preserved in the narrow streets that gave off the square. Here Sophia, surrounded by servants and awed by the formality, settled down to a more rigorous schooling, learning French and English simultaneously 'until I trip over words, speaking three languages at once, using whatever familiar word first comes into my mind'. The Louvre, which Henry James described at about this time as imparting to him as a boy 'a sense of freedom of contact and appreciation' which became the opening of a new world, was one of Sophia's most important schoolrooms, though she did not feel about it as James did. Afternoons were spent visiting the Théâtre Français, and the Jardin des Plantes, and studying the architecture of the Sacré Coeur, the Madeleine and Notre Dame. In the evenings, when alone, the Schliemanns read aloud to each other from books of verse and philosophy.

They were not alone all that much, for Schliemann had made a number of acquaintances during his Sorbonne days, men like the celebrated historian Ernest Renan – he had read and praised Renan's treatise on Averroës, the twelfth-century Spanish-Arab philosopher – and Emile Egger, professor of classics and philology. Paris, with its air of culture and learning – the Goncourt brothers, Gautier, Flaubert, Dumas and Zola were all alive and working – and its bustle was the perfect city for Schliemann. According to the Goncourt *Journal*, which covers this period, Homer was much discussed, and on the whole revered, during the literary evenings and in the cafés in which the writers met; and Renan was one of Homer's greatest admirers, carrying back to the Schliemann household some of the feelings of the French intellectuals for his hero. Sophia, however, complained that while her husband was 'surrounded by his learned friends ... I sit endlessly by like an untutored child'. By day, Schliemann was again busy with his enormous and ever-mounting correspondence, sending out dozens of letters to new archaeological acquaintances and to newspapers in London, New York and Paris itself. If there was something a little over-eager in his enthusiasms, he was also acquiring a certain stature, due not simply to his money, but to his boundless desire for knowledge.

Early in January 1870, Schliemann learned that his eldest daughter, twelve-year-old Natalya, had died in St Petersburg. With his customary theatricality, he locked himself in his room, claiming that had it not been for his desertion of his first family, she might well still have been alive. Days of morbid self-indulgence followed, while the seventeen-year-old Sophia, not much older than Natalya herself, felt increasingly ill and miserable. For some weeks now, Sophia had been talking of headaches and 'illness in my stomach' because of 'Heinrich's insistant demands on me to learn more'. After the bright blue light and warmth of Greece, she found Paris cold, damp and bleak. These pains were now diagnosed as gastrointestinal complications exacerbated by exhaustion and loneliness. Schliemann, even when he had detected a certain note of dejection in Sophia's spirits, had failed to see how demanding his life could be for a young girl, accustomed to the daily intimacy of a large family. She was agonizingly homesick. On one of his trips away, in answer to a sad letter of hers, he wrote: 'My dearest wife: Pray if you are not in a good humour do *not* write to me, because such laconical letters as you wrote yesterday and the day before break my heart and *increase* the pain in my ear. I am very sorry to hear that you are suffering from giddiness but that is the natural consequence of the 4th of the month, on which day you used to have your periods ...' Father, governess, teacher: in Sophia he had found his perfect, malleable, companion. It was not, however, even at this stage, all one way. Behind the anxiety to please and the awe in which she held her new husband, Sophia was growing up. One evening, she announced that she was too tired to accompany him to the opera. Schliemann let her rest for a while, then urged her to make an effort. She refused, and Schliemann went out on his own. Something about her new stubbornness unnerved him, and after the end of the first act he hurried home. She was loving, but not contrite. Years later, recalling his feelings that evening, Schliemann wrote that her determination had made him realize how much he already depended on her: '... after the opera, so paralysed and frightened, I knew I loved and needed a woman of her grandeur'. At last consulting a doctor about her health, Schliemann was told to hire a cook who could prepare Greek food, find a gymnastics teacher, and introduce her to young women her own age. Instead of the opera, he now took her to see Houdini, whom she greatly preferred.

When a message arrived from Frank Calvert that the Turkish authorities had at last signed the *firman* for him to dig at Hissarlik, the Schliemanns packed up the house and set off back to Athens. Schliemann, whose swings of moods could be extremely disconcerting, and whose ready sense of optimism was matched only by the depth of his descent into despair, noted gloomily that 'our happiness would be complete if only her health were good. But alas ! it seems that fate has ruled that lasting conjugal happiness is not to be mine.'

The year 1870, even by Schliemann's restless standards, and despite a marriage that was barely three months old, was to be one of quite exceptional travel. It was not so much where he went – the world tour had satisfied most longings for the East and for exotic places – as the frequency with which he came and went. Leaving Sophia for the most part in Athens, in the care of the somewhat grasping Madame Victoria, Schliemann made trips throughout mainland Greece and the Greek islands, to the Black Sea, Bulgaria, Austria, Switzerland, France, Scotland and around Turkey. The month of May saw him at his most frantic : the first and second days in Constantinople ; then off to Central Europe, moving every few days, often by extremely uncomfortable means, involving long hours in carriages on rough tracks. Everywhere he went, he spent entire days in the museums, recording in his diaries precise details of the collections he examined. During the whole of 1870, he spent just seven weeks in Athens. To Sophia, who not surprisingly wrote him reproachful letters about his continual absences, he replied urging her to keep her mind on more important matters: 'You should fall straight away on your knees and thank God for all the blessings He has showered on you . . .'

The year opened depressingly, for on reaching Piraeus Schliemann was informed that the promised *firman* had in fact not yet come through. Six days later, he moved Sophia from their rooms in the Hotel d'Angleterre back into her parents' house and set off, alone, for Syra, in the Cyclades, where he complained of live objects in his soup and lice in his bed, but, Homer in hand, thoroughly explored what ruins he could find, quoting to himself the *Odyssey* and Homer's praise for an island

> not overpopulated, but fine for grazing
> sheep and cattle, rich also in wine and grain.
> No lack is ever known there, no disease,
> wars on its people, or ills that plague old men . . .

From Syra, he moved across to Delos, balking at the cost of the steamer but writing triumphantly in his diary that the monuments 'seen by Pausanias are most certainly covered with the soil of time'. More and more often Schliemann was now speculating about what lay beneath the ruins of the classical sites he explored. Then came Paros, Naxos, Nios and Santorini, before rejoining Sophia in Athens, where he noted that 'together we shall wait most patiently until the *firman* is granted, and only then shall we leave this glorious city'.

His patience lasted four days. Short trips from Athens, to sites where Sophia could continue her education, were planned, with departures at dawn by carriage, and picnics among the ruins. Phyle, home of Thrasyboulos after the Thirty Tyrants expelled him from Athens, perched, Schliemann wrote in his diary, 'like a nest of birds on a high rock. Big stones are joined together without cement.' In the plain of Marathon, the couple discussed Herodotus's account of the Persian Wars. At Delphi, the shrine to Apollo, where the French were already excavating, he took the opportunity to learn 'all I could to be useful when I go soon to Troy to begin my work'. On all these expeditions, whatever the season or the weather, Schliemann seldom failed to fit in a dawn swim in what he continued to believe to be healthy saltwater, though his earaches were now bothering him increasingly.

Wherever they went, armed bodyguards went with them, since bands of brigands known to attack travellers roamed right up to the very outskirts of Athens. It was at about this time that banditry, thought by many to be condoned by the Greek authorities, grew so menacing that relations with Britain were threatened. A party of tourists, in two carriages, were attacked on a return trip from Marathon to Athens. Four of them, an Italian nobleman and three Englishmen, were taken captive; the other three were sent on with demands for a ransom. Schliemann was apparently one of the people who offered to raise the money for the ransom, but both the Greek authorities and the British Minister in Athens hesitated, hoping to find ways of rescuing the prisoners, who were now moved by the bandits to a more secure hiding-place near Dilessi. As the armed police and soldiers closed in, the four captives were killed. The Dilessi murders almost caused the collapse of the British government, after the Prime Minister, Gladstone, refused to endorse punitive action. These attacks on tourists and foreigners alarmed Sophia's family, but seem to have been dismissed very lightly by Schliemann, who simply went on planning more excursions.

At least some of his restlessness at this point stemmed from his poor relations with Sophia's family who, now connected by marriage to what must have seemed a dream of wealth beyond all imagining, were wheedling from him all they could. Sophia was embarrassed, but the forceful Madame Victoria was relentless. Most of Schliemann's ill-humour and edginess, however, came from the fact that the *firman* had still not been signed. When April came, he decided that he was prepared to wait no longer, and, despite Sophia's anxieties, and the fact that she refused to accompany him, he booked a passage on the SS *Menzalieu*, and sailed, second-class and in discomfort, to the Dardanelles. There he hired a horse to take him to Erenköy to find Frank Calvert, generous owner of part of the mound of Hissarlik. Calvert was ill and in bed. Schliemann, dressed in a suit, a bowler hat, gloves and white shirt, rode on again, taking with him a bodyguard. At Ciplak, the nearest village to Hissarlik, he found a room, took on two workmen, hired some donkeys and, pickaxe and shovel in hand, set out for Hissarlik. Sitting on the top of the hill, he wrote in his diary that he could see 'the handsome Paris and fair Helen landing at this spot in their flight from Sparta . . . With my flesh creeping and with goose-pimples covering my skin', he conjured up the great wooden horse being pulled to the city gates. His good humour appears to have been restored: the entries in his diary are leisurely, satisfied. He recorded sleeping well, having drunk milk rather than wine the night before; that his breakfast consisted of eggs, bread and coffee; and that the Troad was full of crickets, which seemed to live as harmoniously with one another as the Turks and the Greeks. It was very cold, particularly at night.

April 1870 was not destined to launch Schliemann as an archaeologist. Though he soon had four workmen cutting a trench with shovels from east to west across Hissarlik, turning up some coins, clay pots, fragments of a broken cup and a leather ring, all of which he described meticulously in his diary, along with the amount of rain that fell and the precise depth of his cuttings, the lack of his *firman* was to prove disastrous. Even as he reported that his muscles were responding well to the hard physical work, 'because I have kept my body strong with swimming', and was musing poetically that they were 'matched with the channels of my mind and rivers of my soul', the Turks were closing in. Peasants claiming to own the land on which he was digging appeared – for by now he had moved beyond Calvert's land – and demanded payment. Reluctantly, Schliemann gave them some money, but next day they were back, with more claims, this time in a hostile mood. Schliemann was not only cautious with his money: he was absolutely determined never to be blackmailed. Recording in his diary that he had dug into soil 'which lay on top of Priam's palace in the area where I shall uncover the Ilium of Homer', he stopped excavating, paid off his workmen and returned to Athens to bully, cajole and pester anyone who could be of any use to him, to help secure the elusive *firman*. Whatever uncertainty he had previously felt about Hissarlik vanished when he found a vase with 'human ashes', as well as a terracotta bust with what he was convinced were Helen's features. He now had no doubts at all: Schliemann reported to the *Augsburger Allgemeine Zeitung*, that the site was indeed that of Priam's palace.

Back in Athens with Sophia, he filled his days by learning Turkish, locking himself up in his room with a dictionary and exercise books and, apart from meals, emerging only three weeks later, claiming that he had mastered a vocabulary of six thousand words and was now able to write a letter in fluent Turkish. Later, the editor of the *Levant Herald*, a man called Whittaker, was to tell a story about his first meeting with Schliemann. 'One morning ... a knock came at the door and a visitor entered in the shape of a little man with a round bullet-like head, very little hair and a reddish face ... "I understand," said the visitor, "that you are better acquainted with Turkish than most of the other foreigners here : how many words are there in the Turkish dictionary ?" Whittaker, cautiously, suggested a figure of so many thousand. "Thank you, Mr Whittaker," said the little man ; "in that case if I learn so many words a day, at the end of six weeks I shall know all the words of the language" ; and he departed. At the end of the six weeks a knock came again at the door and the same little man entered the office. "I am very much obliged to you, Mr Whittaker," he said, "you were quite right in your calculation, and I now know all the words contained in the Turkish dictionary.'"

Schliemann was now in a position to resume his assault on the Turkish authorities in their own language, though Calvert, appalled to hear about his unauthorized excavations, wrote that he could not 'conceal how injudicious I think it is of you to have made a boast of what you did – and we must suffer the consequences and get the *firman* when the government are in better humour'.

Schliemann was again restless and anxious, and went off to Marseilles to buy provisions for what he continued to insist would be the next season's dig at Hissarlik: spades, camp beds, cooking utensils, a saddle for himself and one for Sophia, coffee, sugar, twelve bottles of cognac and some curry. Some of his discontent found its way into a bragging, pompous letter in French to his son Sergei, who was not doing well at his school in St Petersburg: 'I was heart-broken to hear that you have not been making progress. In this life one must keep on progressing or one becomes discouraged. Try to follow your father's example ... who has always proved how much can be achieved with a will of iron. I accomplished miracles during the four years from 1842 to 1846 in Amsterdam. I did what no one else had ever done and no one will ever be able to do.' He had, he informed Sergei, not only become a merchant, but the most wily and prudent merchant in the entire market. He had then travelled, highly successfully, and produced a 'scientific' book, translated into four languages, which had been universally admired. 'Today, I am an archaeologist, and all Europe and America are dazzled by my discovery of the ancient city of Troy, the Troy that archaeologists from all over the world have searched for in vain for the last 2000 years ...' Schliemann's boasting could be overwhelming; but there was also something pathetic about it. At this stage, he had not even begun to dig at Troy.

In the autumn, Sophia realized that she was pregnant. It was clear that she was no longer in a condition to accompany Schliemann on a new visit to Hissarlik, so he left for the Dardanelles alone. He found the plain of Troy swept by an icy wind, but it neither prevented him from digging nor from taking his dawn swims in the freezing sea. His almost daily letters to Athens urged Sophia, his 'most darling wife' to rest, to eat sensibly, to walk slowly and take the greatest care never to bump into anything in case the 'precious thing you bear may be troubled or hurt'. Only after a fortnight, during which he never seemed to get warm, did Schliemann agree to stop excavating and set off for home, pausing only for further altercations with the Turkish government in Constantinople. Reaching Athens in time to celebrate the new year, Schliemann wrote : 'Will my rightful *firman* be mine ?' That he might not actually be entitled to it, he never appears to have considered.

'Il ne faut pas qu'on s'ennuie' was the motto of Napoleon III and his Second Empire. Fêtes, balls, gambling, financial speculation and Haussmann's building programme all served to keep boredom at bay. Parisians had come to believe that their city was the capital of civilization, and as such somehow invincible. When, on 19 July 1870, France went to war with Prussia, the Napoleonic legend helped to persuade the French that defeat was impossible, and that even the 'Barbarians' would never dare to attack Paris.

It soon became clear, however, that the French were hopelessly outclassed by superior Prussian generals and artillery, and that the French army, which had boasted of being 'ready to the last button', was in fact profoundly disorganized. Within weeks of going to war, came news, not of victory, but of defeat, at Worth, Weissenburg, Mars-la-Tour, and Gravelotte. Metz was besieged. At Sedan, on 4 September, the Emperor and the French army capitulated.

The men who took over power in Paris, proclaiming a government of National Defence, had been part of the opposition under the Second Empire. They were now called upon to carry on a war not of their making. As the Imperial Eagles were torn down, and flags bearing the words 'Liberté, Egalité et Fraternité' went up, calls went out for volunteers for a National Guard. Three hundred thousand men responded. The decision was made to defend Paris by drawing back within restricted fortifications, and all those who had moved away from their slums to the outskirts now returned inside the fortified city. The Gare du Nord became a flour mill, the Gare de Lyon a cannon factory, and the Gaîté Théâtre was given over to producing uniforms. On 18 September, the Prussians reached the city ; the next day Paris was cut off by a ring of German soldiers. Balloons and pigeons carrying dispatches in hollow zinc balls became the sole means of communicating with the outside world. When finding a way to make them travel in a given direction proved difficult, a pupil at the Polytechnique suggested having a long pole, at the end of which would be tied a large piece of raw meat ; four hungry eagles could then be tied to the balloon by ropes, and would fly in the direction of the meat. The only problem was that there were no eagles in Paris. As the cattle, sheep, pigs and then horses – some 70,000 of them – were eaten, and as anxiety about dwindling food stocks spread, the two elephants in the Paris Zoo, Castor and Pollux, were sacrificed. Their trunks, cut into slices, made excellent steaks, and a fashionable restaurant in the Passage des Princes added 'escalloped elephant meat, scullion sauce' to its menu.

By the end of December, the Prussians had their artillery in place, and the bombardment of the city began. For twenty-three days, Paris was continuously bombed; fires caught, and spread; 1400 buildings were damaged. It was an exceptionally cold winter. Together with the incessant shelling, the Parisians had to contend with temperatures that fell to 15 degrees below zero, so that the Seine froze over, as well as with an almost total lack of fuel for heating: what gas remained was reserved for filling the balloons and the wood had long since disappeared. There was no hot water, and very little soap. Epidemics – of dysentery, smallpox and cholera – broke out. On 3 January 1871, Jules Favre, Foreign Minister after the fall of Napoleon, went to Versailles to negotiate an armistice with Bismarck. Paris had held out for 131 days; it was now down to enough flour for just ten more.

During the siege, Schliemann had worried intensely about what might happen not just to his home, but to the various factories and warehouses, as well as flats, in which he had tied up a considerable part of his money. He attempted to cross through the blockade but was turned back by the Germans. Schliemann was a man who seldom seems to have experienced much physical fear. Bribing a postman called Klein from nearby Lagny to lend him his uniform and his passport, he entered the city in disguise. Though Klein was only just thirty and Schliemann nearing fifty, he managed to make his way through the lines, surviving, he was later to say, by flattery. Three times, he told a friend, he was stopped by the Germans, and each time, 'by addressing every lieutenant as general, and every common soldier as colonel, I managed to overcome all obstacles'. Given that spy mania had gripped the besieged city, and that every stranger was suspected of being an infiltrator, it is surprising that the German Schliemann was not arrested and shot by the French.

To his relief, 6 Place St-Michel was intact, though the house next door, which he also owned, had received a direct, but not very serious, hit. His increasingly valuable collection of archaeological finds was unharmed. 'I gave the books in my library as many kisses as I would have given a child snatched from death's door,' he reported. Spring was on its way and the few remaining chestnut trees were in bud. Schliemann remarked that no carriages were to be seen because all the horses had been eaten, and that the theatres continued to play only by day rather than after dark, because there was no gas to light them. The city, he said, was as 'clean and beautiful as ever', and the Parisians as lively, his scholar friends continuing to meet for heated and timeless discussions. Schliemann seems to have been beset by more than his usual amount of self-doubt, for he swung between longings for Sophia and Athens, and misgivings about his marriage, and particularly the poisonous influence of Madame Victoria on Sophia.

On 18 May Sophia gave birth to a girl, Andromache. The baby was to have been called Odysseus, but fortunately plans had been made for the eventuality that it was not a boy. Schliemann arrived back in Athens just in time for the birth, but not before receiving a plaintive letter from his wife, who was constantly buffeted between her voracious mother and the dictatorial but fretful Schliemann. 'I cannot understand why so much energy is spent to obtain this world's goods,' she wrote, 'and often so little made to secure a friend.'

He had now been pressing for his *firman* for Hissarlik for over two years. Whenever he settled in any one place for long enough, he poured out streams of agitated and begging letters to Calvert, to other contacts in the Dardanelles and to Wayne MacVeagh, the American Ambassador to the Sublime Porte, who had been pressed into service on his behalf. Even Schliemann was no match for Turkish bureaucracy, intrigue and procrastination. The continuing saga over the *firman* had become further confused after a meeting with Safret Pasha, the Minister for Public Works, from which Schliemann came away convinced that he had received at least a verbal promise giving him the right to buy land and start digging. Yet the *firman* still did not come. At one point, learning that the verbal promise meant nothing – it is not clear whether this had all been a misunderstanding – Schliemann lost his temper, and his letters to the Turkish officials turned bullying and accusatory.

And then, in the summer of 1871, word reached him that a sealed packet had been delivered to Athens from the American Embassy in Constantinople. The *firman* had arrived – itself little short of a miracle, for his pestering, hectoring manner, his quick, forbidden raids on Hissarlik, and his exaggerated promises seem to have done more to alienate than placate the Turkish authorities. The last obstacle in his quest for Troy had finally been removed.

8

BELONGING TO
THE DARK NIGHT

In the second week of September 1871, Schliemann left Athens for what was to be the real start of a remarkable archaeological career. He was forty-nine, a short, wiry man with dark brown eyes, high cheekbones and a rather heavy mouth. Neither marriage nor financial success had softened a watchful, suspicious look. If nothing else, the coming season at Hissarlik was to seal for ever his commitment to Homer's lost heroes. Sophia remained with four-month-old Andromache in Athens – though it is only from diaries and the dates on his letters that it is now known that she did not accompany him. Schliemann himself, in his accounts of this first major excavation, was to write: 'My dear wife, an Athenian lady, who is an enthusiastic admirer of Homer, and knows almost the whole of the *Iliad* by heart, is present at the excavation from morning to night.' This is one of the lies that have played so powerfully into the hands of his critics. Schliemann, for whom the truth sometimes appears to be no more than an inconvenience, quickly disposed of, was keen to build up Sophia as his partner and an archaeologist in her own right. It was an image he needed.

He paused in Constantinople, where he was appalled to learn that Safret Pasha's assurances about the hill of Hissarlik had been overtaken by events. The Turkish government itself now owned the hill. Ahmed Pasha, Governor of the Dardanelles and the Archipelago, explained that since the opening of a new museum in Constantinople, the Turks were eager to acquire ancient art objects themselves. After so many battles and so many tedious delays, Schliemann was in no mood to give up. He embarked on a two-pronged assault on Turkish officialdom, giving extravagant dinner parties for the Ministers in the evenings, and spending the days badgering the apparently endlessly obliging American Ambassador Wayne MacVeagh, to bring further pressure on the Turks with threats and promises on behalf of the United States – of which Schliemann was, after all, now a citizen. For all his bombast, there was something about him that must have appealed to men in authority, for many went out of their way to help him.

Possessed of a seemingly binding permission to start digging, Schliemann left for the Dardanelles at the end of September, only to face a further thirteen days' delay while Ahmed Pasha procrastinated, demanding more details as to the exact location of the proposed excavations. Schliemann, quick to despair, sent off another beseeching letter to the American diplomats. 'Pray, for Heaven's sake', he wrote on 8 October, 'do all in your power to hurry the matter through ... for the inactivity in this place of vermin, *literally kills me morally and physically* and I cannot return to Athens without having worked at least for six weeks at Troy, for so much has been spoken in the newspapers of my ensuing excavations that ... the whole press would describe me as a ridiculous fool ...' It was no longer just a question of ambition : Schliemann's very standing was now at stake, and there is something touching about his readiness to admit it. The Americans, who, like Frank Calvert, were immensely obliging, now put pressure on Kiamil-Pasha, the new Minister of Public Instruction, and on the Grand Vizier. The flowery titles of these eminent Turks, and the many ceremonial meetings, sometimes give Schliemann's launch into the archaeological world an air of music-hall comedy.

On the evening of 10 October, Schliemann set out from the Dardanelles on the last leg of his journey to the plain of Troy. It was an eight-hour ride. He carried with him the precious *firman*, now containing three important caveats. All the finds had to be divided, one half for Schliemann, the other for the new museum in Constantinople ; all uncovered ruins had to be left in the exact state in which they had been recovered ; and all expenses were to be borne by Schliemann. The first of these three provisos was to lead to mayhem.

'We do care about the authenticity of the tale of Troy,' wrote Byron. 'I venerate the grand original as the truth of history ... and of place ; otherwise it would have given me no delight.' The Hellespont, the narrow crossing at the mouth of the Dardanelles, swum by Byron, faced the Troad. For Schliemann, it was not so much a question of delight as of necessity. He had come to believe, more strongly than ever, in Homer 'as in the Gospel itself'. The day had arrived when he would at last be able to vindicate the poet as the true historian of his age.

Whatever truth was eventually to emerge, the hill of Hissarlik was undoubtedly set in the very landscape Homer so vividly described. The correct and matching topography of the area was a card Schliemann set great store by. A traveller reaching the alluvial plain in the middle of the nineteenth century could not fail to be struck by the great sweep of flat land, ideal for the battle between Achaeans and Trojans, with the mound of Hissarlik rising almost a hundred feet above, having at its back the ocean and the 'swift-flowing' Hellespont, and before it layers of hills reaching up to the summit of Mount Ida. It was a place at which all the winds seemed to meet – Homer's 'windy Ilium' – and where the sea was constantly darkened by a 'soundless swell', pushed one way at the mouth of the Hellespont by the north wind, the other way by the south wind.

On the shore, the land stretched away into salt marshes, lagoons and sand dunes. Fig trees, willows, and tamarisks grew in great number, as they had when Odysseus spoke to Eumaeus of reaching the city walls and 'crouching under our arms, near the town, in the thick bushes, the reeds and the marsh'. The Scamander, with its steep banks planted with trees, was as Homer had described it in the *Iliad* : 'The elms burned, and the willows and the tamarisks, the lotus was also burnt and the rushes and the cypress, which grew in abundance along the beautiful stream of the river.' Its waters were as 'fast-flowing', 'eddying', 'silver-eddied', and 'with mountain shores', as in Homer's text. Had Herodotus himself not spoken of Ilium, with its acropolis and a temple consecrated to Minerva, on the very site of Priam's Pergamos ? Homeric Ilium, declared Schliemann as he got down to work, could thus 'not possibly be any- where else than on the Ilium of the Greek colony, and this in accordance with the common opinion of all antiquity'. Standing looking out across the plain, he noted with satisfaction : 'The view from the hill of Hissarlik is extremely magnificent.'

Excavations began, with Homer in charge and a Turkish overseer called Georgios Sarkis, a former secretary of the Chancery of Justice in the Dardanelles, appointed by the government to keep an eye on Schliemann's every move. Schliemann was particularly irked by having to pay his wages, and referred to him scathingly as 'the eyes and ears of the government'.

In the *Iliad*, the temple of Pallas Athene was said to occupy the highest part of the hill, and the defence wall, with Priam's citadel, the bottom. Schliemann resolved to attack on both fronts, by cutting a wide north–south trench through the entire mound. His scheme was on a scale seldom even contemplated before : that of opening up an enormous area and making a general assessment of what it contained. Only by digging straight down to solid bedrock, Schliemann argued, would it be possible to separate Greek from pre-Greek civilizations. Before Schliemann, no comparable stratigraphical investigations had ever been carried out in the Near East, and no one, therefore, had any precise idea about the way in which the cultural strata of different eras lay superimposed one upon the other. Schliemann's strategy was not just grandiose : it was crude, chaotic and brutal, for by cutting straight down, demolishing great strips of soil and all it contained, without proper measurement or description, a vast amount of invaluable historical knowledge was bound to be lost. In his efforts to 'shed light on the prehistoric Hellenist world, which was completely in the dark', Schliemann was to be ruthless. It was, declared a number of classical scholars who soon heard what he was doing, more like 'rape' than archaeology.

Schliemann set up camp in Çiplak and rose at dawn each morning to ride the couple of miles across the plain to Hissarlik. He was proving to be the most hard-working of archaeologists, always on the move, looking at everything, directing everything, exhorting the workmen to dig faster, deeper, harder. To Sophia, he wrote outpourings of endearments and reproaches, most of the time in Greek, but sometimes in French or English in order for her to practise her languages. 'My dearest wife, my much loved Sophie. The pain your attitude towards me caused me the day I left ... was so heart-breaking, so immense that I have been completely unable up to now to write to you.' When he learned that she had been ill, he begged her to send him a telegram every day with news of how she was.

He was immensely lucky in a servant he now employed, a Greek living in Asia Minor called Nikolaos Zaphyros Yannakis, who was to become his bodyguard and factotum and stay with him until his early death. Schliemann trusted Yannakis in a way he seldom trusted anyone, getting him to pay the wages of the workmen and providing him with a money-belt and funds so that he could offer bribes when all else failed. Trust did not seem to include respect, however, for Schliemann could not prevent himself from remarking that Yannakis 'gives me no assistance in the works as he neither possesses the gift of commanding, nor has he the slightest knowledge of what I am seeking'. But he did do him the honour of addressing him by his real name, rather than the nicknames he bestowed on the workmen, of 'monk' or 'corporal' or 'doctor', according to their 'more or less pious, military or learned appearance'.

The first official season, not under way until the middle of October, was by necessity short. Autumn in this part of Turkey is famous for squalls and driving rain. Excavations opened with eight workmen, soon increased to thirty-five, then to seventy-four. There was far too little equipment, Schliemann rapidly running through the supplies he had brought with him from Marseilles. When no more wheelbarrows could be found locally, the men were forced to fall back on ordinary baskets for carrying away the rubbish. This method turned out to be agonizingly slow – for Schliemann was determined to 'reach the native soil before the winter rain sets in' – and he commandeered four carts drawn by oxen. Rubbish, the debris from the vast cutting, became a major problem, as it had to be disposed of at some distance from the excavation; and when, as they went deeper, this increasingly involved immense blocks of stone, the workmen all tended to pause in their digging while they listened to the 'thunderous noise' of the blocks as they rolled down into the plain below.

Schliemann's first team of workmen was Greek, from the nearby village of Erenköy, and he was soon maddened to discover that, being orthodox Christians, they insisted on taking Sundays off. But then he worked out that this would not apply to Muslims, so he brought in Turks to work on the Christian holidays. Schliemann took a close interest in his workers, becoming intrigued by the differences between the various groups, noting in his diary that the Turkoman women – quite a number of women came to dig and carry stones alongside the men – were not only unveiled, unlike the Turkish women, but stronger and prettier, and that the Turkoman men, when evening fell, took the first woman to hand and made love to her. The workmen were forbidden to smoke, for Schliemann maintained that tobacco reduced energy and powers of concentration.

Even Schliemann's critics admit that his habit of keeping methodical diaries of his digs was valuable. He had devised a system of daily entries, written for the most part at the close of each day's work, giving the date (confusing, since he used Julian and Gregorian calendars at will, sometimes both, and at times incorrectly), the number of workmen and what he paid them, comments on the weather and a list of all significant finds. The entries for the 1871 season open in German, then switch to French. Every few weeks, on Sundays or on feast-days, he wrote summaries at far greater length, and these were to be the rough drafts for the despatches he now started sending to the *Augsburger Allgemeine Zeitung*, and later for his book on Troy. From these, and from letters Schliemann wrote, it is possible to follow the progress of the excavations as well as his swings of mood – to some extent, at least, for Schliemann's forte was never consistency and the various accounts do not always agree.

The further down into the mound of Hissarlik he went, the more mudbrick architecture came to light, wall upon wall, as well as occasional coins. At 13 feet, the Roman remains dried up, to be replaced by mussel-shells and fragments of pottery. Schliemann noted that the early inhabitants must have been very fond of fish, easily obtained since the bay had undoubtedly been rich in schools of migrating mackerel and tuna, as well as oysters, sea urchins and shellfish.

Then came 'round articles with a hole in the centre', like humming tops or whorls, some silver wire, and two copper nails. Schliemann was both disappointed and confused. 'I find much in this stone period,' he wrote, 'that is quite unexplicable to me.' He stumbled on, down and down, destroying everything on his way. 'Unfortunately', he remarked in his diary, 'we are obliged to destroy the foundations of a building 59 feet long and 43 feet broad', as it was of far too late a period to be of interest to a man searching for Troy. He plunged on down. At somewhere between 30 feet and 32 feet, his workmen came across more pottery, lances, axes, knife-blades, saws, needles, bodkins, and more whorls, many of them new not just to Schliemann but to archaeology, but nothing yet so sensational as to make him feel that Troy was near. The deeper he dug, the tougher going it became, the more the debris built up, and the more his inner doubts grew. Days of despair became more frequent. He had lost all hope of ever finding Troy, he noted bleakly in his diary on 1 November. When low, or out of sorts, Schliemann readily speculated about abandoning the site altogether, or turning it over to an established archaeological society. The presence of so many Stone Age objects, he admitted to James, Frank Calvert's brother, 'perplexes me every day more and more'. The problem was the depth at which these things were coming to light. If there were stone-period remains in the top layers, how could he hope to find Homer's bronze or iron city, from a much earlier date, beneath them ? Encouraged to keep on with the excavations by the invariably supportive Calvert brothers, Schliemann went on digging and was rewarded by some metal objects and some more sophisticated pottery. In a characteristic surge of ebullience, he was soon writing of Hissarlik 'which no one before me has ever thought of bringing to light by excavations ... my success at Troy makes me a thousand times more joy than the most lucky business operation I ever made in my life.'

In the middle of November, the rains arrived. Schliemann used the enforced inactivity to write up his notes and to send off letters, in French, Greek, German and Italian, to scholars and historians, his 'honoured colleagues' throughout Europe, telling them of his finds and asking for their advice. The tone of these letters is respectful, modest and anxious. Alone at Hissarlik, with the eyes of the archaeological world focused on him, not least because of the way that he himself had courted publicity, he often felt in need of support and guidance, writing to men like Alexander Conze, the Austrian archaeologist soon to begin work at Samothrace : 'I sometimes lack the sound counsel of a man like you, and if you could advise me, I would be tremendously obliged to you.' When warmer weather returned, he handed out quinine to his workmen against malaria borne by the mosquitoes that plagued the plain, and complained that he was constantly summoned 'not only to cure wounded men, but camels, donkeys and horses', as well as one young girl covered in ulcers, to whom he recommended his own remedy of castor oil and regular bathes in the sea. The girl's ulcers did in fact dry up, which earned him considerable local admiration, and he also had some success using tincture of arnica for the swelling of the animals' joints. 'Gratitude', he remarked somewhat sourly in his diary of 21 November, 'does not appear to be one of the virtues of the present Trojans'.

After two days of violent storms, Schliemann called an end to the season on 24 November. He did his best to hide his disappointment at the lack of more spectacular finds, saying that the enormous difficulties he had encountered had only increased his desire to 'reach the great goal which is at last lying before me, to prove that the *Iliad* is founded on facts ... I shall spare no trouble', he announced before leaving the Troad, 'and shun no expense to attain this result.'

Two of his finds in particular intrigued Schliemann. He spent the months until better weather allowed him to resume digging consulting classical scholars and reading widely in the archaeological libraries and museums across Europe.

The first of these was the head of an owl decorating a number of figures, sometimes with a 'kind of helmet' on its head. Schliemann, who in his usual excited manner was soon seeing owls on every urn or vase, was convinced that this was a goddess – but which one ? From Athens, he fired off letters and, waiting for replies, studied books and journals, where he soon discovered that early owl-headed vases were at some point in history supplanted by the owl as a bird, and by statues of Athena, with a human face. As letters came back, describing similar objects excavated at other archaeological sites, so Schliemann felt able to declare that his owl goddess 'must necessarily be the tutelary goddess of Troy, the Ilian Athena', and that this fitted perfectly with Homer's many references to 'thea glaukopis Athene', the goddess Athena with the owl's face. Through progressive civilizations, he concluded, Athena must have been given a human face, and her early owl's head must have been transformed into her favourite bird, the owl. Suggesting that classical scholars had in fact mistranslated Homer's 'glaukopis' as 'grey-eyed', when it should in fact have been 'owl-eyed', he played with a number of philological and archaeological ideas and themes before fashioning an entire iconography of Athena from the pottery found at Hissarlik, and establishing triumphantly what he maintained was kinship between Trojans and Athene-worshipping Athenians.

The other find that kept him in continuous correspondence with scholars was his discovery of a swastika scratched or painted on to some of the objects his men had excavated. Swastikas, he was sure, must have some fundamental significance, and his first thought was to link them with the Indo-European 'ancestral' races of Bactria and India. Historians replying to his questions spoke of similar signs found in Persian cuneiform inscriptions, and Schliemann was soon sketching out an idea that the symbol was a universal one, 'employed for unknown numbers of centuries', and Aryan, so that an Aryan link bound the Trojans and the Hellenic people, as well as Europeans generally. Aryan ideology had in fact become a fashionable topic, and both Emile Burnouf, former honorary director of the French Archaeological Institute in Athens, and Professor Max Müller, the Anglo-German Sanskrit scholar, subscribed to it. Symbols fascinated Schliemann, and these finds led him to contemplate a far more ambitious plan than simply discovering Homer's Troy : nothing less than revealing the 'development of mankind, and any clue to his inter-relationship throughout the world'. Reading the papers and letters sent to him by Burnouf and Müller may indeed have made him more careful about what to look for, but they did nothing to curb his immense ambitions.

Schliemann's speculations were not going unperceived in the close-knit and jealous world of classical scholarship. While some museum curators and historians dealt with his questions with interest, keeping open minds as to his interpretations, others were beginning to object to his hasty assumptions and apparent bumptiousness. There were rumblings of scepticism. Nineteenth-century archaeology was not known for its kindliness and the attacks already had a sour tinge to them; they would become steadily more bitter and cutting in the years to come. A retired German army officer called Ernst Bötticher, later to cause Schliemann immense unhappiness, declared that his brain was 'like one of the sponges brought up by naked divers'. At a public meeting in Berlin the two men tussled over lines from Homer, the irascible Schliemann offering his adversary the advice that he would do far better in life to keep control of his emotions. In the pages of *The Academy*, an English journal, he voiced his rage against his critics: 'They can never pardon me, a former merchant, a self-taught scholar, for having solved by gigantic excavations ... Ubi Troja Fuit.' It was the German historians and scholars who were most ambivalent about Schliemann; and the Germans, for this very reason, were the people he most courted and most wanted to impress.

By 1 April, 1872, Schliemann was back at Hissarlik. Though he was later to claim that Sophia was with him, she did not in fact arrive until May. Excavations resumed at dawn. Schliemann now had a definite plan in his head: he intended to reach down to the level at which he believed he would find Priam's citadel below later Greek and Roman settlements, and to do so he felt he had no choice but to sink a shaft straight down into the middle of the mound. While he longed to find actual Trojan inscriptions, he accepted that the vast Cyclopean walls of pre-Greek cities, indicating a royal stronghold, built on natural rock, would provide him with satisfactory proof of Homer's Troy. Though he was perfectly capable, on occasion, of sounding modest and respectful when it came to dealings with more established and renowned colleagues, he seldom discussed his actual excavation methods with anyone. Frank Calvert suggested that instead of making one vast destructive hole, he dig a web of smaller trenches; Emile Burnouf advised him to take the time to record precisely at what depth, 'in what bed of earth', every object was found. Schliemann paid no attention to either of them.

The third season at Hissarlik was like a military operation. Schliemann hired a railroad engineer named Adolphe Laurent, who made a series of calculations about the amount of debris that would need removing, and a Greek former miner, Georgios Photidos, who had worked in Australia as a pitman and tunnel maker. He had sent to London for 'best English wheelbarrows, pickaxes and spades', brought in screwjacks and windlasses, and hired ever greater numbers of workmen. 'You see,' he wrote to Frank Calvert, 'I must firmly believe to find Troy, for otherwise I would be a crazy man to work on with 120 and 125 men ...' To make certain no object, however small, escaped him, or disappeared into the pockets of the workmen, he promised them a halfpenny for every object, even of no apparent value, that they brought him. Those who tried to forge things, on the other hand, such as crude figures carved on to pottery, had their wages docked. Since every object 'belonging to the dark night of pre-Hellenic times' was to him a 'page of history', he had no intention of losing anything. The 1872 dig was to last four months. Schliemann's diary, written in Greek or German, runs to over 300 pages and includes rough sketches.

Wanting to remain close to the site at all times, Schliemann built himself three small houses, roofed over with waterproof paper against the rain, which served as bedroom and office for himself and Sophia, and storeroom for the objects brought to the surface during digging. Here, on wet days, Sophia measured, numbered and described, while he wrote his diary, leaving some of the pages to be covered in crude, but numbered, drawings, kept up his mounting correspondence and did the accounts. Schliemann's meticulousness on paper extended across his entire life: the reports on his three houses – cost of materials, size of the planks of wood and so on – are as precise as those on his finds. Photidos was found to have a scholarly hand, and made out perfect copies of all records in Greek. In the evenings, they talked of their beliefs, or so Sophia was later to claim, reminiscing on the early archaeological days: 'How often my dear Heinrich and I spent hours, so important to our inner selves, contemplating aloud on the verities of mankind'. One suspects that most of the contemplating was done by Schliemann. What does emerge from accounts of this time, however, is the sense that Sophia was becoming a most necessary companion to him, someone this man who trusted no one could trust, and that despite her age – she was still just twenty – she was turning out to be resilient, capable and extremely sensible. And there is no question that she both loved and admired her tetchy and highly insecure husband. 'My only concern,' she wrote to her mother on a day on which Schliemann had inveighed against the slow progress they were making, 'is that my Heinrich shall not have suffered in vain.' On another occasion, after Schliemann had come across a piece of ivory shaped like a flute, and played a note on it: 'How pleased I was to see my Heinrich so happy. Few are given the opportunity to share such moments with him.' In his choice of second wife, Schliemann was extraordinarily lucky.

Conditions could not have been described as easy. Once the 'incessant and intolerable hurricane' that plagued the first days had died down, owls kept everyone awake with their shrieks until Schliemann, jumpy even without noise, asked the men to shoot them. Pallas Athene did not choose to intervene. Frogs croaked ceaselessly, and were harder to silence. The walls and ruins were full of scorpions and centipedes with forty rather than a hundred feet which dropped from the rocks on to the men digging in the trenches below, and from the ceilings of the Schliemanns' living quarters. Vipers wriggled out from behind the stones. Though many of the men were bitten, Schliemann was surprised to observe that they suffered no ill-effects from the poison if they drank a potion brewed from a weed that grew in the plain. For a while, his business instincts aroused, he wondered whether to conduct experiments and see if the weed had the same result with the venom from cobras. The weed, however, proved powerless against another highly poisonous snake called the antelion, brown in colour and no larger than a large worm, whose bite was rumoured to lead to rapid death. Had the storks not eaten a large number of these snakes, Schliemann was to say, the plain of Troy would have been totally uninhabitable.

The food available in this remote spot rapidly became monotonous, for there was no fresh meat except for mutton, and practically no vegetables of any kind beyond wild spinach and a few potatoes, though as the months went by, the plain around Hissarlik was covered with wildflowers. Food parcels, sent by the generous Schröders, his former employers, were received with gratitude: Chicago corned beef, ox tongues, cheese and peaches, and even, on one occasion, 240 bottles of English pale ale, which Schliemann noted was good for his constipation.

The season of 1872 did not start particularly well. Though Adolphe Laurent calculated that 666 cubic metres of soil were being removed every day – he had worked out that 78,545 cubic metres needed removing altogether – and increasing numbers of pots, in black, yellow and brown, were coming to the surface, many of these were in pieces and none bore any trace of painting. The Greek Easter closed the site for six days, and no amount of bribes would keep the men at work, who claimed that if they agreed to carry on digging, the 'saint will strike us'. Schliemann, brooding and irritable, calculated that the holiday alone cost him $200. His relations with the workmen were further soured when they went on strike after being repeatedly forbidden to smoke, but this time Schliemann emerged the victor, by sacking them and sending to nearby villages for others to take their place. The original workmen were soon begging to be re-employed, and he seized the moment to lengthen the working day by one hour, so that it now started at five in the morning and lasted until six at night, with two breaks in the day of an hour each. He was not altogether unreasonable. When the larger stones and rocks from the excavations were hauled away in carts drawn by oxen to make new buildings in the surrounding villages, he made no objection.

As the pits descended ever deeper and some of the trench walls started to give way, there was a growing risk of a serious accident. Most of the men by now had cuts and grazes on their feet from falling stones from the trench face and Schliemann developed a terror that a disaster would strike, so bad that he would be forced to suspend work. His fear was at least partly justified when six men were briefly trapped by falling debris and vanished from sight, and for a few minutes seemed to have been crushed to death. But they were pulled clear, with no more than scratches, and work resumed. There were times, in the early weeks, when Schliemann felt so depressed about the rising costs and insignificant finds that he wondered whether to abandon Hissarlik altogether, and move to a more promising site in Greece, like Mycenae or Delphi, places where earlier excavations had proved more rewarding. He would be perfectly willing, he announced one day, to excavate such sites at his own expense, keeping what he found only until his death, after which it would all go to a museum built by him and bearing his name. 'It seems,' he lamented, 'that the Olympic Gods wished to withhold forever prehistoric traces in the Troad from the eyes of men.' Sometimes, now, he talked of retiring to Paris.

Then, in May, Schliemann's luck changed. Vases appeared, with his owl's head, and remains of an imposing building which he firmly declared could only be Priam's palace. 'I have reached virgin soil at last at 18 meters of depth,' he wrote off quickly to Emile Burnouf,' . . . many traces of a high civilization . . . magnificent black pottery or painted black and white with pictures of arcs and arrows . . .' Though his claim to have reached the very bottom now seems to have been exaggerated, he did find what he called a Homeric *depas amphikypellon*, an elongated two-handled goblet.

Soon after, excavating by now on 'my honoured friend' Frank Calvert's side of the hill, came an even more remarkable find, if not exactly Homeric. This was a marble bas-relief, a heliosmetope, showing Apollo crowned with a spiked diadem with ten long rays and ten shorter ones, his hair flowing free, reining in four horses. After noting in his diary the exact measurements of each ray, and exclaiming over the 'grandeur and classical beauty of the style and happy character of the composition', Schliemann recorded that he had never in his life seen anything as 'masterly'. Though many centuries later than Homer's Troy, it was still a superb find.

Next came a cache of bones, which Schliemann announced were obviously those of a six-month-old embryo. Though historians, who learned of Schliemann's finds from the pages of the *Augsburger Allegemeine Zeitung,* or from the bulletins he issued in his letters, and to *The Times* in London, soon confirmed that the Apollo was indeed of immense value, they were somewhat sceptical about the bones. Had Herr Doktor Schliemann, asked a Professor Mann Meister, now added obstetrics to his many other skills ? Was he planning on becoming a metallurgist, a chemist and an astronomer as well ? Schliemann remained jubilant, particularly when an ancient wall began to appear; though neither precisely a tower nor on bedrock, he quickly proclaimed it to be the 'Great Tower of Ilium' which Andromache had climbed when she heard that the 'Trojans were hard pressed and that the power of the Achaeans was great'. 'I am among the ruins of Homeric Troy !' Schliemann wrote in his diary on 18 June. Some of this jubilation was dampened and turned to rage, however, when he heard that Ernst Curtius, the distinguished Hellenist soon to begin digging at Olympia, having at first supported Schliemann in his siting of Troy at Hissarlik, had now switched back in favour of Pinarbaşi, declaring in the process that Schliemann was nothing other than a 'dilettante treasure seeker'. Curtius had visited the plain of Troy in 1871, but had come away more impressed by von Hahn's excavations at Pinarbaşi, where he walked, he declared, 'to the springs, where the Trojan women washed their clothes', than by Schliemann's purported 'Priam's palace' at Hissarlik.

Curtius was not alone in his growing disapproval of Schliemann and his hasty and boastful announcements: at scholarly gatherings throughout Europe there was much talk about the 'romantic financier with the destructive manner of a grave robber'. However often Schliemann used the words 'presume', 'suppose' and 'perhaps', he was never quite able to keep a note of exuberance and triumph out of his statements.

The more sober and pernickety of the archaeologists found it very irritating.

By July there were seldom fewer than 120 men and women on the site, though 'marsh fever', probably malaria and treated by Schliemann with quinine, cut down the numbers for a while. The equipment for the dig had been increased to include battering rams, iron levers and more English spades and pickaxes, and as many as eighty wheelbarrows to cart away the rubbish. Three foremen supervised the work, as well as Schliemann himself, an endearing if peculiar-looking figure in his stiff collar and sun helmet, with his high-pitched nervous laugh and strange gliding walk. Sophia, who did some of the supervising herself, returned to Athens on 27 June.

On 4 August, as the hot sun beat down on the dry and dusty plain, and temperatures climbed regularly into the 100s, came the first find of treasure: three gold earrings and a gold dress pin. The men were now exhorted to work yet more vigorously, and more and more debris was cut out and borne off to be tipped away from the mound. Every day now, votive offerings were appearing, together with statues, tools, jars, household utensils and animal skeletons, to be photographed and sketched by an artist Schliemann had engaged. It was exhausting and unpleasant work, a strong wind blowing from the north driving dust into the faces of the men as they dug. Schliemann, refusing to be discouraged, used this dusty wind as yet another proof that Hissarlik was Troy. Only across this plain in Asia Minor did perpetual winds blow so relentlessly: here, beyond doubt, was Homer's 'windy' and 'stormy' plain.

On 14 August, after the three foremen, the factotum Nikolaos Zaphyros and Schliemann himself had all fallen ill with 'malignant marsh fever', made more intolerable by the 'terrible heat of the sun', Schliemann announced that excavations were over for that year. He left Hissarlik in good spirits, declaring that he was now certain that Troy II – the second city from the bottom – was Priam's city. Though not altogether precise about the different layers on the site, he maintained that there were four strata preceding that of Classical Greece. Letters were despatched to the European centres of classical history. 'I flatter myself,' Schliemann wrote, 'that as a reward for the gigantic work I have done, for the enormous expense that I have incurred and for all my privations in this wilderness and pestilential climate, but above all in consideration of my success the civilized world will give me the right to rebaptize these sacred precincts with their right names . . . of immortal glory which must fill every man's heart with joy and enthusiasm . . . I rebaptize them Troy and Ilium and I christen Pergamus of Troy the acropolis where I write these lines.' From this day on Schliemann's letters and despatches were to be headed 'Pergamus of Troy'.

He was, as so often, too eager and too optimistic. The 'civilized world' was far from ready to yield up its approval; much more in the way of proof, and a far more rigorous excavation technique, would be needed before Schliemann received the praise he so longed for.

In the summer of 1923, Frances Bacon, a descendant of the Calvert family, was going through the contents of the Calvert house in the Dardanelles when she came across a bundle of letters marked 'Schliemann correspondence'. She packed them up and sent them off to the American School in Athens, to join the other Frank Calvert papers, and with them went a short letter of her own. It contained a telling phrase. 'I think,' she wrote, 'Mr Calvert did not quite like it because Dr Schliemann never gave him credit for directing him to Hissarlik.' She was being generous. Schliemann behaved extremely badly towards Frank Calvert, who not only pressed him to excavate his own part of the mound of Hissarlik, agitated endlessly for his *firman* and gave him essential advice and guidance, but seems unquestionably to have been the person who first drew Schliemann's attention away from Pinarbaşi and towards Hissarlik. What happened between them during Schliemann's third season was something of a dry run for much that was to follow. The incident also reveals his total contempt for the deal he had struck with the Turkish authorities, when they released the *firman*.

Calvert was an interesting man who has seldom received his due in the Schliemann story. A well-read and very able figure, with a pointed face and a long beard, he knew a great deal about the geology and palaeontology of the area and, by the time Schliemann reached the Troad, had long since been host to distinguished travellers who had come to visit Pinarbaşi and Hissarlik in the middle of the nineteenth century. Early on in their relationship, Calvert and Schliemann had reached an amicable agreement, founded, as Calvert was later to put it, 'on mutual confidence as gentlemen'. Schliemann was to be allowed to dig Calvert's section of the mound, in return for a half-share in everything that came to light.

All went well until 13 June, 1872 when the workmen uncovered, on Calvert's land, the marble bas-relief of Phoebus Apollo reining in the four spirited horses. Schliemann's declaration that it was a 'masterpiece of the first order' naturally pleased Calvert. It was indeed a fine bit of sculpture, the finest ever found at Troy, and archaeologists quickly confirmed its inestimable artistic value. The problem was that it was the only one : to whom was it to go ? Even before addressing this question, Schliemann's first reaction was to have pieces sawn off each end 'for it can lose *nothing* by that operation and it will gain that much that it can thus be loaded on one cart and transported to your home. If there is a man at the Dardanelles capable of sawing marbles pray send him here at once.' If Schliemann's proposal sounds like vandalism, it has to be remembered that Victorian archaeologists were often cavalier in the treatment of their finds.

Calvert, certainly the more scholarly of the two men, found the idea of breaking up the Apollo repugnant and urged Schliemann not to reduce its immense value as a work of art. After a prolonged exchange of letters about the logistics of shipping such an enormous block of marble, the Apollo was eventually despatched surreptitiously to Athens on the deck of the Greek boat *Taxiarches*. Not without difficulty, however. It is clear that Schliemann had never had any intention of revealing his more valuable finds to the Turkish authorities, who would then rightly have claimed their share, and transporting a large piece of sculpture in secret under the noses of vigilant Turkish guards entailed considerable craftiness. By late August, the Apollo was standing in the garden of Schliemann's house in Athens, and Schliemann was having plaster copies made in order to send them off to the University of Rostock, which had granted him his doctorate, and to the classical antiquities departments in Berlin, Munich and Vienna, as well as to the British Museum in London.

It was now a question of sorting out with Calvert how much the Apollo was worth, for Calvert had readily agreed to sell him his half-share. Schliemann was practised in subterfuge. Well aware of Calvert's opinion of Sir Charles Newton, Keeper of Greek and Roman Antiquities at the British Museum, he wrote innocently proposing that Newton be asked for an evaluation. Calvert instantly protested, as Schliemann must have known he would, saying that Newton was 'renowned as being one of the greatest screws – and always offered a tenth of the real price of a thing and then will ask for something to be deducted, or another object to be thrown into the bargain'. The 'screw'-like Newton was one of the curators to whom Schliemann had presented a gypsum copy of the Apollo.

The Calvert brothers proposed valuing the bas-relief at £500, and Frank generously said that he would accept £125, half his actual due. Schliemann wrote back with an offer of £40 : 'I assure you on my honour of my firm belief that *no* man will ever offer you even this.' A further request, to make it at least £50, was firmly turned down, and Calvert accepted the £40. No sooner was the deal concluded than Schliemann began boasting to friends of his excellent bargain, adding that he personally believed that the true worth of the Apollo might be as high as £2500. Not long afterwards, Calvert was enraged when he learned that he could certainly have held out for £400 – a figure worth some £14,000 today. By then, Schliemann had also haggled over the value of some inscriptions found on Calvert's land at Hissarlik among the ruins of the temple of Athena, which he had argued were of no historical importance of any kind, insisting that the price he was prepared to offer was a 'big price such as nobody else would offer'. In his transformation from businessman into archaeologist, Schliemann had not shed an instinct for driving a ruthless bargain. Nor had he conquered a streak of profound dishonesty, soon to flower in most of his coming relations with the Turkish government.

9

SINGING OF THE CITY

Many years later, when Sophia was an old lady living in Athens, she was to say that when the Schliemanns returned to Hissarlik in 1873 for their fourth excavation, they sensed that something very important was about to happen. There was no question that they needed some dramatic discovery : nineteenth-century archaeology craved dazzling finds in order to prove its validity. More than that, Schliemann believed that gems and worked gold were an important element of the lost, great prehistorical eras he was determined to recover, and he maintained it so loudly and so persistently that his detractors took pleasure in dismissing him as no more than a crude 'treasure seeker', and a failed one at that. Whorls, terracotta fragments, idols and a few small gold earrings were all very well, but had Homer not talked of King Agamemnon 'armed in gleaming bronze', of round shields 'plated in bronze', of the 'flashing of bronze, men slaying and men slain' ? Had the word 'gold' not been used to describe cups, pins, beads, studs and, of course, jewellery ? Had Paris, Hector and Achilles not revelled in their ornamental belts, earrings and necklaces ? Had Helen not been referred to as 'Argive Helen and her wealth' ? If Hissarlik were indeed Troy, where were the traces of all this wealth ?

Schliemann arrived in the Troad foolishly early, on 31 January, when a bitter wind was still sweeping across the open plain and temperatures seldom rose above freezing point. At night the wind blew out the lamps in the wooden huts, the water froze solid, and he kept warm only by his 'intense enthusiasm for the great work of discovering Troy'. He caught a cold. To Frank Calvert (the dispute over the Apollo was still to come), he wrote that he sat at his desk with 'thick gloves, all the water on my

table is covered with thick ice, and the ink freezes in my pen'. Comfort
was not a feature of excavation life. Fortunately Sophia was not with
him – though once again he was to say that she was, and took pains to
label his diary for the 1873 season 'Henry und Sophie Schliemann's
Buch'.

Digging resumed on 1 February, despite a threat by the Turkish
government to rescind his *firman*, on the grounds of suspicion that
Schliemann was not honouring his undertaking to share his finds with
the new museum in Constantinople; but he had, once again, dragooned
his long-suffering British and American diplomat friends into negotiating if not a new *firman*, then at least an undertaking that his excavation could proceed. The find of the bas-relief of the Apollo on Calvert's
northern slope had convinced him that he must have been on the site of
a temple to the god. He was loath to share anything more with Calvert,
so he now moved over to the southern slope in search of earlier, more
spectacular, Homeric finds. He was not altogether hopeful. His intention,
in 1873, was to carry out one last season at Hissarlik – where the
'pestilential' climate had come to fill him with premonitions of an early
death – during which he would fully expose 'Priam's' citadel.

By the beginning of the third week in February Schliemann was
lamenting that a combination of the acute cold, thunderstorms and
Greek church holidays had prevented him from accomplishing more
than a total of eight full days' work, and that he had been obliged to
turn the only stone hut over to the workmen who, unlike him, had no
warm clothes and would otherwise have 'perished through the great
cold'.

But then the icy wind died down, and spring covered the plain with
yellow buttercups. The storks returned to build their nests on the villagers' roofs, but so, unfortunately, did the owls, who took possession of
the holes in the excavated walls and once more tormented Schliemann's
nights with their 'hideous' screeching. By 1 March, there were 158
labourers on the site, working from five in the morning, by which time
the horses employed to drag the carts of debris away had finished their
barley, until sunset, with the usual two hour-long breaks. Even the
attempts at bribery by a merchant from Smyrna, who promised the men
more money than they were getting from Schliemann if they would
abandon the excavations and dig up the liquorice roots that grew in the
plain for him instead, did little to slow up progress. By 15 March
Schliemann was writing that the digging was now proceeding with 'great
zeal, favoured by glorious weather and an abundance of workmen'. With

the first signs of warmth in the air, Schliemann resumed his daily swims, accompanied to the water's edge by a group of Bulgars and Albanians armed with rifles, pistols and daggers against the bandits who, as in Greece, sought out rich traders and foreigners to kidnap or plunder. By the 1870s, travellers in Asia Minor had been warned never to move around the countryside without guards, not least because without them there could be no claim against the authorities for compensation. In the area of Trebizond alone, it was rumoured, fifty-three people had been killed by bandits in just a few months.

Further mishap, causing Schliemann to remark somewhat laconically that 'life in this wilderness is not without danger', came in the shape of a fire which broke out at two o'clock one morning in the hut in which he was sleeping. The north wind, which had been blowing steadily all day, carried sparks from the open fireplace to the wooden walls, which caught instantly and filled the room with smoke before Schliemann had time to summon help. He rose from his bed, seized a large basin of cold water and threw it at the flames. 'I did not lose my presence of mind,' he noted.

Finds were now coming to the surface in ever greater number, at such a rate in fact that, since Schliemann was unwilling to slow down, it soon became impossible to keep a precise record of every object, or to record the exact depth at which it had been found. Sickles, nails, weapons, whorls, coins, copper utensils, owl-headed vases, terracotta pots, statuettes and ever more walls and blocks of stone and marble : every few minutes came shouts from one part of the mound of Hissarlik or another, for Schliemann, with characteristic impatience, had decided to start work this year in several places at once, sinking shafts and opening new terraces with bewildering speed, not made easier to follow by his habit of referring in his writings to the 'northern slope' or the 'southern section' as the spirit moved him.

Visitors could be forgiven for thinking that, instead of establishing order, he sometimes seemed to spread chaos, turning 'Priam's palace' into 'Priam's pigsty' as one critic put it, and constantly buffeted by swings of mood, from exuberance to despair. For by now there were many visitors to the site, historians and classical scholars drawn by what they had read in the *Augsburger Allgemeine Zeitung* or *The Times* : among those who came were Sir John Lubbock, whose *Prehistoric Times* had opened up the debate on early archaeology, and who did a little digging of his own nearby ; Alexander Conze, who was now excavating at Samothrace ; and even the vacillating Ernst Curtius, who seems

momentarily to have encouraged Schliemann to turn his finds over to
the Germans, probably sensing that the German government needed
persuading as to the importance of funding archaeological expeditions.
There was also Count Ludolf, the Austrian Ambassador to Constantinople and the Hereditary Prince of Saxe-Meiningen, a young man
who was to become a personal friend and ally. If nothing else, the scale
of Schliemann's programme, the vastness of his ambitions and the
energy he spent in publicizing them, were bringing him a measure of
the international fame he so craved, even if he found aspects of it
irksome.

Frank Calvert – some time before he realized that he had been cheated
over the Apollo frieze – wrote a balanced article for the *Levant Herald*,
giving a sober assessment of what had so far been found at Hissarlik.
Though his predictions that Schliemann's Troy II actually predated the
Trojan War were both accurate and prescient – no one was to come
out in agreement until Mycenae was later excavated – they enraged
Schliemann, who instantly dismissed Calvert's contributions to the
debate as totally insignificant. Relations between the two men were now
to become acrimonious, with Schliemann accusing Frank Calvert of
causing trouble, and Calvert protesting that, had he not guided Schliemann to Hissarlik and offered him his piece of land, 'you would never
have undertaken the work, and reaped the benefit of my experience' and
that 'your mode of dealing makes me take due precaution'. Furthermore,
he cast doubts on Schliemann's qualities as a gentleman. Their squabble
found its way into the pages of the scholarly *Athenaeum* as well as those
of the *Manchester Guardian*.

By the time Sophia reached the Troad, on 7 April, nine giant clay jars,
almost seven feet tall, buried deep in the earth and thought to have held
water and wine, had come to light – the first jars of this kind and size
ever seen – as well as a brilliant red terracotta hippopotamus, with a ring
on its left side, which led Schliemann to speculate that Troy must once
have had commercial contacts with Egypt, for Herodotus had spoken of
the hippopotamus being worshipped as a sacred animal by the ancient
Egyptians. Skeletons with helmets, lances and other weapons, as well as
pots and vases, all followed, though some of the terracotta objects, too
frail for the haste with which the workmen had been instructed to dig,
reached the surface shattered or cracked, though some, of course, would
have been broken long before. Although there was still no trace of gold
or silver, and very little of bronze, Schliemann's mood was good, even
if he continued to feel perplexed by the mixture of things turning up in

apparently single deposits which he felt could hardly belong to the same age. Pushing this disturbing fact to one side, he continued to insist that his Troy II was Homer's Troy, both because it lay at a depth consistent with Priam living a few generations after the city was established, and because of the impressive stone foundations he had uncovered the previous year.

In May, news came from Athens that Sophia's father was seriously ill. She hastened home but arrived too late to see him before he died. Schliemann sent a gentle and affectionate letter: 'If you cannot master your grief, then come back to me by the first steamboat ... There can be no excavations without you ...' The year 1873 was a poor one for Sophia. On arriving at the Troad early in April, she had been attacked by one of the workmen, apparently intent on rape. How serious this attack was is not clear, for surprisingly few references to it were ever made, either by Sophia herself or by Schliemann, and within days she was again involved in the excavation, sometimes in charge of one of the more distant sections on her own. Whether the incident dented her resolve to be a partner in her husband's work is not known, but letters and diaries suggest that, despite Schliemann's insistence to the contrary, Sophia was never much taken with archaeology. Her life at Hissarlik had been improved after Yannakis, having been asked to find a female companion to join her, had vanished for three days and returned with a pleasant young woman. Asked by Schliemann how long she could stay, Yannakis replied: 'For as long as I stay.' He had taken the precaution of marrying her. His new wife was never to be known as anything but 'Helen', Schliemann evidently not extending the courtesy he gave to Yannakis alone of addressing her by her own name.

Summer was approaching, and the hot nights meant that the workmen stayed at the site, sleeping in the open; as a result, to Schliemann's delight, they worked longer hours, from 4.45 in the morning until 7.15 at night. A number of promising finds began to be brought up, encouraging him to think that the city of his heroes was finally coming to light. First came an ancient circuit wall, then a sacrificial altar, a paved road, a city gate, and a small building, with several rooms. These, he declared, were Athene's altar, the road leading to the Scaean gates, the gates themselves, and, obviously, King Priam's palace. To deter the workmen from carrying off the vast and regular paving stones in the road to join all the others that had gone to building their houses, Schliemann did a very peculiar thing. He had it put about that Christ had taken this path when he came to visit King Priam, and had a picture of Jesus hung on one of the excavated walls in order to further intimidate would-be looters – a story he told later in the German edition of *Tro-janische Alterthümer* but which was left out of the English version, possibly on account of Victorian religious sensibilities.

Schliemann had for some time been planning to write up his account of his four seasons at Hissarlik and was already in contact with a publishing house in Leipzig called Brockhaus. The projected book was to include not just the drawings made by the artist whom he had employed that year, but engravings and woodcuts, as well as several thousand photographs taken by a professional photographer. Sending some advance material off to Brockhaus, Schliemann wrote piously that his sole desire was to 'make the subject widely known, to destroy fake theories, and produce general enthusiasm for Ilium'.

To others, he was somewhat less modest. At the end of May, Sergei, who seems to have been one of the main recipients of his father's more pompous attempts at self-aggrandizement, was sent a long letter explaining how Schliemann had not only already removed over 250,000 cubic metres of debris and uncovered more than half of ancient Troy, but dug up most of the 'monuments of immortal glory' and collected enough important antiques to fill an entire museum. 'But now,' wrote Schliemann wearily, 'we are tired, and because we have attained our goal and have realized the great idea of our life, we will forever terminate our excavations here at Troy on June 15.'

No one, to this day, is absolutely sure when Schliemann found his treasure.* But what he produced was undoubtedly treasure, of a quantity and with enough gold, silver and bronze to dazzle even his enemies. A combination of his own obfuscations – whether to protect himself from the Turkish authorities, to boost his own and Sophia's glory, or simply because the moment was too exciting for rational thought – as well as his various uses of the Gregorian and Julian calendars, and the reminiscences of other people, have only served to obscure the occasion still further. The consensus today seems to be that the find took place early in the morning of 31 May 1873, probably between eight and nine o'clock. The story of this momentous hour in Schliemann's life, and in the

---

* cf. Donald F. Easton, 'Schliemann's Discovery of "Priam's Treasure" : Two Enigmas', *Antiquity*, LV, 1981, and D. A. Traill, 'Schliemann's Discovery of "Priam's Treasure" : A Re-examination of the Evidence', *Journal of Hellenic Studies*, 104, 1984.

life of nineteenth century archaeology, has been told, picked over, and examined so often in the last 125 years that it probably makes most sense to tell it from his side first – though even he gave slightly different versions in his diary, letters and published accounts – and from the reports of other people who do not contradict him. Even in the sober, matter-of-fact description that he gave in his book on Troy, published the following year, Schliemann was unable to conceal a sense of over-powering delight, subdued but unmistakable.

Excavating started that day, as usual, at dawn, which fell somewhere around five o'clock. The workmen's first rest came at nine thirty and Schliemann was later to report that the treasure had come to light 'before breakfast'. Schliemann himself was straightening the side of a trench when 'I came upon a large copper article of the most remarkable form, which attracted my attention all the more as I thought I saw gold behind it'. Fearing what the sight of gold would do to the 'greedy' workmen, and in order to 'save it for archaeology', Schliemann called out 'Paidos' – rest time – justifying the early break by declaring that he had just remembered that this was his birthday, and that to celebrate the occasion the men could have a longer period of rest.

With the workmen gone, he took a large knife, and began digging gently into the side of the trench 'which it was impossible to do without the very greatest exertion and the most fearful risk of my life, for the great fortification-wall, beneath which I had to dig, threatened every moment to fall down upon me'. Fortunately, Sophia was nearby, and now 'stood by me ready to pack the things which I put into her shawl and to carry them away'.

First to surface, according to Schliemann, was a large 'copper shield', in the shape of an oval salver with a knob in the middle; then came a flat-bottomed copper 'cauldron' with two handles; then a silver vase and a copper plate, apparently moulded together by the heat of a great fire. Now came gold: a six-inch-high bottle, a cup, a second cup with large handles, both of them 'wrought with the hammer', and a third cup, made of electrum, gold mixed with silver. Silver knife-blades and copper lances followed. All these treasures were packed tightly together, one piece next to another, in such a way as to suggest to Schliemann that they had been gathered up in great haste, as either the 'hand of an enemy or the fire' overtook the person carrying them. From the way the treasures were found, Schliemann thought that they must have been put into a wooden chest which was then abandoned on the city wall, only to be 'immediately covered to a height of from 5 feet to 6 feet with the red ashes and the stones of the adjoining royal palace'. He was encouraged in this idea by finding a four-inch-long copper key, greatly resembling 'a large safe-key of a bank', not far away.

This, however, was not all. The treasure was safely borne away in Sophia's shawl to the wooden hut, the door closed, and the Schliemanns had time to examine their finds more closely. Only later did they discover that the large silver vase contained jewellery – two gold diadems, a fillet, four exquisitely worked gold earrings, fifty-six other gold earrings, six gold bracelets, two small gold goblets and 8750 gold rings, perforated prisms and dice, gold buttons and other 'similar jewels'. How splendid it all was! and how deliciously clear! Here was the wealth of King Priam, the jewellery belonging to fair Helen, to Andromache and to the ladies of the Trojan court, hastily gathered up by some member of Priam's family, or perhaps even by a faithful servant, while the city went up in flames, much as it had done in the illustrations of the fall of Troy in Jerrer's *Universal History*.

While the Schliemanns marvelled at the treasure, the Turkish over-seer, Effendi Amin, appointed by the government to keep a permanently wakeful eye on Schliemann, heard from the workmen that something odd had happened. 'If you had seen the haste with which he erupted into my room,' Schliemann later wrote to a friend, 'and loudly demanded, in the name of the Sultan, that I immediately open up all my chests and all my cupboards, to which my only answer was to throw him out of the house, you would have taken pity on him.'

In the course of that morning, a German scholar of Greek from Bremen called Dr Heinrich Bulthaupt, arrived at Hissarlik, bearing a letter of introduction from Frank Calvert's brother, Frederick, the owner of a farm at Thymbra, four miles away. Possibly wishing to resume more cordial relations with the Calvert family, and seeing a solution to the immediate dilemma of what to do with the treasure, Schliemann received his visitor warmly, and later wrote a note back to Frederick Calvert. After various civil greetings, he went on: 'I am sorry to inform you that I am closely watched and expect that the Turkish watchman who is angry at me, I do not know for what reason, will search my home tomorrow. I therefore take the liberty to deposit with you six baskets and a bag begging you will kindly *lock* them up and *not* allow by any means the Turks to touch them. In order to use reciprocity I take great pleasure in presenting to your lady my half share in all what has been found this year on your brother's field ...

'The villagers betray me to the Turk so that I cannot anymore take their horses. So, when I want to remove the baskets, pray, lend me for three hours in the night three horses ... please do not refuse me for I am quite in despair; having spent here more than 100,000 franks I cannot take away a little broken pottery.'

If the letter seems to combine a typical Schliemann wheedling tone with defiance, and an absolute disregard for the *firman* he had signed, it should be remembered that the American Chargé d'Affaires in Constantinople, John Brown, had long been urging Schliemann to be secretive about any valuable finds. 'When you find any *small* objects', he had written in March the year before, 'put them in your pocket; if you do happen to fall upon any fancy statues, we will see about it here ... The Imperial Museum here is a dead letter like anything else, which does not make money. Money is the order of the day, in that you must *not* find any large amount of Gold or Silver in your diggings.' Brown went on to remind Schliemann that a British archaeologist, 'making helpful researches at Ephesus', had carried off all he found to the British Museum.

That same evening, two other German visitors arrived at Hissarlik. The elder was Gustav von Eckenbrecher, who had been among the first people to point to Hissarlik as the possible sight for Troy; the younger was his artist son, Themistokles. The account they left of their two days at Hissarlik says little about the treasure, but, along with one of the rare sketches of Schliemann at work, it does give a clue as to the state of his mind that day. Climbing the steep slope to the huts, 'at the top Schliemann came to meet us – a sunburnt, stocky figure of medium build. On his head, which was shaved quite bald, was a straw-hat bound all around in Indian fashion with white muslim. His linen paletot was covered with the dust of the excavations and his whole face even more so ...' Schliemann offered his visitors his own room, which contained a 'very spacious bed', and then excused himself, 'for he had pressing business to attend to and could no longer look after us for the present'. Later, the party assembled for dinner – bread, an 'authentically Asiatic roast of mutton tail' and 'excellent Tenedos wine' – and sat outside as night fell, 'talking of many things, and recalling the events that happened here in remote antiquity'.

By piecing together at least some of the various accounts, it seems that Effendi Amin, having been denied access to Schliemann's chests, set off to obtain authorization to search the hut, and probably for some gendarmes to return with him to help enforce the order. Since he would most likely have had to travel as far as Çanakkale – roughly twenty-five miles away – he was not expected back until the following day. This left Schliemann time to pack up the treasure and send it off to Thymbra, in the care of Yannakis.

The precise details of how the treasure made its way to Athens are lost, but, with the help of various documents that have recently come to light, it appears highly likely that, with Frederick Calvert's assistance, it was taken to the *Taxiarches*, the Greek boat on which the Apollo frieze had travelled, at Karanlik. A Greek foreman, Spyros Demetriou, recomended to Schliemann by Sophia's brother in Athens and later to accompany Schliemann to Mycenae is thought to have boarded the *Taxiarches* with it. With the assistance of another friend of Sophia's brother, a shipping agent called Tzelent, the treasure reached Athens without discovery or interference. Schliemann's letter to Tzelent, arranging for the consignement, is revealing: 'You would much oblige me if you explain to the director of the customs-house that I am a benefactor of Greece, but I have been working for three years in the Troad on behalf of the glory of Greece and I send all the antiquities I excavate to Greece and am bequeathing them to the Greek nation. So I warmly beg you not to open the chests in the customs-house, because they are all sealed.'

Schliemann's diary for these days is terse. Even given the fact that, when he was very busy, his daily entries frequently noted little more than numbers of workmen and amount of money paid, it is unusually cursory. Whether he was feigning overwork in order to conceal the value of the cache, or afraid lest Effendi Amin read the diary, or so busy that he had no time to do justice to the treasure, no one will ever know. The excitement must, in any case, have been immense.

Schliemann had earlier told his son Sergei that he would be closing the dig in the middle of June, and this he now did, no doubt fortified in his decision to whisk the treasure out of the country by a further letter of support from his American diplomat friends in Constantinople, who wrote saying that 'It would be worse than throwing away the articles which you have discovered to permit any part of them to go into the absurd collection of rubbish which the Turks call their "museum"'.Even allowing for the fact that this was a personal note, and not an official letter, the contempt felt by the Western diplomats in the late nineteenth century for the Sultan and the Turkish government is unmistakable and revealing.

There is one trouble with Schliemann's story : it is at least partly false.

Things did not happen entirely the way he described them. How profoundly he lied, and whether his version was so distorted as to cast serious doubt on the Trojan treasure, was a question that was to haunt him in the following months, and that continues to this day to exercise his critics. One absurdly obvious lie, which he was quick to own up to, was that Sophia was with him at Hissarlik on 31 May. After her father's death, she had stayed on in Athens with Andromache to await Schliemann's return. Schliemann himself admitted as much in a cheerful letter written to his new friend, Sir Charles Newton, at the British Museum, not long afterwards: 'On acc. of her father's sudden death, Mrs Schliemann left me in the beginning of May. The treasure was found end of May; but, since I am endeavouring to make an archaeologist of her, I wrote ... that she had been present and assisted me in taking out the treasure. I merely did so to stimulate and encourage her, for she has great capacities. So f.i. [for instance] she has learned Italian here in less than 2 months.'

As for fooling Effendi Amin, the Turkish overseer, Schliemann readily admitted soon afterwards that 'I succeeded in doing so by suddenly singing out that it was my birthday, by feigning to drink freely and by making my Turk drink copiously that famous liquor called "cognac", a word which hereafter I shall never be able to hear without breaking out in shouts of laughter'. But Effendi Amin was a Muslim, and it was unlikely that he drank alcohol.

Unimportant slips; but other inconsistencies were not to be resolved as smoothly. Schliemann's slipperiness was beginning to lend his enemies powerful weapons.

'My hopes have been surpassed,' wrote Schliemann to his Schröder friends in London, 'my mission is fulfilled.' By the third week in June he was back in Athens. Now, at last, he could take stock of the beauty and immense value of his treasure without fear of having it removed by the Turks. The jewellery was carefully unpacked, examined, weighed, numbered and described. It was indeed a scarcely believable find, all he had hoped for, and far more. Within days, crowds of curious visitors, hearing about the gold, which had made him, Schliemann remarked, 'the paramount favourite', arrived at the gates of his house. In the letters he now poured out to friends and curators all over the world he gave precise measurements, page after page of painstaking details: one of the two diadems, for instance, he described as being made of thin gold plate and wire from pure ingots. It consisted of a fillet '22 inches long and nearly $\frac{1}{2}$ inch broad, from which there hang on either side 7 little chains to cover the temples, each of which consists of 50 double rings, and between every 4 of these rings is suspended an hexagonal leaf having a groove lengthwise ...' To his relations, and to people he knew well, he included a photograph of Sophia, a strangely passive and detached expression on her face, wearing the jewellery and the gold diadem. Here, truly, was his Helen of Troy.

Once the collection had been properly catalogued, Schliemann put it on display at his house in Athens. Though he knew perfectly well that trouble could only follow if the Turks got wind of what he had done, his pleasure seems to have been such that he found secrecy, and modesty, impossible. The time had now come to write up the story of his excavations at Hissarlik, and to assess what he had unearthed. It must have been a vastly satisfying moment. His letters and diaries, as well as the reports he began to put together for his coming book, exude an almost disbelieving air of triumph.

For Schliemann, Homer had always been a real man, just as the heroes he described in the *Iliad* and the *Odyssey* were real people, the sort of people he most admired, honourable, courageous, energetic, without self-pity – and clean, the ritual washing in water that was 'clear', 'light' and 'desirable', making men resemble gods.

The objects he had pulled up out of the earth at Hissarlik all went to prove the *realness* of the Greek heroes – the cauldrons and the cups and the gold jewellery. A new world had thus been 'revealed for archaeology', which included not just the gold but, as importantly, the pottery, which Schliemann was one of the first archaeologists to insist was a crucial historical tool. His finds of potsherds, he wrote soon after his return to Athens, 'are far more durable than city-walls or fortification-walls. They give us two termini for the date of the enclosing walls; they can neither be older than the oldest potsherds, nor later than the latest'. No one, until then, had thought this out so thoroughly, and the recognition of the importance of pottery, which Schliemann was to return to again and again, was to become one of his most enduring claims to scholarship.

What he had in fact done at Hissarlik, even if his techniques has been those of an amateur and his destructiveness regrettable, and even if he lacked the crucial bits of knowledge not available until he started excavating Mycenae, was to realize his long-held dream of finding Troy, of rediscovering a lost world, or rather a civilization whose traces had grown faint but for their echo in Greek myths and legends. Against the scepticism of men far better educated and connected than he was, he had actually demonstrated that the Troy of Greek tradition could perfectly plausibly be identified with the hilltop at Hissarlik. Absolute faith in Homer had paid off.

True, one distinctive detail in Homer's landscape stubbornly continued to resist identification : the two 'fair-flowing springs, where two fountains rise that feed deep-eddying Skamandros. The one floweth with warm water, and smoke goeth up therefrom around it, as it were from a blazing fire, while the other even in summer floweth forth like cold hail or snow or ice that water formeth'. But Schliemann had now become convinced, after close examination of the plain of Troy, that the Scamander had changed its bed in the course of the centuries, and that the waters described by Homer might in any case not have been very exactly depicted, but rather a melding of several different features in the Troad.

True, too, that what his excavations had shown was that the walls of Troy had enclosed an oval space of only about 200 yards from west to east, and 175 yards from north to south : a citadel, therefore, and not a city, protecting only the king's house and the homes of the nobility, while most of the people lived outside the walls, probably on a plateau to the east. 'Troy,' he confessed, 'was not large ... I had wished to be able to make it a thousand times larger', adding, somewhat disingenuously, 'but I value truth above everything'.

But none of this was, in Schliemann's eyes, important. What he had done was to uncover five separate cities – they were to become seven in the years to come – one piled on top of the other, to the depth of 50 feet, with Homer's Troy, complete with Scaean gates and Priam's palace, at the second-lowest level. Though this later was to turn out to be wrong – Priam's Troy, in so far as it can be shown to have existed, occupied another level altogether – Schliemann's exuberance broke through all boundaries of modesty. In his triumph, he could afford to be generous. 'Homer', he felt obliged to admit to Charles Newton and other colleagues, in words soon to make their way almost unchanged into his published reports, 'is an epic poet and no historian'. But epic poets naturally 'exaggerated everything with poetic licence'. Homer, he now accepted, had never seen the 'great tower of Ilium, nor the divine wall, nor Priam's palace'. For Homer had only come to Troy three hundred years after its sacking by the Achaeans, and by then its ruins had been covered by a ten-feet-deep layer of red ashes 'and another city stood upon that layer'. But this, too, was unimportant. For Schliemann, with his treasure, had proved that Troy, for all its stone implements, had been immensely rich, and, being rich, 'it was powerful, had many subjects, large dominions, and ... many auxiliary troops'. The *Iliad*, in short, was 'based upon real facts' ... and there 'really was a Troy ... and the *Iliad* – albeit in exaggerated manner – sings of this city and the true history of its tragic end'.

'I flatter myself,' Schliemann wrote to Newton on 23 July, 'that by the discovery of Troy I have a claim to the gratitude of the whole civilized world.' Either through the kindness of 'divine providence', or by his own skill at excavating Troy, Schliemann had turned into an archaeologist. He had become famous. But, once again, he was to find that he had overestimated not only the gratitude of the civilized world he so constantly invoked, but its generosity of spirit.

10

AN HOUR OF
GREAT NEED

While Schliemann was sorting through his treasure, and seeking safe places in which to conceal it, the *Levant Herald* published another article on the subject of Troy and its remains. This one had none of the courteous and measured tones of Frank Calvert's earlier contribution. On the contrary, it took a strong moral line. Schliemann, argued the anonymous correspondent in the Dardanelles, had not only cast strong doubts on himself as a 'gentleman and a man of trust', by whisking the treasures so contemptuously out of Turkey; he had compounded his dishonesty by boasting about it. 'It is bad enough that the Ottoman government should have been defrauded of its due', the article went on, 'but it is far worse that that fraud should have been practised in the name of science ... It casts a slur upon science itself, by making its name a cloak for deception, and degrading its pursuit to the level of predatory traffic.' Schliemann had not merely offended in his won right: he had done irreparable harm to archaeologists everywhere, who would now be denied permission to excavate by governments understandably suspicious of their honesty.

Other critics were no more charitable. Even those who did not impugn his honour began to question the very nature of the find itself. If Schliemann had lied over the matter of Sophia's presence at Hissarlik, had he perhaps not also lied over the gold and silver he claimed to have found? Was it possible that he had bought similar objects and passed them off as Trojan? Had he employed forgers to make replicas in order to swell the size of the find? Had the various bits of gold and jewellery perhaps come from different parts of the mound at Hissarlik and then been artfully melded into a single find by Schliemann later? For people looking for dishonesty, there was much to feed on. Schliemann's early reports of the treasure had been brief, and had left vital things out : why, his enemies demanded, had he not written more fully and with more excitement at once ? Surely he must have thought to look into the silver vase as soon as he pulled it up out of the earth : had he perhaps added the jewellery to the treasure as an afterthought ?

Some of the doubts were silly and provocative. Others were soon cleared up. Schliemann, and his supporters, were quick to remind the world that the treasure had been brought out of Turkey too rapidly to allow much time for description, that to produce forgeries of that quality and at that speed would have required planning and expertise not available to him, and that to have found and purchased items which fitted in so perfectly with the other Trojan finds suggested a coincidence of a quite astonishing kind. But not everyone was either prepared, or, indeed, keen, to be convinced. When, some time later, a British traveller called William Borlase visited the Troad, in a mood of considerable scepticism about Schliemann and his finds, he seems to have been delighted to learn that the 'faithful Nikolaos Zaphyros', Schliemann's factotum, with his 'honest and intelligent face', had quite another version of events.

Nikolaos maintained that it was he who had in fact helped Schliemann dig up the treasure and carry it away to the hut. He further reported that the find was made not on the inside edge of the city wall, as Schliemann claimed, but 'close to the outer side of the wall', that it had not all been closely packed together but 'contained in a little place built around it with stones, and having flat stones to cover it', that Schliemann's 'key' lay not nearby but at least two hundred yards away, and, most damagingly, that though there had indeed been bronze objects, he could recall very little in the way of silver or gold. Borlase, who, on landing at the Dardanelles, had been irked to find that the Turkish authorities imposed guards on all travellers ostensibly to prevent them pilfering as Schliemann had done, admitted that he had never really believed a word that Schliemann had said. 'Never for an instant' had he dreamed 'that Troy had ever existed anywhere in all the size and splendour of the poet's rich fancy any more than I had supposed that Arthur's Camelot was all that it has been described to be ...' Dismissing 'Herr Schliemann's exuberance', and his 'almost poetic imagination', he concluded that his reports had been cleverly 'calculated to convey an impression totally out of accordance with what any person of ordinary intelligence can see for himself by the most cursory inspection'.

Within Greece, Schliemann's adopted country by virtue of his marriage to Sophia, the archaeological world, taking pleasure in labelling Schliemann as a 'German smuggler of American nationality', closed ranks, the University Library in Athens proclaiming that in their eyes he was nothing but a 'thief'. A professor called Athanasios Rhousoloulos needled away at his claims with statements so provocative that the readily choleric Schliemann was reduced to spluttering fury. To Newton in London, he complained that Rhousoloulos 'rages against me in the newspapers like a furious dog'. Sounding very much like a small boy, he said that he had felt impelled to invite '*all* Athenians to come to my house to convince themselves with their own eyes of the atrocious calumnies of that foul fiend'. When another Greek academic called Comnos attacked him, Schliemann wrote an article for *The Academy* – like all archaeologists of the time, he used the columns of respectable journals to describe his finds and refute his critics – saying that Comnos was nothing but a 'crazy man fit for a lunatic asylum', and threatened to leave Greece for ever, taking all his treasures with him.

Many of these attacks could be dismissed as absurd. But it was not as easy to rebuff the views of other European scholars with careers in archaeology of their own. Professor Brentano in Frankfurt protested that the ruins of Hissarlik were in fact no earlier than the Greek classical period; Professor R.C.Jebb in Scotland, a man later to become obsessed by Schliemann's opinions, attributed them to the Romans; while in St Petersburg, Professor Stephani speculated that the treasure was Russian, brought to Hissarlik by Goths and Scythians some time in the fifth or even sixth century AD.

Schliemann's position was soon made more precarious by news from the Dardanelles that the Turkish police had arrested a number of his workmen after the wife of one of them had appeared on a Sunday evening decked out in magnificent gold earrings and pendants. Envious friends had hastened to pass on the information to the Turkish authorities, who arrested her husband and threatened to hang him if the jewels were not instantly handed over. Back in the possession of the Turks, they were despatched to the new Imperial Museum in Constantinople, and put on display. Soon after, a second workman was arrested and accused of concealing more gold; but by the time the police came to search his house, the jewellery had been melted down and refashioned in the shape of a traditional Turkish necklace.

From the Dardanelles now came further rumours of 'spoliation and destruction' at Hissarlik. Bertram Hartshorne, travelling in the Troad, complained in a letter to *The Times* that while the site was indeed being protected against looting tourists and foreigners, the local villagers were being allowed to carry off whatever they wanted and to 'do every species of mischief with impunity'. Sculptured stones and pillars were being broken up and carted away for building 'or used for doorsteps and staircases, while others are to be seen lying about in stables and cattlesheds'.

In the weeks following his return to Athens, Schliemann had been remarkably sanguine about what Turkey would, or indeed could, do about what unquestionably amounted to his wholesale theft of the treasure. He had misjudged the anger and determination of the Turks. Alerted by Effendi Amin's warning that Schliemann had been up to something very suspicious, the authorities now arrested the unfortunate man and accused him of negligence. Though Schliemann had complained repeatedly about Amin's officiousness, and mocked his efforts at supervision, he now felt sufficiently guilty to write off to the authorities, begging for Amin's release 'in the name of humanity', and pointing out that the excavations had been conducted on five fronts simultaneously and that no one man could possibly oversee all five at once. The Turks, surprisingly, took a conciliatory tone; at least at first. Through the Turkish Imperial Museum came a suggestion that Schliemann should hand over at least a number of the objects he had unearthed and failed to declare – for example, some of his 'owl-faced' vases. Schliemann, using the American Ambassador as his intermediary, high-handedly refused, but countered with a brazen proposal that he be granted a new *firman*, allowing him to dig for a further three months at Hissarlik, and hand all he uncovered during that time directly to the museum. The Turks did not bother to reply.

The Sublime Porte now decided to play a tougher game. Putting pressure on the Greek government, they angled for an order for the treasure to be confiscated. For a while, Schliemann's life was made as unpleasant as possible. Guards posted strategically around his house made it virtually impossible for him to move about; his money and assets in the bank were blocked; when he travelled, he found his hotel rooms ransacked.

A stalemate had now been reached. A return to Turkey was out of the question. The American Ambassador, clearly exasperated by the way that Schliemann's bragging had played into the hands of the Turks, warned him on no account to try to enter Turkey, lest he be arrested and tried. Perhaps nervous himself at the degree to which he was compromised, the Ambassador wrote saying that since 'you seem to attach so high a pecuniary value to the things found by you at the Troad ... I must beg to return to you the stone idol which you sent me'. It should be recalled that it was he who had told Schliemann, 'if you once get your treasures to America they will be safe from Turkish pursuit'.

Schliemann himself acted with his customary defiance and panache. Foolishly, since he cannot have been unaware that every move he made was reported back to the Turks, he wrote off to his agent in Paris, Monsieur Beaurain, asking him to find the name of a trustworthy goldsmith able to make copies of the gold and silver pieces in the treasure. Discretion, he urged, was imperative. 'Please talk about objects found in Norway and for God's sake don't mention Troy.' Beaurain was understandably reluctant to enter into what he rightly took to be a highly illegal transaction, but he did write back with the name of a respected Parisian goldsmith called Froment-Meurice. Though there is no evidence that Schliemann ever did contact the goldsmith, a rumour was soon circulating in academic circles that some, if not all, of Priam's treasure had been forged by an Athenian craftsman.

Schliemann needed friends. Help was to come from a somewhat unexpected quarter. For some time now he had been considering the idea of selling the Trojan treasure to one of Europe's major museums and at various times took soundings in France, Germany and England. At the end of July 1873, little over a month after his return to Athens, he had written to his acquaintance at the British Museum, Sir Charles Newton, informing him '*quite confidentially* of my willingness to sell to you my collection'. Money, it appears, was less on his mind than any status he might be able to acquire, for the figures he proposed fluctuated wildly. Newton replied at once. Warning Schliemann that the British government had just put up £27,000 for another collection, so that funds were for the moment low, he urged him to send the Troy pieces immediately to London to be put on display for 'it would be much more difficult to interest the public in the matter only from description'. Newton was the recipient of some of Schliemann's more dense and energetic letters. In reply, just a few days later, came an extraordinarily long and detailed letter, accompanied by photographs, minutely itemized, with many Greek terms thrown in.

Newton's support was crucial to Schliemann, who spent the autumn of 1873 and spring of 1874 fending off attacks, and showering newspapers and journals with articles and letters justifying his position. On his more robust days, he admitted that he had indeed entered the field of archaeology relatively ignorant, compared to his more learned colleagues, and accused them fairly light-heartedly of professional jealousy. When goaded and embattled, he hit back in Homeric flows of invective, accusing his detractors – in their own language, be it German, French, Russian, English or Greek – of slander.

Towards the end of 1873, a new figure unexpectedly came over to Schliemann's side. Max Müller was the Anglo-German scholar who held the Chair in Comparative Philology at Oxford, and who believed that language was the 'living and speaking evidence for the whole history of mankind'. An expert in comparative religion and mythology, he had never thought much of Homer as a historian, considering him principally an imaginative poet. In the autumn of 1873, Müller published an article in *The Pall Mall Gazette*, saying that he did not agree with Schliemann's theory about Hissarlik and Troy. Schliemann, extremely perturbed by this attack, wrote to ask Newton to send him copies of everything Müller had written, adding, in an English that for once lapsed from its usual formal accuracy, that 'I am armed up to the teeth and able to overthrow at once every one of his arguments'. His weapons for once proved persuasive, and Müller joined Schliemann's band of supporters. With Müller on his side, and now Charles Newton, who came to Athens to see the Trojan collection for himself, dined with the Schliemanns on Christmas Eve, and left warmly supporting his theories, Schliemann felt somewhat reassured. It was as well that he did, for his critics, particularly among the German archaeologists, seldom missed an opportunity to attack.

At the Christmas party held by the German Archaeological Institute in Rome in 1873, Ulrich von Wilamowitz-Moellendorff, a classical scholar, later famous for his works on Greek literature, appeared disguised as Sophia Schliemann. The party, complete with poems and charades, was an annual event among the German community.

Wilamowitz-Moellendorff, who from the first had taken a severe view of Schliemann's claims, decided to make the 'self-made man' the butt of a hilarious evening. Having a talent for parody, he dressed up as Mecklenburg peasant, with a large shawl, rang the bell at the Institute and sent in a card with the words 'Madame Schliemann, née Providence', then entered with what he later described as 'French gush' and reduced the room to laughter with a mock hexametric epic ridiculing the purported discoverer of Troy. In the first months after the publicity about the treasure, Schliemann alone had been made the target of attack; but because he proved so eager to paint Sophia as his assistant, so she too was allotted her share of ridicule.

Throughout all this, Schliemann continued with his writing. In the spring of 1874, *Trojanische Alterthümer* (*Troy and its Remains*), appeared first in German, then French. It included eight pages devoted to refuting the attacks of one critic alone, and dismissed the others with the words: 'Being engaged with my superhuman works, I have not a moment to spare and therefore I cannot waste my precious time with idle talk'. In a letter to a friend, Schliemann remarked gloomily that it was the fate of all 'discoverers to be envied, ill-treated, pursued and libelled and all this will only cease with my death'. The English version of the book was not published until the following spring. If he had hoped to silence his critics, Schliemann was disappointed. In their reviews, archaeologists and historians pointed to his 'unscholarly' approach and his over-hasty conclusions, and speculated freely about whether a man who robbed treasures, then offered to sell them around the world, could really be trusted at all. The 'atlas' that accompanied the book was declared to be poorly illustrated and badly laid out. In Germany, the country whose approval Schliemann continued to court most avidly, the professional body of classicists mocked; newspapers scoffed; and popular comics printed cartoons making fun of the Schliemanns. Even when he was able to rise above the cruder attacks, Schliemann found the scepticism of his peers unbearable. Neither now, nor at any other point in the years to come, was he able to accept that at least some of these scholarly disquisitions were simply part of the intellectual debate. True, his reviewers challenged his impetuous labelling of the walls he had uncovered at Hissarlik as the 'Scaean gates' or 'Priam's palace'. But he appeared little comforted by the fact that an ever-growing number of internationally respected figures, like Max Müller and Charles Newton, were now ready to concede that the mound of Hissarlik could finally be accepted to be Troy.

The quarrel with the Turkish authorities, and now with the Greeks, on whom the Turks had continued to put pressure, finally came to a head in the late spring of 1874, when a Greek court ordered that the entire Trojan collection be sequestered. Since it had been split up and distributed for safekeeping among Sophia's various relations around mainland Greece and the islands, and could not, therefore, be found, the order went out to sequester Schliemann's house and furniture instead. Schliemann appealed, writing hastily to beg Newton to value the Trojan pottery at £300 and the treasure at no more than £1,000. 'I require it,' he wrote, 'in an hour of *great* need and grief.' Given that Schliemann had mentioned the figure of £50,000 when offering the entire collection to the British Museum, Newton must have found the request somewhat comic.

Schliemann had first visited Mycenae in the summer of 1868, during his wanderings around the Peloponnese. For a devoted pupil of Homer, this was the capital of the Achaeans and their overlord Agamemnon; it was also 'rich in gold'. For an archaeologist, it was a magnificent site, high on a hill above the plain of the Argolid, with steep rocks falling away to one side and two ravines close to the fortification walls; but what made it so perfect was the fact that its identity had long been accepted by scholars. Unlike Troy, there was no question of having to force an unpopular theory on to sceptical historians; nor were there any strata to cut through and sort out. Some ruined walls, and the famous Lion Gate, had been exposed; the rest was waiting to be excavated.

During his years of digging at Hissarlik, Schliemann had thought constantly about both the Trojans and the Achaeans, and by the time Priam's treasure was unearthed, he had come to the conclusion that the ties between Asia Minor and the Greek mainland and its islands were a great deal closer than had previously been thought. In 1873, believing that his work at Troy was at last finished, he approached the Greek government for permission to excavate at Mycenae. As he pointed out to them, his home was now in Athens, his wife was Greek, and he was perfectly prepared to turn over all he found to a Greek museum – after his death, of course. The government was friendly, apologetic, but adamant: they reminded him that under Greek law all antiquities that lay either above or below the soil were the inalienable property of the nation. Schliemann's reaction was much the same as it had been when the Turkish *firman* was so long denied him. Telling a friend crossly that he and Sophia were 'disgusted' with life in Athens, and that they intended to return to Paris, he made plans to visit Mycenae secretly. More than most people when dealing with intransigent governments, Schliemann cannot be said to have learned from his mistakes.

Late in February 1874, accompanied by Sophia, his old friend Emile Burnouf, and Burnouf's daughter, who was to draw any finds that came to light, he set out for the Peloponnese. When the party reached Mycenae, they pretended that they had the government's permission to carry out a survey. Twenty workmen were hastily recruited, and within a few days thirty-four small trenches had been dug within the existing citadel walls. What appeared was not very exciting: some terracotta figurines, much broken pottery and a plain, undecorated, stela. Schliemann kept his spirits up by deciding that the figurines represented the goddess Hera, Homer's Hera, the patron goddess of Mycenae and the Argolid, with her main shrine a few miles away round the mountain.

For five days, the party dug, collected, recorded and drew, undisturbed. Then the local Prefect received word from Athens that no permission had been granted for Schliemann to dig, and that excavating was to stop immediately. A basket containing some of the finds was confiscated, but when, on closer inspection, it was seen to contain nothing of any distinction, it was returned. Though the Schliemanns were now forced to set off back to Athens, the Greek government was surprisingly forgiving. At the end of March came the news that they were prepared to issue a permit for Schliemann to excavate Mycenae, but on their own, strict, terms. Before Schliemann had time to react, however, it was cancelled, on the grounds that the suit brought by the Turkish government was still pending, but the understanding was that it might well be awarded once the court case was resolved.

For the rest of 1874, and the early months of 1875, Schliemann was exceptionally restless. When in Athens, he kept up his anxious, quarrelsome, correspondence with the archaeological world, and oversaw, by telegram, his business interests around the world. Much as he had during the months of waiting for his *firman* for Hissarlik, he made short trips around mainland Greece and the islands, inspecting other possible sites, should Mycenae not be made available to him. His frustration grew when he learned that Olympia had been granted to the Prussian government and to his enemy Ernst Curtius to dig. Evidently eager to endear himself to the Greek authorities, he readily agreed to pay for the knocking down of an ugly Frankish Venetian tower, 80 feet high and made of large slabs of marble and stone, that had been erected on the Acropolis by the Venetians during their occupation of Athens. Its removal cost him £465. As the tower came down, thousands of owls were ousted from their holes in the walls.

In the spring of 1875, what Schliemann called his 'bloody battle' with the Turkish authorities was at last resolved. He was ordered to pay the Turkish government, in the form of the Imperial Museum in Constantinople, 50,000 francs – £2,000 – against an undertaking that they would make no further claim on Priam's treasure. Money, at this stage in Schliemann's life, was not his foremost concern, his business transactions continuing to bring him in a substantial income. In an expansive gesture, as calculating as it was lordly, he sent five times the sum,

250,000 francs, together with a number of his less valuable Trojan finds.

The gold, silver and bronze, as well as countless weapons, vases, pots and figurines, now belonged to him. He brought them back to Athens from their secret hiding-places with Sophia's relations, and stored them in the vaults of the Greek National Bank. The diadems, earrings and rings in particular intrigued him, for they seemed to have no resemblance of any kind to 'Hellenic, Roman, Egyptian, or Assyrian' pieces, and he was eager to understand just how these early Trojans had manufactured such jewellery. He approached Carlo Giuliano, an increasingly successful jeweller in London, who made granulated gold jewellery in the manner of the Etruscans, Greeks and Romans, and had sparked off a fashion among English society ladies for what became known as 'archaeological jewellery'. Sophia was not the first society lady to wear real or copied classical jewellery for a portrait. Giuliano reported to Schliemann that, in order to make such thin wire, the Trojans must have used only ingots of very pure gold, making them so fine by pulling it through the holes of a drawplate. To carve such minute stars and charms, he said, the Trojans must have put the gold on to hot charcoal and melted it with a blowpipe, then perforated it with a round punch. But 'how the primitive goldsmith could do all this fine work ... without the aid of a lens', Giuliano confessed, was an enigma.

The treasure's immense usefulness as a weapon with which to bargain for concessions had never been lost on Schliemann. One possibility that occurred to him was that he might now turn it all over to the Greek nation – once again, only after his death – in return for being allowed to excavate at Mycenae; and possibly at Delphi and Delos too. Another was that it might go to the British Museum in London; but the British government had balked at the price, Newton declaring that the £50,000 for which Schliemann asked was 'out of all proportion' to its value. In the months and years to come, Schliemann was to offer the collection to France, Italy and Russia, at different times and for different prices, but never, possibly because he had such a dim view of its culture, to America.

In Athens, deliberating over his next move, and waiting to hear about Mycenae, Schliemann let it be known that were he to be given permission to excavate a major Italian site, perhaps in Sicily, then he might be willing to move his fortune to Italy, building a house for himself in Naples or Palermo, setting up and endowing a museum, and donating to it his entire Troy collection. From week to week, he vacillated. His mood, however, was buoyant. The treasure was now his; the worst of the academic attacks on him seemed, for the moment, to be over; his book *Troy and its Remains* was about to be published both in England and in America; and he and Sophia were on excellent terms, exchanging affectionate letters whenever Schliemann was away from Athens.

In the early summer of 1875, he set off for a tour of the European capitals, to seek the personal approval of the academic world he continued to crave.

William Ewart Gladstone, Prime Minister of England for the first time between 1868 and 1874, was a profound believer in the historical truth of Homer's epic poems. Like Schliemann, he passionately wished to prove that Homer was 'one man describing a real world', and that he had 'lived near to the time of the events he described' – perhaps as little as fifty years after them. A brilliant classicist at Oxford, Gladstone had been fortunate in graduating at a moment when the world appeared ready for a reappraisal of Homer's poems and their history, and when the new disciplines of comparative philology, geology and archaeology were all throwing up fresh speculations as to the origins of man and the nature of early civilizations. Though politics kept him immensely busy, he 'let no day pass without having Homer in his hand'. By the middle of the 1870s Gladstone had made his own Homeric pilgrimage when Commissioner for the Ionian islands, and had already published four works on Homer, all of them intended to extend the 'fruitful study of the immortal poems', and to establish just where the poet actually fitted into history. He was now looking for a further weapon with which to refute the extreme scepticism of historians like George Grote and to provide some of the evidence called for by Grote in his influential and widely read *History of Greece*, published in 1846. What was needed, Gladstone declared in his enormous three-volume study, *Homer and the Homeric Age*, was to 'recover as substantial personages, and to bring within the grasp of flesh and blood some of those pictures, and even of those persons, whom Mr Grote has dismissed to the land of Shadow and of Dream'. Gladstone was to become Schliemann's most ardent and valuable admirer.

Schliemann's name had first been mentioned to Gladstone in the autumn of 1873, during an evening in London with Charles Newton. As the respected Keeper of the prestigious Department of Greek and Roman Antiquities at the British Museum, Newton was a man Gladstone trusted; together they discussed Schliemann's finds, and Newton was able to say that Gladstone had shown great interest in Schliemann's report that his analysis of the bronze objects in Priam's treasure had yielded only pure copper, and no tin. By the end of the year, Schliemann and Gladstone were writing directly to each other – a correspondence that was to last until 1884, when Schliemann blamed Gladstone for Britain's occupation of Egypt – and Gladstone had congratulated Schliemann on the remarkable story of his youth, saying that it had left him considerably impressed by the archaeologist's energy. On receiving a copy of *Trojanische Alterthümer* early in 1874, the Prime Minister praised Schliemann for establishing facts of 'the highest importance to primitive man'. It was to Gladstone that Schliemann wrote that he hoped to 'wrench Olympia from the Prussians' and to find enough work there to last him for the rest of his life.

Better was to follow. The Society of Antiquaries in London was a scholarly club of men interested in the whole field of archaeology now being opened up throughout Europe and the Near and Middle east. At a meeting held on 30 April 1874, Newton, not long back from his visit to the Schliemanns in Athens, gave a talk on the Trojan finds, describing them as definitely 'non-Hellenic and pre-Hellenic'. This, somewhat cautious, endorsement had been applauded by Professor Max Müller, and capped by the society's chairman, Lord Stanhope, who pronounced himself convinced that the recovered city was Troy. Even before the meeting, Müller had written to Schliemann telling him how much interest and curiosity the question of the treasure had awakened in English educated circles. Afterwards, Schliemann's fame was greatly increased by almost an entire column in *The Times* dedicated to the gathering and the discussion about Troy.

Gladstone had not been able to attend; but he had not abandoned his Homeric interests. In the June issue of *The Contemporary Review* appeared a long article on Homer's place in history, in which he described Schliemann's excavations as very important, and his work as revealing to the world a 'real objective Troy . . .' and showing how the 'excavations and the poems thus far greatly fortify one another'. For a man until now more mocked than praised, Schliemann must have found Gladstone's words very sweet, made all the sweeter by Gladstone's eminence and his serious influence on Homeric scholarship, even if the statesman had not altogether escaped criticism and ridicule himself for his blind faith in the epic poet. For his part, not surprisingly, Schliemann approved warmly of Gladstone's work. A copy of his book *The Place of Homer in History*, found with Schliemann's papers, has been closely annotated.

There are several contradictory remarks; but a great many 'excellents'.

All this augured well for Schliemann's planned visit to London in the summer of 1875. Before setting off for Paris and then England, he had received a letter from Newton, telling him that Spencer Walpole, president of the Literary Society, wished to invite him to one of its regular dinners, that Lord Stanhope of the Society of Antiquaries wanted to fix an evening, as did the British Museum's Keeper of Coins, the orientalist, Reginald Stuart Poole. Several of the popular weekly and monthly magazines, the *Illustrated London News*, and *The Academy* among them, had requested that he call at their offices, though among Schliemann's papers there is a revealing note from Charles Appleton, editor and founder of *The Academy*, dated January 1875, refusing a draft of £25 'which you no doubt meant kindly: but which is a violation of all the rules of journalism'. Schliemann had evidently offered to pay to have an article published.

Unlike the Germans, who had shunted the classics off to a specialized corridor in their general education, the English continued to regard them as the foundation of all true learning. Gladstone was not the only eminent politician of the day to be well versed in Greek and Latin: many other active figures in public life read, memorized and enjoyed their Plato and their Lucretius, and no other ancient Greek author was as closely studied as Homer, both as a master of literature and as a guide to early Greek culture. 'There is always something new to be learned about Homer', Sir John Myers was to write. 'Like the leaves on the trees, critic falls after critic, theory after theory, and school after school.' Unlike the Germans, the English Victorians also admired amateurs. If Schliemann's lack of formal scholarship irritated the German academic fraternity, his enthusiasm and energy, as well as his remarkable treasures, were found endearing and impressive by the educated British public.

This was to be Schliemann's third visit to England, and the most satisfying. In the 1870s, England, still the leading power in Europe, was in the middle of an extraordinary revolution in religious outlook, education, health, work, leisure, and technical and scientific discoveries. Though still divided and subdivided into classes, with land the socially recognized form of wealth, and politics, the services and the Church the most acceptable professions, 'society' had broadened out since his last visit to take into account the new fortunes being made in shipping and manufacture, soon to be fields for investment for both professional people and the aristocracy. Despite Queen Victoria's strait-laced example to the country, a certain ease in behaviour and morals, a definite light-heartedness, was being felt: the crinoline had gone and the bustle was coming; ladies played golf and did archery (in India they played badminton); and though there was still no smoking in mixed company, and a woman's property was her husband's, the electric light, the tele-phone and the 'horseless carriage' were all on their way in – even if an Act of 1865, forbidding vehicles with engines to travel at more than four miles an hour (and even then they had to be preceded by a man carrying a red flag to warn drivers of horses), had not been repealed. Prince Albert was dead, the Indian Mutiny was long since over, Lister's antiseptics were reducing gangrene, Stanley had just found Livingstone and Cam-bridge had opened its first women's college.

The Great Exhibition of 1851 had triggered two decades of exhi-bitions – and an intense curiosity about the strange, the new, and the very old. As the official catalogue had put it, 'The results of the Exhibition are pregnant with incalculable benefits to all classes of humanity.' A Captain Lane-Fox, later to take the name Pitt-Rivers, was at work col-lecting all that was 'ordinary and typical' – tools, furniture and utensils – from all over the world, in order to trace 'the succession of ideas by which the minds of men ... have progressed from the simple to the complex.'

Into this changing world, Schliemann fitted perfectly. True, he was a foreigner, but Germans were regarded as more serious than the French and the Italians, and his very foreignness somehow obscured – among people resolutely insular – his modest beginnings. For a country search-ing for proof of man's antiquity, intrigued by novelty, flirting with agnosticism, opening its doors to evolutionary theory and anthropology, and at the forefront of inventions and new technology, he had much to offer.

From the moment of his arrival in England, on 10 June 1875, Sch-liemann was courted and fêted. Dinner invitations flowed in; newspapers reported his movements; the presidents of London's many literary and historical societies urged him to attend their meetings. Gladstone, with whom Schliemann was in touch on the second day of his visit, was very friendly; in return, Schliemann pronounced *The Place of Homer in History* the 'masterpiece of a great scholar'. On 24 June came the meeting of the Society of Antiquaries at Burlington House, Piccadilly. Introducing Schliemann, Lord Stanhope spoke of a man who had 'con-ferred a service which cannot be overestimated or forgotten in the history of primaeval inquiry itself'. Schliemann's talk, 'The Discovery of Homeric Troy', lasted an hour and a quarter; after which Gladstone spoke at great length, declaring that 'light was now beginning to pierce the thick mist which had hitherto obscured such remote subjects of antiquarian research'. Dr Schliemann, he said, was a spectacle, rare to British eyes, of the 'most pure, single-minded and ardent devotion to the cause of literature and knowledge ... the most splendid example of disinterested sacrifice'. Next day, *The Times* reported that both men had been loudly applauded.

After this, came a reception at Lord Lansdowne's house, to which Schliemann was taken by Gladstone. They must have made a strange pair, Gladstone tall and imposing, of Scottish ancestry, and Schliemann, the German former grocer's apprentice and merchant, small, wiry and anxious. To Sophia, who was staying in Brighton with Andromache, Schliemann wrote: 'Never in my life have I seen such richness in rooms and toilettes ... I made many acquaintances, as Gladstone introduced me to everybody ... The meat must have cost at least 20,000 francs: imagine, there were even quantities of magnificent grapes.' His delight is touching. The next morning, he called on Gladstone, who noted in his diary: 'Fourteen to breakfast: ten of us a Schliemann party: we have a long Homeric discussion.' One evening, Schliemann dined with the Lord Mayor at the Mansion House; on another, he was invited to stay by John Lubbock, author of the classic *Prehistoric Times*. 'I was received,' he later wrote, 'as if I had discovered a new part of the globe for England.'

To add to his pleasures, his book *Troy and its Remains* had now been published both in England and in America. The London press treated it kindly, devoting considerable space to a full discussion on Homer and the existing state of classical studies. Following the book's appearance, a debate began on both sides of the Atlantic, with the professor of classics and history at the University of Wisconsin, W.F.Allen, not only supporting Schliemann's contention that Hissarlik was Troy, but defending his statement that the goblets and vases decorated with an owl's face were indeed of 'owl-eyed Athena'.

Social, literary and academic London had taken to Schliemann; in the years to come his visits to England were to provide him with his moments of greatest triumph. Though he continued to have stern English critics, he was also acquiring an impressive body of English supporters, some of whom, in time, were to become real friends. In a letter to the French traveller and geographer, Charles Gauthiot, written from Brighton on 8 July, Schliemann, with some bitterness, contrasted his reception in Paris, where he had paused on his way to London, with the warmth with which he had been received in England. How much of the French chilliness was to do with the recent war with Germany is not clear. Even though they were perfectly well aware that he had 'discovered a whole new world for archaeology', Schliemann reported that the French had none the less greeted him as a 'German traitor', and that none of his former friends had returned his calls. In London, on the other hand, and here Schliemann moved into his more boastful vein, 'I am the subject of continual ovations . . . all over London I am received with indescribable enthusiasm, learned societies are packed out when it becomes known that I am there . . . all the members of the Court wish to see me, all the foreign princes and princesses send me invitations . . .

Even if doubts remained in most people's minds, both about the date of Priam's Troy, and the crucial question of whether it had really been besieged and burnt by the Greeks, Schliemann's years in the cold seemed to be coming to an end.

'At the pressing invitation of the charming and wise Queen of the Netherlands, we are going first to Holland, then to Sweden, Denmark, Germany and Italy . . .' Schliemann wrote to a friend before leaving England. During the short European tour that followed, seldom pausing in any one place for more than a couple of days, he seemed at times more concerned with his worldly success than with archaeological matters, though he rarely failed to visit the main museum of the cities where he stopped, particularly when it contained early historical finds. He had earned his social success. It must have done much to boost his frail self-confidence.

From The Hague came a first letter to Sophia: 'My darling wife, my very beloved Sophia. At this moment, 10 o'clock in the evening, I have just come back from the company of the most gracious, the most charming of Queens, who has invited me to supper at the Palace . . . To my joy, she finds extreme charm in my conversation. And three times she forced me to stay when I wanted to leave.' In the course of the evening he had promised the Queen some 'statuettes' and planned to ask Sophia's brother, Spiridon, to look for some 'nice ones at very low prices.' Even to Sophia, he could not prevent himself from adding, 'I can't pay much because I have to give them away.' Queen Sophie, who was genuinely interested in the ancient world, was to receive from him a number of Tanagra figures, smuggled out of Greece, a crime she seems to have condoned. To a friend from The Hague, Schliemann wrote: 'Her

Majesty is always inviting me for breakfast, lunch and dinner. She has read much, and is gifted with a quite extraordinary memory ...'

From Copenhagen, where he admired the museum of prehistoric antiquities and complained that Danish women were exceptionally ugly, he moved on to Stockholm, where he received a letter in English from Sophia, causing him to write back quickly to praise her progress in the language, and to declare himself delighted with the news that one of his archaeological foes, Comnos, had been 'destituted'. In Roebel, where he went next to visit his sister Dorothea, he was so incensed by a fresh attack on him by Frank Calvert in the *Manchester Guardian* that he declared himself unable to eat or drink until he had composed a reply. Everywhere he went, restless or admiring, he gave talks on Troy.

It was in Germany during this trip that Schliemann met a man who was to play a determining part in the next stage in his archaeological career. While in London, Gladstone had advised him to contact Professor Rudolf Virchow, an authority on face urns, and to consult him about the strange pots and vases found at Hissarlik. Though Schliemann and Virchow, to the end of their lives, were never to agree on the 'owl-face', they became friends.

Rudolf Virchow was an earnest-looking man, with small round glasses and a beard. Like Schliemann, he seems seldom to have smiled. As a professor of pathology at the Bavarian University of Würzberg, he had pioneered cellular pathology, the theory that the basic units of life are self-reproducing cells. He was a man of many interests and a great deal of energy, and by the mid-1870s was already a member of the Prussian Parliament, and soon to become one of the leaders of opposition to Bismarck and something of a symbol of a democratic Germany. He was also an anthropologist, founder of the German Anthropological Society, and had carried out a study of German schoolchildren. Like Schliemann, he was possessed of immense ambition; in Virchow's case, it was to acquire 'an all round knowledge of nature, from the Deity down to the stone'.

In superficial ways, in fact, the two men, products of the nineteenth-century search for knowledge, were extraordinarily similar. Both now in their mid-fifties, they came from modest families in rural north-east Germany. They shared a taste for extremely hard work, an excellent command of foreign languages, and an obsession with Homer. Just as important, they agreed that classical archaeology should be viewed not as art, but as history. By the time they met, Virchow had already excavated a number of sites in eastern Germany, unearthing pottery not altogether unlike the vases at Hissarlik, and he was now turning towards the Near East, in the hopes of testing out his belief that the European civilizations had their distant roots in the East.

In character, however, Schliemann and Virchow were very different. Where Schliemann was impetuous, choleric and prickly, Virchow was dry and detached, with a certain coldness of manner. 'Icy enthusiasm' was something he valued. His sobriety and reflectiveness were to prove extremely useful in the years to come. Schliemann, at fifty-three, had made a most important friend.

By September, Schliemann had reached Rome, where he spent two weeks exploring possible sites around the volcanic lakes of Albano and Nemi, before travelling on down towards Sicily. Though increasingly determined to return to Hissarlik, and ever more convinced of the rightness of excavating at Mycenae, he roamed around the island, pausing at Segesta, Taormina and Syracuse, sometimes for little more than a few hours, looking for traces of prehistoric civilizations, hoping to find archaic settlements similar to Troy. Palermo, he told Sophia in a letter written on 13 October, was 'la perla di tutta la Sicilia'.

Just two miles off the western shore of Sicily, in a lagoon opposite the town of Marsala, lies the island of San Pantaleo; on it stands the city of ancient Motya, famous as a Carthaginian stronghold, besieged in 397 BC by Dionysius the Elder, tyrant of Syracuse, who sent 80,000 men and an entire fleet of ships to take it. The catapult, so it is said, was used for the first time against the walls of Motya. Despite being abandoned to its fate by Carthage, Motya held out for many months; when it finally capitulated, all its inhabitants were slaughtered. Though classical scholars of the sixteenth and seventeenth centuries had been interested in ancient Motya, few early travellers or guidebooks ever referred to it. To Schliemann, however, Motya had promise. He arrived there on 19 October and immediately opened a new excavation diary. It is written in English, and fills five pages.

Hiring eighteen workmen, he spent five days carrying out trial excavations, beginning on the south-eastern side of the island, where he thought some of the city walls had been washed away. Though he quickly uncovered the remains of a large house, some pillars, and a considerable amount of pottery, both painted and unpainted, fine and crude, he was disappointed. By 22 October he was noting morosely in his diary that there was no archaic pottery, and no potsherds, earlier than the fifth century BC. 'There being nothing to find and no historical riddle to solve,' Schliemann announced, 'I shall not continue the excavations.'

(He was, it later turned out, wrong: Motya has yielded exciting archae-ological finds.) In any case, he was not enjoying himself. His workmen spoke a dialect he could not follow, and they were the worst he had ever employed; he blamed some of this on the inbreeding of the remaining nineteen families who occupied the island. There is also some suggestion that his relations with the archaeological authorities were strained.

The brief flirtation with Motya was to occupy only a few lines of Schliemann's published work. Fleeing the 'great dirt and uncleanliness' of the island, he set off for home, to learn whether or not the great prize of Mycenae was to be his.

11

NOTHING BUT
THE GLORY

The *Iliad* says nothing about the famous wooden horse. Set in the last year of the siege, it ends before the death of Achilles and the fall of Troy, with the funeral rites of Hector, 'tamer of horses'. It is from the *Odyssey* that we follow the 'much enduring' Odysseus on his ten-year journey home to Ithaca, and that we learn that Menelaus did return to his palace of Sparta with the kidnapped Helen.

Agamemnon, 'king of kings', did not fare so well. Returning to Mycenae and his wife Clytemnestra, he discovered that his place had been taken by her lover Aegisthus. 'Agamemnon set foot on the soil of his father with a happy heart', Homer has Menelaus recount in the *Odyssey*, 'and as he touched it, kissed his native earth ... Aegisthus set his brains to work and laid a clever trap. He selected twenty of his best soldiers from the town, left them in ambush and, after ordering a banquet to be prepared in another part of the building, set out in a horse-chariot to bring home the king, with his heart full of ugly thoughts. Agamemnon, never guessing that he was going to his doom, came up with him from the coast, and Aegisthus feasted and killed him as a man might fell an ox in its manger. Not a single one of the king's following was left, nor of Aegisthus's company either. They were killed in the palace to a man.'

But where at Mycenae did the assassins bury the bodies ? Aeschylus, Sophocles and Euripides all carried on the tale of the ill-fated house of Atreus, but it was the second-century AD Greek traveller and geographer, Pausanias, who described the aftermath most clearly. Pausanias was widely regarded as a faithful reporter of sites, for 'without him, the ruin of Greece would for the most part be a labyrinth without a clue, a riddle without an answer'. In his *Description of Greece*, he reported that, according to local tradition, Agamemnon and his companions, as well as his father Atreus, were buried within the walls of Mycenae, while Clytemnestra and her lover were buried outside. 'There is the grave of Atreus,' he wrote, 'and graves of those who came back from Troy with Agamemnon . . . and one grave holds Teledamus and Pelops – for they say that Cassandra bore these children to Agamemnon, and that Aegisthus slaughtered them when still babies . . . Clytemnestra and Aegisthus were buried a bit outside the wall; they were not considered fit to be inside, where Agamemnon himself and those slaughtered with him lay.'

Travellers and scholars who came later, Pausanias in hand, interpreted his words literally as meaning on one or other side of the vast city walls, but did little to verify them. Schliemann disagreed. Mycenae, as he had noted on his earlier surveys of the site, had two distinct and separate sets of walls: one went all the way round the acropolis, the other encircled a far wider area outside the battlements. Was it not more likely, he asked, that the royal sepulchres of Agamemnon and his comrades lay within the acropolis walls, and those of their murderers without?

Homer had led Schliemann to Priam's palace; why should he not do the same with Agamemnon's tomb, this time with Pausanias's help? The discovery of Troy had proved the *Iliad* to be a work of history; was the *Odyssey* not likely to be one, too?

In the spring of 1876, some months after his return from Motya, the suit between Schliemann and the Turkish government having finally been resolved, the Greeks decided to grant Schliemann his permit for Mycenae – very possibly helped by a few words from Gladstone, for they were eager to restore good relations with England after the Dilessi kidnappings and murders. Not everyone wished him well with his new site. 'Schliemann', remarked an anonymous and mocking critic in *The Times*, on learning that the man who had discovered Troy was now to excavate Mycenae, 'continues to deny the world of intellectuals who have devoted their *entire* lives to the world of the past. But, let him proceed and prove himself to be the butt of our amusement. Graves will never be found within the citadel walls unless the destroyer of Troy seeds graves during the night.'

Doing their best to ignore these words, the Schliemanns set out for Mycenae and the plain of Argos, taking with them a vast amount of equipment and a very toughly worded permit. The number of workmen Schliemann could use was limited, and only one area of the site was to be excavated at a time; all finds were to be turned directly over to the

Greek government. In return, Schliemann was to have first rights of publication. The Greek Archaeological Society in Athens, when spelling out these terms, had taken the sensible precaution of sending one of its firmer and more experienced officials to accompany the party. Panagiotes Stamatakes, a gifted archaeologist in his own right, and by all accounts an impressive and intelligent man, was to have a miserable autumn. Schliemann had no time for 'trouble-making government clerks'.

Guidebooks were more poetic in the nineteenth century than they are today. The men who wrote them preferred to overlook the local inhabitants and the poverty and dwell instead on Arcadian vistas and mellow light. 'In the interior,' said John Murray's *Handbook for Travellers in Greece*, published in 1854, 'the horizon is rarely without eagles, vultures, or other large birds of prey, while rollers spread their brilliant wings to the sun by the side of the traveller's path; gay hoopoes strut along before his horse, opening and shutting their fan-like crests; and now and then a graceful snow-white egret stalks slowly by in searchful meditation'. To those who wished to visit Greece in order to shoot, Murray's guide recommended the winter months, when there was an abundance of 'woodcocks and wildfowl of all kinds, from pelicans to jacksnipes'. But the guidebooks were not all poetry; practical hints were included, some of them of a sturdy, Victorian kind. All travellers to Greece, wherever they went, were encouraged to take with them a 'large and stout cotton umbrella', as well as a green veil against the sun, and they were urged to wear flannel next to their skin at all times. Above all, they were 'during meal-time to keep the mind disengaged from business and seldom to devote the time of sleep to study or to society'. Danger was to be looked ever 'in the face', while 'in sickness' the tourist was to be 'determined (Deo Juvante) to resist its pressure, and to recover from it'.

Owing to the rivalry between the great European powers over what remained of the Ottoman Empire, Greece had been swarming with diplomats and military missions since the beginning of the nineteenth century, as well as with foreign travellers and artists who, having for many years seen the Italian grand tour as indispensable to the educated mind, had turned to the Greek ancient world for inspiration. Their ardour had only been increased by the Greek uprising, and there was a tendency now to see the Philhellenic movement as a romantic crusade. The artists and scholars sketched and drew, mostly in watercolour, pictures that were intended to convey the 'feel' of the past, to evoke a lost paradise in a land of classical perfection. Where sites lacked the ideal romantic setting, the artists furnished suitably hazy vistas and well-placed trees themselves. Hugh William Williams, whose watercolours were appropriately soft and elegiac, was praised by Hazlitt for giving 'at once an impressive and satisfactory idea of the country of which we have heard so much ... Some splenetic travellers have pretended that Attica was dry, flat and barren. But it is not so in Mr Williams's authentic draughts ...'

The early travellers seldom confined themselves to sketching. They also removed everything that could be moved, bits of pillar and painted pottery, mosaics and statues, and took them home, to be given to museums in London, Paris or Berlin, or to furnish their own sitting rooms and start their own collections. Already by the 1820s, fifty years before Schliemann began to dig in Greece, most of the classical sites had been visited and picked over by acquisitive enthusiasts. His covetousness and underhand tactics when confronting a new excavation – as well as the Greek government's tough attitude towards him – have to be seen against a background of these early collections, such as Lord Elgin's spectacular removal of most of the Parthenon frieze and sculptures to the British Museum, and his pronouncement, on being made Ambassador to the Ottoman Porte in 1798, that he intended to make his Embassy 'beneficial to the progress of the Fine Arts in Britain'. Among the requirements of membership of the Xenion, a club of young men in London in the mid-nineteenth century, was not only 'enthusiasm for Greece, Ancient Literature and Fine Arts' but an understanding that anything of value that they came across would be spirited back home. As Williams observed on his travels : 'Whatever relics could be picked up, readily found purchasers among the strangers and merchants who visit this interesting country ; consequently they are spread over a great part of Europe, and there is hardly a collection of any note, which cannot boast of some specimen of Greek art.' Schliemann was just one in a long line of looters.

What these early travellers were referring to, of course, were the remains of the great Classical Greek period, the fifth century BC, with its temples and sanctuaries at Delphi, Epidaurus and Olympia. But by the middle of the nineteenth century attention was moving backwards, to the earlier 'dark ages', and to a desire to demythologize the past. 'We do not know the Greeks,' Nietzsche was to write, 'as long as this hidden and subterranean access to them remains obstructed.' Interest in topography was spreading. Schliemann was arriving at precisely the right moment.

Of all parts of Greece, the Peloponnese, with its three toes pushing down towards Africa, was among the most admired, and, by the time Schliemann and Sophia arrived in the summer of 1876, one of the best charted. A group of French scientists had not long finished a detailed study of the flora, architecture and archaeology of the area, producing an immense and richly illustrated three-volume survey. 'There is probably no part of the world,' said the popular Murray guide, 'which will more fully repay a tour of a month or six weeks ... The scenery ... is of the rarest grandeur and beauty, and stamps itself on the memory with distinctness. The cloud-capped Acropolis of Corinth, the primaeval remains of Tiryns and Mykenae ... all these are among the choice places of the earth which, once seen, live in perpetual freshness in the imagination.' And of all of them, Mycenae was judged by many to be not just the finest, 'in some respects unequalled in interest by any object in Greece', but one of the great archaeological wonders of the world.

The site itself was magnificent, lying, as Homer had put it, on a plain 'in the depth of the horse-feeding Argos', between the three peaks of Mount Euboea. Rising above the plain to form a series of terraces a thousand feet long and five hundred feet wide, ringed by the ruins of bastion walls and surrounded by high, dark, bleak mountains, and ravines which funnel the winds, the citadel is just visible from the flat fields stretching south to the Bay of Nauplion. Once a prosperous, if cursed city, founded according to Pausanias by Perseus, Mycenae had lived through a long golden age of immense wealth and artistic supremacy before crumbling into ruins.

The Schliemanns reached Mycenae at the beginning of August 1876. It was high summer, and the plain – Homer's 'very thirsty Argos' – was hot, dusty and windy, the landscape bleached and the fields pale yellow with a stubble of corn. Oleanders were growing in the dry river-beds. Argos was famous for its sheep, and its fierce sheepdogs. Approaching on their horses, Schliemann and Sophia would have ridden up the winding path to the citadel. Looking up, they would have seen the great gate, once closed by a massive wooden door, under a stone lintel with the famous relief of the two lionesses – or, some say, two griffins – standing face to face, now partly covered with rubble and vegetation. Behind the gateway lay sixteen-foot-deep walls, a circular terrace, and the jumbled ruins of once imposing buildings, all covered with lichen; on the slopes beyond the walls, leading down to the plain, were the remains of a lower city.

There was no hotel, and the Schliemanns rented a two-room house in the village of Charvati, a little less than a mile from Mycenae. Paying very little attention to anything the permit had stipulated, they began to hire workmen, formed them into three teams and started excavating at three places at once, both inside and outside the Cyclopean walls – so called, according to Greek tradition, because their vast size suggested that they had been made by giants. Before the digging could begin, the men had first to clear away the debris and vegetation from around the Lion Gate, though the Greek Archaeological Society had done some clearing in the 1840s, shortly after the society was founded. Real excavations began on 7 August. Sophia was put in charge of supervising an immense 'treasury' that stood close to the entrance. There were several of these 'treasuries', which looked like vast ovens, partly covered in earth, their entrances just visible through the undergrowth, some with their domes caved in.

The first few days were hot and unpleasant. Schliemann, who had told Müller that what he feared most from excavations now was the sun, wrote at one point to say 'the life is terrible here; there is *no shade*, all is dirty and the privations of all kinds are literally overwhelming'. Though sixty-three men had been employed, and worked from six in the morning until six at night, the early finds produced nothing exceptional, the sun remained overpowering and the winds blew dust continuously into their eyes. For all this, Schliemann appeared to be in remarkably good spirits. Despite the hardships, he noted in his new excavation diary. 'I cannot imagine anything sweeter than to excavate Mycenae, because every potsherd is a new page of history.' Soon the men began to bring up clay figurines and animals, knives, buttons, hatchets, needles and arrowheads – all pleasing, but nothing, yet, to suggest a royal tomb. Sophia, who had been working with thirty labourers and two horse-carts, uncovered in her smaller 'treasury' some archaic pottery, a number of necklaces made of glass beads and several vases decorated with geometric patterns. Schliemann, ever anxious to show her off as a skilful archaeologist in her own right, made much of her neat work, and her willingness to crouch for hours in the mud, picking delicately through the earth with a penknife, taking immense care not to chip any of the finds.

Schliemann's mood soon soured as he realized that Stamatakes was planning to take his orders seriously. Bickering and blustering began. When Schliemann ordered his men to open several trenches at once, or moved at too fast and too destructive a pace, Stamatakes countermanded his instructions and the men stopped work. Schliemann, furious at the way that an excavation for which he was paying was being ruled over by a 'government spy', sent off furious letters to Athens. So did Stamatakes, who informed his superiors that Schliemann was ruthlessly destroying anything Roman or late Greek, that he was now excavating in seven places at once, and that unless he was sent some assistance he wished to be recalled. His task was not an enviable one. Schliemann worked from dawn until two o'clock in the morning, dashed around from place to place, paid no attention to anyone, changed the programme at will and also the method of paying the men. 'Utter confusion' reigned, lamented the Greek overseer. Stamatakes was an interesting man. Though without formal university qualifications, he had been appointed assistant to the Ephor General of Antiquities in 1866, at the age of twenty-six, and been responsible for drawing up an inventory of all antiquities in private hands. Before his early death from malaria in 1884, he was himself to be made Ephor General – the country's most senior archaeological post.

For the moment, however, he was battling to supervise the men – there were 125 employed by the middle of September – catalogue the finds and write frequent reports for the Society in Athens, while on increasingly ill terms with both Schliemanns. Sophia, who took a lofty line about her husband's scholarship, had turned out to have a gift for mimicry, and entertained visitors with imitations of Stamatakes's rages. The Greek, for his part, referred to Sophia as the 'fanatical Mrs Schliemann'. As the sun beat down, the tall, furious Greek and the small, wiry German archaeologist, under his immense sunhat, shouted at each other across the trenches. Telegrams, letters, emissaries travelled back and forth to Athens with complaints. When Stamatakes ordered the men to stop digging in one section, Schliemann, he reported in his despatches to Athens, 'began to insult me coarsely. Unable to control my temper, I replied with similar insults. Later his wife came up and began to abuse me in front of the workers, saying that I was illiterate and fit only to conduct animals and not archaeological excavations.'

All this would have been disastrous had it not been that Mycenae was proving an immensely rich site. As the hot summer turned into the softer autumn, and the days grew shorter, so the men reached deeper levels and came up with ever finer objects, as well as exposing part of what Schliemann took to be a Cyclopean water-conduit with, close by, twelve recesses made of large slabs of stone which he assumed were small cisterns. A tombstone appeared with a hunting scene and a chariot drawn by a horse; then another, with a naked warrior, grasping the head of a stallion whose outstreched legs suggested that he was running, and holding in his uplifted hand a double-edged sword. This, said Schliemann, must surely be an exact picture of the Trojan war chariots.

In the second week of October, digging was suspended. The Emperor of Brazil, Don Pedro II, had sent word that he would like to visit Hissarlik and Schliemann hastened away to the Dardanelles to act as host, noting in his diary his delight when he discovered that the Emperor was able to quote at length from the *Iliad*. An account of this visit has been left in a letter written to Mathilde Marie de la Tour by Comte Arthur de Gobineau, a diplomat accredited to the Emperor by Napoleon III. De Gobineau seems to have taken an immediate dislike to Schliemann. The party landed from their boat at five o'clock in the morning and rode across the plain to visit Troy. 'The great Schliemann', remarked de Gobineau, 'is nothing but an impudent charlatan, a liar and an imbecile. All this spoils the Troad a bit for me . . .' A German professor joined the group, and turned out to be, in de Gobineau's eyes, as pompous and self-regarding as Schliemann. The rest of the visit passed under a 'cloud of pedantry', though de Gobineau was able to relieve his boredom by making fun of Schliemann behind his back. Don Pedro had made de Gobineau promise not to argue with Schliemann. He kept his word, but agreed so fulsomely with every word the archaeologist uttered, that 'inane things' were said and the Emperor 'laughed until he cried'. Later, visiting Mycenae, de Gobineau reluctantly admitted that what the Schliemanns were unearthing might well lead to 'having to change our opinion on the origin of art', and even he seems to have enjoyed a torchlight party in 'Agamemnon's tomb', the Treasury of Atreus, its 'floor strewn with laurel branches'. Why Schliemann should have irritated de Gobineau quite so much is never made clear.

By the middle of October the rains in the plain of Argos started. Torrential downpours turned the dusty site into a sea of mud. But still the finds kept coming: decorated pottery, vases, and, even more exciting, the discovery of a number of 'sepulchral slabs' – both sculptured and unsculptured – which, announced Schliemann, 'undoubtedly mark the sites of tombs cut deep in the rock', and could be the sepulchres 'which Pausanias, following the tradition, attributes to Atreus, to the "king of men" Agamemnon, to his charioteer Eurymedon, to Cassandra, and to their companions'. However, he admitted that there was no way in which Pausanias could actually have seen these tombstones, since at the time of his visit, somewhere around 170 AD, 'all the sepulchral monuments had for ages been covered by a layer of pre-historic debris, from 8 to 10 ft thick, on which an Hellenic city had been built'. Then, in the middle of November, came one of those occasions which forever mark a person's life. It was Priam's treasure all over again; only better.

Noting that the upright tombstones he had uncovered stood, not in natural soil but in artificial fill, Schliemann had ordered the men to explore further. They dug down: nothing came to light. They dug on. Then came a few gold-covered buttons. Since Schliemann believed that plunderers had been at the tombs before him, he was not expecting a great deal. What was more, it was still raining hard, and it was proving difficult to find workmen. According to his diary, it is clear that he was thinking of abandoning at least that section of Mycenae. But at this very moment came an incredible discovery.

Working within the inner walls, under the upright slabs, Schliemann opened a tomb and found the remains of three human bodies, their feet turned to the west, and their heads to the east. On each lay diadems of gold, piped with copper wire; scattered among them were fragments of a silver vase, plated with gold and richly ornamented, as well as many obsidian knives. Then came more bodies, which, from their size, and the presence of female ornaments, Schliemann concluded were women. One, to judge by the teeth, had been extremely old. As they were uncovered, they were seen to be 'literally laden with jewels'. It was not just the gold but the bodies that made it so hard to believe: the actual remains of men and women – possibly the very heroes Homer spoke of. This was the stuff of dreams.

In the next few days, further digging within the citadel on a spot that stood out from its surroundings by virtue of its undisturbed black earth, suggesting that it had lain untouched since 'a remote antiquity', brought to light a fourth shaft grave. First came some fragments of 'archaic' pottery and more obsidian knives. And then, at a depth of $26\frac{1}{2}$ feet, lying not far apart, came the most awesome sight of all: five more bodies, 'smothered in jewels'. Nearby lay a silver cow's head with long golden horns, and a golden sun on its forehead – surely representing the goddess Hera, the patron deity of Mycenae. There were also many bronze swords and vases, copper cauldrons, and a sizable golden goblet, with handles in the shape of pigeons – surely Nestor's gold wine cup, described in the *Iliad* as 'studded with gold pins and decorated with two golden doves'.

The skulls of the five bodies were in an advanced state of decomposition, and only two could be saved. However, three wore masks. One that caught Schliemann's attention had an oval, youthful face with a high forehead, a long Grecian nose and a small mouth with thin lips; the eyes were closed, but the hairs of the eyelashes and eyebrows were well marked. Another was that of an older man. Its round face bore a smiling mouth, full cheeks, a small forehead and eyebrows and eyelashes 'tolerably represented'. The eyes were closed. The smile was knowing; it suggested mystery and resignation. Near the head of one of the other men lay an odd, twisted, mask, in the shape of a lion's head. At first, Schliemann took this to be a helmet, and put it to one side; later, examining it better, he came to believe that it was also a mask, to be worn over the head, though others later suggested that his first assumption had been right, and that it was a helmet, worn much as Alexander the Great's men wore lions'-head helmets, their muzzles resting on the forehead.

But what was overwhelming about this fourth grave was the sheer quantity of gold – which Schliemann was soon describing as crowns, breastplates, massive golden goblets, tiaras, brooches and pins. There were 400 pieces of gold that looked like coins; over 150 gold discs; minute double-headed gold battleaxes. More, far more, than the treasure of Troy. There were also two large golden signet rings, one representing a hunter with his charioteer, in a chariot drawn by two stallions, their legs portrayed in such a way as to suggest that they were travelling at great speed, the other a battle scene with four warriors, one apparently vanquished by the other. What made these rings so extraordinary was the beauty and skill with which the pictures had been engraved.

Schliemann dug on. Directly north of the fourth grave, he now uncovered his fifth and last grave; like the third and fourth, it was outstandingly rich, though it contained only one body, which quickly crumbled. Efforts had clearly been made at the time of burial to preserve the bodies, for they were coated in some kind of white clay, designed to keep the moisture out – perhaps the remains of shrouds or robes; but as they were exposed to the air, they fell away into dust.

The mud had now dried out in the sun, and Schliemann returned for a closer look at his original tomb, which had at first seemed empty. He pushed further down into the soil and soon came across three more bodies, squeezed tightly together within the inner walls, laid out east to west. Two wore gold masks. One had flesh still hanging on to the skull: this was to prove Schliemann's most exciting find. 'All its flesh', he wrote, 'had been wonderfully preserved under its ponderous golden mask. There was no vestige of hair, but both eyes were perfectly visible, also the mouth, which, owing to the enormous weight that had pressed upon it, was wide open, and showed thirty-two beautiful teeth.' The face seemed to be that of a man of about thirty-five, and he wore a large gold breastplate; golden leaves were scattered over his forehead, chest and thighs, and a flattened mask covered his face. Schliemann did not, as is often said, send off a telegram to the King of Greece with the words : 'I have gazed upon the face of Agamemnon'. That was invented later. What he did do was to hastily summon an artist to draw the body, in case it crumbled away, while sending off for a druggist to try to preserve it. For two days he watched over the body, terrified that it would shrivel and vanish before it could be preserved. When the druggist came, he managed to solidify the figure, by pouring alcohol over it, in which he had dissolved gum sandarac. The body stayed intact, and was later despatched, with triumph, to Athens, where the torso and skull are to this day, in the vaults of the National Museum.

The treasure in this first tomb, the last to be explored by Schliemann, had less of the richness of the fourth shaft grave. Robbers, over the centuries, had clearly removed all but a modest number of objects, like some gold cups, a silver jug, fragments of a bronze sword, and a jar with two silver handles. But then another gold mask, buried at the south end of the tomb, came to light, with a long thin nose, a large mouth and lips, and a particularly prominent beard and moustache, its ends turning upwards in the form of crescents.

The world, both locally and in the capitals of Europe, had been following Schliemann's daily finds, for both Stamatakes and Schliemann himself regularly sent off bulletins and reports which were published in newspapers in Greece and abroad. One Athens paper had already congratulated Schliemann on his 'lucky fingers'. Now, as news of a well-preserved figure of the mythic golden age spread 'like a rolling fire through the Argolid', huge crowds began to gather round Mycenae. 'It is believed that ancient Mycenae has come back to life,' reported the *Argolis*. 'Everyone has been seized by a fever of curiosity.' A cordon of soldiers was posted round the citadel walls, causing Schliemann to remark, as he looked out on their watchfires at night, burning brightly above the plain, that the scene reminded him of the watch kept for Agamemnon's return – only now it was to keep away fortune-hunters and unwanted visitors. Every evening, as darkness fell, the Schliemanns rode back to their house in the village, carrying their finds in blankets, which were then counted, numbered and locked away. 'I have found an unparalleled treasure ...' wrote Schliemann to a friend in Athens. 'All the museums of the world put together do not possess one fifth of it. Unfortunately nothing but the glory is mine.'

It was all, however, rather more complicated. What, precisely, *had* Schliemann found ? In his personal diaries, written in the days following the discovery of the tombs, he confessed to being unsure as to whether these really were the ones described by Pausanias. But as the days went by, and the glory of what he had excavated grew on him, so his doubts shrank. The shaft graves, he began to declare in the despatches he was sending off to *The Times* – later to form the basis of his book on Mycenae – were undoubtedly those of Agamemnon and his companions. Telling Max Müller that two of the bodies had been covered by 'at *least* five kilograms of pure gold', he spoke of his 'firmest conviction' that he had unearthed Pausanias's tombs : 'The treasure I found is so immense, that the Greek and Roman jewels of all the museums in the world do not make up one quarter of the quantity; and as to the quality, the Mycenaean treasure stands alone ...'

To the King of Greece, Schliemann now sent word of his great find : 'With extreme joy I announce to Your Majesty that I have discovered the tombs which tradition, echoed by Pausanias, has designated as the sepulchres of Agamemnon, Cassandra, Eurymedon and all their companions ...' The letter included a somewhat wistful note : 'These treasures alone will fill a great museum, the most wonderful in the world, and for centuries to come thousands of foreigners will flock to Greece to see them. I work only for the pure love of science, and accordingly I have no claim to these treasures. I give them intact and with a lively enthusiam to Greece. God grant that these treasures may become the cornerstone of an immense national wealth.' One wonders what Stamatakes made of these generous-spirited words.

In a little less than three weeks, Schliemann had excavated five shaft graves – containing more gold than has since been found in any other similar Greek grave. Then he stopped, possibly because five had been the number of graves mentioned by Pausanias. He had been hard at work for four months more or less without a break, and the winter was closing in. His relations with Stamatakes were now almost unbearable, and in a letter to Müller he claimed that the unfortunate overseer 'would have made an excellent executioner'. The Greek government, finally aware of the extraordinary nature of Schliemann's finds, were also beginning to crowd in on him with new stipulations and new caveats. The excavations, towards the end, had been repeatedly stopped to give

time for some official or other to make his way to Mycenae. On 27
November, in a mood of considerable frustration, Schliemann wrote to
Müller: 'these immense treasures make the Greeks tremble at their
shadow'. It had in fact been not with Sophia, once again absent at one
of the moments of his greatest glory, but with a professor sent from
Athens, that Schliemann had opened his last grave and found the mask
with the particularly fine features.

Schliemann now set off back to Athens, where, in the remarkably
short space of eight weeks, he turned his *Times* despatches into a book:
*Mycenae: A Narrative of Research and Discoveries at Mycenae and
Tiryns*. Max Müller, who was in Dresden, had been acting as his intermediary with the London newspaper, correcting Schliemann's Germanic
English. Praising him for his great success at Mycenae, Müller urged
restraint and prudence: 'Never mind the attacks of the press ... You are
envied – that is all, and I do not wonder at it. You have 'enviers' in
England too, and it is very important that you should not have any
misunderstanding with *The Times*.' Schliemann was angling for Gladstone to write a preface for his book on Mycenae, writing to him to say
that he was confident Gladstone would not be able to refuse a 'man who
has for years and years submitted to all hardships and privations in the
most pestilential climate'. Evidently Gladstone hesitated, for when he
finally agreed, the letter from Schliemann was fulsome. The preface, he
declared, would be the 'most brilliant reward to which my ambition
could possibly aspire'.

In January 1877, an engineer called Vasilios Drosinos, who had helped
Schliemann before, was sent back to Mycenae to make a ground plan of
the shaft graves. While going very carefully over the site, he came upon
what he thought might be a sixth grave, but outside the circle and to the
south. Stamatakes, who happened to be at Mycenae that day, agreed
to sanction more digging and almost immediately a gold vessel was
unearthed, followed by some golden goblets, and a number of signets,
one of immense detail and beauty. Schliemann must have been irked.
Later that year, when *Mycenae* was published, he had no alternative but
to sound admiring. Drosinos, 'my most excellent engineer', was warmly
praised for being so 'keen sighted'.

The moment had come to take stock of just what his excavations at
Mycenae had revealed, and where they fitted into the tales of the Trojan
War. The task was not an easy one.

Even as he dug, Schliemann had been aware that not all his assumptions

about the shaft graves were likely to remain unchallenged for long. As
the news of what he was bringing up out of the ground spread around the
archaeological centres of Europe, and more particularly as his confident
assertions began to be absorbed by his critics, so murmurs of disbelief
turned into open doubt and disagreement. That the stone slabs, standing
vertically around the graves, were some kind of bench created around
an agora, and made sacred by virtue of the royal tombs below, as
Schliemann claimed, was immediately questioned. Dating also quickly
became a topic of intense speculation, as the question of embalming or
burying the dead at that period was fiercely debated. More and more,
the entire timing of the purported Trojan War began to be challenged,
as was the question of whether the bodies uncovered at Mycenae could
possibly have been contemporaneous with the finds in Schliemann's
Troy II.

A decade of public hostility had turned Schliemann into a more
cautious man. While others went to great lengths to attribute to him
very precise identification of the bodies, Schliemann remained vague,
preferring neither to correct nor to dispute words put into his mouth by
others. Vagueness suited his purpose. Emil Ludwig, Schliemann's first
biographer, commissioned by Sophia in the 1920s to write her husband's
life, has a story that when faced by scepticism on his return from
Mycenae, Schliemann exclaimed: 'What? So this is not Agamemnon's
body, these are not his ornaments? All right, let's call him Schultze.'
Ever afterwards, in conversation, he spoke not of Agamemnon but of
Schultze.

What could not be challenged, however, was the magnificence of
Schliemann's finds. Even latter-day critics, who continue to complain
about his ruthless archaeological methods and the ease with which he
lied, have trouble proving his Mycenaean finds to be forgeries or fakes.
Forgery, in so short a space of time, and under the ever watchful eyes of
Stamatakes, seems out of the question, and the purchase of items to
boost the find highly unlikely, given the circumstances of the excavation,
and the statistical improbability of being able to get hold of identical
items. The market in antiquities was still extremely new. True, in the
early days of the dig. Schliemann did report finding fragments of pottery
in his second shaft grave which in fact came from another part of the
grave circle: they seemed to him very like the pottery he had found at
Troy, and he desperately needed evidence to make Agamemnon and
Priam contemporaries. He also seems to have shifted two figurines from
one part of the site to another – but this may have been a genuine error,

made in the confusion of the vast excavation; and he does not seem to have moved anything else. And the treasures of Mycenae were indeed fabulous: not only the fact of finding so much gold, but the sheer quantity of the pieces and the artistry with which they had been fashioned. Like the earlier finds at Troy, the treasures suggested a cosmopolitan and cultured world of trade and contacts extending throughout the Mediterranean: alabaster from Egypt, ivory from the Near East, amber from Northern Europe.

The first to see these objects and the wealth of Mycenae were, not surprisingly, the Athenians, for the Greek government hastened to put them on display. Before doing so, however, the curmudgeonly Germans were given a glimpse, and they were quick to treat Schliemann's new finds with contempt. Curtius and the other German archaeologists now digging at Olympia, reported Charles Merlin, the British Consul at Piraeus, in a letter to Charles Newton in London, 'don't think much of them. Their importance has been grossly exaggerated.' The letter continues, in language curious among Victorian gentlemen, with some gossip. 'Schliemann's geese are all swans. He recognized Agamemnon's remains the moment he saw them, and the Greeks swear that he rogered his wife in public on the spot, in an ecstasy of antiquarian delight.' But in February, when he was at last able to visit the exhibition, held in the National Bank in Athens, having jostled his way through crowds of eager diplomatic ladies, Merlin was 'immensely impressed' and prepared to concede that the Mycenaean finds were indeed different from anything he had ever seen before, though he continued to doubt whether they were in fact as old as Schliemann maintained. Merlin was evidently much influenced by Curtius, for he repeated Curtius's theory that they really belonged to a different period altogether. He was also clearly swayed by Curtius's personal dislike for his fellow German archaeologist. 'It is a pity', he told Newton, that Schliemann 'is so vulgar in his manner, and gives his opinion as if there is no one who knows anything but himself'. To his wife, Curtius had written that the gold of Mycenae was of 'such incredible thinness that the hero Agamemnon must have been but a beggarly prince'. (On this score, Curtius was wrong: a lot of the gold was quite thick, and that from the three richest graves has since been estimated to weigh a total of 15 kilograms, according to the Mycenaean scholar, Oliver Dickinson.) One of the gold masks, Curtius went on to suggest dismissively, could perfectly well prove to be a Byzantine head of Christ.

Schliemann, as he settled down in Athens to contemplate his treasure and write his book, believed that what he had done at Mycenae was to prove beyond all possible doubt the historical accuracy of Homer's epic poems. All earlier anxieties now faded away. He had in fact done both less and more than this. The existence of a Trojan war, the links between Troy and Mycenae, were still far from clear, and continued to float dateless and uncertain in the minds of many archaeologists of the day. However, what Schliemann had actually done was to present the world with a lost civilization, which in time would be pinpointed by historians who followed after him as a Mycenaean Age, the first great civilization to flourish on the European mainland, some time between 1550 BC and 1050 BC.

His finds at Mycenae far outshone anything he had dug up at Troy, in terms both of value and beauty. The gold cups, the buttons, the bracelets, the swords and the vases, these were the equal of any archaeological discoveries, even in Tutankhamun's tomb in Egypt – in the artistry of some of the individual items, if not in quality and weight – and that was not be excavated for another fifty years. An amateur, a German businessman with an obsession about Homer, had, in just a few months, revealed a chapter of the past about which almost nothing had been known. The finds at Mycenae were to transform all existing views on prehistory, and to open an entire new field for archaeological exploration. In time, this would lead to the discovery of Minoan Crete and the deciphering of Linear B, the script of the later palaces, as an archaic form of Greek. But that was all in the future. For the present, an unknown grocer's apprentice, from the obscure village of Ankershagen in north-east Germany, had succeeded in casting light on a remarkable age, long before the dark ages descended on Greece. It was, indeed, an extraordinary achievement.

Mycenae was to be the peak of Schliemann's career as an archaeologist. Everything that he did afterwards – and some of it was very important – was something of an anticlimax. Though he remained loyal to Homer, he became more cautious with his ebullient assertions, preferring to defer to experts whose opinions he had earlier so blithely disregarded. It was left to others to dig further, find more, and establish that what Schliemann had done was to unearth remains of the beginning of Mycenaean civilization, more than three hundred years earlier than the period to which many scholars have attributed the events described in the *Iliad* and the *Odyssey*. Schliemann himself never returned to Mycenae, and after the publication of his book, seldom discussed his excavations there with anyone.

The excavation of Mycenae, however, profoundly altered the way the world regarded him. His critics remained outspoken, but to the public he had become the man who, single-handed, had revealed to them a sumptuous past. Schliemann was, at last, famous.

By the late spring of 1877, with a draft of *Mycenae* completed, the moment had come to receive the accolades he felt to be his due. And where better than in England, the country which had honoured him so pleasingly before ?

Long before Schliemann arrived in London, a warm current of approval for him had begun to spread among British archaeologists and historians. 'Schliemania' was said to have gripped the public. The weekly illustrated magazines were far more leisurely and discursive in those days, and the *Illustrated London News* had sent several artists over the months to Mycenae, who came back with sketches of the site and of the increasingly popular Schliemanns. Before the reproduction of photographs was introduced in the mid-1890s, woodblocks were used in the illustrated journals, and artists were sent off to sketch every event worthy of attention : no other moment of history was ever drawn as vividly as the Victorian era. All through the spring of 1877, the magazine devoted two and sometimes even three whole pages repeatedly to the Mycenae excavations. On 24 March appeared a flattering portrait of Schliemann, 'offered as a tribute of personal respect, in recognition of his laudable endeavours and large pecuniary sacrifice'. Other picture magazines, like *Life*, *The Graphic*, *St James's Gazette* and *The Builder*, began to describe his work, often using pictures of the Schliemanns hard at work to illustrate their stories.

Strangers had now begun to write to Schliemann with praise, or questions, or requests. Robert Browning, who was planning to publish a new translation of *The Agamemnon*, sent a plea to be allowed to illustrate it with photographs of the Mycenaean treasures. A man called Norris J. Foster wrote from Birmingham to ask for Schliemann's autograph, 'that I may keep it as the handwriting of him who has done more towards enlightening the present generation on Grecian history, than anyone alive'. Letters from scholars, admirers, heads of university colleges and secretaries of committees poured in : from this year on, Schliemann would seldom receive less than two thousand letters in any one year.

His English season was to be a time of honours, banquets and speeches.

Everywhere he went, his words were taken down by reporters and printed at length in the daily papers, in tones that were gratifyingly respectful. Schliemann reached London on 22 March, only just in time to be the guest of honour at a meeting of the Society of Antiquaries at Burlington House. Lord Stanhope had died, but Gladstone was present and congratulated him 'upon the success of his labours', expressing great personal gratitude for 'the enlargement of knowledge in an age rather degenerate by the noble and high-minded enthusiast'. After prolonged cheers, Schliemann was made an Honorary Fellow of the society. *The Times* next day devoted an entire column to the 'illustrious discoverer'.

Other ceremonies, as pleasing, followed. Throughout April and May, Schliemann was entertained by the Royal Academicians, by the Royal Historical Society and by the Institute of Architects – where Gladstone, by now in opposition but who was, once again, present, spoke of the honour coming Schliemann's way from the 'heart and understanding of the English people', and where he was presented with a diploma for his 'deeds of danger and daring'. The Salters' Company made him their guest of honour at a banquet at which Schliemann made much of his childhood, dreaming in 'his poor little village'. The officers at the Tower of London invited him to dine. But it was during the evening reception at the Worshipful Company of Grocers that Schliemann really came into his own. 'I feel infinite pleasure in thinking that I am myself a grocer,' he declared, in reply to a fulsome toast, 'and that in praising here the grocer's business I praise a trade which I have followed up with unremitting zeal for a period of twenty-eight years ... The habit I had acquired in my long career as a grocer not to do anything superficially but to proceed in everything with tact, system and perseverance has been of immense advantage to me in my archaeological excavations; and I feel bold to say that had I not been a grocer, I could never have succeeded in discovering Troy or the five Royal sepulchres at Mycenae ... Without commerce that could be no ambition, and without ambition there could be no science. Thus, without commerce, men would be brutes.' It was strong stuff, and the grocers cheered. To Sophia, Schliemann wrote that he had become the 'lion of the season'. Hodge, the artist, was pestering to do his portrait for the Royal Academy; while a well-known London photographer wanted to add his portrait to those of the 'leading men in Medicine and Surgery'.

A glimpse of the triumphant Schliemann appears in a memoir of Tennyson, written by his son in the 1890s. They had been invited to meet Schliemann at a dinner given by Lord Houghton at Almond's

Hotel. During the evening, the talk turned to the Troad. Hissarlik, announced Schliemann, was no bigger than the courtyard of Burlington House. Tennyson's son continues: 'As we were leaving the room after dinner, Schliemann, duly impressed with the splendour of the entertainment, remarked to us of our host: "Our Lord is a very gracious Lord, is he not?"'

British lords may have remained a source of mystery and splendour to Schliemann, but he was invariably most elegantly and correctly dressed for every occasion, his obsession with personal neatness and cleanliness having, if anything, grown over the years. For this visit to London he had taken with him his own valet; just the same, he was often to be found brushing and rebrushing his suits as he put them on. For many years now, Schliemann had been buying his clothes, or having them made, in London, where he had found a shirtmaker to design him a particular style of collar, with a lower cut than was then customary, which drew attention away from his somewhat short and thickset neck, while at the same time suggesting a greater height. Schliemann owned, he calculated one day, fifty suits, twenty hats, and forty-two pairs of shoes.

Several of the societies which now competed with each other to bestow ever greater honours on Schliemann spoke of their sadness at not being able to receive Sophia as well. Lord Talbot de Malahide, president of the Royal Archaeological Institute of Great Britain and Ireland, referred to her in a speech as the 'first lady who has ever been identified in a work so arduous and stupendous' and said that her reputation was now one which 'many will envy – some may emulate – but none can ever surpass'. The institute wrote to ask Schliemann whether Sophia might be persuaded to come to London to attend a special celebration in her honour.

At this time Sophia was three months pregnant, and not feeling very well. A telegram reached her, in French – 'Tu as absolument besoin distraction divertissements. Viens mon ange adorée ...' – and she set off obediently at once for London. Schliemann urged her, before leaving, to have one last swim in the healthy sea. She arrived in early June. Whether she wrote her own speech, or whether Schliemann wrote it for her, is not known, but at five past five on Friday 8 June, she was escorted from the top of the sweeping staircase of the Royal Archaeological Institute, by Gladstone on one side, and Lord Talbot on the other, into the room in which she was to speak. Schliemann's pride was such, he was later to say, that his arms, shoulders, legs and hands trembled so hard that he

could barely walk; and he wept unashamedly and copiously. As for
Sophia, she spoke out resolutely on the subject of Troy and Mycenae,
and her own role in the excavations, and on the importance of the ancient
Greeks and the language of Plato. She ended with an appeal to 'English
ladies to teach their children the sonorous language of my ancestors, so
that they may be enabled to read Homer and our other immortal classics
in the original'. There was much cheering. Sophia was just twenty-six.

A few days later, having dined with the Lord Mayor, and turned down
many other grand intellectual and social invitations, the Schliemanns
were made Honorary Fellows of the Royal Historical Society. Since
Schliemann was an American citizen, the *New York Times* had sent a
reporter to the reception. He evidently found the occasion extremely
tedious, complaining that the audience of three hundred (he made little
of the fact that a further eighteen hundred people had to be turned away)
had long-suffering expressions, and the ladies 'contemplative eyes and
unfashionable shawls', but he did remark on Schliemann's 'calm, patient
eyes' and 'round, compact head and persevering chin' and said that
Sophia, whose English was 'broken', was a 'handsome, olive-com-
plexioned' woman. After this, the Schliemanns set off back across the
Channel. Gladstone and Lord Talbot were among those who saw them
on to the boat train at Victoria.

After the glory of London, Paris was a little flat. The house at 6 Place
St-Michel was let, and the Schliemanns, having paused for a short
holiday in Boulogne, rented an apartment in the Rue de Tilsit. Schliemann's earaches were now an almost constant part of his life, and he
was forever seeking new specialists and new cures. The Schliemanns
were regular visitors to Europe's many spas.

In August, *The Times* printed an article drawing attention to Schliemann's offer to bring his entire Trojan collection, including all the
gold and silver, to be put on show at the South Kensington Museum.
The suggestion had evidently come from Gladstone. Abandoning the
pregnant Sophia in Paris, Schliemann hastened to London to plan the
exhibition, and to finish seeing *Mycenae* through the presses. He continued his love-affair with England, writing to Sophia towards the end
of August, 'I live here in a dirty stinky inn in a splendid country ...
But what an enormous difference between the English and the French
character! What charming, sincere and sociable people here!' He was

observing, he added, the 'strictest incognito' for he had a great deal of work to do.

Sophia was both ill and lonely, and also very short of money, Schliemann having fled with his customary haste. She now had to fall back on borrowing from friends, a position she found humiliating, and one which was later used to prove Schliemann's extravagance during excavations, for it was assumed that all his fortune had been eaten up at Troy and Mycenae. (There was never any question of it: Schliemann was a very rich man.) Andromache, now aged six, arrived in Paris to join her mother. For a while letters between Paris and London were bitter. 'My heart', Sophia wrote to him, 'do you not consider me one of your occupations? I know I am worth nothing, but do not show it to me.' Schliemann chose to take offence and complained irritably that she did not speak enough foreign languages. (Sophia's next letter was written in four different languages.) Even so, he failed to be with her either for Christmas or when she later gave birth to a son, though he made it back to Paris in time to see the boy christened Agamemnon. There had been plans to call him Odysseus, but Schliemann wanted to mark his latest triumph. During the ceremony, which took place in a Greek Orthodox church, Schliemann is supposed to have placed a copy of Homer on the child's forehead in order to invest him with the poet's spirit. These were not good times in the Schliemann marriage. Sophia was no longer quite so pliant, nor Schliemann so enraptured. When his moods turned sour, his endearments dried up. 'My own Sophithion, adored wife and everlasting friend', became just her name, and on his many crossings of the Channel to attend to business in France he did not always take the time to call in on his wife and children. 'Is it not enough,' Sophia wrote to him one day, 'that I remain here in poverty by your request? Do not complain that I cannot manage what I do not have ...' Before signing herself 'your wife', she wrote a question mark. Even so her spirit of self-sacrifice and patience is impressive. 'Why? Why do you demand, yet ignore? I thank God for you, yet wonder what manner of man you are ... I know the fate of every woman who is joined to a genius.' Even when angry, Sophia never seems to have doubted that the man she had married was the most gifted archaeologist of his day.

The Greek government had, surprisingly, agreed to let Schliemann add a small number of his Mycenaean finds to his Trojan collection; as they began to reach London, Schliemann took an active part in setting up the exhibition, constantly seeking reassurance from Max Müller. The two men had first been drawn together by a certain similarity in their backgrounds – both came from poor rural German families – and by the single-mindedness with which each of them pursued their life's ambitions. But their friendship had become closer when Müller's young daughter suddenly died and Müller was devastated. 'I would give all the world to be able to find words to console you,' Schliemann had written to him. 'I feel all the immensity of your loss.' Schliemann had, after all, lost his own daughter, Natalya, at the age of twelve. With friends in trouble, Schliemann could be both generous and sensitive. Together with the letter, he had sent some minor but interesting Mycenaean fragments he knew would intrigue Müller. Müller wrote to say that they had given him the first glimpses of pleasure since the death of his child.

Schliemann had kept three albums of diary during the Mycenaean excavations, and these, together with his reports to *The Times* and a lavish number of drawings and photographs – over a thousand of the pottery alone – became the basis for his book, *Mycenae*, which appeared towards the end of the year, and was dedicated to Don Pedro II. It is both more readable and more scholarly than his earlier books – both his friend Emile Burnouf and an English editor called Philip Smith had helped him with it – and was soon selling well. Archaeological jewellery was still the fashion, and one society hostess, after seeing pictures of the Mycenaean jewellery, begged him to let her 'copy the beautiful design for a tiara ... I call it Klytemnestra.' Schliemann's love for England and the English, he now told Sophia, 'is growing hourly more and more intense'.

To Gladstone, Schliemann boasted that *Mycenae* had 'probably had a larger sale than any archaeological work ever published'. He had been right to press Gladstone to provide a foreword. Gladstone was one of the very few people able to state a belief in Homer's historical reliability that far exceeded anything permitted to professional archaeologists, and yet remain respected. Once Gladstone had written that he basically accepted that the 'half-wasted, half-burned' remains at Mycenae were the 'ashes of Agamemnon and his company', Schliemann himself could safely take a vague and detached position. It was Gladstone, and not he, who had stuck his neck out.

Not everyone shared Gladstone's certainty. Archaeologists, writing their lengthy reviews in British journals, complained that *Mycenae* lacked enough precise details about the bodies and where they had been found, and continued to insist on the need for more proof. Even Charles Newton, Schliemann's friend from the British Museum, felt obliged to say, in his notice for the *Edinburgh Review*, that a number of basic problems were, as yet, unsolved.

For all his new-found respectability and outer semblance of calm, it was never hard to provoke Schliemann. His temper was soon sparked by the publication, in *Fraser's Magazine*, of William Borlase's attack on him from the Troad, in which he reported Yannakis's remarks that the finding of the treasure had been quite different from Schliemann's own account of it. Schliemann now spluttered on about libel and misrepresentation, and accused Frank Calvert, who had entered the debate with further misgivings about Hissarlik, of being a 'foul fiend'. Schliemann seems to have suffered particularly at the hands of German academics. The strength of their hostility, some of it of an undisguisedly personal nature, is evident from the memoirs of Prince von Bülow, who visited Olympia with Ernst Curtius in the summer of 1877. Von Bülow found his companion, by then a widely respected archaeologist and the author of a best-selling book on Greek history, both charming and distinguished. But he added: 'Only one thing about him disturbed me: his ceaseless carping criticism of Heinrich Schliemann ... It pained me that a German intellectual of the type and reputation of Curtius should do his best to stigmatize as a bungler and a charlatan such a passive, naïve, yet not the less fine, enthusiast as Schliemann, a man filled with holy zeal for knowledge.' It would not have been necessary to be a diplomat, he concluded, to 'see that every word he spoke breathed jealousy against the successful rival in the archaeological field'. It was the Germans, perhaps because of Schliemann's origins, or the fact that he did not belong to their close-knit academic world, who were invariably most maddened by his spectacular finds.

The attention paid to him in England, and the success of *Mycenae*, had, however, finally succeeded in instilling in Schliemann a small degree of the confidence he had always lacked. For the first time he was now able to hear out his accusers without invariably succumbing to rage and bluster. 'All the venom of the German scholars,' he wrote to a friend, 'will not yet suffice to hurl the 50 feet high and 300 feet thick raised hill of Hissarlik into the sea of oblivion.' He was also now capable of producing scorn and contempt himself, writing to Müller that if the Prussians failed to find anything at Olympia, 'it is merely because they work like ignorant fools, without tact, order or system and throw all the rubbish ... within 50 yards of the site they excavate' – strange words for a man whose own excavation techniques had been described as careless and destructive. 'Tact' and 'system' had both been values extolled in his speech to the grocers. He must have felt to some extent vindicated, for the German Anthropological Society, of which Rudolf Virchow was a founder, now made him an honorary member. He was praised, as the words on the scroll put it, for 'having brought to light from centuries of limbo the royal residences of Priam and Agamemnon'.

With *Mycenae* selling well in England and Germany, and about to appear in France, and the exhibition in London attracting admiring crowds, Schliemann was again free, though his health was poor and the pain in his ears excruciating. 'I want rest,' he told Müller, 'which however I shall not find before the grave, because I am accustomed to great activity, and could not stand it to live a single day without some serious occupation.' Schliemann, once again, was becoming restless.

12

A FAIRLY
HEEDLESS WORLD

Troy was, and remained, Schliemann's first and greatest love. He returned to it again and again for the rest of his life. There was something about the vast sandy plain, with the eagles and vultures circling overhead, and the immense horizon stretching away to the islands and the mountains that drew him; something about the poetry of the Trojan War and 'windy Ilium' that had settled on his imagination. There was, too, a small and uncomfortable feeling of doubt that never quite went away. Was Hissarlik *really* Priam's Troy? Why did Troy II not match better with Agamemnon's Mycenae? Did the site perhaps still conceal some clue, some new treasure that would silence his critics and provide him with evidence of a kind no one ever again would be able to dispute, that he, Schliemann, had been the man to prove the tale of Troy correct?

Despite their financial settlement, the Turks continued to feel aggrieved by Schliemann's behaviour. True, they had the money, but there were many at the Sultan's court and in the archaeological service in Constantinople who felt somehow cheated. The Trojan treasure, whatever its history, had been found on Turkish soil, and so it belonged to them, and not to a wandering German who was already known to be trying to sell it to one of the European powers. Schliemann's request for a new *firman*, to continue with his excavations at Hissarlik, was turned down.

Enraged, Schliemann reverted to his old tactics, lobbying his diplomat friends, sending off beseeching telegrams to politicians and scholars, Ambassadors and Consuls, hectoring, bullying. However, after his triumph at Mycenae, Schliemann was a man with powerful friends. The letters that poured off his pen and went to colleagues and contacts in France, Austria, Italy, England and Spain were listened to, and acted on. Gladstone and Bismarck, both canvassed for help, responded. There was now nothing to do but wait.

To ease his restlessness, and fill the time before the powerful voices had their effect, Schliemann returned to his earliest site, Odysseus's palace on the island of Ithaca. He was not unsuccessful, uncovering the ruins of 190 houses, and a spring of water which neatly matched Homer's lines on the watering of Eumaeus's swine; but after three weeks and no trace of a palace, and very little prehistorical material, he decided to dig no further.

The cajoling worked. The Turks capitulated and at the end of September 1878, Schliemann returned once more to the Troad. His excavations were becoming more professional and more precise each time, and he had now fined down the list of implements and tools. This year, he began by putting up felt-covered wooden barracks on the north-west slope of Hissarlik, from where it was just possible to glimpse Europe, beyond the Hellespont. It had nine rooms for himself and Sophia, visiting friends, the overseers and servants. There was also a wooden hall, to double as dining-room and storehouse, a hut for tools and machinery, another for ten gendarmes – the Troad had become no safer for rich foreigners and travellers over the years, continuing to be, as Schliemann wrote to a friend, 'infested by robbers and murderers' – and a stone house to act as kitchen. There was also a stable for the horses.

The contract drawn up with the Turkish authorities was clear: all antiquities to be divided, two-thirds for the Imperial Museum in Constantinople and one-third for Schliemann. Hemmed in by restrictions, watched over by zealous officials, Schliemann's spirits were low. 'I am quite discouraged,' he wrote to Layard, who was by now Ambassador in Constantinople and had evidently worked hard on securing the *firman* for him, 'and often think I shall not live till my projected departure.' Both of his overseers had fallen ill, and he was having to take their place, single-handedly directing the digging, though he welcomed the presence of the gendarmes who, he maintained, made sure that nothing was stolen. 'The vexations on the part of the Turkish government are *overpowering.*'

The 1878–9 Troy campaign started in earnest on 1 March. One hundred and fifty workmen had been taken on. The weather was still agonizingly cold, and a strong north wind, that blew day after day for over two weeks, made it impossible to keep warm, even inside the new huts. Only exercise, energetic work in the trenches, made any difference. Long before sunrise, despite the wind and the cold, Schliemann insisted on riding over the plain to the Hellespont to swim, ignoring the advice of his ear specialists, accompanied by his platoon of guards. Since the first part of the journey was usually made in the dark, there were times when the men lost sight of him altogether. One morning, his horse slipped, and animal and rider plunged into a clump of bushes, horse on top. It was some time before the muffled but unhurt Schliemann was discovered and pulled free.

Soon, the storks returned to the Troad. In their wake came Emile Burnouf and Rudolf Virchow; their presence and the temperate and steadying influence they exercised over Schliemann was to make a vast difference in the years to come. They brought order, where before chaos had flourished. In the evenings, as dusk descended over Hissarlik, the three men sat outside, looking across the plain towards the sea, talking of Homer and the heroes of the Trojan War.

The new plan was to uncover the entire circuit of walls that surrounded the mound. As the workmen dug, and almost the whole western half of the citadel was cleared, so new caches of treasure began to surface – necklaces, earrings, bracelets, pins – buried in and among the walls of the section earlier identified by Schliemann as Priam's palace. Most of them were concealed in terracotta vases. Though none were quite as extraordinary as his original discovery, they did contain much gold, including lumps of unworked gold, silver and electrum. Finding treasure was now becoming almost routine. And once again, there was something about the way the treasure had been packed away and hidden that suggested panic and haste. To Schliemann, it was all further proof of the fall of Troy.

Schliemann was becoming far more reserved and reticent in his claims. Gone were the days of instant telegrams and wild assertions. When he spoke of his finds, now, he mentioned 'royal residences' and 'gates', rather than 'Priam's palace' and the 'Scaean gate'. At least some of this new modesty was due to his old friend Burnouf, a man of exceptional versatility, who, to his scholarship as an expert on Oriental religions and Sanskrit, added the skills of engineer, geologist, surveyor, draftsman and author. Burnouf had done his best to promote Schliemann among the wary and disbelieving French archaeologists, and had written appreciative reviews of *Mycenae*. His role at Troy was that of mapmaker, producing diagrams of the excavations for the next planned volume on Troy, and his visit had been sponsored by the French government.

During the early weeks, he came to distinguish a slightly different series of layers than Schliemann's existing five, and proposed a further breakdown into two more. Schliemann, who accepted his idea, now spoke of the lower five as being 'prehistoric'; the third, he called 'Homeric Troy'.

But it was really Virchow who did the most to shape Schliemann's growing professionalism. In the early days of their acquaintance, Schliemann had been impetuous and easily sidetracked; under Virchow's guidance, he was to become more judicious and reflective. In discussions with Virchow, who wandered backwards and forwards across the plain, collecting botanical specimens, he began to widen his view of the site of Troy to take in the surrounding terrain, with its animal and plant life. *Ilios*, the book that resulted from this fifth season at Hissarlik, was to contain six pages on the zoology of the Troad, with observations on the plentifulness of tortoises ('it would not be difficult to catch some hundreds of them in a day'), of the venom of the water snakes which inhabited the many pools on the marshy plain, and of the abundance and consequent cheapness of the leeches. Commercial implications continued to intrigue Schliemann. As for the birds, Homer, he declared, had probably mixed up cranes and storks, for he never mentioned the latter, of which there were hundreds, in his poems. Schliemann could not resist repeating Homer's lines: 'The Trojans went with clanging and noise like birds; as when the clanging of the cranes rises in the face of heaven, who, after having escaped the winter and the tremendous rain, fly with loud cries over the streams of ocean, bearing murder and destruction to the Pygmaean race.'

Virchow, like Burnouf, was a man of many skills. One of these was in medicine. Learning that there was no qualified doctor for the whole of the Troad, he was soon spending much of his time visiting the local villagers, instructing them on how to turn the plentiful juniper and camomile of the plain into potions and cures. He returned from his wanderings with useful information about malaria and hookworm, which later proved valuable for research. The men of the region, he declared, were for the most part healthy, and, compared to 'specimens in what we call civilized cities', sturdy and well built. His one serious complaint was against the priests, who forced the villagers who were Christians to fast during Lent, which left them weakened and vulnerable to disease.

Before he departed at the end of his three-week visit, Virchow and Schliemann spent five days exploring the Troad, stopping to examine sites that were usually either Hellenistic or Roman. Together, they climbed Mount Ida. There is a story, possibly apocryphal, though Virchow himself repeated it, that Virchow used the occasion to turn Schliemann's thoughts towards presenting his Trojan treasure to Germany, his native country. Sitting on a grassy slope, he is said to have picked a sprig of flowering blackthorn and presented it to Schliemann with the words : 'A nosegay from Ankershagen.' What Schliemann made of this curious, oddly sentimental, statement or said in reply is not known ; but the suggestion is that a seed had been sown.

When Virchow finally left, planning to pause in Athens on his way back to Germany, Schliemann wrote off to Sophia, begging her to entertain Virchow well, and giving her the names of the men she should invite to meet him 'But no women'. There was something about Virchow that made Schliemann listen, even when the words would have been unacceptable coming from anyone else. After his stay in Athens, Virchow wrote to say that he thought Sophia was very lonely, and that she should not be left quite so much on her own. In a correspondence that touched on every subject from recent scientific discoveries to the identity of specific archaeological finds, there were also patches of intimacy, and Virchow soon became the family adviser on Sophia's stomach-aches, the children's diets and Schliemann's persistent earaches, though Schliemann paid no attention to his friend's entreaties to him to abandon salt water swims in very low temperatures. Often extremely busy himself, both with politics and with his scientific work, Virchow's answers to Schliemann's many letters occasionally took the form of notes. 'As I am very much pressed for time,' he wrote one day, '(1) Give Agamemnon no milk for some time, but instead soup or tea for supper ... (4) the lecture on Troy at Strasburg you must give in German ... I shall write you immediately about a governess ...' Virchow's recommendations were calm, reassuring and practical, and they exercised a brake on some of Schliemann's agitation and exuberance. When an inappropriately expensive wedding present reached Virchow's daughter, he entreated Schliemann to be more moderate in the future.

But moderation was not in Schliemann's nature. Even his undoubted respect and affection for Virchow could not prevent an outburst of bitterness and fury when, early in 1880, he learned that Virchow was planning to publish a paper of his own on a site called Hanai-Tepe, not far from Hissarlik, and that he was intending to describe not only skulls – which Schliemann conceded were his subject – but pottery – which was not. During the weeks spent together in the spring of 1879, the two men had agreed that Virchow's views would take the form of a paper to be included in Schliemann's coming book. News that Virchow was going his own way prompted a furious telegram: 'Publish nothing about Hanai-Tepe. Else friendship and love for Germany both perish.' To his publishers, John Murray in London, went instructions that no more proofs should be sent to Virchow.

After the telegram, there followed a letter. Its tone was anxious, bombastic and childish. It contained a mixture of reproach and threat. Virchow evidently agreed to postpone publication, and the two were soon exchanging friendly letters once again on the subject of Bavarian beer and cold baths. In many respects, Virchow was just as ruthless as Schliemann; and he was far shrewder. Whether or not he now consciously decided to enter into some kind of elaborate game with Schliemann, he spent the next two years flirting with his invitations, hesitating and then declining all of them, with excuses about political appointments, grandchildren, university commitments. But his letters remained cordial, and his advice excellent. Schliemann, Virchow told him again and again, was too restless: he needed to slow down, reflect more, not always rush into print before thinking things through. 'You do everything half, quarter, or eighth fashion, or even less, and have to revise later.' At a moment of tranquillity, when Schliemann's mind was possibly occupied by other things, Virchow went ahead and brought out his paper on the skulls of Troy, dismissing it to Schliemann as a small and insignificant pamphlet. Their friendship remained intact.

The fifth season – or second campaign – at Hissarlik had been demanding. Schliemann, taking Sophia with him, went off to the cool of a spa in Bavaria to recuperate. His ears were again bad. But his spirits were high, for the German newspapers were beginning to adopt a more friendly tone in their reports on his work. He told Layard that he was being 'immensely appreciated here ... and nobody now doubts that I brought to light Homeric Troy'. Schliemann never lost his warm respect for grand people. Prince Bismarck, he informed Layard, had shown him 'much kind attention; he is a genius of a superior order, and even of archaeology he speaks as if he had studied all his life that science ...'

Ilios: The City and the Country of the Trojans is the longest book Schliemann ever wrote. With well over 800 pages and 1600 engravings, it is in fact longer than *Troy and its Remains*, *Mycenae*, and his later *Troja* combined. The English edition is dedicated to Layard; the American to Gladstone; and the German to Virchow, who generously declared that the former 'grave-digger' had now indeed proved himself to be a scholar. As it was Virchow, Schliemann does not seem to have taken offence at the 'grave-digger' slur.

Instead of publishing the results of the 1878-9 excavations as a long supplement to his earlier book on Troy, Schliemann had decided to use the moment to summarize his entire Trojan work at Hissarlik since 1873. Having at last, and somewhat painfully, learned the value of expert help, he included nine appendices by other scholars. Frank Calvert, with whom Schliemann was once again on good terms, contributed a paper on a tumulus at Hanai-Tepe; Max Müller an essay on the swastika; and the Irish classical scholar, John Mahaffy, one on Homer's Ilios. For this book, editorial help had come not simply from Burnouf and Virchow, but from an Oxford scholar on Assyria and the Hittites called A.H.Sayce, with whom Schliemann had been corresponding for some time. Sayce, who was to become one of Schliemann's closer friends, had agreed to edit the proofs. On his return to Oxford in February 1880, from a season's excavating in Egypt, he found detailed notes from Schliemann on how he was to go about it, together with a cheque for £100. Given the length of the manuscript, the sum was perhaps not quite as generous as it sounds; and Schliemann's instructions have a daunting ring to them. 'You will find many passages,' he wrote, 'which ought to be transferred to other places. You will find others which must be given in footnotes. You will see where I have used certain authors too much, others too little ... You have carte-blanche to do as you please.' Sayce was not the only one of Schliemann's growing band of friends to be subjected to much hard work on his behalf. In a letter to John Murray, in March, Schliemann wrote sternly: 'Burnouf is a zero as a reviser, he has not changed a word, nor suggested an idea. Virchow is precious for the excellent ideas he submits and the changes he suggests. But the most precious of all is Sayce, who desires to make the book in the highest degree worthy of its author ...'

Sayce did his best. The tone of *Ilios* is modest; the self-contradictions have been reduced to a minimum. But there are parts of the book which remain dense and unclear, particularly when it comes to describing precisely where certain finds were made, and on what date. Pottery, once again, is heavily stressed, Schliemann having become still more convinced of its importance. 'In treating of the objects of human industry found in the debris,' he wrote, 'I begin with the most important – Pottery – because it is the cornucopia of archaeological wisdom for those

dark ages ...' Even so, the dating of the Trojan War, and its links with
Mycenae and Agamemnon's tomb, continued to remain unproven : there
was growing certainty that Homer, living at a later time, could not
conceivably have witnessed anything himself. 'I wish,' declared Schliemann mournfully, 'I could have proved Homer to have been an eye-
witness to the Trojan war ! Alas I cannot do it !' This particular note, a
little naïve, a little rueful, clearly appealed more to British academics,
who liked willingness to admit error and have a change of mind, than
to German ones, who considered it symbolic of Schliemann's lack of
seriousness.

It was left to Virchow, who wrote both a preface and an appendix to
Ilios, to sound a more positive note. He was satisfied, he declared, that
Hissarlik did indeed answer all the demands of Homeric topography :
standing on the top of the mound, and accepting that the rivers had
altered their course over the years, he claimed that it was perfectly
possible to look out over the battlefield, with Imbros and Samothrace
just visible, as Homer said they were. Schliemann, unnerved by the
hostility of his critics, had become somewhat reluctant to make grand
assertions. Virchow felt no such inhibitions. 'The question of the *Iliad*
is not simply the old question – "Ubi Ilium fuit ?" No, it embraces the
whole. We must not sever the story of the gods from the story of the
men. The poet who sang of Ilium painted also the picture of the whole
Trojan country ... All this is inseparable. And therefore it is not left to
our choice, where we should place Ilium ... we are compelled to say : –
Here, upon the fortress-hill of Hissarlik, – *here*, upon the site of the
Burnt City of Gold, – *here was Ilium*.' Fine words, particularly when
accompanied, as these were, by praise for Schliemann's courage. There
was more to come. 'And why not call him Priam ? Whether Priam ever
existed or not, the prince of the golden treasure who lived on this spot
comes near enough to the Priam of the *Iliad* to make us refuse to forego
the delight of giving the place his name ... Do not let us cut ourselves
off from all poetry without the slightest need. Children that we are of a
hard and too prosaic age, we would maintain our right to conjure up
again before our old age the pictures which filled our youthful fancy.'

All this can only have been soothing to Schliemann, but it was still
not quite enough. Doubts remained, particularly as the level he had
identified as that of Priam's city stubbornly refused to turn up the
remains that were expected of it. The mound of Hissarlik had still not
yielded its best secrets.

Once again, the critics split into supporters and sceptics. *Ilios* was published in both England and Germany in November 1880. As befitted the work of one of the leading and most controversial archaeologists of the age, it was reviewed everywhere, and at great length. *The Builder* was fulsome : 'This book is unique. The expression is bold, but it is fully justified by the work . . .' Schliemann's style, this reviewer declared, was not 'unworthy of the pen of Bunyan or Defoe'. *The Times* had long been a supporter : *Ilios* was 'magnificent'. '. . . Of this class of explorers none have accomplished so much or gained so great a distinction as Mr Henry Schliemann. No other has brought to this peculiar work such a rare combination of talents and qualifications.' *The Edinburgh Review* spoke of the 'Galahad of this Trojan quest'.

Other papers, however, took a sterner line. *The Pall Mall Gazette* mocked what it called the 'omnium gatherum' of the nine contributors, comparing them to the fashionable gatherings of a London society hostess called Rosie MacKenzie. Schliemann was accused of being unscholarly and muddled, of having a verbose style, of being 'chaotic'. A few old enemies rallied, turning in trenchant and dismissive attacks, for the most part from the safety of anonymity. Schliemann was once again in a fury, and begged Sayce to 'confound the false statements' of one of his 'libellers', warning him, as he had once warned Virchow, that if he failed to do so, 'then I cease to be your friend'. Sayce was clearly a sensible and kindly man, and refused to take offence. Urging Schliemann to show restraint, he set about identifying one of the more provocative critics, the Scottish Greek scholar R.C.Jebb, and chastized him severely in the pages of *The Academy* for neither bothering to learn the 'elementary principles of archaeological science' nor taking the trouble to visit Hissarlik himself.

At the end of the day, most critics were now inclined to concede that the site of Hissarlik was indeed the right site for Troy – assuming that a Troy and a Trojan war had existed – and that Schliemann, if nothing else, had made a serious contribution to prehistoric archaeology. What puzzled some of them, however, was why Schliemann had chosen *Ilios* as the place to publish a 67-page autobiographical memoir, touching on his forlorn past, his skills as a businessman, and his lifelong passion for antiquity. Scholarly books were not usually so personal, though Schliemann had always introduced a personal note into his writings. Virchow had done his best to persuade him to leave all the autobiographical material out, but had failed. 'It is not from any feeling of vanity', Schliemann justified his decision to a friend, 'but from a desire to show how the . . . pickaxe and spade for the excavation of Troy and the Royal sepulchres of Mycenae were both forged and sharpened in the little village of Mecklenburg ...' He wanted the world to know how 'in the autumn of my life', he had been able to realize the 'gigantic projects I formed when I was a poor little boy'. The myth had taken shape; had Schliemann now begun to believe in it himself? On his many journeys, lecturing to learned societies and committees, old memories, in the spirit of small-town-boy-made-good, were seldom omitted for long.

At the end of the autobiographical fragment comes a curious financial note, a formal answer to the charges that he was bankrupting his family with his extravagance. Explaining his business interests, Schliemann reported that he still had a yearly income of £4000 from the rents of four houses in Paris, as well as another £6000 from other sources. He put his expenditure at £5000 – leaving £5000 to be added each year to his capital – in current money £200,000. There is something both engaging and touching in his choice of the most improbable places in which to justify and present himself in the most admirable light. The treasure from Troy, he added sanctimoniously, would thus never be sold: as 'I love and worship science for its own sake, I shall never make a traffic of it'. Books seemed to him good places in which to deliver messages. And there were, after all, readers ready to believe and to admire: 'Although we part from Dr Schliemann's book with indifference,' noted *The Spectator*, 'we part from Dr Schliemann himself with no feeling but that of admiration.'

It was left to *The Academy* to have the final word: 'There was a time when to indulge in hostile cricitism of Dr Schliemann, his works and ways, was to incur odium. Now it has become a habit – so much so, that there appears to be something almost heroic in the author of this colossal piece of literary toil coming forward and offering it to a fairly heedless world.' The British like underdogs.

During their honeymoon in Italy, Schliemann had promised that one day he would build Sophia a mansion of her own in Athens, looking out over the sea. It was not until 1878, ten years later, that he at last considered the moment had come to start building; but the house that went up was on a scale and of a grandeur that even he, in his days as a prosperous merchant, could not have imagined. It was the palace of a dreamer; a celebration of Homer and his epic poems; a self-monument to the man who discovered Troy.

After the Great Powers had imposed on Greece a German king, the young Prince Otto of Bavaria, in 1833, efforts were quickly made to give the new Hellenic capital of Athens a European look. In the years that followed, despite the political turmoils that were to overthrow Otto and replace him with another young prince, the eighteen-year-old son of the heir to the Danish throne, and despite a more or less permanently unsettled state, Athens continued to grow and to prosper. In 1833, fighting between Greeks and Turks had reduced the devastated city to a population of barely 4000; by the late 1870s it was nearing 80,000, but travellers observed that the well-built houses of the rich, 'rather German in appearance', continued to vie for space with miserable dwellings carved out of the ruins. Half-buried columns and huge fragments of early Greek walls caused at least one visitor to remark: 'It may be considered a heroic act to wander through Athens on four wheels; every street is filled with stones and building materials, while the streets are so narrow that it is impossible to turn'.

Most of the new houses followed the same basic plan: a neo-classical façade, with a base in marble or stone, and marble staircase, balconies, and highly decorated balustrades. The rich Athenians, at least, lived well.

In the late autumn of 1878, while Schliemann was launching his second Trojan campaign in the Dardanelles, builders started work on a plot of land he had bought on University Street, a wide, new avenue at the foot of Mount Lycabettus. Though not far from Syntagma Square, where cosmopolitan Athenians and foreign visitors came to stroll every evening, it was quiet and central. Having written off to a friend in Indianapolis for designs of American houses he had particularly admired, Schliemann had put the project into the hands of the Austrian architect, Ernst Ziller, though Ziller was there more to oversee than to design: as with most aspects of life, Schliemann knew precisely what he wanted. His mansion had long been clear in his mind.

On his return from Troy, he set about drawing up the final specifications. The house was to be of both stone and marble, three storeys high, with rooms on the ground floor in which to exhibit his growing archaeological collection, a great hall, a formal dining-room, several sitting-rooms and bathrooms. His library and study were to be on the second floor, together with the bedrooms and dressing-rooms. All three storeys, and every room, including the kitchens, were to have mosaic floors, laid by two Italian craftsmen who were brought from Livorno with their families. Devoting much the same intensity to his mansion as to his excavations, Schliemann chose the wood for the doors, selected the marble and arranged for it to be quarried, drew up lists and schedules and kept the accounts. Furniture was ordered from Vienna, chandeliers from Paris. Bathroom fixtures, kitchen equipment, even the furniture for what became known as Sophia's 'boudoir' were picked out by him, with an eye more to the functional than to the pleasing. How far Sophia was ever consulted is not known, but no trace of her hand in anything emerges from the detailed bills and instructions found among Schliemann's papers in Athens. It is sometimes as if she never existed.

Schliemann, who combined a curious mixture of extravagance and frugality, set no budget for the new house. Day by day, it grew, more sumptuous and more extraordinary. From the street, marble staircases curved up towards an open balcony, with French windows opening on to an immense hall. When the basic structure was at last finished, a team of Bavarian artists arrived to paint both walls and ceilings with murals, some from sketches drawn by Schliemann himself, others of objects and patterns from his Troy excavations. A frieze, in the style of Pompeii which he had so much admired during his travels in Italy, showed figures digging at Mycenae and at Troy, Schliemann himself wearing black horn-rimmed spectacles and the two-year-old Agamemnon sitting on a rock. In the years to come, as Schliemann continued to make more finds, so paintings of them were added to the decorations on the walls. The ceilings, for the most part, were pale, in pastel colours; the walls bright, even gaudy. The swastika featured prominently among the classical designs on the bronze and iron gates and railings, as well as on the balconies and fences. In the late 1870s, University Street was still relatively empty. Schliemann had been able to buy several acres of land, and this was now laid out by Italian landscape gardeners: there was a lawn, a grove of citrus trees and banks of flowering shrubs, kept watered by a windmill pump. Schliemann, who had grown interested in plants when Virchow visited the Troad, decided to introduce some eucalyptus trees to Athens after learning that they possessed healing properties; he gave orders that pigeons and hens should be kept, but not eaten. There was also a cat.

Iliou Melathron, the house of Ilium, as Schliemann named his mansion, was christened by a ball on 14 February 1880. The guests and their carriages were greeted at the gates by Bellerophon (grandfather of Homer's hero Glaucus, killer of the Chimera, a fire-breathing monster 'lion in front, serpent behind, goat in the middle'), and Telamon (King of Salamis and father to Ajax), for Schliemann had thought to provide his servants with classical names. The ball was judged a social success, but did not end without an incident which, if true, softens somewhat the conventional view of a humourless Schliemann. The following morning, a messenger arrived from the Greek Council of Ministers. On the roof of Iliou Melathron had been placed a row of naked classical statues; the messenger brought a request that they be removed. Schliemann might well have fallen into one of his customary rages; instead, he laughed. He and Sophia summoned up as many seamstresses as they could find, and when dawn broke next day the passing Athenians were amazed to see that the naked statues were now fully clothed. Crowds gathered. Schliemann let it be known that the garish coverings were there by order of the Ministers. There was much laughter. Before long, a second messenger arrived, begging Schliemann to undress his statues.

Iliou Melathron was spartan, in appearance as in regime. There were no curtains and no comfortable chairs, the ancient Greeks having furnished their houses simply, though when Sophia later gave him a rocking chair, Schliemann had it placed in the garden and could sometimes be seen dozing in it after lunch. Meals were plain – a lot of fruit and fish – and because he was always in a hurry, the food had to be ready on the table when he appeared. On occasion, a business acquaintance, agent or antique dealer could be seen hovering in a corner of the dining-room, with Schliemann addressing him over his shoulder from where he sat at table. Since he intended his children to grow up fluent in at least some of his many languages, each meal was conducted in a different one, decided before they began to eat. If ever they forgot and slipped back into Greek, they were fined and had to put a coin in a box kept for that purpose in the middle of the table, which was opened from time to time and the money shared out.

From the very first days at Iliou Melathron, Schliemann imposed a routine on the household. It was he, not Sophia, who gave the orders. Inflexible as a young man, he remained inflexible. All messages that arrived at the house for him had to be delivered in classical Greek, for he had retained his great love for the language and intended to keep working at it until he died. Among his papers in Athens are pages in ancient Greek translated from the *Arabian Nights*, copied out in his neat, steady hand. Every hour of the day had its programme. He rose at three in summer, five in winter and unless the weather was unusually bad, rode the three miles to the sea to swim, sometimes taking Andromache or Sophia with him. For the rest of her life, Andromache would tell the story of being woken before dawn to go for these swims, and recount how her father was so fanatical about the children's health that he took a thermometer to the church for Agamemnon's christening, in order to test the temperature of the holy water, despite the fury of the priest. After his swim, Schliemann retired to spend the morning in his study – outside, on the wall, had been engraved Pythagoras's words : 'All who do not study geometry, remain outside' – a room full from floor to ceiling with books, except for a few bare patches of wall on which he had hung fading views of Indianapolis and New York. Stock Exchange prices arrived each morning from Paris, London and Berlin.

Schliemann answered all his letters himself, standing at a high desk as he had in his merchant days, and still doing calculations in Dutch. However busy he was, he insisted on finding time to read and reread the *Iliad*, of which by now he had an enormous collection of copies, both leather-bound and the Tauchnitz paperback editions, which he took with him on his travels and annotated in pencil. Sayce, on a visit to Athens, remarked not only on the excellence of Schliemann's classical library, but on the phenomenal memory Schliemann himself had of its contents. In his memoirs, Sayce tells the story of one of the regular Friday night gatherings at the American School, during which disagreement broke out over a passage of Lucian's *Dialogues*. The professor presiding over the meeting asked one of the students to fetch a copy of Lucian. 'Where-upon Schliemann,' wrote Sayce later, 'who had been sitting silently in a corner of the room, remarked : "I do not think it is necessary that Mr X should trouble himself ; I think I remember the passage". He was right : he could recall it perfectly and at length.'

The Schleimanns were hospitable, on an ever grander and more inter-national scale, and travellers frequently arrived bearing letters of intro-duction from friends and classical scholars all over the world. It was always Schliemann who replied, pressing them to come for a meal, and very seldom were the answers not written, without mistakes, in the language of the visitor's native country. He was a good host, and a good listener, but he would rarely discuss his own work. There is an odd story, left by Lewis Farnell, a Fellow of Exeter College, who lunched with the Schliemanns while visiting Athens. Farnell, who was impressed by Schliemann, observed that he was a 'blend of the rich German bourgeois and the dreamer', dismissed his fellow guests as 'mainly parasitical', and then made a curious remark. 'Agamemnon,' he noted, 'was a bright boy with a Greek profile that did not look altogether natural ; and we were told that it was the result of much twisting and manipulation of his infant-features.' Schliemann was indeed obsessed by all things Greek and classical ; but that he pummelled his son's face to make him have a Greek profile is fanciful to an absurd degree. There was something about

Schliemann that always seemed to prompt this kind of malice.

For all the guests, and all their scepticism, Schliemann was a fond father, and spent what time he could with his children while in Athens, making it a rule never to work later than six in the evening. 'His discoveries were his children,' remarked one visitor, and 'he was ready to fight for them as a lioness fights for her young'. Their education was of constant – and sometimes rather overbearing – concern to him. Language, for example, had to be used economically and he soon instituted a custom whereby unnecessary words were dropped: if a child called down from upstairs, saying 'Please come upstairs', he was told to drop the 'upstairs' on the grounds that it was redundant. Meals were punctual; lights, everywhere in the vast house, had to be out by ten o'clock. When he was away, Sophia and the children could be found having picnics in the corner of one of the enormous formal rooms, preferring the floor and rugs to the chilliness of the dining-room table, the meals brought to them in hampers from the kitchens. The image is an endearing one, if a little sad. It was all very splendid; but it was not cosy.

If anything, Schliemann had grown more spartan and self-disciplined over the years. Not long after the move, he developed a cyst on one lip; he had it cut out without anaesthetic. For someone so continuously tormented by earaches, he was singularly uncomplaining. He also grew neater and more precise. Arriving in Iliou Melathron, he had decided that only his second-best clothes could be entrusted to an Athenian washerwoman; his best linen and silk were now sent to be washed in London, Schliemann having made what he considered a very good deal with an English laundry. He calculated that he sent off 218 shirts each year.

Sophia was now twenty-eight. Schliemann was almost sixty, a slight figure with a large head, thinning hair and a clipped voice. He took snuff, kept a silk handkerchief in his pocket, and wore a number of different, elegant, hats. For the year 1879, his accounts say that he spent £13 on his London hatter. Asked to give his favourite colour, he would reply blue, the colour of the indigo which had made his fortune. Amelia Edwards, author of *A Thousand Miles up the Nile*, has left a brief portrait of the Schliemanns from a visit she paid to Athens. Dr Schliemann, she wrote in *The Graphic*, was a 'man of middle height and middle age, stoutly and strongly built, with a massive German head, capacious brain-case, square jaws, and brilliant dark eyes'. Though she was not introduced to Sophia, she caught a glimpse of her strolling in the garden, dressed in a long white morning gown, 'a tall, fine woman, pale of complexion, with dark eyes and hair, and a stately bearing'. Schliemann's hunch had been right. It had not taken very long to turn her from a Greek schoolgirl into a woman of considerable authority.

Their marriage was a good one, in spite of Schliemann's many absences. When apart, they often wrote to each other every day, and Schliemann's letters are full of endearments. 'I burn four candles,' he told Sophia, 'but the room is still dark, whereas your eyes would light it up. Life without you is unbearable.' He worried about her health, bullied her about her education, and missed her when he was away. For her part, she was always anxious about his ears, and soothing when he was attacked by his critics. Wherever he was, Schliemann continued to rule the household. 'Make the nurse look four times every night to see if Agamemnon is properly covered,' he instructed her by letter during a trip to Brindisi.

Like Sophia, the children had to be continuously acquiring knowledge. Expeditions to museums and sites were obligatory, and they were often very long and drawn out. But as a father, Schliemann was not without magic. Emil Ludwig tells a story about Andromache, then aged eight. The little girl asked her father what the word 'eternity' meant. 'Imagine, Andromache,' Schliemann is said to have replied, 'a block of marble as long as from here to the Piraeus, and that once every thousand years a piece of silk is drawn along it. By the time the marble has been chafed through, that is eternity.'

Schliemann intended to make the most of his Trojan treasure. He knew it to be a valuable card in the world stakes of archaeological respectability, and he was going to play it very carefully indeed. There was nothing for him to gain from Agamemnon's mask and the other Mycenaean finds – over which squabbles had already broken out, the town of Nauplion claiming that they should go there and not to Athens – but the Troy gold was definitely his. In *Ilios*, he had made a most Delphic utterance : the treasure, he had announced, would go to 'the nation I love and esteem most'. The question was : which country was that ?

It was perfectly true that Virchow, during their walks in the Troad, had been persuasive. Germany was, after all, Schliemann's native country and there was something infinitely pleasing in the idea of what the gift, and any ensuing recognition, would do to his many German rivals and detractors. How very satisfactory to be able to silence one of the most outspoken of them, Ernst Bötticher, who had already publicly dismissed the Trojan collection by saying that it was far too insignificant to take up precious space in the German state museum. But the Germans had never done much for him, except to deride his work, as Schliemann explained to a Berlin friend : 'If I leave it in my will to a German city, it can never be Berlin, for I have never had a single word of appreciation from there and have always been treated with the most odious hostility.' There was of course the Louvre in France, where he still owned property, and England, though the British had been tiresomely evasive when he offered to sell the treasure to the British Museum, and even Russia, where he had been toying with the idea of putting on an exhibition in the Hermitage in St Petersburg.

Sophia was pressing hard for him to present the treasure to Greece, possibly as a gesture of defiance since she apparently felt slighted at being ignored by the court and not invited to royal functions after the Schliemanns had been accepted everywhere else as celebrities. Even the Americans might have been contenders for the treasure, had they responded differently when, in March 1878, Schliemann had let it be known that he would like to be made US Consul for Athens or the Piraeus, 'and would of course amply reward the Smithsonian Hall in Washington by gifts of antiquities for the honor the govt. might bestow upon me by their nomination'. The matter reached the State Department, but Schliemann heard no more.

As the months went by, and the debates and secret negotiations went on, the question of where the treasure should go slowly resolved itself. While writing *Ilios*, Schliemann had returned in his mind to his boyhood in Ankershagen, and he now discovered a lost fondness for his youth. Though he was not to revisit his home village for another few years, he did get in touch with a number of people he had known as a boy, making much of his rise to fame in the world, and his ability now, should he want to do so, to confer favours on those who needed them. Even Minna Meincke, his childhood love, who had married before he had the chance to return to claim her, was written to with a burst of sentimental nostalgia. Evidently Minna, who was now a stout and provincial widow in her late fifties, was not all that keen to have her story included in Schliemann's reminiscences, though she appears to have given in after he wrote her a brisk and characteristic letter : Minna's very name would be forever famous not only in Germany, he told her, but wherever *Ilios* was read: 'All I have written can only redound to your credit. What other German women have been immortalized in similar fashion ?'

Virchow had also played his cards well. Honorary membership of the German Anthropological Society, which had come at exactly the right moment, pleased Schliemann greatly, particularly after the Crown Prince attended a lecture he gave in Berlin in the summer of 1880. And even his health now conspired to draw him back to Germany, for his attempts to relieve his constant earaches repeatedly drove him to take cures at the famous German spas.

Just the same, Schliemann wanted something tangible in return for the Trojan gold. He was not interested in money, but honours were different; and these he coveted almost above all things. Virchow did his best, acting as intermediary with the German government, while trying to rein in Schliemann's more grandiose fantasies. It was a time-consuming process. The director of Berlin's museums, Richard Schöne, the Prussian Minister of Education, Herr Puttkamer, the Hereditary Prince of Saxe-Meiningen, even Bismarck, were all brought in to play their parts; at last Schliemann capitulated. The cost to Germany was not insignificant: the treasure was to be placed under Prussian administration and to be unpacked and arranged by Schliemann himself; it was to be exhibited in a special wing of the new ethnological museum, bearing Schliemann's name in large gold letters; Schliemann was to be made an honorary citizen of Berlin – an honour so far bestowed only on Bismarck and Field Marshal Helmuth von Moltke, for their victories in the Franco-Prussian War. More difficult to negotiate were the Prussian order *Pour le Mérite*, a medal for his 'longtime assistant', Sophia, and membership of the Prussian Academy of the Sciences in Berlin, of which not even Virchow was a member. 'You did not give your collection to Berlin for the sake of receiving decorations,' wrote Virchow somewhat sharply to the ever hungry Schliemann.

In the winter of 1880, the matter was at last settled. The Trojan gold was to go to 'the German people in perpetual possession and inalienable custody'. To Max Müller, Schliemann now wrote: 'The German people have libelled me for seven years, but now they have come round and my *Ilios* is highly appreciated by them. Besides, in getting old, my attachment for my mother country *increases* … and I prefer to present the dearest jewels I have to my libellers because they are my countrymen.' Schliemann left Athens for London to start packing the 4300 items still on exhibition in the South Kensington Museum into forty large cases, which he closed with his own personal seal. They reached Berlin in January and, on Schliemann's specific orders, were delivered straight to the vaults of a bank. He was not sorry to be removing the exhibits from London, since he considered that the British curators had made a poor job of cataloguing and labelling the various items, and in any case, what more agreeable than to receive a personal letter from the Emperor Wilhelm I, thanking him for his 'patriotic gift', a testimony to his attachment 'to the fatherland, and a collection of the greatest importance to science'?

It is worth remembering the magnificence of the Trojan collection: terracotta vases, urns, coins, medals, knives, lances, copper battleaxes, figurines with owls' faces, the red terracotta hippopotamus, jugs, and, of course, the famous treasure – the huge silver vase, cups in gold, silver, electrum and bronze, many thousands of small gold rings, eardrops, buttons and needles, a gold headband, gold bracelets and the gold diadems, one of which alone was made of 16,000 pieces of gold threaded on to gold wire. There was nothing quite like it anywhere in the world.

Early in July 1881, the Schliemanns travelled to Berlin and installed themselves in a suite in the Tiergarten Hotel. Imperial Berlin, in the 1880s, was very splendid. On the seventh at one o'clock, a magnificent ceremony was held at which the Mayor of Berlin, Herr Forckenbeck, read out a proclamation making the former grocer's apprentice from Mecklenburg an honorary citizen of the Imperial capital, the Reichshauptstadt, Berlin: Schliemann, he declared, 'by his combination of practical activity with idealism' had become a 'pattern for all German citizens.' Sophia was escorted by Prince Wilhelm, the future Emperor. That evening, a banquet in honour of the new citizens was held in the Rathaus, the city hall, attended by several representatives of the German nobility, many esteemed German academics, and Schliemann's sisters. The Royal Berlin orchestra played the March from *Tannhäuser*. At the close of the evening, messages of congratulations from the Kaiser, the Crown Prince and Bismarck were read out. Schliemann, later, was to write of the ceremony that he felt 'uncertain of fact, time and sequence, because my very soul is elevated'. But he was not yet finished, either with archaeology, or with honours. That glorious day, he noted was not an end, but a 'semi-colon of a paragraph in my life'.

13

A CIVILIZATION
AT PLAY

Schliemann's days as an archaeologist were far from over. Apart from anything else he wanted – needed – to find evidence confirming his theory that the Mycenaeans had spread their civilization widely throughout Greece. Obtaining, with no trouble, permission to carry on with his excavations in Greece, he turned to a ruined site in Boeotia, north of Thebes, called Orchomenos, standing on a bleak clifftop, ringed by high mountains. Homer had called it a 'mighty' city, 'rich in gold', a description he had given otherwise only to Troy and Mycenae. Pausanias, who had passed by Orchomenos on his travels, described it as 'famous and glorious as any city in Greece', and wrote of two springs, Lethe (forgetfulness), and Mnemosyne (remembrance), that flowed from the rocks into the river in the gorge. This time Schliemann took with him not only Sophia, the two children and a nursemaid, but his English friend A.H.Sayce, and Ernst Ziller, the Austrian architect of Iliou Melathron, as well as a member of the Greek Archaeological Society. Workmen were recruited, in Schliemann's usual high number, and soon immense trenches had been sunk in and around the ancient citadel and its Cyclopean walls.

An early visitor to the site was Arthur Evans, whose father had known Schliemann, and who had been much intrigued by the Trojan exhibits at the South Kensington Museum. In appearance, the two archaeologists were somewhat alike : Evans was also small, wiry, impeccably and formally dressed on the hottest of days. Both men were possessed of enormous vigour and stamina, and, at some point in their lives, rich enough to embark on a life of excavations without public support. But Evans, who came from a secure intellectual background, was plagued by none of Schliemann's agonizing self-doubt. At first, his sister Joan was later to write, Evans 'laughed a little at the odd little man', but as he began to take in what Schliemann was uncovering, a 'bright new world' was revealed to him, which was to change his life. From this point on, the Greek Bronze Age became his obsession. 'I have myself an almost uncanny memory of the spare, slightly built man,' Evans himself was to write, many years afterwards, 'of sallow complexion and somewhat darkly clad, wearing spectacles of foreign make, through which – so the fancy took me – he had looked deep into the ground.'

This time, the famous Schliemann luck settled on Sophia, who had been sent to oversee the excavation of the treasury, identified by Pausanias as that of the legendary King Minyas. It looked from the outside very like the treasury of Atreus at Mycenae. It was here, in a small side chamber, that Sophia suddenly caught sight of some pieces of green limestone, which turned out to be fragments belonging to the ceiling that had since collapsed. When these were pieced together, one by one, a very laborious process, they turned into a marvellous geometric pattern of spirals, rosettes and leaves. Sayce observed that they reminded him of Assyrian sculptured ornaments, Ziller that they looked very like Oriental carpets. Later, Orchomenos's fine ceiling, like the friezes at Mycenae and Tiryns, came to be regarded as one of the high points of Mycenaean artistry. Orchomenos yielded no gold or treasure, but it did supply Schliemann with more pottery, mostly in the form of grey polished pieces. He judged these to be unique, not having come across them before, and called them 'grey Minyan ware'; but they were to turn up later in excavations all over Greece and parts of Asia Minor, as well as in Troy itself. Orchomenos provided another link in Schliemann's Mycenaean age; but this time he published no book, only a report, and closed the excavation down after two brief digs.

Sophia's work at Orchomenos was one of her main contributions to Schliemann's archaeology. Despite his continuing efforts to portray her everywhere as his 'full partner', Sophia had in fact spent very little time at Troy, not much at Mycenae and none at all at Tiryns. Their letters to one another when apart – his written in French, English, Italian, German or Greek, hers mainly in Greek or German – talk of family matters, not archaeology. Schliemann, while remaining choleric in public, had become less irascible at home, while Sophia's basically sensible nature was by now less buffeted by his outbursts. Her tone, when she wrote, was calm, and very loving. The doubts and insecurities of the early years had vanished, even if she continued to reproach him. 'My darling, what sort of life is this?' she wrote during one of his many absences from Athens. 'Always apart? Am I to go on writing to you forever, and are we to be apart forever? ... Don't you think that it would be nice if you were to live near your poor wife, who idolises you, who knows married life only in dreams?' If biographers have tended to give Sophia only a shadowy role in his life, it is because, compared to Schliemann's intensity and his tormented need to succeed, she appears staid and for the most part unruffled.

It was at this moment that possibly the most crucial person in Schliemann's entire archaelogical career entered his life. He was a twenty-seven-year-old German architect called Wilhelm Dörpfeld, who had been working with the German team at Olympia. Virchow and Burnouf had convinced Schliemann that the only way to understand a site properly was to bring the training and knowledge of experts to bear on it; and, at Samothrace, Alexander Conze had for some years now been proving the value of architectural grounding. However, Dörpfeld was not just an architect, but a fine draftsman, and he possessed unusual powers of observation. The two men could scarcely have been more different: where Schliemann was imaginative, creative and impatient, with a constant need for approval and respect, Dörpfeld was phlegmatic, confident and highly conservative. While Schliemann was cosmopolitan and a linguist, tied to no nationality and no religion, Dörpfeld was a believer and spoke only German with any fluency. While Schliemann played with the truth, Dörpfeld held it in high regard. Almost the only thing the two men shared was a profound trust in Homer, yet Dörpfeld unquestionably felt both affection and loyalty towards his older mentor. The partnership they formed was to last until Schliemann's death, and in some ways beyond. Dörpfeld, it would soon be said, was Schliemann's greatest discovery.

Their collaboration began tentatively. Dörpfeld agreed to do a drawing of the Orchomenos ceiling, Schliemann having been convinced by critics that drawings were still clearer and better than photographs to illustrate books. After this, Schliemann approached Dörpfeld to join the new season he was planning at Troy. At first, Dörpfeld refused, since all Schliemann was offering was a short contract; having just married, he wanted a secure job. A different man, an Austrian architect called Joseph Höfler, was taken on instead. But then Dörpfeld learned that he had been appointed to the German Archaeological Institute in Athens – of which he later became director – which allowed him to take on temporary positions. He arrived to join the others in the Troad in March 1882, at a salary of £35 a month. The price was high; but Schliemann would never regret his new assistant.

Firmans to dig at Troy continued to plague Schliemann. Whatever the promises, however clear the understandings, every visit to Hissarlik led to new battles and new subterfuges. Once again, the Turkish authorities were vacillating about Schliemann's proposed campaign; once again, Schliemann turned to friends and colleagues for help. By now, he seldom wasted much time on junior officials. His world was firmly international, his players the leading men of the day. If mere scholars failed, he turned to Consuls and Ambassadors; if they failed, he called in Crown Princes and statesmen. His new-found attachment to Germany made him appeal first to the Germans, hoping to stir up their sense of pride when he pointed out to them that while British archaeologists were given free rein all over Mesopotamia, German archaeologists still had trouble securing even limited access to one small corner of Turkey.

Over the years, Schliemann's interests had become more political; fame had given him a taste for intrigue. When the German diplomats posted to Constantinople failed to secure his *firman*, he called for them to be replaced. He also announced to the world that he was no longer in agreement with Gladstone's policies, and that his real hero was Bismarck. Defying Virchow, who was locked into the liberal opposition to Bismarck, Schliemann remarked that he, personally, was all for imperial conquest. 'Since the fatherland now once again recognizes me,' he wrote to his new champion, 'I can henceforth only turn to the German legation in Constantinople.' Since much of this badgering involved playing off different statesmen and different countries against each other, it led, not surprisingly, to some ill-feeling, particularly as Schliemann's notions grew more grandiose by the hour. Why not make some kind of deal and return Alsace-Lorraine to the French? he asked Virchow. To others, he complained openly about the inefficiency of the German foreign office.

At last, in January 1882, the new *firman* arrived; but it was not the one Schliemann wanted. It confined him to the hill of Hissarlik, and did not, as he had requested, extend to the Troad at large, which he had been exploring on a private visit of his own. Criss-crossing the plain on a horse for two weeks, he had been searching for more evidence to add to his theory that Homer knew not just about Troy, but about the area surrounding it as well, and that the poet would be able to lead him to other sites. For Schliemann, despite his brave words to the contrary, was still not altogether happy about Troy, and remained haunted by the discrepancies between the poems and the finds. Schliemann's Troy, he had to admit, did not really match the glories of Homer's Troy. And if Homer had invented his Troy, then who was to say that he had not invented the whole of the *Iliad* ? Since Schliemann was still unprepared to concede publicly that Homer's account was anything other than the truth, more evidence had to be produced. The flaw lay not in the theory, but in the excavations. It was a question of more, deeper, better work. Perhaps Troy was really only a citadel after all, and the city itself had extended beyond the walls ? To prove this, he needed to go far outside the limits of the *firman*.

And so he battled on : more cajoling, more threats. It was only after the excavations had actually begun in March that the right *firman* at last came through. Once again, the campaign was to be on an enormous scale, and hugely ambitious ; and this time, it had a truly international flavour. Apart from his various Greek and Turkish valets, cooks, water-carriers and foremen, there was the German Dörpfeld and the Austrian Höfler, a Polish engineer and a Greek photographer – Schliemann's 'General Staff' as they were sometimes called – as well as two Turkish overseers. To the second of these, a man called Beder Eddin Effendi, Schliemann took an instant loathing. Beder Eddin, he would say, was arrogant, conceited and extremely ignorant ; in fact, he had never before been sent such a 'monster of a delegate'. There were also the many workmen, some Greek, some Turkish and some Levantine Jews. Since a number of 'opulent' men had recently been carried off into the mountains and ransomed by brigands, Schliemann chose eleven bodyguards from the 'strongest and most trustworthy Turks of the Dardanelles', though he was soon furious to find that they had been suborned as spies by Beder Eddin.

The excavation site itself was in good order, Schliemann having left watchmen to guard over the buildings and the equipment in his absence. Apart from putting new waterproof felt over the barrack roof, and moving some of the huts a bit further apart from each other, to lessen the risk of fire, there was little to do. Digging began immediately.

The first days were unpleasant. The agreeable south wind that had greeted their arrival was replaced by a strong, cold, north wind, which turned every few days into a gale, and blew dust relentlessly into the workmen's eyes. Since very few of them owned spectacles to keep the dust out, most were forced to swathe their heads in shawls, reminding Schliemann of mourners at an Italian funeral. The wind blew, without interruption, for fifty-eight days; the cold was such that the snow on Mount Ida would not melt, and the plain produced very few of the brilliant yellow and white wildflowers that had made the Troad so magical in previous years. However, the cold and the absence of rain did keep the frogs at bay, and Schliemann's nights were no longer tormented by their incessant croaking; and, in the middle of March, first the cranes, then the storks, arrived.

This excavation was going to be different. Schliemann had undertaken to re-examine the whole site, going down layer by layer, studying everything he came across with extreme care, including all things Hellenistic or Roman, as well as to sift through the debris so casually thrown away on his earlier digs. Dörpfeld and Höfler were precise, trained, professionals and their expertise was to mark the entire five-month campaign; and it was to transform all previous knowledge of the site.

Out of the chaos of earlier inchoate digging there emerged a new structure and a new series of layers. Troy I, it now began to seem clear, had been succeeded by a second, larger, city, which had used Hissarlik merely as an acropolis and for its grander buildings, and which itself had a lower town. Schliemann, never a man to wait for confirmation, announced that here, at last, was a Troy worthy of Homer. This time, the evidence produced by his able and considerably more cautious assistants confirmed his words. As they dug, and as they sorted through the chaos and began to reassign new roles to buildings, and join walls up in different ways, so a detailed picture of a prehistoric palace fortress began to emerge, one with roomy buildings and vast ramparts. Measurements were taken; plans made; maps drawn up. Schliemann's palace, the one he had so readily labelled Priam's, but whose paltriness continued to haunt him, was found to cover an older and larger building, standing close to where the treasures had been found. A collection of three different buildings – part of them lost through Schliemann's earlier destructiveness – was seen to fit well with Homer's description of Priam's palace. Then the circuit wall was traced far beyond its earlier span, and two new gates came to light. Dörpfeld proposed a new sequence of strata which made the large second city, Troy II, Homer's city. This was not, of course, the first time Troy II had been so named, for Schliemann himself had identified it as Homer's city, changing his mind for a while later and labelling Troy III as the right one. These switches, and the consequent reassignment of the treasure and the burnt debris up and down the strata, say something about how unsure Schliemann, who went on sounding confident in public, continued to be of what he was actually uncovering.

The 1882 campaign turned up some double-handled goblets which Schliemann, with the ebullience with which he often reported his better finds, and which contrasted so glaringly with the dry tones of his German colleagues, estimated would take ten bottles of Bordeaux wine each. More copper and bronze bracelets, and more battleaxes appeared, but what pleased him most was a figurine with an owl's head, its beak protruding between round eyes.

Meanwhile, in and around the Troad, Schliemann and his team started to examine the mounds or tumuli which local history held were the burial places of the Homeric heroes. Though Schliemann himself had long been rather sceptical, he now uncovered items of the same kind as at his earliest Trojan settlement, and came to believe that he had identified the tomb of Achilles himself, some 250 yards from the Hellespont, just as Homer had described it : 'a great and goodly tomb on a jutting headland upon the wide Hellespont, that it might be visible far off from the sea, to men who now are, and to those that shall hereafter be born.' He thought he had found Patroclus's tomb too, not far away.

The Turks did not like these forays into the plain of Troy. They began to suspect that the foreign archaeologists, measuring and mapping their way among the marshes and the rivers, were in fact spies, intent on charting Turkish fortifications along the coast. Word arrived that all excavating was to stop, and when Schliemann demurred, Beder Eddin threatened to have him and his companions chained and sent to Constantinople as prisoners. Only later did the new German Ambassador to the Sublime Porte, Count J.M.von Radowitz, manage to have the ban lifted, and it was not until November, after the excavations had been closed down for the winter, that Dörpfeld was able to draw the ground and floor plans he needed, in the middle of the heavy rains that had settled on the Troad.

By then Schliemann was in Marienbad recovering from malaria, which strong doses of quinine, usually effective, this time seemed slow to cure. As he took the waters and consulted doctors, he planned his new book. *Troja : Results of the Latest Researches and Discoveries on the Site of Homer's Troy* was written in English, but this time Schliemann translated it into German himself. *Troja* was dedicated to the Crown Princess Victoria of Germany and the American edition included a lofty inscription : 'To all who are searching for the light thrown on history by the science of archaeology'. A bound copy went off to the King of Greece.

Like *Ilios*, the book contained a number of appendices. Sayce, in a fulsome preface, spoke of Dr Schliemann's skill, energy, perseverance, enthusiasm, devotion, and of his phenomenal grasp of languages and ancient Greek literature, and asked sternly: 'Why is it that Dr Schliemann's example has not been followed by some of the rich men of whom Europe is full ? Why cannot they spare for science a little of the wealth that is now lavished upon the breeding of racers or the maintenance of a dog kennel ?' Reviews were on the whole admiring, the *Quarterly Review* concluding that 'There was a Troy, and Dr Schliemann has found it. The new ten years' siege is finished by a victory won, not by hollow stratagem, but by unwearied labour in the trenches, animated by high enthusiasm, directed by signal skill, and illustrated by wide and varied learning.' *The Times* declared that anyone who continued to doubt that Hissarlik was the site of Troy should be prepared 'either to suggest a better or to abandon the research as hopeless'. The newspaper was now scathing about those who continued to see Homer as pure fiction. 'It may be time then for the enthusiastic Homeric reader, who cares a great deal about poetry, and nothing at all about antiquities, to cry out that he is hurt ...' The Victorians could be vitriolic when censorious; but their flattery was no less extravagant.

But had Schliemann really found Homer's Troy ? Yet again, his own published words are confident. In a remote antiquity, he declared, in the plain of Troy, had stood a large city, destroyed by a fearful catastrophe. It had an acropolis, temples and some other large buildings, on the top of the hill of Hissarlik; and its lower city reached out east, south and west. In all, it answered perfectly to the 'Homeric description of the site of *sacred Ilios*'.

His work at Troy, Schliemann announced, was now finally over. He had given ten years of his life to it. 'How many tens of years a new controversy may range around it, I leave to the critics; *that* is their work; *mine* is done ...' Once again, some of this at least was bravado. He was not as certain as he sounded.

The year 1883 was to have been a period of rest. Instead, Schliemann fiddled with proofs and foreign translations, spent five weeks in Ankershagen, where he rented his old family home back from the current pastor, in exchange for a generous sum, renewing his friendship with the now plump and matronly Minna Meincke in her black silk widow's dress, and parading his successes to those who remained alive from his modest past life. In June, he travelled to Oxford to receive an honorary doctorate, in the gratifying company of the King of the Netherlands. He took a cure in Hesse; visited Paris; went to look for the burial grounds of Leonidas's three hundred Spartans, felled in 480 BC at Thermopylae, but was soon obliged to send a telegram saying 'unauffindbar' – untraceable – to Virchow, to whom he had promised half of the skeletons; and was just as unsuccessful at the Marathon Soros, burial Mound of the Athenian dead after their victory over the Persians in 490 BC. As ever, he spent little time at Iliou Melathron.

What peace Schliemann might have found when not being pricked and stung by the murmurings of his detractors was broken by fresh attacks from his old enemy Ernst Bötticher, and his more recent foe, the Scottish historian R.C.Jebb. There was something in Schliemann which infuriated the literal and conscientious Jebb and, whether behind the curtain of anonymity or on a public platform, the Scotsman continued to nip and torment. Urged by friends like Virchow and Philip Smith to pay no attention, Schliemann preferred to listen to Sayce, who had himself suffered at Jebb's hands and who now wrote to say: 'We must "kick" him until he is never able to bark again.' Archaeological feuds took a more naked form in the nineteenth century.

In September came news of the death of Schliemann's factotum, Nikolaos Zaphyros Yannakis, who had drowned in the Scamander, within sight of the walls of Troy. Yannakis was a drinker. Frank Calvert's niece, Edith, reported in a letter to Schliemann that Yannakis, returning home late one night, had decided to take a short cut 'over a deep and boggy place into which he fell head foremost'. Yannakis's wife, the Helen whom he had married so suddenly in order to provide Sophia with a female companion, was now destitute. Whether Schliemann bore Yannakis a grudge for the stories he had told William Borlase about the Trojan treasure is not known, but he did send off a cheque for £8.

Schliemann himself was far from well. The frenetic energy he put into his life was taking its revenge: his ears hurt continually, there were fears that something might be wrong with his kidneys, and he was no longer able to throw off infections as he once had. He fretted over delays, wrote innumerable and often irascible letters, some starting in one language and finishing in another; his handwriting grew ever more cramped, his tone more imperative. Schliemann had always loved telegrams; these now poured out with renewed urgency. Sayce, worried about Schliemann's health, urged him to spend the winter in a warm climate, and to give up all thoughts of new archaeological sites for the present. 'You have spent yourself too fast,' warned Müller, alerted by Sayce to Schliemann's condition. 'You ought now to rest, rest on your oars, rest on your laurels, and you may still do much good by encouraging others ...'

But Schliemann was in no mood to retire, and leave the glory to younger archaeologists. In any case, there were still many among his critics who continued to doubt the vast claims he made for Troy and Mycenae. The site he turned to next was never to yield him quite the splendours of his earlier excavations; but it produced another piece in the jigsaw of prehistoric Greece that he believed to be his own.

Even the ancient Greeks regarded Tiryns with awe. This fortress of immense stones standing above the plain of Argos, nine miles southwest of Mycenae and close to the shore, was said to have been the birthplace of Hercules, and Pausanias had likened its walls in splendour to the Pyramids of Egypt. It was from Tiryns of the Great Walls that black ships had set off for Troy, joining the fleet under the command of 'warlike Diomedes'. Schliemann said that Tiryns was the most beautiful place he had ever seen, as beautiful as the 'ascending peaks of the Himalayas, the luxuriance of the tropical world on the Islands of Sunda', the Great Wall in China, the valleys of Japan, the Yosemite valley in California and the high peaks of the Cordilleras, a lofty claim that can hardly have failed to irritate those whose travelling had been confined to Europe. By the end of the nineteenth century Tiryns was a mound of ruins, with galleries that had been used for hundreds of years as sheepfolds.

On 14 March 1884, Schliemann and Dörpfeld arrived in Nauplion, a small town just south of Tiryns, dominated by the citadel of Palamedes, believed by the ancient Greeks to be a distinguished astronomer and present at the siege of Troy where he invented the game of draughts to distract the besiegers during their long wait. Spring had arrived in the Argolid. In the distance, snow could still be seen on the high mountains, but in the plain the fields of corn were full of scarlet anemones and purple cistus, and the lemon and orange trees had fruit. On the hills, among the olive trees and cypresses, could be found irises and wild hyacinth. The two men took rooms in Nauplion and began to supervise the unpacking of their equipment: forty English wheelbarrows with iron wheels, twenty large iron crowbars, shovels, pickaxes and hoes. The Greek authorities, to whom all Schliemann's finds were once again to go, did all they could to help. Sixty workmen were hired, and one of them was detailed to do nothing but fetch drinking water in barrels from a spring and carry it to the others. This time Schliemann was to take a more supervisory role, indicating where he wished digging to begin and walls to be torn down, while Dörpfeld acted as surveyor, engineer and mapmaker, as well as chief overseer of the buildings. Schliemann remained in charge of treasure and pottery.

It was to be a most harmonious dig. The party soon settled down to Schliemann's exacting routine. Schliemann himself rose at 3.45 and went off to swim in the dark, a boatman from Nauplion rowing him out to the open sea. Once on shore, he drank a cup of black coffee without sugar and rode the couple of miles to Tiryns as the sun rose, sending his horse back to Nauplion to collect Dörpfeld while he breakfasted on corned beef, bread, sheep's cheese, oranges and retsina. His new friend, John Mahaffy, who came to visit the site, missed him at breakfast, but at last tracked him down in the trenches, 'going from group to group, inquiring, watching, exhorting his men'. These were for the most part Albanians, women as well as men, in brightly coloured local costumes, with what Mahaffy described as soft 'woollen cream-white capotes' that they put on when not working. At midday came lunch and a rest, which Schliemann took using a stone as pillow, which later turned out to be part of a Byzantine church. As darkness fell, he rode back to Nauplion. Dinner consisted of soup made from Liebig's Extract of Meat, fish or mutton fried in olive oil, more cheese, oranges and retsina. The spring vegetables – broad beans, peas and artichokes – were ripe, but he considered them inedible and unhealthy cooked in olive oil.

Schliemann's digs were now famous affairs. Travellers to the Peloponnese rarely missed a visit whenever they were near a site; and his delight in their company is touching, particularly when the visitors were people with titles. Lord and Lady Pembroke dropped in on Tiryns, as did the Crown Prince of Saxe-Meiningen. ('So distinguished', noted Schliemann with satisfaction, 'by his love of science and learning'). Carl Schuchhardt, who later wrote a book about Schliemann's archaeology, remarked that, unlike Goethe, who barely bothered to greet his visitors, Schliemann was a most courteous host, warm and tender when within his circle of family and friends, even if, as he grew older, he became more stubborn.

This year, rewards came fast. If anything, Schliemann had under-estimated the importance of Tiryns. As the weeks went by, a vast palace emerged under their spades, richly decorated, its courtyards opening out into halls and storerooms; there was a fine colonnaded inner court, a hall with a large circular hearth, very like one found at Troy, and a bathroom, with the remains of a terracotta tub resting on an immense block of limestone. The remains of palace walls, as they were exposed to the light, were seen to include decorative relief blocks, inlaid with blue glass paste and serpentine or painted with frescoes of hunting scenes; some floors were covered with mosaics of pebbles, a few of which were painted in four basic colours, yellow, white, red and blue.

If the graves and masks of Mycenae had shown the dead of a lost prehistoric past, buried in all their splendour, the palace of Tiryns spoke of a civilization at play. In the second season at Tiryns, another fresco, showing a young man leaping over the back of a bull, was found, adding to this feeling of lightness and exuberance, though only later, after the excavations at Knossos, was the closeness of Tiryns to the Minoans apparent. This was architectural sophistication and artistry of a kind never either seen or expected from prehistoric Greece. The journalists who had gathered at Tiryns during the first few days to watch the great Schliemann at work had found archaeology very much slower and more boring than they expected, and had left long before the palace had started to unfold, the *New York Times* man remarking that 'Schliemann's luck has run out'. It was therefore Schliemann himself who announced his major new find, in a series of letters and reports despatched around the world, in which he claimed to have uncovered a giant palace, decorated with 'Doric' columns, 'one of the most astonishing discoveries of the century'. His prehistoric palace, he told readers of *The Athenaeum*, could not fail to give rise to 'universal amazement, for nothing like this has ever turned up'.

To Schliemann, as the days passed, and more of the palace and its objects – vases, pots, jewellery – turned up, it seemed to provide yet more proof that the ancient Mycenaean cities enjoyed flourishing international contacts. Both Mycenae and Tiryns, he concluded, had been built and inhabited by Phoenicians, who arrived in the Aegean in a remote prehistoric age, and were expelled by the Dorian invaders somewhere around 1100 BC. Like the other Mycenaean cities, Tiryns had come to an abrupt end in a fire. One of Schliemann's recurrent themes, in keeping with his love for Homer's heroes, was that archaic Greece had been peopled by men of exceptional heroism which the modern world singularly lacked. Only figures like Tsar Alexander II, who had emancipated the serfs and been assassinated in St Petersburg in 1881, he said, could compare with them. To Dörpfeld, the great palace of Tiryns suggested something else: he saw it as one more link in an unbroken chain of Greek architecture, with its beginnings in Troy and its peak in the Parthenon in Athens.

Despite the extraordinary completeness of their find, the excavations at Tiryns attracted surprisingly little excitement. Sayce was quick to write to say that it was the 'fitting capstone of all your wonderful discoveries', and Schliemann had the pleasure of being greeted by his name written in flames from oil lamps against the sky during a visit to Breslau; but otherwise it was all a little flat. *The Prehistoric Palaces of the Kings of Tiryns* appeared in three languages and four editions simultaneously. It was a rather more sober book than its predecessors, and this time Schliemann conscientiously acknowledged the help of his assistants, particularly Dörpfeld, something he had seemed reluctant to do previously. There was no mistaking Dörpfeld's importance: for at least part of the last two seasons at Troy he had been in charge on his own, and he had contributed to *Tiryns* a number of fine maps. John Mahaffy, who had helped with the English edition, had found close association with the volatile Schliemann awkward, all the more so as Dörpfeld kept coming back with new revisions. At one point, considerably irked, Mahaffy suggested that Schliemann would do well to inscribe Shakespeare's words – 'Too swift arrives as tardy as too slow' – on the walls of his great palace. Mahaffy was another of Schliemann's colleagues who refused to take umbrage when Schliemann became cantankerous; after one clash, he ended a letter: 'I am very sincerely, indeed most truly, your packmule, J. Mahaffy'. For a man most often described by biographers as friendless, Schliemann came, towards the end of his life, to inspire great affection in people he worked with.

Anything that Schliemann touched was now news. In the long reviews – some of them twenty or even thirty pages long – that appeared in the quarterly magazines, Schliemann was praised for his wonderful sympathy for the early Greeks, for the thoroughness of his research, for being as 'indefatigable' with his pen as with his pickaxe. *Life* magazine called *Tiryns* 'the event of the publishing season'. Archaeology, noted the *Quarterly Review,* had been blind and dumb while it remained the 'handmaiden of literature'; but in becoming 'one of the servants of history, she has found both eyes and tongue'.

Schliemann was tired, nervous and increasingly deaf; but he remained in somewhat boastful mood. 'I am fatigued,' he wrote to a friend, 'and have an immense desire to ... pass the rest of my life quietly.' However, his very success denied him rest, for 'wherever I put my spade I always

Sophia with the Schliemanns' two children, Andromache and Agamemnon, probably in the early 1880s.

The Lion Gate, Mycenae. The figures above are Schliemann (standing) and his assistant Wilhelm Dörpfeld (sitting). The woman with the white hat, is Sophia Schliemann.

Schliemann's discoveries at Mycenae. 1, gold mask, supposed to be of Agamemnon, found with skeleton in Agamemnon's tomb; 2, silver cow's head, with golden horns, emblematic of the goddess Hera, or Juno; 3–4, golden tankard and goblet; 5–6, thin gold plates and buttons, dress ornaments, found with skeleton.

Rudolf Virchow (left), who provided Schliemann with archaeological expertise, and Wilhelm Dörpfeld, who became his assistant.

Schliemann's excavations in the Acropolis of Mycenae.

Schliemann giving an account of his discoveries at Mycenae before the Society of Antiquaries at Burlington House, London in 1877.

Schliemann (right) aged 67; and below with Sophia in Berlin.

Berlin in 1945; and (below) the flak tower in the Zoo, where Schliemann's Great Treasure was discovered by the Russians.

discovered new worlds for archaeology' and so he owed it to civilization to keep going. Or perhaps, since fortune was a 'capricious woman', what he should really do was imitate Rossini. 'When Rossini had written *Guillaume Tell*,' he explained to Müller, 'he wrote no more, for he was sure that he could never produce anything like it in grandeur. I ought to do the same in *Greece* at least.'

Tiryns was indeed a city worthy of Homer and his heroes, one more site rescued from the distant mythological past. It might easily have been the crowning moment in Schliemann's archaeological career; in fact, it paved the way for yet another monumental battle.

In the early months of 1886, before the critical storm broke that was to engulf him, Schliemann turned his attentions to a new site, a natural successor to his excavations at Troy, Mycenae, Orchomenos and Tiryns. Crete had first entered his plans in 1883; he was now to worry away at it for the rest of his life. What he might have found, and where it would have taken him, no one can guess, but there is little doubt that he was aware of its immense possibilities, and that he was convinced that it contained a Bronze Age palace. Homer, he pointed out, had called Crete a 'ravisher of eyes'.

For archaeologists in the 1870s and 1880s Crete was a political nightmare. The island was owned and ruled over by Turkey. After a Cretan insurrection in 1866, the Sublime Porte had promised a number of reforms, and the Khalepa Pact of 1878 – named after a suburb of Khania, the Turkish capital of Crete – did inaugurate a period of relative prosperity and peace, with a measure of self-government for the island, and an elected Assembly. However, the Christian Cretan deputies, who were in a majority in the Assembly, were firmly opposed to allowing archaeological excavations of any kind while their island remained under Turkish rule.

Crete, however, was fast being recognized as an archaeological prize. By the second half of the nineteenth century it was abundantly clear that there would be much in the way of fame and trophies for the person and the country allowed to excavate the island. Towards the end of December 1878, Minos Kalokairinos, a Cretan from the town of Heraklion, had made a number of soundings along the southern edge of what had been a Greek and Roman city called Knossos, and in so doing had uncovered the beginnings of an enormous palace, clearing several rooms and terraces and bringing to light a number of large storage jars. His excavations had been halted by the new Turkish Governor-General of Crete, John Photiades Pasha, acting on the orders of the Cretan Assembly. Not, however, before the British Consul to Crete, Thomas Sandwith, had been to inspect Kalokairinos's site and written to Charles Newton urging him to pay a visit to Crete and see for himself what was being turned up. Newton failed to make the journey, but interest in Knossos spread rapidly among the French and American archaeologists, all of whom were blocked by the Cretans who, well aware of the covetous and grasping behaviour of the European archaeologists, had no wish to see their treasures despatched to the capital cities of the European powers.

Schliemann, as was painfully well known, was not a man easily put off. Early in January 1883, he had written to Photiades, a friend from the days when Photiades was Turkish Ambassador to Athens, begging him to forward a request to the Cretan Assembly that he be given a *firman* for Knossos. The official answer was no. Unofficially, there was a feeling that if Schliemann came to Crete in person and put his case before the Assembly, there was just a chance that he might succeed. 'I will try to make the Impossible possible,' he wrote to a friend. However, the Assembly met only rarely, and circumstances continued to stand in the way of a personal visit, so that it was not until the spring of 1886 that he at last found time to visit Crete.

Schliemann and Dörpfeld, by this point inseparable archaeological companions, arrived in Knossos in May. Like many of their peers, the two men were convinced that the Mycenaean civilization could not have emerged in isolation, and that Crete, standing between mainland Greece, Egypt and Syria, might well provide the missing link. Knossos, outside Heraklion, was judged the most likely place for the palace of the fabled king Minos, with his labyrinth constructed by Daedalus. Crete, Schliemann told Gladstone, was 'still virgin soil to archaeology', and there was enough on the island to provide him with work for the rest of his life. Virchow approved of Schliemann's decision, and Müller had written, with considerable prescience, that Crete was surely a 'perfect rookery of nations' and that 'there, if anywhere, you ought to find the first attempts at writing, as adopted to western wants'.

No *firman* to dig was forthcoming from the Sublime Porte, despite the interventions of the German Ambassador, Schliemann's helpful friend Count von Radowitz. What was perhaps more significant, his influential contact, Photiades, had been replaced and was no longer in a position to help him, while the powerful Cretan Archaeological Society remained implacably opposed to all excavations. For a while, Schliemann refused to be deflected. One can obtain anything . . .' he remarked, 'one has only to choose the right means.'

As soon as they reached Crete, it was evident to both Schliemann and Dörpfeld that Knossos, like Hissarlik, was an artificial stratified mound Wandering around the chambers that Kalokairinos had excavated five years earlier, and examining the vast walls protruding from the debris, they became convinced that Knossos was indeed another prehistoric palace. The vast storage jars were exactly like the large *pithoi* found at Troy, and the bits of pottery were plainly of the same shape and size as those from Mycenae and Tiryns, and bore the same decorations. 'I should . . . not at all wonder . . .' Schliemann wrote off to Müller, 'if I found here on the virgin soil the remnants of a civilization, in comparison to which even the Trojan war is an event of yesterday.'

Surprisingly, perhaps, Schliemann made no attempt to petition the Cretan Assembly in person, even though it happened to be meeting in Khania at the time, but turned instead to Dr Joseph Chatzidakis, a prominent Cretan physician and politician, and the founder of the Heraklion museum. How helpful Chatzidakis actually was is not clear, but a new setback developed at the site of Knossos itself, when the Turkish owners of the land on which the buried palace stood, demanded an exorbitant price, vastly swollen by insisting that Schliemann buy not only the patch of land he needed, but an entire derelict estate that went with it. There were, Schliemann was informed, 2500 valuable olive trees on it; characteristically, Schliemann decided to check for himself and found only 889. Probably sensing that even were he to raise the money to buy the estate, he would still have trouble securing his *firman*, he resolved to wait, urging the Turkish owners to find another buyer for the land and the olive trees. Though he was to visit Crete once more, in February 1889, and though he continued to believe that the island possessed information crucial to his prehistoric world, the remarkable later finds at Knossos, which proved right so much of what he had claimed and completed his vision of a prehistoric Greek civilization, were not to be Schliemann's.

In any case, in the summer of 1886, Schliemann had more pressing problems to deal with. His enemies were gathering.If there is something of a wounded animal at bay in Schliemann's stand against his detractors, there is also something perplexing – and unpleasant – in the vehemence and enthusiasm with which they gathered for the kill.

The first call to battle was sounded in the pages of *The Times*, the newspaper which above all others had supported Schliemann so admiringly throughout his excavations at Mycenae. It came from the pen of an American called William Stillman, who had been appointed *The Times* correspondent for the Mediterranean. Stillman was an odd figure. A traveller and adventurer from New England, greatly interested in archaeology, he had spent several years in Crete as American Consul at the time of the insurrection against Turkish rule, and had himself applied for – and been refused – permission to dig at Knossos. Stillman's private life was tragic: at the end of the 1860s his wife, who suffered from bouts of madness, committed suicide; not long afterwards, his much-loved thirteen-year-old son died. Stillman's contempt for Schliemann seems to have exceeded even that of Jebb. He was, warned a friend who had suffered at Stillman's hands in New York, 'a mortal enemy of mine, as well as of yours'. Furthermore, Stillman was mean and envious, and a 'despicable reptile'.

In the spring of 1886, while Schliemann was occupied with Crete, Stillman was one of a party of English and American academics and historians who had visited the plain of the Argolid and called in to inspect both Mycenae and Tiryns. With him were F.C.Penrose, a respected scholar renowned for the precision of his measurements of classical Greek buildings, and Lewis Farnell who had visited Schliemann in Athens. On their return from the Peloponnese, Stillman settled down with his pen. His first attacks appeared in *The Times*, beginning on 24 April. Schliemann, Stillman opined, had made a fundamental error: Mycenae was nothing but a classical Greek site of approximately the fifth century BC, which had been invaded and overrun some time in the third century BC by the Celts, who had occupied a number of the older ruins and used them as a sepulchre for one of their chiefs, filling it with looted Greek treasure. All that Schliemann had in fact done was to 'ransack' a Celtic tumulus 'for bones and trophies of Homeric heroes'. His so-called tomb of Agamemnon had therefore nothing at all to do with a Trojan war, even if such a war had existed, but was merely the 'remains of some obscure barbarous tribe which reoccupied the ruins of the old cities and established a temporary rule there during the decay of Greece'.

This attack was painful enough. But Stillman wished to press his point home. Schliemann's datings for both Tiryns and Mycenae were simply 'the most extraordinary hallucinations of an unscientific enthusiast which literature can record'; while his finds were no more than 'wretched barbaric work of no archaeological character'. Schliemann's very theories, he repeated to the *Evening Post*, were 'simply stupefying'.

His professional point made, Stillman now came out with a more deadly personal attack, of a kind apparently fashionable in the late nineteenth century. Schliemann, he declared, both in *The Times* and in an article for *The Academy*, was a destructive and disorganized excavator, easily deluded and far too keen on worldly triumphs. 'Through want of method and archaeological knowledge, he has not by them added a single scientific fact (I speak advisedly) to what we knew either of Troy or of pre-Hellenic archaeology.' Strong words; there were more to come. Schliemann's photographs were also of 'utter worthlessness'. Possibly most offensive of all, Stillman's concluding tone was deeply patronizing. There was, he said, something very 'tragic in this collapse of an antiquarian crusade heralded with a grand flourish of trumpets, and alleged to have terminated in a signal triumph'. He ended with some advice: 'If these ruins are to be further ransacked in the unscientific way in which they have been begun, it were better for science that Dr Schliemann let them alone.' If he could not be persuaded to do so, well, then he should at the very least 'associate himself with some exact and scientific archaeologist'.

This was too much; it was not only Schliemann's honour that was at stake, but Dörpfeld's too. Even the quick response of some of the other papers – *The St James's Gazette* declared that 'so fickle in its loves, *The Times* is the Queen Elizabeth of journalism' – was not nearly enough to soothe Schliemann's fury. In any case, a major archaeological war had been launched, and the prominent archaeologists of the day did not intend to miss the fun. Like the Trojans and the Achaeans, they now formed up into two camps. As the archaeological world began to seethe, newspapers not only in England but throughout Europe and America reported their views, and old critics of Schliemann took the opportunity to complain that he left his excavations in such a state of chaos that it was hard to figure out what period they belonged to. Dr Michael Dettner, a librarian from Athens, visited Tiryns and came away, so he said, distressed by the 'impiety' of Schliemann's method 'which borders on vandalism'.

Since the dispute had become so public, and the protagonists were so famous – Schliemann versus *The Times* – a public arena was needed in which to fight the battle out. The Society of Antiquaries in London, the acme of scientific respectability and the setting for some of Schliemann's finest hours, offered their premises in Burlington House for an open forum, to be held under the auspices of the Hellenic Society. The meeting took place on 2 July. On one side stood Schliemann and Dörpfeld, who had already led the counterattack in the *The Times*, and behind them, if only in spirit, friends like Sayce, Müller and Mahaffy, who wrote that Schliemann's enemies 'the pedants, have been discomfited and brought to confusion' and recommending that they commit 'archaeological suicide' much as their colleague Dr Brentano, an old foe of Schliemann's, had done. (Brentano had recently killed himself.) On the other side were such figures as Jebb and, it seems, Emile Burnouf, who had come down in favour of Stillman, but not Stillman himself who had refrained from travelling to London to attend. What was at issue was the nature of Schliemann's claims for his sites: were they truly prehistoric, as he maintained, or were they in fact Byzantine ?

The large hall of the Society was overflowing; many people, unable to find seats, stood. The two cases were put; papers were read; speeches were made; opinions were aired. *The Times*, whose coverage of the occasion has a somewhat penitential air, noted: 'The combat was truly heroic.' 'Apollo,' remarked *Life* in its next edition, 'had sent his fiercest rays, but Pallas Athene stood over the discoverer of Troy with her shield.'

When it was all over, when the various differing views had been sifted through and appraised, the victory was judged by the *Manchester Guardian* to have gone to Schliemann and Dörpfeld, not least because there was a feeling of disapproval that Stillman had not bothered to put in an appearance. What was more, he was known to have refused Dörpfeld's offer to conduct him personally around Mycenae and Tiryns. Though *The Times* insisted that Schliemann had not entirely satisfied his critics, nor 'demolished' their correspondent, there were few doubters left at the end of the day, particularly after the eminent English authority on architecture, Dr James Ferguson, threw his weight behind the two Germans, and Arthur Evans, by now Keeper of the Ashmolean Museum in Oxford, condemned *The Times* for its 'preposterous perversities'. Soon, the other newspapers were accusing Stillman of ignorance and jealousy.

The following year, Penrose agreed to visit Mycenae and Tiryns, accompanied by Dörpfeld. When he returned to London he wrote an article for *The Athenaeum*, completely rejecting his initial Byzantine hypothesis. Of Stillman, who was transfered to America, no more was heard.

14

PALLAS ATHENE
INTERVENES

The last years of Schliemann's life have a haunted, sad feel to them.
Though very obviously happy with Sophia, and devoted to his
two children, he wandered the world, usually on his own, often
in considerable pain from his ears. He seemed unable to settle. Wherever
he went, he was always looking for finds to compare with those of Troy
and Mycenae; and he was always disappointed.

Physically, he looked older, with skin reddened and worn by the years
in the sun, his forehead made higher by his receding hair, and his
moustache trimmed in such a way that it looked wispy. Sometimes
he seemed to stutter; and his lips twitched. Time had made him less
combative, but more obsessive, and his daily routines had an ever more
desperate air to them. He slept very badly.

Early in 1886, before his visit to Crete, Schliemann had taken off for
a sudden expedition on his own to Cuba, Santo Domingo and Puerto
Rico. Seldom, he wrote to friends, had he enjoyed himself so much. At
the end of the year, his battles with Stillman over, feeling that he had
been vindicated by men who considered him their equal, and hoping
that a warm climate might soothe his ears, he decided to spend the
winter months in Egypt. His plan was to do the journey in style, renting
a large houseboat with sails and travelling up the Nile as far as the
Second Cataract at Wadi Haifa. He engaged a crew of ten; the entire trip
was to cost him £1500 – an immense sum in the 1880s. At the last
moment, Sophia lost her nerve and decided that she should stay behind
in Athens with the children; and so Schliemann set out alone, taking
with him a consumptive servant he had christened Pelops (founder of
the Pelopid family after whom the Peloponnese is named). Not only did

the hot Egyptian sun fail to cure him, but Pelops grew worse, and was eventually put on shore to die in an Egyptian hospital.

The journey, however, was a success; if Schliemann was lonely, he did not say so. On board his houseboat he rose at the late hour of seven, walked up and down the deck for thirty minutes, ate three eggs, walked some more, studied Arabic and read Euripides. At the end of the day, before settling down to write up his diary, he had himself put ashore and walked for an hour and a half in 'the health-giving desert sand'. When the party reached Abu Simbel, he marvelled at the vast reliefs on the temples, describing them as 'the world's most powerful works of art'. Everywhere he went, he took medicines with him, to hand out to the sick, much as he had done many years before at Troy, only this time he recited from the Koran rather than Homer, and advised them to bathe regularly in the Nile. Though he soon came to dislike his 'Mohammedan' sailors, complaining that they were dirty and disloyal, he greatly admired the Nubians, whose fine features, natural nobility and eyes 'fiery enough to melt ice', reminded him of the Homeric heroes and whose women, despite the jewellery that cut into their faces, he considered extremely beautiful. When not visiting the temples, he stayed on board, writing in his 257-page diary, studying the cloud formations as he paced the deck, and constantly pausing to record the temperature and the changing depths of the river and to copy down, in his neat and precise hand, any hieroglyphic signs he came across. He had lost none of the curiosity of his earlier travels to the East. The letters he sent home were cheerful, most of them written in several different languages. To his children, he was invariably loving and also teasing: 'Schliemann to Andromache', he would begin. 'The best of daughters! Rejoice!'

To Sophia, he wrote mainly in Greek, long, affectionate letters in which he described his dreams and enquired after hers, with growing interest in their meanings. When he dreamed of money, he worried that it might mean that there were difficulties on the way. One day, he spoke of having seen Sophia in a dream in a very agitated state; another day, he said he had seen her 'entering 900 drachmas for wine' in her account book. When she wrote back to say that she had dreamed of visitors from abroad, and of seeing crows, he became anxious about what this could portend. By this time, Schliemann would say that he really preferred to speak and write only in Greek – not modern, but ancient Greek. 'Only Homer interests me,' he told a friend. 'I am increasingly indifferent to anything else.' Though not, apparently, completely indifferent to his own fame. There remained until his death something very touching about his insatiable need for recognition and reassurance. The distinguished Orientalist E.A.Wallis Budge was in Aswan at the time of Schliemann's visit and has left a revealing story about his behaviour.

There had been no instructions from any of the organizations in Cairo about a public reception for Schliemann, so that when one of his servants suddenly appeared with news that 'his great master' was anchored nearby, no one, for a while, reacted. But then Henry Wallis, an artist currently drawing the Aswan tombs, announced that he felt that some gesture should be made, and together with a British army officer called Major Plunkett and Wallis Budge, had himself rowed out to the house-boat. A butler greeted them, showed them into a reception room and served coffee and cigarettes.

Major Plunkett, speaking for the three of them, offered to guide Schliemann around the tombs. Wallis Budge, in his account, goes on : 'Dr Schliemann replied very stiffly : 'It is very kind of you to be so amiable. I should like to place my archaeological science at your disposal by showing and explaining to you the tombs, but I have not the time as I am going up to Halfah.' He then reached out one hand, and lifted up a paperbound copy of the Greek text of Homer's *Iliad* ... and went on with his reading.'

Plunkett, it seems, paused, took a cigarette, lit it, and 'in a sweetly soft voice' asked if they had Schliemann's permission to withdraw ; when it had been granted, the three men retired 'with as much dignity as was possible under the circumstances'. One can only guess at the degree of Schliemann's injured pride.

Schliemann was back in Europe for the rest of 1887, spending much of his time on the move, travelling between Italy, Germany, France and Greece, with pauses to recuperate at Iliou Melathron. Early in 1888 he set off for a second trip up the Nile. His plan, this time, was to do a little excavating of his own. He had his eye on a site in Alexandria, which he had come to believe concealed the lost mausoleum of Alexander the Great. At first, the authorities, reminded of Schliemann's eminence by the German Embassy in London, appeared eager to grant him permission to dig wherever he wished. But the spot he had pinpointed turned out to lie directly beneath an extremely holy shrine, and the religious authorities in Alexandria refused to allow him anywhere near it. Instead, they offered Schliemann a site on the outskirts of the city, near a railway station, and here, having sunk a twelve-metre-deep shaft, he discovered a life-sized marble bust which he announced was nothing less than a Hellenic head of Queen Cleopatra VII. The bust was soon whisked secretly out of Egypt, and Schliemann wrote to Bismarck to tell him of the new 'masterpiece' he was adding to his collection donated to the German nation. It was altogether a most satisfactory find. Schliemann had often spoken of his desire to excavate a bust of Cleopatra. But the diaries of this excavation are missing from his papers in Athens, and more than one critic has added the Cleopatra head to the long list of alleged forgeries, thefts, exaggerations and, in this case, purchases, passed off as finds.

This year, Virchow had agreed to join Schliemann in Egypt, with the intention of looking for skulls in order to study the cranial characteristics of both ancient and modern Nile valley inhabitants. Their friendship, which had continued to pass through awkward patches, seemed more settled. The two met towards the end of February, and set off on a mailboat up the Nile from Cairo to Aswan, briefly held up by attacks from dervishes, fought off by Anglo-Egyptian troops stationed in the area. They spent one week at Abu Simbel, where they discussed excavating Kadesh, and another at Luxor on the way back. As they moved slowly up and then down the Nile, they paused, in order for Virchow to collect his skulls, and for Schliemann to look for ancient ceramics, glassware and any weapons, to add to his Berlin collection. The trip gave rise to the odd story recounted both by Emil Ludwig and by Lynn and Gray Poole in their life of the Schliemanns, *One Passion, Two Loves*, but never put down on paper by Schliemann himself. At this time Schliemann is said to have told Virchow about the episode that had taken place during his first voyage around the world in 1854. Wishing to visit Mecca, which was strictly forbidden to all infidels, he had himself circumcized, darkened his body all over by lying in the sun, and, dressed in the white robes of a pilgrim, visited Mecca, and entered the holy Kaaba. A myth? It is unlikely now that anyone will ever know. Such a pilgrimage is perfectly in keeping with Schliemann's ambitions and audacity.

One of the last portraits of Schliemann comes from the archaeologist Flinders Petrie, who was digging at the temple site of Medinet el Fayum. Schliemann and Virchow, together with an anthropologist called George Schweinfurth, arrived at a moment of immense excitement, when a sudden find was yielding mummies, pottery, papyri and figures. 'Schliemann,' Flinders Petrie was to write many years later in his autobiography, 'short, round-headed, round-faced, round-hatted, great round-goggle-eyed, spectacled, cheeriest of beings; dogmatic but always ready for facts.' By his tone, he would seem to have felt well disposed towards Schliemann, but when, in a later book about the methods of

archaeology, he included a chapter on ethics and wrote: 'to turn over a
site without making any plans, or recording the positions and relations
of things, may be plundering, but it is not archaeology ... to wantonly
destroy a monument by cutting pieces out ... is unjustifiable', it is quite
possible that Schliemann may have been one of the guilty archaeologists
he had in mind. As for Virchow, although Petrie found him 'calm' and
'sweet-faced' and admired his beautiful grey beard, he had a theory that
Virchow had made some kind of mischief about his work while in Cairo.

Schliemann was back in Athens by the end of April, and was soon
immersed in the finishing touches to the new German Archaeological
Institute, which had been designed by Iliou Melathron's architect, Ernst
Ziller, and was to include a frieze of Greek inscriptions chosen by Schliemann and painted on to the walls of each room. The façade was
decorated with pictures of the Muses, and the interior, under his direction, was to be in the 'Pompeian' manner. The institute, he wrote, with
considerable pride 'is a magnificent building, worthy of the Institute of
the greatest nation on earth'. Visitors to Iliou Melathron during these
times spoke of the atmosphere being that of a cross between nineteenth-
century refinement and the more rugged life of the early Greeks, with
Schliemann seated at the head of the dining-room table, like a 'tough
old Ulysses', sketching out his plans.

There were vast piles of letters waiting for him on his return. By the
late 1880s, Schliemann had begun keeping an index to his own letters,
in the front of the copy-books he used for all his correspondence. Letters
went off to Bismarck and Gladstone, Sayce and Schröder, Virchow, and
his publishers Brockhaus and John Murray. Since he was away from
Athens so much, it was Sophia who received the greatest number. While
his letters to her are often filled with instructions and directions, hers
are full of anxiety about his health, and often contain gentle but definite
reproaches about the amount of time he spent travelling and away from
her. It is clear that by now the pain in Schliemann's ears was appalling,
and growing worse, and that he suffered intensely from his increasing
deafness. Sayce, one of the friends most concerned about him, wrote
sympathetically: 'Your letter has filled me with grief ... Your health is
of paramount importance, and everything else ought to be sacrificed to
it.'

And yet Schliemann kept on travelling, and digging, and searching.
In November 1888 he was back in the southern Peloponnese; from
Kythera, he sent a telegram to *The Times*, claiming to have discovered a
temple under a Byzantine chapel. He moved across to Pylos, where he

searched for – and failed to find – the palace of King Nestor, 'master of the courteous word ... whose speech ran sweeter than honey off his tongue'. From here he went to Sparta, where he found nothing, then to the island of Sphacteria, where he maintained that he uncovered some ancient masonry from the days of the Peloponnesian Wars. By the spring of 1889 he was off yet again, to the sites and cities of the northern Peloponnese, and then to the Ionian islands, to contemplate the great battle fought and lost by Mark Antony at Actium in thirty-one BC, ending up on Ithaca, the scene of his archaeological awakening. To Virchow, Schliemann poured out letters as detailed and driven as any that he ever wrote, talking of things he had seen, and things he hoped to do. He still had plans for Knossos, though when he reached Crete that spring, he found that the matter of the derelict estate had not been settled, and that political intrigues continued to make a *firman* most unlikely. 'The Cretans are all liars,' he declared, echoing the Apostle Paul. Some days, he admitted to having lost all enthusiasm 'to start the great work'; other days, he insisted that he would never 'abandon hope'.

For many years now, Sophia had urged her husband to pay no attention to the critics and archaeological foes who buzzed around him. A man like him, she would say, who had been decorated and honoured by so many countries and academic institutions, should ignore their trivial and envious remarks. Among the several thousand letters written to Schliemann during the final years of his life there are many from friends like Virchow, Sayce and Müller begging him to pay no attention to the attacks, to rise above such things. Schliemann could not; it was in his nature to feel hounded by every hostile review, every dismissive remark. One of the hardest things to explain is precisely why he inspired such passion – mostly of a negative kind. He had, quite simply, more enemies than most people of his time and profession, people who felt so very strongly that they would continue their often unreasoned assaults long after these had ceased to be relevant, and even when they had begun to harm their own reputations by doing so. The anguish that filled Schliemann whenever he was attacked, and the exaggerated and inappropriate energy he put into refuting his opponents, may be part of the reason for the strength of their feelings. In his sixties, widely acknowledged as one of the most important archaeologists of his day, Schliemann was no more able to practise moderation than he had ever been.

Stillman had, it is true, been successfully silenced; but another enemy was waiting. Though Ernst Bötticher acted alone, and remained on his own, without supporters, and though he commanded very little respect in the archaeological world, he was to prove more troublesome than most who had gone before him. His niggling, in the late 1880s, was all the more trying in that Schliemann's former critics had now for the most part entirely accepted not only that he had discovered the site of Troy, but that he had awoken the world to the glories of the Mycenaean age. Even Ernst Curtius, the excavator of Olympia and Schliemann's most persistent doubter, had swung round behind him. After paying a visit to Mycenae, Curtius had appeared at Iliou Melathron with a letter for Schliemann, in which he apologized for his past scepticism and hostility and said that he did not wish any shadow of ill-feeling to stand between them any longer.

Bötticher was the former artillery officer in the German army who, in 1883, had launched an offensive against Schliemann; it had grown more insistent and more bitter year by year. His argument was perfectly straightforward, if peculiar. He maintained that the mound of Hissarlik excavated by Schliemann was not a human habitation at all, but a burial ground; not a city, but a necropolis, probably Persian in origin. Furthermore, he declared that Hissarlik was not Troy either; that Pinarbaşi, the much debated site some four miles away, was in fact the true site of Troy.

Bötticher's claims would have been dismissed altogether had it not been for the fact that Schliemann himself had been so insistent in the early days at Troy that what he was finding was a 'vast number of funeral urns' with human ashes. However, since then, there were far larger and more persuasive bits of evidence – circuit walls, palaces, ramps, houses – to show that Bötticher's theory was absolutely mistaken. Despite *Life's* mockery of Bötticher as a 'queer antagonist', whose mind had been distorted by a 'wrong twist', the German ex-artillery officer continued to insist that he was right, and that Schliemann and Dörpfeld had in fact tampered with the evidence, torn down walls in one place in order to join them up in another in such a way as to support their own theories, as well as produced false maps. Even Virchow was accused of fraudulence, with the suggestion that he and other friends of Schliemann were on his payroll. Bötticher was as obsessive and dogged a character as Schliemann, and his sheer persistence won him a following. For all the absurdity of his views, he managed to have his pamphlets published, read and discussed, and even to place articles in respected academic journals.

Schliemann became haunted by Bötticher. He begged and bullied his friends to write articles in his defence; he declared that the artillery captain was making him ill, and threatened that unless Bötticher was silenced, he would stop sending treasures to Berlin. When the two men met at the International Anthropological Archaeological Congress held in Paris in the summer of 1889, Schliemann was beside himself. Not even the new Eiffel Tower, and the opening of the fourth World Fair, both events guaranteed to enchant him in other circumstances, could really distract him from Bötticher's assertions. They seemed to him so unreasonable. If the dead had been buried on the hill of Hissarlik, where, then, had those people passed their lives? Why was it that no cities had been found?

And then Pallas Athene of the 'Flashing Eyes', daughter of Zeus, intervened. She came to him, Schliemann told Virchow, on the morning of 13 September 1889, and told him to reopen the excavations at Hissarlik, and to invite Bötticher, together with a number of respected archaeologists, to inspect the site. (Though it has been suggested that it was Dörpfeld, rather than the Goddess of Wisdom, who had the idea first.)

The meeting was set for 1 December, and Schliemann offered to pay everyone's expenses. A *firman* was produced by the Turks in a record period of time. Major Bernhard Steffen, a German officer known for his maps of Mycenae and the Argolis, and Professor Georg Niemann of the Academy of Fine Arts of Vienna University, who had excavated at Samothrace, agreed to become neutral arbitrators.

Between 1 and 6 December the three men, together with Dörpfeld and Schliemann, tramped around Troy. On the sixth, the arbitrators voted unequivocally in Schliemann's favour, and drew up a document to say so. Bötticher, who seems at one point to have dismissed some of his own more provocative remarks simply as a desire to stimulate serious debate, refused to sign, and returned home to renew his attacks and insinuations in the pages of the *Levant Herald*, a paper which had always been willing to give space to Schliemann's detractors.

Bötticher's willpower, and the tolerance of the archaeological world at large, seem to have been remarkable. Despite scholarly refutations of the German officer's words, despite much-publicized disparaging comments on his own integrity and honesty, a second conference was now arranged at Hissarlik. This time, a group of eight internationally known academics, with wide experience across the whole field of archaeology, was brought to Troy, once again at Schliemann's expense.

These learned men, from Germany, America, France and Turkey, inspected the mound of Hissarlik in the last days of March 1890, then issued a formal protocol entitled *Mémoires presentées par divers savants*, in which they categorically endorsed the work of Schliemann and Dörpfeld. Their plans, it was decreed, 'correspond accurately to the existing remains ... We affirm that in no part of the ruins have we found any signs that point to the burning of corpses.' Bötticher, at last, was routed.

As it turned out, he had done Schliemann a very good turn. Later, Virchow was to say that Bötticher should have been not castigated, but thanked. For it was he who provoked Schliemann into returning to Hissarlik for fresh excavations; and these were to prove as important, perhaps even more important, than anything he had done before.

After the experts left, Schliemann and Dörpfeld returned to their work. It was Schliemann's twelfth visit to Troy. One of his ambitions, now, was to uncover a true necropolis, somewhere near the mound of Hissarlik, as a final way of refuting Bötticher's claims. The lower city, and an area just outside the walls, were designated as new parts to excavate. Rails had been laid down since the last dig, and the debris was hauled away much faster. The excavating proceeded at great speed, even if Schliemann lamented that Dörpfeld's insistence that each stratum be minutely inspected, stone by stone, was holding everyone up. In fact, events moved quickly. Within a few days, two entirely new large buildings began to emerge out of the ruins. They were not just very similar to the palace complex at Tiryns, but they contained ceramics of an unmistakable Mycenaean design. Most convincing of all, perhaps, they included a number of jars with stirrup-like handles, which archaeologists were coming to accept as the most telling signs of Mycenaean occupation. No similar find had been made in any other part or layer of the mound of Hissarlik. But what was most interesting and most unexpected was precisely *where* these buildings lay. For they were not in the second city, commonly now accepted to be the Trojan city, but in the sixth city, far closer to the surface and thus agreed to be far more recent. Schliemann and Dörpfeld took note; but they were inclined to be cautious. The report they issued was extremely tentative, not least because, in spite of all the vindications of Schliemann's theories, there were still classical and Mycenaean scholars like Adolf Furtwängler, who continued to claim: 'Schliemann is hugely celebrated ... but is and remains half crazy and confused, having no idea of the meaning of his excavations ... – a cruel, but not totally unfair remark, for Schliemann was never to develop a true archaeologist's perception of the culture of the Mycenaeans or how to define it.

In any case, Schliemann at least was distracted by something else altogether. Pallas Athene was at work again. The latest find consisted of four magnificent polished and carved stone axes, three of them apparently in green nephrite and one in violet lapis lazuli. '... Toward the end of June I saw Pallas Athene in front of me,' Schliemann wrote to Alexander Conze, 'holding in her hands those treasures which are more valuable than all those I uncovered at Mycenae. ... I cried for joy ... I thanked her from the bottom of my heart and begged her fervently that henceforth she should watch over me.' The gods and goddesses were fickle creatures; but a lifelong believer could not fail to respect their powers.

The axes should, of course, have been given to the Turks, who now vigorously supported Schliemann's work; though they took the whole pieces for their museum, they allowed him to keep many of the incomplete fragments he managed to excavate. But there was something about treasure that, for all his hard-acquired archaeological respectability, never failed to entrance Schliemann. His instinct was to conceal it. Letters despatched from him at this time are full of secrecy and hidden allusions. Though nothing is known of the details, it seems that the axes were spirited out of Troy to Athens, from where, rechristened Egyptian in origin in order to further confuse any pursuer, they were sent on to Berlin. The honest and scrupulous Dörpfeld appears to have acquiesced in what was, after all, a theft.

At the end of July, the excavations at Hissarlik were declared over for the year. There was much still to do, now that the new buildings had been cleared. 'I intend to resume them vigorously on the 1st of March next,' Schliemann wrote to Victor Emmanuel of Savoy, the future King of Italy, who was one of the many visitors to Troy that spring.

He was never to see Troy again. For much of the 1890 season, Schliemann had been almost totally deaf, complaining of exhaustion, the heat and constant thirst. Every day he tried to clear his ears by taking water through his nose; it seemed to help a bit. In April, Virchow came to visit him; during a walk on Mount Ida he noticed that his friend was so deaf that he was unable to make himself heard. He offered to examine Schliemann's ears and, though hampered by lack of instruments, thought that he could see some kind of bony obstruction; he recommended a visit to the best ear specialist in Germany, a man called Schwartze with a clinic in Halle. As the pain grew worse, and his hearing more limited, Schliemann at last agreed to take his advice. But he insisted on going alone. Sophia was later to say that while he packed, in Iliou Melathron, he wondered out loud who would wear his clothes after his death.

Schliemann's last weeks are not easy to describe reliably. There are many slightly different versions of what happened, more or less romantically embellished by friends, relations and biographers. They were, however, the very stuff of high Victorian drama.

On 12 November, Schliemann was operated on in the clinic at Halle; the operation lasted one and three-quarter hours, and bits of floating bone were removed from both ears. He began to hear a little better, and was soon sitting up in his hospital room reading the *Arabian Nights* in Arabic, and working on the proofs of his report on the most recent Troy season. To Dörpfeld, clearing up some misunderstanding that had arisen between them, he wrote: 'We have accomplished great things together, and many great things still remain to do, which we can only do together ...' He declared that he was on the mend, even if at one point the pain seems to have been so acute that he refused to see Virchow, who had travelled from Berlin to visit him. Professor Schwartze wanted him to stay on in the clinic, fearing that the inflammation might spread, but Schliemann was anxious to reach home in time for Christmas and discharged himself early. And yet, instead of travelling straight to Athens, he decided to break his journey first in Leipzig, in order to see his publisher, Brockhaus, and then in Berlin, where he wanted to discuss some property deals.

Before catching the train from Berlin to Paris, Schliemann had breakfast with Virchow; the two men discussed a possible expedition to the Canary Islands, in search of lost Atlantis – for had Homer not spoken of the islands as enjoying eternal spring? There was talk, too, of a journey with Sayce, who had been delayed by a snake-bite in Egypt. Though Sayce made light of it in a letter to Schliemann, the bite says something of the dangers faced by archaeologists in the nineteenth century. Had he not instantly cut the wound open, and cauterized and burnt a large area of his leg, he would certainly have died. To Sophia, Schliemann wrote, in classical Greek, a most touching letter: 'Words fail me to celebrate our marriage. At all times you were to me a loving wife, a good comrade, and a dependable guide in difficult situations, as well as a dear companion on the road and a mother second to none. It has always been a pleasure to me to watch you in the panoply of your virtues. Therefore, today, I promise that I shall marry you again in a future life.'

Though the train was extremely draughty, and the temperature in Paris had fallen to 32 degrees, with thick frost, Schliemann sounded cheerful. 'Long live Pallas Athene !' he wrote to Virchow. 'At last I can hear again with my right ear, and the left will get better.' To Sophia, to whom he confessed that his ears still hurt, he explained that it was because he had forgotten to protect them from the cold with the wadding his surgeon had given him. The pain was, however, bad enough for him to seek out a Parisian doctor, who removed some more bony material.

Still, Schliemann delayed. He now decided on a quick trip down to Naples on the way home, to see the results of the new excavations at Pompeii. The weather remained bitterly cold. Reaching Naples his ears were hurting so much that he sought out another doctor, but this man seems to have been more impressed by the eminence of his patient, and more interested in archaeology than medicine, and merely took the time to accompany him to Pompeii. Two telegrams went off to Sophia ; they are Schliemann's last messages to the outside world. The first, despatched from the Grand Hotel in Piazza Umberto, said that he would be arriving home on the Saturday morning. The second, sent the following day, 23 December, spoke of starting a new cure and therefore having to delay his arrival for a few more days.

On the afternoon of Christmas Day, 1890, as he was crossing the Piazza Santa Carità on foot, Schliemann collapsed. Unable to speak and partly paralysed, he was carried to a nearby hospital, but since he had no identification on him and seemed merely dazed, he was refused a bed and taken to a police station. There, a prescription was found in his pocket, with the name of the doctor he had consulted. When summoned, the doctor was able to tell the police who Schliemann was, and hastily arranged for him to be carried back to the Grand Hotel. Once in his room, the doctor opened his left ear : the inflammation had spread. Henryk Sienkiewicz, the Polish Nobel Prize-winner, was to recall seeing 'a dying man ... brought into the hotel. His head bowed down to his chest, eyes closed, arms hanging limp, and his face ashen ... After a while the manager of the hotel approached me and asked : "Do you know, Sir, who that man is ?" "No." "That is the great Schliemann !".' Poor, "great Schliemann" ! He had excavated Troy and Mycenae, earned immortality for himself – and was dying' ...

Next morning, the whole of Schliemann's right side was paralysed.

Eight of Naples' most eminent doctors gathered to discuss what should be done. As they talked, Schliemann died.

When the news reached Athens, and was picked up by the newspapers, telegrams began to arrive at Iliou Melathron. They came from Germany and America, Russia and France, England and Italy; they were sent by archaeologists and historians, statesman and crown princes, soldiers and friends. Dörpfeld, and Sophia's eldest brother, Yiango, travelled together to Naples to bring Schliemann's body home. Nine days after his death, his coffin, inside which had been put copies of the *Iliad* and the *Odyssey*, was placed under a bust of Homer in Iliou Melathron. Though Sophia had refused the King of Greece's offer of his personal guards to accompany the coffin from the ship that brought it to Piraeus, she accepted a ceremonial guard of Evzones to stand at the corners of the coffin. The King and the Crown Prince held vigil; scholars, foreign dignatories, and Athenian friends filed past.

Not long after Iliou Melathron had been completed, Schliemann had asked Ziller to design a mausoleum for his family. It stands in Athens's main cemetery, on the hill of Colonus, south of Ilissum. The position is magnificent. On Schliemann's instructions, Ziller had the marble decorated with a frieze: one side has scenes from the *Iliad*; the other, of Schliemann and Sophia supervising the excavations at Troy.

On Sunday 4 January, 1891, the funeral service was held in Iliou Melathron. The king had insisted that Schliemann be given a state burial, with full honours. The now very elderly Archbishop Vimpos, who had brought Sophia into Schliemann's life, officiated, helped by the Protestant Chaplain to the Royal Household. The American Ambassador, Archibald Loundon Snowdon, gave the address; a scholar of neo-Hellenic literature, Dr Rhangabe, recited verses in Greek, written in the Homeric hexameter; Dörpfeld spoke a farewell: 'Rest in peace, you have done enough.' The words could not have been more fitting. And at the last, Sophia recited Helen's farewell to Hector, from the twenty-fourth book of the *Iliad*: 'Twenty years are come and gone ... my tears flow both for you and for my unhappy self.'

The coffin was placed on top of a gun-carriage, drawn by eight black horses, and carried to the mausoleum. From here, Schliemann had told Sophia, their spirits could look out over the Acropolis, for eternity. It was a sombre, respectful occasion. Schliemann, who had so often and so painfully felt neglected, would have been pleased.

Schliemann would have been pleased, too, by the world's reaction to his

death. He died, at the age of sixty-eight, a man of substance. The grocer's
apprentice from Mecklenburg left a mansion and a mausoleum, in which
Sophia would join him only in 1932, after a state burial of her own, in
Athens; property and investments in Indianapolis, Paris, Germany and
England; a museum wing bearing his name and filled with his finds in
Berlin; 150 large volumes containing copies of his letters, written in
twelve different languages; fifty-two pairs of shoes and boots and fifty
suits. In his will, his first wife, his brothers and sisters and his two
surviving Russian children were all well provided for. (One peculiarity
in the will, which long mystified biographers, was a gift to Sayce of 'ten
thousand francs in gold', rescinded by a codicil: only much later did
Sayce explain that he had been told of the bequest and informed Schliemann that he neither needed nor wished for such a 'recompense' for
the help he had given him over the years.) During his lifetime, Schliemann had been awarded twenty-nine degrees or diplomas from
various universities, museums and academic societies; and he could
count among his friends the foremost historians and archaeologists of
the day, as well as a satisfactory number of crown princes, dukes and
counts.

The obituaries, of which there were several hundred, reflected all this.
Newspapers and magazines were generous to Schliemann in death in a
way that they had not always been in life. Many chose to dwell on the
rags-to-riches theme, pointing to his great successes as a merchant,
sometimes contrasting the shrewdness of his business acumen with the
simple faith he brought with him to archaeology. Schliemann had, wrote
his friend John Mahaffy in *The Athenaeum*, 'the childish simplicity of
genius'. Some celebrated the patience and persistence of this 'self-taught,
indomitable' man, which amounted at times to a fundamentalist faith
in what he was trying to do, and cited his finds as rewards for these
selfless labours. Percy Gardner noted that Schliemann had been a man
who dealt with his enemies 'in the spirit of a theologian who had to
combat an insidious heresy'. Occasionally this religious note took flight:
Schliemann seemed, to some writers, to have belonged to an age before
Christianity, believing strongly in providence, but managing at the same
time to blend a 'certain amount of natural Teutonic heathenism' with
the 'early Greek heathenism of Homer' – though just what they meant
by all this was never made very clear.

Some other papers remarked that Schliemann had been 'a little stiff
in controversy', and rather prone to take offence. *The Times*, perhaps in
order to compensate for their earlier acerbity, lauded his 'rare force

of character', his 'noble ambition', 'disinterested ideals' and 'unerring instinct'; they saw his life as 'so full of incident, so fruitful of discovery, and so fertile in controversy'. Friends, in these long obituaries, mourned a generous-spirited and insatiably curious man; and occasionally pointed a finger of blame for his untimely death at Bötticher, whose vituperation, as they saw it, had affected Schliemann's health. And if the English professed surprise at the amount of mourning that went on in other countries – for they had come to see Schliemann as their own – both the Germans and the Americans laid claim to him. J.Irving Manatt, an American professor, wrote in his obituary that 'it may as well be remembered that Troy was uncovered under the protection of our flag'.

What in the end, however, all seemed to agree upon was that Schliemann, through extremely hard work and tenacity, and in the face of considerable hostility, had been the man who had drawn aside 'the veil which long ages had lain over the remains of the prehistoric age of Greece'. He was, as the *National Review* concluded, 'one of the greatest pathfinders in archaeology'.

Schliemann would have enjoyed all this; he would have liked the number of obituaries and their warm and approving tone; though he might perhaps have taken most pride in Gladstone's valedictory words. 'Either his generosity without his energy,' observed the English statesman who had done the most to advance his cause in England, 'or his energy without his generosity, might well have gained celebrity; in their union they were no less than wonderful.'

Towards the end of February 1891 a memorial service for Schliemann was held in Berlin, under the auspices of the Mayor and the various archaeological bodies whose praise for Schliemann had for so many years been grudging. So many people wished to attend that invitations had to be limited to members of royal families, to the most important government and court officials, and to the leaders only of the scientific and artistic worlds. A bust of Schliemann was placed in a prominent position. The flowers were superb. The ceremony opened with Beethoven's 'Ruins of Athens'. Virchow, who had been asked to give the address, spoke for an hour and a half. It was left to Schliemann's old enemy, Professor Ernst Curtius, to say that his discoveries had been of value not only to archaeology, but to the whole civilized and educated world.

Sophia, thirty-eight at her husband's death, lived on for many years, using the fortune she inherited to plan and finance a number of orphanages and sanatoriums for tuberculosis patients. Photographs of her show an increasingly dignified, almost haughty woman, with a steady gaze and a solid presence. Emil Ludwig, the German biographer of Bismarck and Napoleon, whom she invited to write about Schliemann's life, describes a day during the First World War in Athens when 'there advanced towards me from out of her magnificent palace a tall, beautiful woman of about sixty, half queen, half Niobe, all in black and wearing a string of pearls.' Sophia died in 1932. Her coffin, covered in the white and blue flag of Greece, was placed in the mausoleum alongside Schliemann's, looking out over the Acropolis. She had been a widow for forty-two years.

It was perfectly true. Schliemann *had* thrown light on an entirely unknown prehistoric world in the Aegean, and turned, as his friend Sayce put it, the heroes of the *Iliad* and the *Odyssey* into 'men of flesh and blood'. He had given archaeology a whole new world. But had he discovered Priam's Troy?

In 1893 and 1894 Dörpfeld, funded first by Sophia, and then by Kaiser Wilhelm II, returned to Hissarlik and resumed the excavations. He went back to the earlier plans, looked again at Schliemann's first digs, and began to dig once more. Under fifty feet of earth, lying to the southeast of Schliemann's city, he uncovered the enormous walls of a late Bronze Age city. Here, at last, were the true signs of Homer's 'well-built' city, with its 'fine towers' and 'broad streets'; here, at last, the ever-missing proof that Troy had indeed been one of the finest fortress cities in the Aegean. Schliemann had quite simply missed it. The site was right; his dating wrong. Where he had dug, Homeric Troy had been levelled to give space for the Roman city of Novum Ilium. In his last season at Hissarlik, not many months before he died, he had in fact stood on the very brink of solving the riddle that had obsessed him for over twenty years. Having, from the very first moment when he reached Hissarlik in 1868, been certain that Homer's Troy lay at or very near, the bottom of the mound of Hissarlik, in that last dig he had found Mycenaean pottery in significant quantities close to the top. He had put nothing down on paper to say that his original city, Troy II, was wrong and that Homer's Troy in fact lay near the surface; but had he, in his mind, faced with the most important intellectual challenge of his life, taken that final step?

No one, now, will ever know. Many of Schliemann's followers and biographers are convinced that he died without that knowledge. What clues there are remain tantalizingly vague, and could be interpreted in different ways, like the letter he wrote to Virchow on 10 May 1890: 'The Mycenaean pots are very remarkable, which allow conclusions to be drawn about the earliest of prehistoric times.' Five weeks later, shortly before he closed the excavations for the season, a letter went off to King George I. 'The fourth stratum.' he informed the King, 'contains especially fine buildings, the same stratum in which were found the previously-named "Lydic" pottery, as well as many vases of the Mycenaean sort ...' The jars, he went on, which appeared to be imported from Greece, could thus 'serve as a tell-tale sign for the chronology of the upper levels of Troy'. There is a definite feeling that Schliemann was groping his way towards something, but what? Dörpfeld, who knew him better than anyone during those last few years, was to say that Schliemann, in 1890, was aware of his mistake. The final words should go to him, as told by Jerome Sperling who took part in the later American excavations at Troy under Carl Blegen and the University of Cincinnati.

Forty-five years after Schliemann's death, Dörpfeld, then in his eighties, arrived on a visit to Troy. 'One evening', recounts Sperling, 'Carl Blegen asked Dörpfeld how Schliemann reacted about realizing his mistake in trying to equate the much earlier remains with Homeric Troy. Dörpfeld replied with a characteristic twinkle in his eye: "I discussed the matter with Schliemann, who listened carefully without saying much. He then retired to his own tent and remained incommunicado for four days. When he finally came out, he quietly said to me: I think you are right."'

If the story is true, the scholar in Schliemann triumphed at the last over the gold-seeker. For Dörpfeld's Troy, the Troy of stratum VI, had little gold and no treasure. To admit this, Schliemann was obliged to face the fact that the treasure he had found, the diadems and the gold and the silver, did not belong to the Trojan War at all, were not worn by Helen, or hidden by Priam, but were the possessions of some other people altogether, living at least a thousand years earlier.

Other archaeologists were soon to add to the story of Troy and the Greek 'palace' age. In the late 1890s, Arthur Evans succeeded in buying the disputed estate at Knossos, and, when Crete finally won its independence from Turkey, he began to dig. The Mycenaeans, so Evans came to believe, were former vassals of a Minoan Empire. What he was looking for were more clues to that past era, and particularly for any written material. Like Schliemann, Evans was impatient and sometimes overhasty in his assertions. But he had all the advantages of new techniques and methods of archaeology and he knew the crucial importance of stratigraphy, the distinguishing of one layer from another by a minute examination of its contents, colour and textures.

Exactly one week after starting to excavate, Evans found what he was looking for – evidence that there had indeed been a prehistoric system of writing. By the end of his first season at Knossos he had brought out of the palace over a thousand tablets with writing on them. The script which he called Linear A had a few stylized strokes taking the place of pictures, while Linear B was made up of characters incised in straight rows. Evans spent the rest of his life trying, and failing, to decipher the tablets.

In the 1920s, two gifted young archaeologists, the Englishman Alan Wace and the American Carl Blegen, excavating on the Greek mainland in search of further remains of a prehistoric Bronze Age, helped establish the sequences of pottery, making it possible to show at least the relative dates of Troy's strata and the shaft graves at Mycenae. Then in 1932 Blegen, with a team of helpers, started work at Hissarlik. He was a methodical, scholarly man, somewhat dismissive of Schliemann's erratic archaeological ways. He was not, he declared, looking for treasure. Indeed, he found none, but he did come across a great deal of pottery and many new walls and houses – enough to allow him to subdivide the site into yet more sections and conclude that Troy VIIA – and not Troy VI, as Dörpfeld held, or Troy II, as Schliemann twice maintained – was Homer's Troy.

In 1938, as war closed in on Europe, Blegen abandoned Hissarlik and moved on to a Mycenaean site in western Messenia, the suspected site of King Nestor's palace. And here he found something far better than treasure. In a room inside the palace, he came across 618 tablets, apparently baked hard after a vase of olive oil exploded and turned them into durable ceramic. Only twenty were intact, but from these and the fragments of the others, it was immediately clear that they were written in Evans's Linear B script. They seemed to be inventories, possibly the everyday record of the palace, what Blegen would later call King Nestor's 'office of internal revenue'. However, Linear B was still indecipherable, and the war brought an end to all archaeology in Greece for the time being.

It was 1950 before the search picked up again, and thirty-eight more Linear B tablets were found, this time at Mycenae. A young linguist called Michael Ventris, not yet thirty and soon to die in a car crash, settled down to examine Linear B. At first believing it to be similar to Etruscan, he assembled a grid of the relationship between the various signs. First a basic structure, then a series of meanings, appeared. What Ventris realized, as he began to read, was that Linear B was not like Etruscan at all, but a language very similar to ancient Greek, 'a difficult and archaic Greek ... but Greek nevertheless'. Though archaic and crude, these were words that Socrates or Plato might have understood. Meanwhile, Blegen had found 300 new tablets at Pylos. Ventris, substituting sounds for syllables, was able to confirm that these were indeed inventories; lists of soldiers, slaves, serving women, military units and commanders. There were names of individual shepherds, and even oxen, and lists of ewes and rams, chariots and military equipment and of repairs and breakages – a world not so much heroic as good at accounting. Most exciting perhaps, certainly for Schliemann, had he lived to see this day, the names of Homer's heroes appeared, even if as ordinary people and not as famous warriors; there was Achilles, and Hector, and Aeneas. Of the twenty-six trades mentioned in the tablets, twenty-three had been spoken of by Homer. From Tiryns and Mycenae were to come more tablets and more details; from Knossos another tablet, with the words 'To all the gods – a pot of honey'.

Linear B provided one of the most vital missing clues. It proved that the rulers of Tiryns, Mycenae, Orchomenos, Pylos and even Knossos were in fact, as Schliemann had argued and hoped, Greeks, and therefore that the inhabitants of the Bronze Age palaces, at the supposed time of the Trojan War, did actually speak the same language as Homer. An older civilization of Minoans on Crete, who reached their golden age earlier, around 1900 BC, had indeed exerted an immense influence over the occupants of mainland Greece, but after 1400 BC they had been subjugated by the people we now call Mycenaeans, and power in the Aegean had shifted from Knossos to Mycenae. And so Schliemann had, on this score at least, been right: the Mycenaeans, with their great Bronze Age palaces, had been Greek, and had enjoyed an immensely cultured civilization. Before he died, Michael Ventris, with his partner John Chadwick, paid Schliemann the ultimate compliment. They dedicated their book *Documents in Mycenaean Greek* 'to the memory of Heinrich Schliemann, 1822–1890, Father of Mycenaean Archaeology'.

The excavating of Troy went on, and continues to this day. Since the late 1980s, Professor Korfmann and a team from the University of Tübingen have been clearing, surveying and digging on and around the mound of Hissarlik, bringing to light further information on each period, and, more important, uncovering a large lower town, and additional evidence of Troy's past. Though ancient Troy does not appear ever to have rivalled Knossos or even Pylos in size, Schliemann would have felt encouraged that the Troy contemporary with Mycenae has emerged grander and larger than his own Troy II.

But what even Korfmann has been unable to do is to offer the final proof that Schliemann craved. To this day, no one can say with certainty what happened at Troy, or whether there was a Trojan War at all. First Schliemann, then Dörpfeld, then Blegen, the three men who devoted much of their lives to Troy, all concluded that they had found Troy. Of the three, it was Blegen and not Schliemenn who was the most outspoken. 'It can no longer be doubted,' he declared, at the close of his excavations, 'that there really was an actual historical Trojan war, in which a coalition of Achaeans, or Mycenaeans, under a king whose overlordship was recognized, fought against the people of Troy and their Allies.' Even though the archaeologists who followed him have seldom been prepared to go as far, saying only that *if* there was a Trojan war, then Blegen's Troy, Troy VIIA is the most likely site for it, a possible story can be pieced together, with evidence from a wide variety of sites and sources. And Schliemann, with his blind faith in Homer, was the man who, as Ventris acknowledged, laid the first seeds. His chronology may have been wrong; but that does not alter the fact that the long history of Troy was linked with the Mycenaean world, as sung by Homer, and as documented by archaeology.

Beginning at Troy, the story could go something like this. The most important question – who were the Trojans ? – remains a mystery, and the suggestion that both Greeks and Trojans were of the same stock is considered doubtful. Somewhere around 3600 BC–3000 BC a band of immigrants arrived on the plain of Troy by ship, though where they came from is not clear. They built a first settlement, which, in approximately 2500 BC, was destroyed by a great fire, only to be rebuilt, somewhat larger, as Troy II. These people produced heavy shallow dishes and two-handled goblets, and they had substantial amounts of gold and jewellery. Troy II came to a violent end around 2200 BC. From then until about 1800 BC, as Troy III, IV and V, the inhabitants of the mound kept the same early Bronze Age culture, enjoying their commanding position in the Troad.

Around 1900 BC–1700 BC came a sudden break with the past. Troy VI appears to have been built by newcomers, who arrived on the plain, bringing with them the horse. Troy VI belongs to the middle and late Bronze Age : free-standing houses, a tower with handsome masonry, a cistern. This settlement, too, came to a violent end, during the first half of the thirteenth century BC, possibly as the result of an earthquake. Its successor, Troy VIIA, the Troy of the large storage jars, identified by Blegen as the Troy of Helen, Priam and Homer's epic poems, was sacked at some time between the middle of the thirteenth century and the early part of the twelfth century BC. The settlements that followed were Hellentic and then Roman cities.

Across the water on the Greek mainland, a somewhat different history was unfolding. A Greek-speaking people seems to have settled in what is today Greece soon after 1900 BC, at a time when Crete was beginning its golden age. Between about 1700 BC and 1600 BC came the sudden flowering of a Mycenaean civilization on the mainland, heavily influenced by the Cretans, and made up of a series of kingdoms at places like Tiryns and Orchomenos, trading with other cities across the whole of the Peloponnese and along the shores of Asia Minor. With the decline and end of the power of the palace complex at Knossos, supremacy passed to the Mycenaeans.

The culture and life of these Mycenaean strongholds, as recounted by Homer and believed by many early archaeologists and historians, was seen as being a world of raiders and slaves, of rich plunder and lavish entertainment, of men who bound their hair with gold and silver threads, who loved jewellery, ornamental belts, and beautifully decorated swords, who worshipped the gods and recognized their divinity in little clay figurines. These Mycenaeans decorated their walls with 'friezes of blue enamel', grew wheat, barley, beans and figs and made olive oil and wine sweetened with honey. They had cheese, but did not drink milk. They kept dogs to hunt with and to guard over their houses ; but no cats. They feared death horribly – the 'darkness' into which Homer has his dying heroes sink. The world evoked by Homer is one of pleasure and heroism, ruled over by capricious and all-powerful gods and goddesses, inhabited by men of superhuman strength, seemingly closer to the gods than to man.

These Mycenaeans, still in this traditional version, were a warlike people, constantly at odds with neighbouring cities, and ever away on raids along the coast of Asia Minor – Homer's greatest praise for a man was that he was a 'sacker of cities'. The rich and prosperous Troy, with its thousand or so citizens dwelling inside the fortified walls, and some five thousand in the city below, was just one of the many cities they sacked, perhaps even at a moment when its defences were weakened by an earthquake, around 1250 to 1200 BC. The Mycenaeans had ships, and the seizure of women was commonplace. The sacking of Troy was thus seen as one of the last great exploits of the Mycenaean world, remembered and sung by the bards as the Mycenaean world descended into a dark age of poverty and isolation.

This version, though inspiring, is now accepted as overly romantic; the truth appears to have been far more prosaic. Though archaeology has not been able to produce Trojan ancestors, it has managed to establish that the most prosperous age of the mainland Greek states, the 'palace' age, when Mycenaean expansion in the Aegean was at its height, fell in the fourteenth and early thirteenth centuries BC – that is, at a time assumed to correspond with the siege of Troy. According to the pottery and decoration found at the various sites, the strongholds were all linked. However, the Mycenaeans of this great age were rather more like bureaucrats than Viking raiders, less glamorous but considerably more orderly. As the Linear B tablets show, these palaces shared the same sort of social structure and administration and some of the stone decoration is so alike that it may have been carved by the same travelling artists. Schliemann would have been pleased that the Mycenaean world does seem to have been as he maintained, one world, with one language : a stable civilization, with strong centralized authority, a hierarchical society, and clear arrangements about levying taxes and military service. The Mycenaean palaces had good contacts throughout the Mediterranean and the Aegean and became rich not so much through raiding as through the careful husbandry of their resources. Greeks and Trojans knew each other and traded actively. Trojan imports from the Mycenaean world seem to start around the sixteenth century BC and continue into the first half of the thirteenth century, not only pottery, but during the later years luxury items like ivory boxes and beads, electrum and silver pins. In return, the Trojans may have exported spun yarn (thousands of spindle whorls have been found at Hissarlik), and fish. Horse-breeding accounted for some of Troy's prosperity.

It was when the economic security of the Mycenaean strongholds began to collapse, possibly as a result of diminishing resources, somewhere around the thirteenth century BC, that tensions in the area grew, with the various states scrapping over what was left. With troubles growing at home, an armed foray against wealthy Troy may have seemed attractive. And so the great Bronze Age settlements, over a period of a generation or more, disintegrated, their end hastened by a possible combination of wars, piracy, poor harvests, epidemics and even an earthquake. Around 1200 BC the power of the Mycenaean palaces was over; the great centres celebrated in Homer's catalogue of ships, as having contributed to the Achaean expedition to Troy, lay in ruins and largely deserted. While the Aegean as a whole had been able to survive the collapse of the Minoan world on Crete, it could not do the same after the disintegration of the Mycenaean. What followed, the long period of the dark ages, lasted until the dawn of Greek classical history.

As for Homer himself, the details of his life remain extremely meagre. All that it seems possible to say is that the author of the *Iliad* and the *Odyssey* – if he was in fact one and the same person – lived between 750 and 650 BC, on the northern Aegean coast of Asia Minor. When the dark ages lifted, somewhere around 800 BC, literacy and epic poetry returned to Greece. The tale of the invasion of Troy, by a vast fleet from mainland Greece, and its destruction, followed by the homecoming of the heroes, looking back as it does to a supposed heroic age when heroes were valiant and rulers stern but fair, became one of the most loved of all the epic poems. It is not impossible that Homer himself visited Troy, soon to become a wealthy Greek city built on top of the ruins of ancient Troy, before the great bay silted up, and power moved to the coast and the new town of Alexandra Troas. Schliemann believed that Troy was finally abandoned only in the fifth century AD.

Though Schliemann and Gladstone and a number of other nineteen-century historians wished to believe that what Homer wrote was an accurate record of the Mycenaean 'palace' age, and a literal account of a heroic war against Troy, it is more generally accepted today that he pulled the various elements of his story from different times – spanning a number of centuries – and different places. The *Iliad* and the *Odyssey* therefore reflect more the life and the culture of the dark-age Greeks than anything Mycenaean, with added scenes and details coming from the ancestral memory of the times when Mycenae and Troy were great palace strongholds. The world of Schliemann's and Homer's heroes – raiders, sackers of cities, warriors – is not the same as that of the orderly men and women depicted in the Linear B texts.

The names of many of the best-known archaeologists are linked to the sites of their greatest discoveries – Arthur Evans to Knossos, Austin Henry Layard to Nineveh. But none compares with Schliemann for the way in which he fused his vision of the past, a past painted by just one great epic poet, with his life's work. Excavating too fast, too chaotically, without recording anything properly, and without the help of the later technology soon to become available to archaeologists, in fact digging, as M.I.Finley put it, much as one might dig a field of potatoes, Schliemann set out to prove that Homer was a historian as well as a poet. He made mistakes, he was often ill and exhausted, and he did invent things – though perhaps from vanity and a sheer need to succeed rather than from conscious dishonesty – but, Homer in hand, he kept on going; and it was Homer, a figure he seemed sometimes to regard as a cross between a surveyor and a war correspondent, who led him to a whole, lost, prehistoric world. Even if embellished by details that belonged to a later age, it was, after all, a real world. Not surprising, then, that Schliemann felt persecuted and outraged by his detractors. 'How many tens of years a new controversy may rage around Troy, I leave to the critics,' he wrote in some understandable despair in *Troja*. '*That* is their work; *mine* is done.'

For a while, after his death, Schliemann's detractors were silenced. But they did not stay silent for very long. As inconsistencies in his accounts of his life and work came to light over the years, so critics began to question not only his integrity; but his contribution to archaeology as a whole. There is no doubt at all that Schliemann embellished aspects of his private life and his personal adventures, in order to emerge in a more romantic and rosier light. And there is little doubt that, at one point or another in his life, he lied about where and when and with whom he made his more spectacular finds; that he added to certain discoveries in order to make them seem more substantial; that smuggling did not seem to him to be a sin; that he did combine several smaller finds to create more impressive treasures; that his methods could be both ruthless and devious; and that his love of treasure was boundless. A flawed character, certainly; but a great archaeologist none the less.

PART THREE

BERLIN AND AFTER

15

DEAD AND
WOUNDED ART

The story of Schliemann's life is at an end; but not that of Troy's gold, the famous diadems and rings, clasps and buttons, necklaces and goblets, earrings and needles that he considered his most valuable archaeological finds. For the treasure of King Priam, as it has continued to be called, was fated to keep on wandering. At the time of Schliemann's death in 1890, his collection from Troy, and much else besides, was safely in the wing of Berlin's Ethnographic Museum which had been given over to his gift to the German nation, and was widely considered one of the marvels of the prehistoric Bronze Age. It was not to remain there.

The treasure, which had already made one long journey from the mound of Hissarlik across the Aegean to Athens, and a second from Athens to Berlin, was to move yet again. It is in Berlin that the tale of King Priam's gold and Helen's jewels reopens – for despite all subsequent archaeological excavations at Troy, Schliemann's treasure continued to carry the names of Priam and Helen when, in the closing years of the Second World War, in the destruction and chaos of the city, it vanished once more. And it might have remained lost to the world, as it was during the centuries in which it lay undisturbed beneath the ruins of successive Hellenic and Roman cities, had it not been for the investigative flair and persistence of a small group of people.

The looting of art by victorious armies has a long and dishonourable history. All those objects perceived by conquerors to be the things most prized by the defeated – their churches and palaces, pictures and furniture, jewels and coins – have been the most coveted and most pillaged. Across Europe, the looting barbarians of the dark ages were followed by the apparently more civilized armies of the Renaissance princes, who in victory simply included in their treaties the transfer of all that could be moved and all that they desired. Revolutionary France, convinced that it was entitled to become the natural 'repository' for Europe's artistic heritage by virtue of its own advanced artistic sensibilities, encouraged Napoleon's instinct to add artistic plunder to military conquest. To Napoleon, conquering was possessing, and possession included treasure; to avoid the awkward charge of theft during his Italian campaign, he rechristened the early Italians 'honorary Frenchmen'; and his sacking of Italy was impressive. The treasures of Modena and Padua, Rome and Milan, flowed smoothly over the Alps into France.

It was not until halfway through the nineteenth century that steps were at last taken to make the cultural heritage of nations in some way inviolate. Pillage became a subject for international treaties, whose clauses exempted art from the rightful spoils of war. The Hague Conventions of 1899 and 1907 included Articles designed to shield works of art from the destructive and greedy tendencies of conquering soldiers. 'All premeditated seizure, destruction, or damage' to churches, charitable or educational institutions, and to all historical monuments and works of art and science', Article 56 laid down, was 'prohibited and should be prosecuted'. Like other treaties, the Hague Conventions were ignored. The First World War saw not just plunder but callous wrecking. The famous library of Louvain in Belgium was set on fire and an irreplaceable collection of ancient manuscripts, as well as a number of unique early scientific instruments, disappeared in what was later to be called a 'shameless holocaust of irreparable treasures, lit up by blind barbarian vengeance'. Appalled by such crude destructiveness, asserting that treasures of this kind belonged not to any one nation-state but to the entire civilized world, the signatories to the Versailles Treaty in 1919 insisted on adding stern clauses about restitution and compensation. As these seemed insufficiently forceful, art experts spent the 1920s and 1930s drawing up a series of tougher international agreements for the policing and protecting of art during times of war. Their new proposals sounded adequate, but they had been accepted only by the United States, Belgium, Greece, the Netherlands and Spain by the time war returned once more to Europe.

Germany had played little part in these debates. In any case, Hitler and the National Socialists had no time for art treaties. Long before war broke out, they had made it clear that all those whom they considered enemies, or of lesser human worth, were exempt from the protecting Articles. The Jews, celebrated collectors of some of the best pictures in Europe, as well as members of the labour unions, church groups, and opposition political parties, were all excluded. To destroy the Jews entailed not just destroying the people themselves but taking their property and possessions, both to raise money, and as a symbol of total power.

As the war spread, Hitler and the German army began to loot, obsessively. By the time unconditional surrender was signed in 1945, pictures, sculptures, tapestries, manuscripts, silver, gold, jewellery, furniture, medieval armour, rare coins and prehistoric treasures had all been stolen, from every country in Occupied Europe, and sent back to Germany. Napoleon had pillaged randomly; Hitler brought to looting not only ideological fervour, but all the meticulousness and precision of his highly organized military machine. It soon became known as the 'strengthening of Germanism'.

Hitler admired the florid German painters of the nineteenth century. He also liked Fragonard and Watteau, Tiepolo and Canaletto, Poussin and Claude Lorrain; but he did not much care for the French Impressionists. After the annexation of Austria, in March 1938, he decided to add to his own small collection of pictures with a view to creating the greatest museum in the world, which would contain collections from every age and every nation. Linz, the birthplace of Hitler's mother, a provincial Austrian town, was to be transformed into the cultural heart of the Thousand-Year Reich, and made into a magnificent new city with fine modern buildings housing separate collections of art. The showpiece was to be a Führermuseum, with a colonnaded façade more than 150 metres long.

In 1938 the plunder of Europe was already under way. Hitler consulted various experts, among them the art historian Dr Herman Voss, and a Linz Commission, under Dr Hans Posse, former head of the Dresden Art Gallery, began to contact the better-known German art dealers, men like Karl Haberstock in Berlin, with instructions to start searching for suitable art. For a while, there was an air of legitimacy about the whole business, for at least some of the acquisitions were paid for, especially if they happened to belong to Aryans and Christians or to state museums, even if the money came from accounts confiscated from Jews. The Jewish collections, however, were quite openly plundered. Corrupt art dealers were soon acting as middlemen, identifying and locating valuable Jewish art works and passing on the information to Hans Posse.

The progress of the war helped the looters. As the German forces marched across Europe, opening up new territories to loot, so Hitler began to see the need for some more systematic method of securing art for his world collection at Linz. He needed an art controller, a man to run what would effectively become a cultural section. He found him in the shape of a semi-educated philosopher called Alfred Rosenberg, the son of an Estonian shoemaker. Rosenberg was not much interested in art himself; the author of *The Myth of the Twentieth Century*, a rambling volume of ill-digested world philosophy, which sold over a million copies in the 1930s, Rosenberg preferred to talk Nazi ideology, of which he saw himself partial architect and chief exponent. Beyond admiring his organizational skills, no one thought much of Rosenberg. Airey Neave, who was to observe him in the dock during the Nuremberg trials, described Rosenberg as 'by far the most boring and pedantic of the accused ... He had the expression of a dreary spaniel ... His appearance was that of an off-duty undertaker in a Boris Karloff film.' Rosenberg may indeed have looked like an undertaker; but he was telling the truth when, asked by the Tribunal to describe his activities, he replied: 'Between October 1940 and July 1941 my organization accomplished the greatest art operation in history.' Only the word 'theft' would perhaps have been more accurate.

Das Einsatzstab Reichsleiter Rosenberg für die Besetzen Gebiete, known as ERR, began life in January 1940 as an 'ideological mission', with orders from Hitler to clear out, 'for scholarly purposes', all Jewish and Masonic libraries and places of worship. What was found in these raids was to be stored for a future academy, a 'Hohe Schule' to be set up after the war as a centre for Nationalist Socialist research, indoctrination and education, where young Nazis would be sent to learn about the moral and spiritual degeneracy of Jews and Freemasons. Rosenberg was very good at his job. When Paris fell, he despatched teams of 'requisitioning officials' to go from house to house, drawing up inventories of all the art objects abandoned in houses belonging to Jews. Within a couple of weeks, 38,000 houses were stripped, and it took 150 trucks of the Union of Parisian Moving Contractors and over 1,500 French labourers to cart their contents away. Not everything, of course, was set aside for the post-war education of young Nazis. The pick of the looted art, like the Vermeers and the Van Goghs, were sent to Hitler, to whom Rosenberg was soon writing, expressing hopes that 'this short occupation with the beautiful things of art which are nearest to your heart will send a ray of beauty and joy into your revered heart'.

As his headquarters for Western Europe, Rosenberg chose the Hotel Commodore in Paris. His storehouse was the Musée du Jeu de Paume, on the corner of the Place de la Concorde, and by the late autumn of 1940, over 21,000 separate works of art had already been assembled, for the most part to be packed up and shipped off to Berlin, though a few special pieces were kept back for private exhibitions in the museum's galleries. Soon, Rosenberg was opening branches in Amsterdam and Brussels. After Field-Marshal Wilhelm Keitel, Commander-in-Chief of the German Armed Forces, issued a decree formally extending the 'collecting of art' from Jewish and Masonic centres to all collections, regardless of the race or religion of their owners, the distinction between state and private property was rapidly blurred. Everything, everywhere, was to be regarded as available; though the words 'safekeeping', and 'taking into custody' of art objects were the ones the Nazis themselves preferred to use at Nüremberg.

Hitler was not the only German who had his eye on Europe's cultural heritage. Goering, Chief of the Air Force and founder of the Gestapo, unlike Hitler, did like the Impressionists. His taste ran to the early Dutch and Flemish masters, as well as French Gothic and Italian Renaissance art; landscapes bored him, but he loved nudes, triptychs and portraits, and especially Cranach's Venuses. Goering saw great possibilities in the art rape of Europe. He already owned a small art collection, housed at his estate, Carinhalle, sixty miles south-east of Berlin. 'Whenever you come across anything that may be needed by the German people,' Goering was soon telling senior officers, 'you must be after it like bloodhounds.' The cost of all this plunder, in human terms, was irrelevant. 'This everlasting concern about foreign people must cease now, for once and for all.' For it was, of course, not just art that was being looted, but everything the Germans needed or desired. More powerful than Rosenberg, and just as tenacious, Goering began to provide the transport to carry the looted art back to Germany. In the next few years, he was to make twenty-one trips to Paris to pick out for himself the pictures he most admired. Goering was not, of course, the only acquisitive German military commander – a colonel in the SS, Dr Kajetan Muehlmann, proved a most competent plunderer in Holland, and later in Poland and Russia – and as other officers and other branches of the German war machine joined in, a certain chaos developed.

There was plenty of art to go round. The first work believed to have been stolen by the Nazis in France was Vermeer's *Astrologer*, taken by the Gestapo from Baron de Rothschild's house in Paris. After the collapse of Holland and Belgium, paintings by Breughel, Rubens, Jan Steen and Rembrandt all began to make their way east. Looting on this scale posed a formidable problem of logistics, and other sections of the German army were soon being called upon to provide extra transport. By the spring of 1941, Rosenberg was able to report that 7,000 cases of looted works of art were already on their way to Germany – only there was no talk of 'loot', but rather of 'collections of materials' moved by 'bearers of culture'. As museums, libraries and private houses were raided, so photographers were ordered to make a record of every major acquisition; these pictures were pasted into albums and sent off to Hitler, like shopping catalogues, to make his selections easier.

In the east it was all rather different. Whatever shreds of legality the Germans had tried to invent before, when it came to looting the art of the occupied countries of western Europe these were now quite simply abandoned. The Western Europeans possessed, after all, a recognizable and impressive history and culture, one which Hitler intended to absorb: the Slavs, and particularly the Russians, like the Jews, were not really human at all. What was not seen as worth plundering, or proved too cumbersome to move, was destroyed.

Czechoslovakia was stripped first. After the German occupation, in March 1939, the looting began. Once again, it was not just art: trolley-buses went, and cotton and iron and food, but they were quickly followed by entire libraries, the contents of scientific laboratories and pictures. Then came Poland. As the German troops crossed the border in September, the newly appointed Governor-General, Hans Frank, and his special deputy Dr Muehlmann, who had done so well in Holland, were given orders to secure all Polish art treasures 'to complement German artistic property'. On 15 November, Frank issued a decree that all 'movable and stationary' public valuables be sequestered. Looting was carried out openly and with considerable brutality. So efficient were Frank and his men that within six months he was able to announce proudly that Poland was now picked clean. To mark the occasion, he had a handsome catalogue printed; it read like the inventory of some magnificent imaginary museum: paintings by the great masters of France, Holland, Italy, Germany and Spain; rare illustrated books and woodcuts; antique porcelain and glass; tapestries, coins and medieval weapons. The National Museums in Warsaw and Krakow had been emptied; the cathedral of Lublin stripped; the houses of the Polish nobility, the university libraries, the monasteries – nothing had been overlooked.

If the Poles were viewed as barbarians, the Russians were regarded as scarcely human. There was something of an almost crusading zeal in the Nazi desire to reduce their most splendid possessions to ruin. The words 'protection' and 'safeguarding' of art, repeated so frequently during the art raids on western Europe, were rapidly forgotten.

Rosenberg was still in charge of looting, with his ERR, when the Wehrmacht crossed the Soviet border on 22 July 1941. When, at four o'clock in the morning, the Luftwaffe bombed Kiev, the Red Army was unprepared. Rosenberg had asked Hitler to second to him von Holst, an expert on the Leningrad museums. He now set up his headquarters in Smolensk, and quickly cleared the city's four museums. The problem with the Soviet Union, for the looters, was the sheer scale of the operation, though the Soviet attitude towards art since the revolution somewhat compensated for it. Scattered over a country several times the size of western Europe lay many handsomely endowed cities, monasteries, museums and churches filled with centuries of superb craftsmanship and careful collecting. Until the revolution, Russia had been one of the richest countries in the world in terms of art: from Peter the Great down, the Tsars had not only commissioned architects and painters from all over Europe to create for them immense and exquisitely decorated palaces and parks, but had bought from abroad many paintings by the European masters. At the turn of the century, major art buyers from America turned to Russia as well as Holland, Italy or France for their purchases.

After the revolution all this changed. Private collections flooded on to the market as owners fled abroad, leaving their pictures to be sold by servants, or confiscated by museums. When, in 1905, Diaghilev had organized an exhibition of eighteenth-century Russian portraits, 2,000 pictures were loaned by their private owners. By the mid-1920s, over half of these portraits had gone abroad. In the 1930s, until the practice was stopped, a number of the remaining paintings were sold by the state to raise money: Titian's *Venus with a Mirror* went to Washington, Rembrandt's *Temptation of St Peter* to Holland. By now, in any case, most of the pre-revolutionary art experts had either fled abroad or were dead, and though curators of the great museums continued to care for their collections, and party leaders continued to take state art to decorate their walls, the whole idea of privately owned masterpieces had become suspect, just as the decadence of non-revolutionary subjects was frowned on. Anything left in private hands was sold, for absurdly low prices, or confiscated. What Rosenberg and his men found, as they moved further into the Soviet Union, were museum collections beyond all dreams, and a few masterpieces either hidden away, or hanging, unrecognized, in municipal buildings. It was simply a matter of how to find and plunder them most efficiently.

When it became clear that the ERR, on its own, was not able cope with loot on this scale, a 'special formation' under the Foreign Minister von Ribbentrop was set up and given the task of keeping close behind the advancing German troops, ready to secure and seize 'their cultural treasures and all objects of great historic value, to select valuable books and films, and generally to despatch them all to Germany'. Von Ribbentrop and his 'battalion' turned out to be a match for Rosenberg and the ERR. Soon, companies of his men, spread out over a huge area, had emptied the laboratories of the Medical and Scientific Research Institutes in Kiev, the Ukrainian Academy of Sciences at Schevtchenko, and the famous library at Korolenko. From Kiev, they took over four million books and manuscripts. Carpets, curtains, jewellery, porcelain – everything went. Freight trains, with forty to fifty wagons piled high with booty, were soon reaching Germany every month. The looters' task was made considerably easier by the Soviet unpreparedness and confusion, and the fact that the safekeeping of art had not been a priority: as the Germans advanced, museum directors had been instructed only to save all metal objects. Bronze candelabra of the nineteenth century were packed up and taken to safety, while Flemish sixteenth-century masterpieces were left for the Germans.

It was not until after the war, at the Nuremberg trials, that the world really learned how devastating had been the German policy towards the Soviet cultural history. Documents produced by the prosecution proved that the German High Command had intended to annihilate some of the cities. One secret order of the Chief of the Naval Staff (Staff 1.a. No. 1601/41), dated 29 December, 1941, and addressed only to staff officers, had laid down plans for Leningrad. 'The Führer', it said, 'has decided to erase from the face of the earth St Petersburg. The existence of this large city will have no further interest after Soviet Russia is destroyed.' While the German troops moved in to attack, von Ribbentrop's art battalion set out to scour the surrounding countryside.

St Petersburg had been the seat of the Russian Tsars since the beginning of the eighteenth century. The Tsarist palaces, outside the city, decorated under the reigns of Catherine the Great, Alexander I and Nicholas I by architects and craftsmen brought from Italy, France and England, were known throughout the world for their furniture, porcelain, Gobelin tapestries, marble busts, pictures and painted silk hangings. On 23 September 1941, while the German soldiers fought for the heart of Leningrad, the art looters reached Petrodverts – or Peterhof – the palaces and park, 29 kilometers to the west, founded by Peter the Great in 1705, and inspired by Versailles. As magnificent as the palaces was the splendid park, designed by the French architect Le Blond with an elaborate system of canals and fountains. After the revolution, Peterhof had become a museum park, and its palaces were opened to the public. Again, the Russians made it all too easy for the German art battalion: preparations for the evacuation of the Peterhof collections had been made in the weeks before the arrival of the Germans, and much had been packed ready into crates. But the NKVD, the precursors to the KGB, had forbidden their removal on the grounds that it would make the Red Army appear to have lost control of the war. The art battalion arrived to find 34,214 art objects and 11,700 books, many of them simply waiting to be transported, together with 14,950 pieces of furniture.

The Germans occupied Peterhof during the two-year siege of Leningrad. What they could not take away, when they finally pulled out, they destroyed. Floors of the palaces were torn up, beams in the ceilings sawn off, ceilings ripped down. The Great Palace, started by Le Blond and completed by Rastrelli, the great master of Russian baroque, was set on fire. The Chinese room in the Monplaisir Palace was torn apart. A nearby pavilion had served as a latrine. In the park, the pipeline feeding Le Blond's ingenious water systems was blown up; the trees were cut down for firewood. As they drove out of the park for the last time, the Germans fired 9,000 rounds of heavy artillery shells into Catherine's English Palace.

The story of the disappearance of the amber room, taken from the Catherine Palace at Tsarskoe Selo 25 kilometers south of Leningrad is one of the most celebrated and puzzling art thefts of all time. It has yet to be solved. In 1707, the Danish craftsman Gottfried Wolfram designed a room for the Prussian King Frederick William I, made entirely of amber panels, separated by mirrors and decorated with mosaics and miniatures. So beautiful was this room that Peter the Great, on a visit to Prussia in 1716, begged to be allowed to take it back to Russia. By 1743, the amber room had been installed in the Winter Palace in St Petersburg: Rastrelli added more Persian amber, and fifty-three pillars covered in mirrors, to set off the amber panels. Like Schliemann's gold, the amber room was fated to keep wandering, a task made simpler by the fact that it had been designed in detachable sections, the amber itself so thin that it was almost transparent, backed with silver foil to enhance the reflections, and inlaid with landscapes made of thousands of minute mosaics. In 1755, the amber room was moved to the Catherine Palace at Tsarskoe Selo, where it survived the revolution to become one of the most valued treasures of the Soviet Union.

One of Rosenberg's groups entered the Catherine Palace with the German troops. While the palace itself was turned into a barracks for the soldiers, the amber room was dismantled and packed up, together with other amber objects collected by Peter the Great, as well as silk hangings, gilt ornaments, furniture, carpets, statues, pictures and books. It was sent off to join other loot at the SS North-East Group headquarters at Königsberg, near the border with Poland. At least the beauty of the amber room had been recognized and respected. The rest of the Catherine Palace did not fare so well, according to the testimonies of various German officers later taken prisoner. The famous parquet floors, carved in different woods, were gouged up; the eighteenth-century yellow silk hangings in the small dining-room, with their pattern of swans and pheasants, were ripped down; the iconostasis in the palace chapel was smashed, as were the violet, blue and white glass panes in Catherine II's bedroom. On the pond in the park, a rare collection of old boats was broken into pieces, while the marble of a Turkish bath was smashed. As they left, the Germans paused to set fire to Rastrelli's 'dining-room for the gentlemen', with its gold mouldings, and to the great hall, with its frescoes by Torelli, Giordano and Brullov.

Perhaps not surprisingly, the Russian campaign is better remembered for its destructiveness than for its pillage. It was as if the Germans had taken particular care to identify all that was most precious to the history and culture of the country, in order the better to destroy it. Novgorod was believed by the Russians to be one of its founding cities; with its magnificent cathedrals and monasteries, it contained not only monuments but much eleventh- and twelfth-century art. The advancing Germans reduced the city to a ruin. Smolensk, another of the most ancient towns, was occupied by the Germans for twenty-six months. In that time, they blew up various palaces and used the stones for fortifications, and burned down libraries containing 646,000 books. As the months of German occupation went by, it became apparent that nothing that lay in the German path would escape destruction. Kaluga, a town south of Moscow, had been the home of Konstantin Tsiolkovsky, the aeronautical designer; after his death in 1936, his house had been turned into a museum, displaying his models of dirigibles, his plans for rockets and his instruments. German soldiers broke up the models, set fire to the furniture, turned one of the rooms into a hen-coop, and used a portrait of Tsiolkovsky for revolver practice. In Taganrog, they destroyed Chekhov's home; in Tikhvin, Rimsky-Korsakov's. The Germans spent six weeks at Yasnaya Polyana, Tolstoy's estate, using the furniture, manuscripts and books as firewood; and several more in Klin, where Tchaikovsky composed *Eugene Onegin*, turning his house into a garage for their motorcycles and heating it by burning the tables, chairs and the composer's personal belongings that had not been looted earlier by other German soldiers.

Pushkin's estate at Mikhailovskoye had been declared a 'state reservation' in 1922, and, in the years leading up to the war, had become a shrine for many thousands of visitors. Piece by piece, building by building, the Germans looted it, set fire to what would burn, and chopped down what was still standing. When they left, they bombarded the village with artillery and mine-throwers. Pushkin's tomb, in the nearby monastery of Sryatiye-Gory, was later found, as a witness told the Nuremberg Tribunal, 'covered with refuse, rubble, wooden fragments of icons, and pieces of sheet metal'. These 'Hitlerite vandals' seemed to take particular pleasure in desecrating what they could not carry away. After plundering the Korolenko Library in Kharkov, the soldiers used the books they considered worthless as paving stones to make the muddy streets easier for their lorries.

As the war grew nastier, as prisoners on both sides were shot, and as the German casualties increased, so the vandalism was not only tolerated but encouraged. A frenzy of destruction seemed to settle over the invading army; it left some idea of what might have happened in the Western European countries had Hitler not had his dream about Linz. By the early spring of 1944, Russia had been laid waste.

Four hundred and twenty-seven museums had been totally destroyed, and all over the Soviet Union, palaces and pavilions, houses and libraries, had been pillaged, burnt and blown up. As many as 1,670 Greek Orthodox churches had been torn down. The cultural inheritance of Russia had effectively been reduced to rubble.

Even so, art was only a very small part of what had been removed or destroyed. More than 1,700 towns and 70,000 villages had been left in ruins; 32,000 factories had been blown up, and over 100,000 collective farms demolished. Along with Peter the Great's silks and paintings and Catherine's amber room had gone horses, cows, pigs chickens, beehives and agricultural machinery of every kind. As many as forty-nine million people are now thought to have died. The sheer brutality of the German destruction of the Soviet Union was important for what was to follow.

The Allies were not oblivious to the plunder of Europe. Intelligence reports from the occupied territories told of looting by German soldiers and of the casual destruction of churches and monuments. In December 1942, after a detailed account arrived of the sacking of Poland, various universities and art societies started pressing for an official body to prepare for the artistic recovery of Europe, once the Germans were defeated. Priority 'targets' were drawn up; they included Goering's estate at Carinhalle, which was by now known to contain a great deal of looted art, and the finding and confiscating of all records kept by Alfred Rosenberg, whom sources identified as controller of 'an important body of looters'. As more information emerged, so lists were drawn up of the names of prominent looters and the collaborators who had helped them.

In America, two prestigious organizations, the American Defence – Harvard Group and the American Council of Learned Societies, pushed President Roosevelt into setting up a Commission for the Protection and Salvage of Artistic Monuments in War Areas, under Owen J. Roberts, a Justice of the Supreme Court. Roberts was given an office in New York and a team of people to make lists and maps of important historical and artistic buildings all over Europe. They soon produced what they called a manual of 'art first aid'. In England, a similar but somewhat more informal body was formed, at 27 Princes Gate in London, under Lieutenant-Colonel Sir Leonard Woolley, the distinguished excavator of Carchemish and Ur, reporting directly to the War Office.

It was by now perfectly clear to everyone that the fabric of Europe's churches, palaces and museums had suffered appallingly from the war; what was less clear was the extent of the looting or the callousness of the destruction. The plan, as the Allies began to reconquer Europe, was to appoint teams of art experts, former art historians or museum curators, to give them cameras, typewriters and jeeps, and send them off to follow the advancing troops. Their first task was to identify buildings that should be protected from looters as well as from soldiers looking for billets, and to produce lists of places requiring urgent art first aid. The fact that only a couple of dozen officers were considered sufficient for this mission gives some idea of how little was really known about the ferocity and efficiency of the Rosenberg and von Ribbentrop looters. The Germans, hearing of these plans, hastened to put out some propaganda. On 1 October 1943, a German radio station warned its listeners that, among the Allies, was an 'organization consisting of thieves and Jews' which was being issued with maps to 'enable them to trace artistic treasures', and that its members, far from being 'historians acting for the sake of science and from an unselfish love of art', were in fact 'Jewish buyers' for the big New York and London art firms. Poachers and gamekeepers : it all sounded almost exciting. But no one, at this time, had any conception of the enormity of the artistic task that lay ahead.

The Allied forces landed in Sicily in July 1943 ; the slow battle for the recapture of Europe had begun. As long as the Axis survived, there had been very little looting of artistic treasures by the Germans in Italy : Hitler bought rather than stole masterpieces of the Renaissance from Mussolini. But as the Germans retreated, they plundered. In July 1944, the German 362nd Infantry Division pulled out of Florence with 307 paintings taken from the Uffizi museum and elsewhere. All over Europe, the German forces were on the move, either pulling back or concentrating their troops. For Rosenberg and the ERR, von Ribbentrop and his art battalion, there was now a new task : that of deciding what to do with the immense horde of stolen art.

By early 1944, the various depots set up by the looters were full. Schloss Neuschwanstein in Bavaria, the nineteenth-century castle built by mad King Ludwig II, for example, which had served as the main depository for the art taken from the French Jews, was crammed to overflowing. Other castles, storehouses, and museum vaults could take no more. With the increasing likelihood of the Allies entering Germany itself, confusion among the looters intensified. Nor was it just a question of concealment and security : much of the plunder, particularly the furniture and pictures, needed certain temperatures and amounts of humidity. One place to provide the right conditions was the salt mines, where the temperature seldom rose above 47 degrees Fahrenheit, or fell below 40 degrees, while the humidity was constant at around 65 per cent. It was to some of these that the art teams now began to take the stolen treasures, sometimes building walls deep into the mines behind which the loot could be concealed. The tables, now, were slowly turning.

The looters were on the retreat; those intent on salvage advancing. A vast treasure hunt was about to be launched.

Eleven days before the Normandy landings, General Eisenhower sent a message to all field commanders. 'Shortly we shall be fighting our way across the continent of Europe ... Inevitably, in the path of our advance will be found historical monuments and cultural centres which symbolize to the world all that we are fighting to preserve. It is the responsibility of every commander to protect and respect these symbols wherever possible.'

The words sounded good. But the Allies were soon struggling, foot by foot, to gain a toehold in France, and few British or American officers had the leisure to debate whether or not the châteaux that lay in their paths were full of priceless tapestries and Louis XIV furniture.

Behind them came, as planned, the art experts appointed to what had been named the Monuments, Fine Arts and Archives group (MFA&A). The trouble lay not with their expertise, but with their number. Two American officers and one British officer made up the entire first art brigade. They had a couple of Baedekers thoughtfully provided by the group, a few large-scale maps, and they were cultivated and thoughtful men. But they had no camera, no typewriter and no jeep. Their instructions were to give first aid to the most injured art (they had no supplies); to inspect and report on the state of the artistic monuments (they had no transport); and to prevent the Allied troops from billeting in historic buildings (three men against several million). In the next few months, they were joined by three more American officers and two more British ones. Since the army plainly considered the entire enterprise absurd, and since even Woolley had mentioned possible 'suspicion and impatience at dilettanti who are anyhow "soft"', it was remarkable that they were able to accomplish anything at all.

These eight men, and the few more who crossed the Channel to join them, turned out to be extremely resourceful. They hitched lifts on army trucks, they stole German cars, and they took bicycles, and then they fanned out, pedalling in the wake of the advancing armies. After the British called for some kind of formal definition of 'art', the group was issued with helpful directives. 'A castle,' said the brief, 'is usually defined as a large fortified building, and a palace as an unfortified stately mansion or residence of royalty.' As they moved forwards, they quickly realized that posting off-limits signs on listed buildings was far less effective than covering them in the white tape that indicated unexploded mines, and that their real job at this stage was less that of bringing first aid to monuments damaged by the Germans than preventing the Allied troops from wreaking further destruction.

The Americans billeted in the Château de Frémigny, as the men from the MFA&A soon pointed out, had done more harm in two months than the Germans had in four years. The way they saw it, the official directives were all wrong: a palace should really have been defined as the 'local honey on the Supreme HQ protected list, where blasted colonels will certainly billet their troops'. As Janet Flanner wrote in her book on art, *Men and Monuments*, the officers of the MFA&A were really 'frantic boarding-house keepers, trying to put thousands of lodgers into the right rooms and out of the wrong ones, and above all trying to prevent them from pocketing everything pretty that belonged to the house'. Billeted American soldiers, in particular, had a tendency to nail pictures of pin-up girls on to priceless carved wooden panels, and there were soon reports of fires in châteaux where soldiers had set up their paraffin cookers on parquet floors. Very few indeed paid any attention to the useful booklet issued with the rest of their army kit, which gave orders not to carve names on pieces of furniture, nor chip bits off sculptures to take as souvenirs, nor clip out corners of paintings, and urged all those billeted in historic buildings to treat them 'as you would expect a stranger to treat your own house'. (Man, noted the author of this pamphlet sternly, was 'distinguished from the beasts by his power to reason and to frame abstract hopes and ideas'.)

The task set for the men of the MFA&A was not just daunting: it was also profoundly depressing. As they travelled across France towards Paris, or in the direction of Holland and Belgium, they began to realize that the war had indeed been terrible for Western civilization. Art, in every direction, was not just wounded; it was dead. There was often little to do beyond write obituaries. One officer, who covered an astounding 13,000 miles in France in two weeks, estimated that 90 per cent of the listed monuments had been hit, and that two out of every three had been severely damaged. Gothic buildings, he observed, with their jagged surfaces and flying buttresses, had survived better than the flatter, smoother Renaissance ones.

As for the second duty of the MFA&A men, that of tracking down art looted by the Germans, or hidden by people in basements, hay-lofts, church steeples, slaughterhouses and lunatic asylums, the enormity of that task seemed, for the moment, too great even to consider.

The people still missing from this story are the German museum curators. True, some had joined the ERR or von Ribbentrop's art battalion. But others, whether by virtue of their age, their integrity or the importance of their jobs, sat out the war years in their own museums, doing their best to protect their collections and, after the Allies began bombing the German cities, trying desperately to find ways of making them safe. Of all these collections, Schliemann's treasures from Troy, and particularly Priam's gold, were considered one of the prizes of the German art world.

Schliemann, when giving his Trojan finds to the German nation in 1880, had specified that he wanted a wing of a museum to himself, one bearing his name in large gold letters over the entrance. While a suitable site was being sorted out, the Troy gold went on show in Berlin's Department of Ethnography, and when the Martin Gropius Bauer was ready, with the prestigious Museum for Pre-and-Early History, it was moved into fine new quarters, where it attracted enormous numbers of visitors. Shortly before the turn of the century, the collection was recatalogued, and 9704 separate items listed, but the true figure was certainly very much higher, as several of the objects were counted together under single headings. When, after World War I, the Versailles Treaty decreed that a number of German museum pieces should be given to the European countries as compensation for some of their own art looted or vandalized by German soldiers during the fighting, Schliemann's treasure was excluded.

In 1926, Wilhelm Unverzacht was made director of the Pre-and-Early History Museum, by this time widely accepted as the most important of its kind in Germany. Unverzacht was a scholarly and conscientious man, very knowledgeable about art and its international dimensions, for he had spent the early 1920s serving on the post-war reparations committee. He had powerful friends in Berlin and among the future leaders of the National Socialist Party, though it is said that when he eventually became a party member it was only to keep his job. Much of the story that follows is drawn from Unverzacht's diary, in which he made long and detailed notes; it has come to light only recently.

In 1934, increasingly aware of the threat that the political turmoil developing once again in Europe could pose to German art collections, the director of all Berlin museums, Otto Kümmle, called a meeting of curators. Unverzacht was one of the men who attended. The contents of Berlin's museums, said Kümmle, were to be divided into three: the first group was to contain irreplaceable items, the second those of great value, and the third everything else. The threat, at this stage, was perceived as coming from the air, given the recent developments in aeronautical technology. Schliemann's collection was considered to fall into all three categories, with Priam's treasure as well as some of the gold and silver finds of his last season at Troy falling into the first group, and many of the pots and vases into the second.

In 1937 came rumours of imminent hostilities. Group one, which by now also included the Apollo from Troy, over which Schliemann had fallen out with Frank Calvert, as well as all the best pieces from group two – pots, cups, jars – were packed into boxes and baskets and taken down to the basement of the Pre-and-Early History Museum. Anxiety for their safety grew after Sudetenland was invaded, and had reached such a pitch by the summer of 1939 that the Prussian Minister of Finance, Johannes Popitz, six days before the invasion of Poland, ordered curators to start moving their more valuable objects out of central Berlin to places of greater safety. Unverzacht closed his museum, and organized round-the-clock shifts of packers.

What happened to the many millions of objects that made up the contents of the Pre-and-Early History Museum – and particularly the vast Schliemann collection – is extremely confused, and made more so, not just by the amount of material that was moved, but by the fact that it was broken up into different groups, which, at different times, travelled to different places, both within Berlin itself and in the surrounding countryside. The story of Unverzacht's war, to judge by his diaries, is one of ceaseless anxiety and activity, as he searched for ever more boxes and baskets in which to pack and move his collections, as he inspected possible stores, vaults, mines and castles, as he held meetings with influential Party members who might have been able to help him, and as he bullied and cajoled all those with transport to carry his containers. The fact that at various times different lists were made of the collections in the Pre-and-Early History Museum, and put in different places, and that some of these lists were lost while only parts of others survived, turned the task later facing the post-war museum curators into a nightmare.

By the spring of 1940, any suitable metal for the war effort still remaining in Berlin's art collections had been confiscated; museum curators fought to salvage what they could. Sandbags were delivered to reinforce walls and ceilings, and windows were bricked over. In January 1941, Unverzacht arranged for his most valuable exhibits – Priam's gold and the Apollo among them – to be transferred to the vaults of a bank, and for part of group two, including some of the Troy pottery, to go to the basement of the Neuer Munze, a section of the Reichsbank.

By the end of 1941, Berlin, the imperial capital of Germany, with its four-and-a-half million inhabitants and splendid baroque palaces, churches, squares and boulevards, was a city at war. Searchlights and anti-aircraft guns were arranged in concentric circles around the city, while fortified gun emplacements had been built in the town centre. Foremost among Berlin's defences were three vast towers – known as flak-towers, an acronym of the German words for aviator, defence and cannon – somewhat like modern crusader castles, designed after the first Allied bombing by Albert Speer's architects. These enormous buildings, with walls 8 feet thick made of reinforced concrete, and window slits protected by solid steel shutters, were situated in the Zoo gardens, in the Humbold park and in the Friederichshain. Shell- and bomb-proof, the towers were 120 feet tall, with five or more levels below ground, and they each had their own water and electricity supplies. On top were mounted 128-mm guns in pairs, capable of firing a salvo every ninety seconds, with eight shells programmed to explode simultaneously. When the guns fired, the earth trembled.

Of the three, the Zoo tower was the largest. Equivalent to a thirteen-storey building, and occupying almost an entire city block, it contained barracks for a hundred gunners, a 95-bed hospital with two operating theatres, air-raid shelters large enough to take 15,000 people, as well as kitchens and a broadcasting station. This self-contained fortress was run from a communications tower on the roof, from where the Luftwaffe directed the defence of Berlin and kept in touch with the various anti-aircraft gun units. Ammunition, buried far below the ground, was brought to the top of the tower in steel lifts, which made almost unbearably loud groans as they were winched up. On the walls of the Zoo tower had been painted slogans, in vast white letters: 'Better dead than slaves', and 'Our honour is called faithfulness'.

The flak-towers were now seen to have another use. As Berlin's curators began to despair of saving their collections, it was agreed that one floor of both the Zoo and the Friederichshain towers would be turned over to them as warehouses. In the next few weeks, Berlin's treasures were delivered by post-office vans for safekeeping – various Greek, Egyptian and Roman antiquities, Gobelin tapestries, dozens of paintings, the Kaiser Wilhelm coin collection, and even the vast Pergamon altar, built around 180 BC by Eumenes II of the Hellenes. On 2 September 1941, after many negotiations, Unverzacht had three sealed boxes – containing, among other things, all Priam's gold and treasures – and thirty crates removed from the Pre-and-Early History Museum and taken to rooms 10 and 11 on the first floor of the Zoo tower. Guards were posted, and identity cards issued to a very small number of people allowed access. In time, many more boxes and crates arrived from the museum, one of them containing a set of microfilm records of everything that had been held there.

With all his most prized objects apparently out of immediate danger, Unverzacht began to search for safer homes for the art objects that remained in the basement of the Pre-and-Early History Museum. At first, he was drawn to places to the east, believing that little danger was liable to come from Russia ; but then, as the Russians looked increasingly likely to mount a counter-attack, so the west seemed more attractive. Disused salt mines and castles were all visited and considered.

Lebus was an old archaeological centre on the River Oder. After many trips there and back, and many discussions with his useful Nazi contacts, Unverzacht was able to arrange for a barge – a far better means of transport than jolting vehicles on rough roads – to be loaded with boxes from the museum. When it reached Lebus, the Hitler Youth helped to unload it. The barge left Berlin just in time to escape a heavy Allied air raid on the city, in November 1943, during which part of the museum was destroyed. Unverzacht, whose own home received five direct hits in the course of the war, continued to spend his time packing, seeking interviews with those in power who could help, and scouring Berlin for empty crates and hiding-places. In time, more consignments went off to Lebus, though 1,200 boxes, containing many pots from Troy, were stuck in the ice for several days when the River Oder froze over ; some went to a salt mine at Schönebeck, others to a castle near the city. A few of the more valuable exhibits were brought to the Zoo tower to join the rest, after Unverzacht was able to negotiate additional space on the third floor. By now, it was becoming extremely complicated to work out just where everything had been hidden.

In November 1943, the Allies began to bomb Berlin continuously. The flak-towers, standing high above the surrounding houses, made excellent targets and the even more concentrated raids of November 1944 scored direct hits on the Zoo and its surrounding gardens. Both Zoo tower and treasure remained virtually unscathed. The animals in the Zoo did not. Incendiaries and phosphorous bombs set the animal houses alight. On 22 November, seven elephants died in the blasted remains of a once ornate Indian temple, two giraffes and sixteen antelopes perished, and the lions and tigers suffocated to death in their cages.

Rumours soon spread around the city that two crocodiles had escaped and had been captured just as they were about to slip down into the city's sewers, that a tiger had entered a fashionable café and eaten a piece of sugar-and-almond cake before expiring, and that a dangerous wolf was on the rampage. Only the story of the wolf proved at all true, and even so it turned out to be an exceedingly timid animal, found cowering behind someone's front door.

Three days later, the RAF returned with 443 Lancasters. This time an aerial mine hit the Zoo's aquarium, and its artificial river, one storey up, designed so that people could watch the reptiles swimming around above their heads, exploded, scattering crocodiles and fish among the ruins. Once again, the Zoo flak-tower remained undamaged. On 3 February, 1945, the bombers were back, with a thousand US Fortresses and 900 Mustangs and Thunderbolts. Aerial photographs showed two square miles of central Berlin in flames. In almost six years of war, the Zoo had been hit by over a hundred high-explosive bombs. By the time the war ended, 750 of the 2,000 animals that had not been evacuated earlier had been killed and many more were to die from cold, shock and lack of water. The seven dead elephants, each weighing between four and six tons, posed appalling problems of disposal. It took a team of veterinarians, working full time and disappearing every so often into the labyrinth of intestines as they sawed, a week to chop up the carcasses and carry them off to be processed as soap and bonemeal. Berliners, so it was said, invented a recipe for cooking crocodile tail in such a way that it tasted very like chicken, and produced remarkably delicious sausages and ham from the dead bears. (According to Norman Lewis, in his book *Naples '44*, when the city was liberated by the Allies, its celebrated aquarium was emptied of its most exotic fish for a banquet to welcome General Mark Clark, who let it be known that he liked fish. The main course was the prize of the aquarium's collection, a baby manatee, boiled and served with garlic sauce.)

In January 1945 came a major Russian offensive, with one-and-a-half million German soldiers confronting two million Russians along an eastern front that stretched almost from the Carpathian Mountains to Prussia. Russian tanks, in their white winter camouflage, pressed on. On 17 January, Warsaw was liberated. On 19 January, the Red Army entered East Prussia. On the twenty-third it reached the Oder. The speed of the Russian advance, said the *Manchester Guardian*, changed the face of the war. 'How far is it now to Berlin?' became the daily question. By the thirty-first, General Zhukov's forces were forty-five miles from Berlin.

A pilot, describing the scene from the air, spoke of the advancing Russian army as a 'huge octopus weaving long tentacles among the Silesian towns and villages'. In under three months, the Russians advanced 225 miles.

The bombing of Berlin, on 3 February 1945, almost entirely destroyed the little that still stood of the Pre-and-Early History Museum. Fires broke out, and were soon too fierce to extinguish. Four hundred packed boxes, awaiting transport to some safer place, were obliterated. Unverzacht moved into the Zoo tower, to stay close to his most valuable collections. As the Allies approached, the growing realization that Berlin itself was soon likely to come under direct ground attack prompted debates about whether or not to evacuate some of the boxes and crates stored in the flak-tower. Despite the lack of transport, a number of boxes were moved to mines at Schönebeck, Grasleben and Merkers in Thuringia, soon to be taken by the advancing American troops.

The most valuable exhibits from the Pre-and-Early History Museum were at this point in their three original boxes on the first floor of the Zoo tower. There was no way of moving them without Unverzacht's permission. Some kind of dispute now seems to have broken out between him and the Berlin authorities, because when an order arrived for the boxes to be evacuated, Unverzacht refused to let them go.

By the middle of April 1945, the Red Army was closing in. All of Unverzacht's collections now lay scattered – in the heavily damaged basements of his museum, in the vaults of the Neuer Munze, in salt mines now in enemy hands. But the three boxes, with the gold, silver, bronze and jewellery from Troy, remained in the Zoo tower; and there they stayed, as the Russians began the final advance on Berlin.

16

IN TEMPORARY KEEPING

Marshal Zhukov, the deputy Supreme Commander-in-Chief of the Red Army, had decided to launch the final battle for the city two hours before dawn, on 16 April 1945. The Allies had long accepted that the war could not end without the fall of Berlin. 'We shall fight before Berlin', had declared the Reich Labour Minister, Robert Ley, 'for Berlin and behind Berlin'. With searchlights and the headlights of the leading tanks switched on, just under half a million Soviet troops prepared for the final offensive against the Third Reich. In the preceding weeks, Zhukov had insisted that the assault troops undergo special training in street-fighting. By 20 April, the first combat units were on the city outskirts. By 26 April, Berlin was surrounded. As they advanced, the artillery reduced to rubble all that stood in its way, while multiple phosphorous rockets were fired at close range, starting fires that spread rapidly through the city. The Red Army tanks forced their way through the barricades erected to resist them, their guns destroying what remained of Berlin's buildings. After them came the infantry, with hand grenades, sub-machine-guns and flame-throwers.

Though the German resistance was fierce, the majority of the 90,000 troops left to guard Berlin were Hitler Youth or Nazi Home Guard, poorly equipped and ill-trained, under the leadership of Goebbels, Gauleiter of the city. The only efficient soldiers were a handful of SS and Luftwaffe, and no more than 25,000 men of the fifty-sixth Panzer Corps, not enough to man the defence rings that had been set up around the city. Old men and boys did what they could. As the Russian troops fought their way towards the Reichstag, much of the battle was conducted in hand-to-hand fighting in the underground tunnels and sewers. A Soviet war correspondent, Nicolai Asanoff, described the city under attack as 'a place of sudden spurts of flame, deafening explosions and avalanches of brick and stone thudding into the street'. Retreating German soldiers had mined some of the pedestrian subways, and when they exploded, the pavements above burst open and flames spurted up into the air. Anyone seen trying to surrender to the Red Army was shot by the SS.

One of the main targets for the advancing soldiers was the Zoo flak-tower, from which the defence of the city continued to be conducted. General Zhuikov's men, fighting their way up from the southern tip of the Tiergarten, broke through the gates of the Zoo in tanks and drove up to the hippopotamus house, from where they opened fire on the tower, aiming for the steel-shuttered windows. The Zoo tower, as had been planned, was acting as shelter for Berlin's civilian population, 30,000 of whom had crammed their way into the building. When the Russians went in, they found people crushed together, terrified, sitting and standing on every step, floor and landing. The two operating theatres and the hospitals were working desperately as casualties flooded in, and amputated limbs and dead bodies piled up with nowhere to put them.

In the Zoo itself, an elephant, a chimpanzee, a few monkeys and some birds had survived the shelling, as had one male hippopotamus, found swimming wretchedly around its dead mate which was floating in the water, the fins of an unexploded shell improbably sticking out of its side. (More mysteriously, when Soviet troops entered the monkey house, they are said to have found Pongo, the largest gorilla in captivity, lying dead in his cage, having apparently been stabbed to death.)

The centre of Berlin was cleared, block by block, by the Russian soldiers. On the afternoon of 30 April, Hitler and Eva Braun committed suicide. Goebbels, who had planned to fight to the finish from inside the Zoo tower, blowing it up in the final stages with himself and all its occupants inside, now tried to negotiate a truce. When that failed, he gave poison to his six children, then shot his wife and himself. On 1 May, the Red Army raised a victory flag over the Reichstag; at six o'clock next morning, Berlin fell. Unconditional surrender was signed at midnight on 9 May. The Russians had mounted an extraordinary military operation to ensure the fall of the city: two-and-a-half million men, 7,560 aircraft and more than 6,000 tanks. Over 300,000 were killed or wounded in the final assault, and many hundreds lost their lives in the storming of the Reichstag. Not surprisingly, when the text of the Berlin surrender was broadcast over Soviet radio, the achievement was

hailed as 'the greatest event in history', a triumph of the Soviet army
and of the new Soviet order.

Berlin was a ruin. At least 100,000 Berliners were dead, their city
reduced to many square miles of rubble, their streets buried under
debris. The marvellous baroque buildings of the Unter den Linden, the
mile-long avenue of lime trees lined with cafés and hotels, where some
of the most elegant people in Europe had strolled before the war, had
crumbled to pieces, showering masonry on to cars and ambulances now
full of dead people. Everywhere, there was a smell of death. The canals
and sewers, home to many Berliners in the last days of the war, were
choked with bodies, as was the subway, after a last-minute decision to
flood it, drowning thousands of those who had taken shelter below
ground. Dazed survivors, who had endured not only four years of
intermittent bombing, but weeks of close-range artillery fire, emerged
from cellars, drainpipes and holes in the ground and wandered aimlessly
around. 'Berlin', wrote the correspondent for the *Manchester Guardian*,
'is a city of the dead. As a metropolis, it has ceased to exist ... I have
seen Stalingrad, I lived through the London blitz, I have seen a dozen
badly damaged Russian cities, but the scene of utter destruction, desolation and death in Berlin ... is something that almost baffles description.' Nearly every familiar landmark that had made Berlin one of the
finest European cities – the Opera House, the famous hotels, the Embassy
buildings and ministries – had disappeared; entire districts had simply
vanished. The Tiergarten looked like a forest after a bad fire.

After the first inferno of shelling and explosions, silence descended
over the city and long lines of displaced people, some of them drawing
handcarts with their belongings behind them, or carrying little flags
showing their nationality, came stumbling along the roads, trying to
avoid the craters, the smashed and blackened vehicles and the piles of
dead bodies. It was, wrote Wolfgang Leonhard, who entered Berlin
with the Russians, 'a picture of Hell; flaking ruins and starving people
shambling about in tattered clothing.'

It had been agreed by the Western Allies that they would stop when
they reached the Elbe, and leave the Red Army to take Berlin on its own.
While the Russian soldiers were still mopping up pockets of resisters,
Colonel-General Berzarin took up his appointment as the Soviet commander of the city and rapidly began to restore order. Instructions went
out to close the banks and freeze accounts; to hand over wireless sets,
cameras, cars and guns to the Soviet authorities; and for all members of
the Nazi Party, the Gestapo and the police to register. A curfew was

imposed from ten in the evening until eight in the morning.

In the wake of the Red Army came a number of Soviet secret service men, as well as German Communist administrators, recruited earlier from Germany and taken to Moscow to be trained. They proved extremely efficient. Water trucks were soon bringing in water to replace that of the reservoir and the canals blocked by rubble and corpses. Within a couple of days, military trains began to arrive at the stations. Every able-bodied German, even women and quite small children, was ordered to start clearing the city. Since the roads were piled high with masonry and stones, and no one could tell where they were, maps of the city were put up at all main squares and crossings. Within a couple of weeks, the electricity was back on, the trams were running and ration cards had been issued to all civilians, though there was no one who was not hungry. Small shops reopened, and the hospitals started to function again. Soon, even the Zoo was back in business, though scarcely an animal house was standing, and the only occupants were the elephant, the chimpanzee and the lonely hippopotamus.

The first Russian troops to enter Berlin had been the elite corps, whose behaviour towards the conquered Germans was soldierly. The second wave was very different. They were mainly supply troops, or back-up services: Armenians, Mongols, Lithuanians, Ukrainians and Tadjiks, rough, exhausted men, many of whom had been fighting the Germans for nearly four years, who had seen what they had done to Russian towns and villages, and heard stories about the extermination camps at Maidanek and Auschwitz. Some were themselves survivors of the German concentration and slave labour camps. They did not feel generous towards the Berliners, and nor were they encouraged to. 'Red Army Soldier,' said one of the posters put up by the Soviet army. 'You are now on German soil; the hour of revenge has struck.' Urged on by hate propaganda, and by their own memories of the war, these Russian troops went on an orgy of destruction, looting and rape. By the time some sort of order had been restored, 90,000 women were said to have been raped; many committed suicide.

In the Summer Palace of the former Tsar Nicholas II at Yalta, on 7 February 1945, Churchill, Stalin and Roosevelt had agreed that after Germany was defeated, the country would be divided up into three zones of occupation; and, after some argument, that France would also take a zone, to be cut out of the territory earmarked for the British and the Americans. The drawing-up of these zonal boundaries had put Berlin deep inside the Russian zone, and though there was talk of making some other city, perhaps Leipzig, the meeting point for the four zones, the argument for Berlin itself proved too strong. It was decided to form an Allied Control Commission, which would run Germany – and Berlin – jointly. On 9 June, Marshal Zhukov announced that he was setting up the Soviet Military Administration for the Eastern sector. But it was some time before the three other partners took up their own positions within Berlin. For two entire months, May and June 1945, Berlin was in Russian hands. This delay was crucial for the fate of the city – and for that of Schliemann's gold. At Yalta, the three leaders had also discussed the future of Germany itself, and the policy that would be followed over reparations, accepting, in a secret protocol, that it was only fair that compensation would largely go to those who had carried 'the main burden of the war', and 'suffered the worst losses'. This, too, was soon to have a bearing on King Priam's treasure.

Long before the Russians surrounded Berlin, random bits of information kept reaching the offices of the MFA&A in London about the extent of the devastation which the art first aid men could expect to find within Germany itself. Woolley had now been appointed head of the MFA&A Branch of the Control Commission for Germany, and by early 1945 German-speaking art experts were ready to tackle the enormous task of sorting out just what it was that the German art looters had actually done with all their plunder. There was very little reassurance to be had after the news reached London, smuggled out by a German art historian, that Hitler had ordered that all historic buildings and works of art inside Germany, whether looted or of German origin, should be destroyed rather than allowed to fall into Allied hands.

As it became obvious that Berlin was about to fall, the decision was taken to increase the number of MFA&A officers to eighty-four. The veterans among them were by now highly experienced, having spent the North African, Sicilian and Italian campaigns assessing the damage to art, clearing and cleaning it and supervising emergency repairs. What confronted them within Germany, however, was on a different scale altogether.

Within days of crossing the border into Germany, a number of documents concerning art works fell into their hands : these contained names of German forwarding agents and art dealers, notes on depositories, and some lists of looted items. Captured Germans provided further clues. From information sent out by an extremely brave art curator at the

Musée du Jeu de Paume in Paris, Mlle Rose Valland, who had been constantly threatened with arrest by the Germans and had none the less managed to discover the coded ERR secret numbers referring to art stores, it was soon possible to establish that the Germans had set up six art depositories above ground – at Neuschwanstein, Chiemsee, Kogl, Seisenegg, Nicholsburg and Kloster-Buxheim. But it was also clear that most of these stores had already been emptied when the Allies began bombing German cities.

Then, early in April 1945, while the Russians were beginning their final assault on Berlin, came the first real breakthrough. An art catalogue, annotated by one of the German teams of looters, was found by an Allied officer in Aachen. It contained references to a copper mine at Siegen in Westphalia. When the men from the MFA&A arrived, they found four hundred important paintings concealed in the mineshafts. Then came the discovery of a second cache, in the Kaiseroda salt mine at Merkers in Thuringia: 550 canvas bags, each containing a million Reichsmarks in gold; 400 smaller bags containing gold bricks; boxes of wedding rings and gold fillings from the victims of Auschwitz and Buchenwald; and pictures and art objects from fifteen of Berlin's state museums – including the Pre-and-Early History Museum. Some of Schliemann's Trojan vases at least were now safe. The men of the MFA& A suddenly acquired respectability; and art recovery, overnight, became a target for all army units.

No group of men proved more resourceful than those of the American Seventh Army. It was due to them that Goering's art train was captured. Throughout the spring of 1945, as Germany collapsed around him, Goering had often seemed more concerned about saving his art collecion than preventing the military defeat of the Third Reich. As the fighting came closer to Carinhalle, he panicked and began despatching trains in different directions with wagons packed with pictures. As Goering gave orders, only to change them again, the paintings, sculptures, carpets and pieces of furniture were shunted backwards and forwards, east and west, up one line and down another, taking shelter from Allied raids in tunnels. In a final shoot-out, the train carrying the bulk of Goering's collection was trapped and a number of pictures blown up. But enough remained for the American army to stage an exhibition, with a placard bearing the words 'Courtesy 101st Airborne'; it included not just art but Goering's gold hairbrushes and golden plates. American GIs, many of whom had never been to an exhibition in their lives, flocked to stare; in the process, two small paintings by Memling and a Cranach disappeared.

Next came the best find of all, in the Alt Aussee mine in the mountains near Salzburg. By now the skills of a detective were considered just as useful to a member of the MFA&A as a good working knowledge of German and some expertise in art history, and indeed the story of the saving of the Alt Aussee depository reads more like a thriller than an army operation. The Germans had been determined to blow up the mine and all its contents before leaving. But they left it too late, and it was not until the area was being overrun by troops from the 80th Infantry Division that a group of senior German officers found time to arrange for a number of crates, stamped 'Marble', to be delivered to the mine. These contained not marble at all, but bombs with detonators. Unfortunately for the Germans, news of what was going to happen got out, and bomb disposal squads were despatched to the mine in time to defuse the bombs. The Alt Aussee hoard, containing art works destined for Hitler's museum in Linz, was indeed an extraordinary find: in the various underground chambers, connected to each other by a network of tunnels, sitting on great wooden shelves built in tiers along the sides, the MFA&A men found Michelangelo's marble Madonna from the Church of Notre Dame in Bruges, Jan Van Eyck's Ghent altarpiece, a Greek sarcophagus from Salonika, paintings by Rembrandt, Egyptian tomb figures, tapestries from Krakow, Vermeer's *Portrait of the Artist in his Studio*, and works by Rubens, Reynolds, Frans Hals and Titian. There were 6,700 paintings.

The great diaspora of European art now went into reverse. The looted art was going home. But the imponderable question now posed itself: Where, exactly, *was* home ? In Alt Aussee, the various pieces had been numbered and catalogued. But as the war began to turn against them, so the German looters had given up making their careful inventories, and in the castles, farms, storehouses and mines which were now yielding up their treasures to the MFA&A, the Germans had left chaos, objects piled up one upon the other, with no clue as to identity or owner. In Munich alone, over 175 different hoards of Nazi plunder were discovered, while it took 120 trucks and 24 railway wagons to carry away the books and documents alone from the mine at Grasleben, to which some of the Troy finds from group two had made their way. The sheer size of the task facing the eighty-four officers of the MFA&A now became horribly clear to them: even if they could identify each piece, how could they find out where it came from or to whom it belonged ? State museums were one thing, but what about private owners, many of whom were now either dead or dispersed somewhere across Europe ?

How would their heirs know what had survived or where to find it? And while the MFA&A began the long process of identification, how were they going to protect all this priceless art, keep it warm and dry and safe from Allied looters? The official documents and papers of the MFA&A branch contain endless references to lack of coal for heating.

Munich was now the central collecting point for retrieved art, and each nation was allocated its own storerooms; other branches opened in Frankfurt, Marburg and Wiesbaden. A paltry sixteen lorries with drivers were seconded to the MFA&A. To these collecting points were now brought Nazis known to have been involved in the looting, to be interrogated by members of a new investigation unit. Here, too, came art experts and museum curators from France, Holland, Poland and Belgium, both to identify their own stolen collections and to help sort out the rest. Slowly, item by item, the pieces began to make their way home, the task of the art detectives made a little easier by the German love of bureaucracy, for a number of additional ledgers and catalogues of the plunder had by now turned up, together with thousands of photographs. In January 1945 Hitler had apparently decided that the entire collection of loot was to be catalogued, and though it had never been completed it provided an excellent starting point.

The MFA&A men, however, had to be more than detectives; they needed to be policemen as well. Looting did not end with the war. As they advanced, the Allied soldiers saw nothing wrong in 'liberating' the odd treasure from the homes in which they were billeted, and neither did the flood of refugees who were fanning out across the whole of Europe trying to get home. Sir Frank Markham, the Secretary of the Museums Association in Britain, was one of the MFA&A officers sent to Germany with the specific brief of tracking down the art stolen by Goering and Himmler. 'My job here is fascinating ...' Markham wrote to his wife in May. 'Three days ago I discovered Himmler's hoard of looted material ... Dutch masters, Gobelins, carpets etc, in a concentration camp, guarded by those who might (and very nearly did) finish up at Belsen ... There was a further hoard at a big farm ... the contents of what appeared to be a museum.' Early in the war, Himmler had restored a twelfth-century castle in the Westphalian village of Wevelsburg in order to open a school for the SS, and filled it with treasures brought from Berlin, most of them medieval. In 1943, the castle had been partly cleared and the art transferred to a farm nearby, where six rooms were filled with Russian paintings and a remarkable collection of antique cutlery.

As the US troops approached, in March 1945, the SS blew up the castle, leaving the former prisoners from a nearby concentration camp to start looting the farm themselves. Over the next few days, streams of skeletal-looking survivors could be seen staggering between the farm and the concentration camp clutching old masterpieces, tapestries and china, medieval armour and volumes of Diderot's *Encyclopédie*. Among the survivors were forty-one German bible students, who succeeded in curbing the looters and stored what they could retrieve in the camp laundry to await the Allied soldiers. Markham, who arrived at the farm with a car and a driver a few days later, obviously felt considerable sympathy for the prisoners in their desire to take away what they could as compensation for the horrors they had suffered. Writing to his wife about the 'Russian slave labour looting and rapining', he added: 'But after 4 years as slaves, they consider it no wrong to take it out on the Boche!'

This feeling lay, in fact, at the heart of what was soon to become a major issue of disagreement between the Western Allies and the Russians. The Russians had lost eight million men in battle, and up to twenty million more through what *The Times* described as 'German oppression, starvation and wartime hardship'. They knew at first hand all about the murder, robbery, slave labour and atrocities perpetrated by an occupying army, and they were learning more about German extermination camps and Gestapo torturers with every passing day. Their country had been pillaged and laid waste by the Germans, and it was estimated that it would take them at least ten years to recover. In April 1945, a book appeared illustrating tortures carried out by the Germans on the people whose countries they had occupied. The Soviet people, who had been led, largely correctly, to believe that, in spite of the Allies, it was really the Red Army who had borne the brunt of the struggle against the Germans, insisted that the 'whole German people' was to blame, and that they should endure many years of punishment and hardship before being allowed back into the comity of Europe. 'We shall forget nothing,' the Russian chief propaganda writer had declared, as the Red Army moved across Germany. 'As we advance through Pomerania, we have before our eyes the devastated, blood-drenched countryside of Belorussia.' Though, after the fall of Berlin, Stalin had insisted that the Soviet Union had no intention of 'dismembering or destroying Germany', it was clear that Russia had serious reparations in mind. This was not just because they had suffered most. They also felt morally superior. In this terrible war, insisted the editorials of the

Soviet newspapers, it was the great moral strength of the Soviet people, 'guided by exquisite, noble ideas', that had really secured victory.

Although Colonel-General Berzarin, Commandant of Berlin, had succeeded in restoring some kind of order to the city, there was not much he could do, even if he had chosen to, to staunch the looting that settled over Berlin while it remained solely in Russian hands. May and June 1945 saw what little remained of the glory of pre-war Berlin stripped and vandalized. It was not just small things that went, like power plugs, door handles and taps; entire factories were dismantled and packed on to lorries and trains to be sent back to Russia, to replace those smashed by the Germans during the years of occupation. Technology, in all its shapes, from typewriters to telephones, was particularly prized by the inhabitants of a country which had itself been comprehensively stripped of all *its* industrial machinery and transport. There was something more brutal and vindictive in all this than the epidemic of looting that broke out in southern Italy as the Germans pulled out and the Allies advanced. There, as Norman Lewis described the situation in *Naples'44*, a damaged and abandoned tank shrank day by day, as unseen looters unpicked it part by part, an orchestra playing at the San Carlo returned from a five-minute interval to find its instruments gone, a cemetery was suddenly emptied of tombstones, and all the manhole covers vanished overnight, leaving treacherous holes in the roads.

In Berlin, art was not forgotten. As the Russian soldiers combed through the ruins, they smashed everything they could not take away. There was, in fact, a Russian officer called Lieutenant-Colonel Piartly appointed by the Soviets as their MFA&A representative; but, despite his high rank, he had virtually no power to control the looters, occupying a place within the Education Department listed as 'subordinate to the theatres and the cinemas'. In any case, Piartly had little time for art; he turned out to be more interested in 'ideological questions, security and political purity of the German institutions and museums staff', according to the MFA&A reports sent back to Lieutenant-Colonel Woolley in London. And so the Russian soldiers were left to get on with their looting. In the shells of the once superb embassies, they ripped and chopped up seventeenth- and eighteen-century furniture, tore apart Chinese carpets, and shattered French Empire mirrors. The more discriminating soldiers, who sincerely believed that they were entitled to help themselves to anything they saw and liked, were soon to be found gathering up jewellery, glass, china and pictures. One early visitor to the city described seeing three Red Army soldiers leading a pitifully feeble horse which was dragging a handcart with a Bechstein piano perched on top; when the horse collapsed into a crater, the Bechstein, with the searing of splintering wood, toppled into the mud. Old plates, or worthless radio sets, were wrapped up in Dürer prints torn from their frames to make them easier to carry away.

It is in this context, a Russian army in the mood to punish and claim compensation, that what happened later to Schliemann's treasure has to be seen.

The final assault on Berlin had taken its toll on European masterpieces. Many of those already looted once by the Germans and buffeted about on the backs of lorries, were about to be moved yet again, and this time some were never to reappear. Art looting had not yet come to an end.

The flak-tower in Friedrichshain resisted the Red Army onslaught for a while, but the combined forces of several tanks and artillery shells eventually managed to reduce part of it to rubble. Flames apparently consumed much of the warehouse floor, containing paintings by Botticelli, Ghirlandaio, Signorelli, Titian and Rubens. What remained in the way of art objects – the Germans were later to say 20,000, the Russians only 11 – was removed and disappeared without trace. The Zoo tower, however, remained intact. During the last heavy bombardments Unverzacht had, like a captain at sea, stayed with his collection, sleeping, so he later said, on top of the boxes, waiting to see what would happen next. In a letter, written some time after the war, he spoke of the last few days as a nightmare of explosions, with shots raining down on to the tower, fires spreading round the surrounding buildings, and thousands of refugees clamouring for shelter. On the evening of 1 May, Dr Werner Stanfinger, senior medical officer in charge of the hospital inside the flak-tower, formally surrendered to the Red Army.

Stalin, too, seems to have had a dream about a museum of world art; but his dream was altogether more ambitious than that of Hitler. He is said to have wanted this to encompass not just art, but science, technology and history, so that the past in all its forms could be put on show to educate and entertain the Soviet people. Though Stalin's own personal taste ran more to the cinema – he is reported to have seen Alexander Korda's *Lady Hamilton* thirty-eight times – he did believe in the educative powers of art, while favouring 'social realism', pictures of cheerful peasants riding tractors, over decadent Western nudes. What happened next, in the saga of World War II and the looting of art, is pieced together from references in Unverzacht's diaries and letters, from the documents found by the two Russian art experts, Konstantin Akinsha and Grigorii Kozlov, in the Moscow state archives, and from clues picked up and put into some kind of order over the years by Klaus Goldmann, director of the new Pre-and-Early History Museum in the Charlottenburg Palace in Berlin, who has devoted much of his professional life to recovering the collections dispersed and stolen during the war years. It is an extraordinary tale.

Before the final push on Germany, Stalin, at a special meeting of the Politburo, apparently authorized the setting-up of a number of 'trophy brigades', under the Committee of Arts of the Council of People's Commissars of the USSR. These were to consist of small groups of art experts, usually fewer than four people, each with the rank of Major, travelling together within the Russian zone of Germany. Their task, like that of the men of the ERR and von Ribbentrop's battalion, was to scour the countryside for desirable art objects and bring them back to the Soviet Union. Though originally intended to be made up of art historians, museum administrators and restorers, in practice these brigades turned into motley teams of people with only the most tenuous links with art. One had a circus manager in charge. Appointments to the trophy brigades were as random as they were absurd. Boris Brodsky, who has since written a book on the Soviet private art collections, tells of a writer friend who was summoned to the Ministry of Culture in 1945, handed the uniform of a major, some money, and a ticket to Germany, and instructed to bring back something good. This friend did not know much about art, but it seemed a promising assignment. The only problem was that he had an enormous head. When the moment came to select a major's cap, not one could be found to fit. It looked as if the whole mission might now be cancelled. But the writer had a friend in the army who was also a major and had an enormous head. After bribing his friend with a vast sum, he returned with a very battered but capacious cap, with which he was finally allowed to proceed to Germany.

Andrei Chegodaev, a prominent art historian in Moscow today, was one of a team of people sent to Silesia to forage for art. When he got there he found that not only was there no art to steal, but that his companions had no interest in the arts whatsoever. He broke away on his own, and eventually returned to the Soviet Union with an extremely valuable collection of art books, discovered lying scattered on the floor of a magnificient country house that had already been looted by retreating

German soldiers. Chegodaev was to return twice to Germany. Once was to keep an eye on the other trophy brigades: by the autumn of 1946 there was no senior Red Army officer who was not on the lookout for furniture, clothes and china to take home with him, so that sealed cars, trucks and even military planes were arriving back in Moscow with the entire contents of rich castles and houses. The second time, Chegodaev went back to pick through what remained of Hitler's archives in the bombed Reichstag, where, in the basement, under a lot of rubble, he retrieved a number of recordings of speeches made by Hitler and several other leading Nazis at the height of the war. He took these back to Moscow on a military plane, piling them up to make a seat for himself on the journey.

There was little of the Nazi precision and orderliness about many of these Soviet brigades. They lacked Rosenberg's tidiness. Not only were many of their members ignorant and chaotic, but the whole enterprise was further confused by the fact that they were not the only official Soviet looters. Other, similarly directionless, groups, under the auspices of the Ministry of Finance and a number of the secret service organizations, made their own trips around the Russian occupied zone, taking whatever they could find. One art expert, a woman called Natalia Sokolova, now dead, has left memoirs describing her own activities as part of an art brigade in Silesia in the late spring of 1945. What she remarked on was the lack of discrimination among the looters, so that the things given to the teams of German women and boys ordered to help pack in readiness for transport to the Soviet Union – chandeliers, carpets, pictures, cutlery – were often of little value. However, not every looter was ignorant, and before the Russian pilfering ceased, over two million art objects of various kinds had made their way over the border.

There was almost no museum in the Russian occupied zone of Germany that did not lose all or the major part of its collection. Wiesbaden lost seventy major paintings. From the Siemens collection went a Delacroix flower picture, Manet's *Two Women in Black* and a nude by Ferdinand Hodler; from the Keller collection, El Greco's *John the Baptist*. Another El Greco, a *Saint Bernard*, and a ballerina by Degas were found in bomb shelters and despatched. Leipzig, Dessau, Schwerin, Gotha, Weimar and Wartburg all lost important works of art. The story of the stripping of some of Dresden's most valuable pictures has been told by Stepan Churakov, a prominent art restorer and a member of the trophy brigades during the war. Twenty-three of the Dresden Gallery's best and largest paintings were found by his trophy brigade concealed in the castle of Meissen. Because the original canvases were very fragile, they had been attached to newer, stiffer ones, and were therefore awkward to carry and virtually impossible to squeeze round the narrow staircases of the castle. The route along the Elbe had been blocked by an explosion, and so the trophy brigade had to load and unload the paintings several times on and off the trucks sent to transport them. At Pillnitz Castle, the pictures were unwrapped, then wrapped again in soft white cloth for the long journey back to Russia, and local citizens were brought in to help, in exchange for a loaf of bread and a bottle of burgundy for every two people. The train carriages allocated to take the pictures on the final leg of the journey proved too small; and so a special flatcar had to be found, and a hut built on top to house the paintings. The train, with sub-machine-gunners to protect it in case of attack, passed without incident through Germany. In Poland, however, the axle broke. And so it went on. Not until 10 August, several weeks later, did the Dresden pictures reach Moscow.

Within Berlin itself, the trophy brigades tackled a prize of a size that might have daunted any but the most determined looters. The immense Pergamon altar, with its famous marble frieze showing a battle between the gods and the giants, had been brought to Berlin in the nineteenth century from the coast of Asia Minor. Many years after the war, an American based in Berlin at the time, Dick Howard, described the day the Pergamon altar was once again dismantled. The man in charge of this operation was one of the most senior figures in the Soviet trophy brigades, a Major Druzhnin, former curator of the Tretyakov Museum in Moscow. He 'nodded taciturnly and forty soldier workmen joyfully attacked the sculptures with pickaxe and crowbar,' reported Howard. 'The friezes were ripped anew from their walls, loaded upon flatcars, and were never seen again. About a hundred other first-class Greek sculptures and architectural pieces . . . went with them.' By the time they had finished with the Department of Greek Antiquity, Major Druzhnin and his men had made off with 70,000 Greek vases, 1800 statues and 6500 terracotta and Tanagra figurines. It was a haul that Rosenberg himself would have been proud of.

The removal of the treasures from the Zoo flak-tower, the three sealed boxes containing Schliemann's gold from Troy, was one of the best-organized thefts of them all. A few hours after the surrender of the tower to the Red Army, Unverzacht asked the senior Soviet officer in charge for help in protecting his treasures. His fear, more than justified

by what was going on all round the city, was that they might otherwise
be looted by the ordinary troops. On 2 May, a number of Soviet soldiers
were posted outside the storeroom. Unverzacht was told to remain at
his post. The next day, a commission from the trophy brigades appeared
at the tower to discuss the future of the collection. It was followed by
Colonel-General Berzarin, who inspected the sealed crates and informed
Unverzacht that a Soviet art team would arrive shortly to supervise the
transporting of the crates to a safe place. What, or where, that place
would be, he did not say. On 5 May, Unverzacht was officially named
'Director of the Flak-tower museum', given a special pass and told to
report directly to the new Russian Commandant in charge of the building. Some wounded soldiers, who had been occupying part of the storeroom, were now, at his request, moved elsewhere. In the days that
followed, Unverzacht made several journeys to inspect what was left of
his museum, and to see whether anything could still be salvaged from
its ruined basement. On 12 May, the sealed boxes were opened,
inspected, found complete and resealed.

There is some confusion about the exact date on which they left the
safety of the Zoo tower storeroom, but by 26 June, when a special
commissar had a final meeting with Unverzacht, they were gone. 'The
best pieces from Heinrich Schliemann's collection have been taken into
safety by the Russian's', Unverzacht was to tell a friend. He never saw
them again. He was later to justify the readiness with which he turned
one of Germany's most prized possessions over to the Red Army by
saying that he could think of no better way of protecting it from the
casual soldier looters, who would surely have broken up the collection
beyond all salvaging; and that, in any case, his experience of the restitutions following the First World War convinced him that the Soviets
would hand them back to the Germans as soon as the terms of peace had
been agreed.

From documents that came to light only when Akinsha and Kozlov
began their investigations, it is possible to follow the path taken next by
Schliemann's treasure. From the Zoo flak-tower it travelled by lorry
to the Russian headquarters, at number 4, Drachenfeldstrasse, in
Karlshorst, to the east of the city. Here, a three-storey building with a
large basement, and a disused slaughterhouse, had been turned into a
central collecting point for things destined to travel to the Soviet Union,
with a second overflow building not far away in a former private castle
belonging to the von Treskow family. Art was of course only a fraction
of the loot now making its way to Moscow, and it had been decided that

only the most valuable items would travel by military plane, the rest remaining to be transported by train.

Some time towards the end of June, probably on the thirtieth, a military plane carrying seventy-three major pictures, including Degas's *Place de la Concorde* from the Gustenberg collection, was due to leave for Moscow. Apart from the pictures, the three boxes from the Zoo flak-tower containing the gold items were included on the transport papers. In the event, the plane proved to be stuffed with fur coats and room could be found for only seventeen of the pictures; but according to the travel documents that went with them, there is no doubt at all that the three boxes were on board. Major Druzhnin, the overseer of the removal of the Pergamon altar, was later to confirm that he, personally, had seen them loaded on to the plane, and had himself signed the papers. These listed the contents as consisting of gold, silver and other objects, belonging to different periods of the Stone Age and to the early Middle Ages, much of it female jewellery and bowls and vases, the most ancient being 'from the treasure from Troja (excavated by Schliemann), that from Eberwald (the 6th c. BC), from Cottbus (the 5th c. AD) and finally from Holm not far from Duzen (the 11th c. AD)'.

Major Kopas, representing the Military Council of the Fifth Army, accompanied the treasures from Berlin to Vnukovo Airport in Moscow, where there was an eight-day delay while customs officers tried to match up lading bills with the contents of the plane, and to disentangle official loot from the confused hoard of fur coats and china, before the boxes were delivered, by lorry, to the Pushkin Museum. Here, on 9 July, they were formally signed for by a senior curator of the museum, Nikolai Lapin. Travel documents, found by Akinsha and Kozlov, confirm every step of this journey.

A Special Commission had been appointed at the Pushkin Museum, after the arrival of the first trainload of trophies from Poznan in April 1945, to sort through the art. The commission itself was made up of experts in the various different fields. One of their tasks was to inspect every item, and match it against any catalogue or document that accompanied it. Protocol No. 83, drawn up in the Pushkin Museum on 12 July 1945, described the contents of box number one as containing 259 objects from the Schliemann collection, including the famous gold diadem which Sophia had been photographed wearing. There were, it later transpired, a small number of discrepancies between the German list accompanying the box and the objects themselves, but these were of a very minor order and thought more likely to have been caused by the

haste with which the list was prepared than by any freelance looting
along the way. As far as is known, Schliemann's treasure from Troy
reached the Pushkin Museum virtually intact.

What happened to it then might have turned out very differently
if post-war politics had followed a different course. For by the time
Schliemann's gold was making its way from Berlin to Moscow, the Red
Army's Western Allies were at last, after many delays, taking up their
positions in their own zones of occupation in Berlin. From the first,
relations were extremely prickly.

The Russians had their own views about reparations. And while the
Western Allies continued to dither over the scope of a formal reparations
committee, and how to calculate replacement values of all that had been
lost, the Red Army and the Soviet secret services continued to help
themselves to what they thought they deserved. When they did reluctantly agree to send liaison officers to sit on the various Allied committees discussing restitution, the Soviet officers remained nonchalant;
they listened, but they promised nothing. And so the debates went on.
What was fair? Was a looted Rubens worth as much or more than a
looted Botticelli? Was a Meissen dinner-set better than a Louis XIV
chair? Come to that, was a destroyed fertilizer factory more, or less,
valuable than a bombed medical laboratory? From America, the
Librarian of Congress, Archibald MacLeish, noted drily that there was
something very peculiar in treating paintings and books as if they were
in the same category as locomotives.

Meanwhile, relations between the Soviets and the Western Allies
continued to sour. When the Americans and the British had finally
entered their sectors of Berlin, they had been greeted as liberators. The
Berliners had found two months of Soviet occupation extremely tough.
They were hungry, dispirited and frightened. Dr A.C.Kanaar, posted to
Berlin in the summer of 1945, was horrified by the 'barbaric' and
'uncooperative' attitude of the Red Army soldiers, and warned that it
was 'high time that Britain awoke to the menace which threatens Europe,
a menace which is not one whit less than that of the Nazis'. In July that
year, 105 Berlin children died as a direct result of starvation. One of the
more bizarre incidents reported to the Western forces occupying Berlin
was the looting, not of goods, but of people. In the district of Luckau, in
the Russian sector, all children between the ages of fourteen and eighteen
were suddenly rounded up and sent off to the Soviet Union, after a call

for a 'Slavonic element' to help rebuild the depleted Russian population. Since the Western Allies were effectively barred access to the Russian zone – though parties of Russian looters frequently made raids into the French, English and American zones – there was very little they could do to help. Major Stephen Terrell, in a long report to the British authorities, noted that the Berliners whom he interviewed all expressed a marked preference to 'be in any other part of the world than that of the Russians'. It all made the popular view that, once 'this vast struggle' was over, Russia would prove herself reasonable and eager to cooperate with her Western partners, sound somewhat hollow.

The Soviets, in fact, were not at all eager to cooperate; they were touchy, suspicious and deeply alarmed that the Western Allies appeared to be trying to set up a large European joint power using the industrial strength of the Ruhr as its base. People returning from visits to Moscow reported a difference of 'outlook so great as to make a common viewpoint an impossibility'. Within Berlin itself, the Western Allies, who had assumed that there would be fraternal meetings between the forces of the four occupying powers, and a certain easy flexibility between the zones, found themselves excluded from all but the most distant and formal contact with their Russian counterparts; Zhukov, insisting that nothing had ever been said at Yalta about access to the various zones, continued to prevaricate. A sense of division and isolation settled over the city. While the Red Army soldiers were constantly being warned against the dangers of the Western attitudes towards 'private property, speculation, predatory instincts, prostitution, offensive lack of esteem for the individual person', the British and Americans complained openly about 'semi-orientals in a generally lower state of social and intellectual development' than their own. An instinctive wariness towards the rougher of the Soviet soldiers is apparent in the words of one British officer, reporting to his superior after taking over an airfield from the Red Army. It was, he said, 'one of the most disgusting experiences of my life ... anywhere that affords cover is a natural lavatory ... baths, liftshafts, cupboards, chairs ...' Never, he added, had he seen such 'wanton destruction ... wire cables shot through, electric light fittings pulled away from walls ... furniture smashed and fouled'. When the leaders of the Allied powers met at Potsdam in July 1945, they found that not only had the Soviets already redrawn the map of Germany, and absorbed a further 3500 square miles of east Prussia, but that the very fittings of their bathrooms at the conference had been looted.

Suspicion soon turned into open hostility and bitterness. The Western

Allies could hardly fail to be aware of looting by the Red Army, but they were powerless to act, not least because the Americans, British and French had failed to agree on a joint policy for restitutions. By March 1946, there was still no formal joint commission and reports and documents of the time contain an endless series of complaints about Russian high-handedness and a growing irritation at the Allied failure to agree on guidelines. When a suggestion was made that all claims should go through one central body, the Russians declared that this would only violate the authority of the four powers; when, at the end of 1945, a Conference on Reparations was held in Paris, the Soviets boycotted it; when an Inter-Allied Reparations Authority did finally take shape, they refused to acknowledge its existence; and when asked for lists of all they had found in their sector, they stalled. Though the British had no detailed knowledge of the workings of the Soviet trophy brigades – whether concerning industrial machinery or art – Sir Frank Roberts, British Minister in Moscow between 1945 and 1947, remembers jokes going around the diplomatic community about the Soviet decision to keep flying Dakotas in and out of Berlin long after their other air routes had been switched over to the far more comfortable Ilyushins. Dakotas had removable seats and plenty of space for large crates and packages.

In any case, the Western Allies were not altogether guiltless themselves. True, pilfering of German treasures had been restricted to individual soldiers carrying off things they took a fancy to. But while negotiations over restitutions were at a particularly delicate stage, a number of senior American military officers suddenly launched what became known, with extreme bitterness, as the Westward Ho plan. This consisted in taking back to the United States from Germany some 202 major paintings – including works by Rubens, Rembrandt, Botticelli and Van Eyck – for 'safekeeping' (using Rosenberg's word), and to be sent on tour around the country. Though there was an immediate public outcry, and several of the senior members of the MFA&A threatened to resign or asked to be transferred to other jobs, it was two years before the pictures – valued at over £28 million – were finally returned.

The MFA&A men had good reason to feel proud. They had done an extraordinary job. No similar recovery of movable objects had ever taken place on this scale before. The treasures looted by Napoleon's army, after all, had been put on show in one or another of France's museums, while the looters, both official and private, were all French. In World War II, less than a hundred men, in the space of only a few years, had unearthed 1,700 depositories of looted art, most of them fortunately in the American zone. Surrounded by chaos, fighting daily battles over inter-Allied rivalries, in the teeth of continuous looting by soldiers and refugees, they had identified obscure pictures, salvaged and protected untold numbers of pieces of priceless porcelain, worked out how to deal with collections from families whose members had been wiped out in the war, and travelled unbelievable distances – one man later calculated that his beat had covered 15,000 square miles.

By 1949, some three million paintings and art objects pillaged by the Nazis had gone home, to fourteen different countries, though claims for compensation continued to pour in. (Those for non-art objects make absurd reading – churchbells, an omnibus, four ponies and fifteen cows, a trawler, a wooden hut and a fire engine from one Dutch village, 12,000 kilograms of mangelwurzel and sunflower seed from a Soviet village. Even the Soviets, though they complained constantly that no amount of art could make up for the museums vandalized and burned to the ground by the Germans, had not done too badly : hundreds of crates of pictures, icons and scientific collections, 15,000 volumes from the Kiev research unit, and a fountain from Leningrad had been retrieved – though not Catherine the Great's amber room, whose fate to this day remains perplexing. Rumours circulated in recent years include a story that it was lost at sea in January 1945, when the ship on which the Gauleiter of East Prussia, Erich Koch, was smuggling out his loot, was torpedoed by a Russian submarine ; and another that it was flooded and destroyed when the mine to which it had been taken for safekeeping was blown up a few months after the end of the war.

As for the art objects stolen by the Nazis from other German citizens, they did not come out too badly either. One of the first tasks undertaken by the MFA&A, when they went into Germany, was to recruit local help. Though the process of denazification was slow – there are reports among the MFA&A papers on a Professor Dr Alfred Stange ('thoroughly unreliable'), and a Professor Dr Richard Hamann ('member of Party ; not ardent') – teams of former art specialists were soon at work sorting out how to restore all the art looted within Germany itself, particularly from the Jews, so many of whom were now dead. When the final tally of stolen art was made, 1,703,000 objects were found to have been taken from German citizens by Rosenberg and von Ribbentrop's men. The tally of personal loot which was not art – household furniture, race-horses, cars, silver fox furs – was valued at $87 million, and stolen gold at $263 million.

At the Nuremberg trials, thirty-nine volumes of photographs of objects taken by Rosenberg and the ERR were produced in evidence. They included a detailed inventory of 21,903 works of art. There were medallions and plaques, tapestries and Coptic textiles, folding screens and weapons, engraved gems and terracotta figures. Had the ERR managed to complete its task of cataloguing all it stole, the judges were told, there would have been somewhere between three and four hundred such volumes. It was, said the prosecution, a case of 'genuine spoliation', characterized by the 'systematic and disciplined' way in which it had been carried out. Both Rosenberg, who continued to insist that he had done everything solely in the cause of 'safeguarding' and 'protecting' the art he took, and Goering, were condemned to death for their crimes against humanity. But the part they played in stripping Europe of its history and culture was not forgotten when the Tribunal formally expressed 'the conscience of the civilized world against the plunder of public and private property, wanton destruction not justified by military necessity.'

By the spring of 1947, disputes over restitution had in any case been swallowed up by the far larger question of the future of Germany itself. While the Russians increasingly opposed the idea of a powerful and hostile neighbour on their very borders, the Western Allies kept pushing the Germans on the road towards economic recovery. After the coup in Prague in February 1948, and the setting up of one-party rule in Czechoslovakia, and with the growing numbers of refugees attempting to flee from the Soviet Union and its satellite states, the Allies stepped up their efforts to create a strong West German nation in order to curb Soviet expansion. What few shreds of cooperation remained between the four sectors turned into confrontation. In March 1948, the Russians walked out of the Control Commission in Germany and blockaded the western sectors of Berlin. The iron curtain descended; the MFA&A men began to go home; and all talk of restitutions, of art or of anything else, ceased.

In 1946, vast areas of the USSR were hit by a severe and prolonged drought. The country sank into a period of shortages and misery. Visitors reported seeing, from their train windows, sidings full of equipment and metal from the factories stripped by the Red Army in Germany, rusting and abandoned. The pre-war years had been marked by the brutality of the collectivization policy, in which some eight to nine million people died, and the reign of terror of 1937 and 1938 had seen at least four million others arrested and untold thousands shot. The return of peace, in 1945, witnessed a return to internal terror, and by the end of the 1940s the numbers of prisoners in Stalin's gulags is thought to have reached six-and-a-half million people. Art, looted or otherwise, was not a priority. In any case, social realism, and not the decadent art of Western Europe, was regarded as the summit of artistic endeavour. 'Patriotism' and 'optimism' were the words to use, and all art had to pass before a censorship committee. Chegodaev, who had been appointed curator-in-chief of the Dresden pictures held in the Pushkin Museum, remembers eminent guests, members of the Politburo and high-ranking army officers being brought to view them in secret. One day, in 1947, he received a message that Stalin was sending his secretary, Poskrebishev, to see the collection. Poskrebishev arrived, said nothing, stared and left; he was a short, stocky man, with apparently no neck, and Chegodaev found him extremely frightening. Next morning came an order from Stalin that the Dresden collection was to be put away and never shown to anyone again. It stayed behind locked doors for ten years.

Cultural austerity was reflected in shoddy buildings and vast new public works, while the paintings and sculptures brought back by the trophy brigades disappeared into museums seldom visited by foreigners, or into locked vaults in their basements. The looted treasures of the West were now an embarrassment, better forgotten. It became unwise to make any reference to them. And when the former minister of state security, Viktor Semyonovich Abakumov, was arrested and his entire collection of lavish furniture and carpets – looted from Germany – confiscated, other high-ranking former looters panicked and tried to get rid of all their rich treasures from the war. Alexander Georgievich Halturnin, who was working in the Ministry of Culture at the time, recalls that he was constantly being approached, in secret, for his advice about what to do with them.

With Stalin's death in 1953 came a slight change. A decision was taken by the Communist Party Central Committee to 'strengthen and further' the friendship between the Soviet Union and the German Democratic Republic, and as a first gesture of goodwill the remarkable Dresden collection of 750 major pictures went home. This was not just good politics. Much was made of a story that these masterpieces had been rescued by the Red Army from a store half under water, in which they had been falling to pieces, showing the trophy brigades in an altogether new and heroic light. As Natalia Sokolova helpfully put it in her memoirs, so poor was the care the Germans had taken of their own

pictures that they had 'lost all moral right to them. Now they belonged
to the Red Army, the only army in the world that carried on its banners
revenge to bandits and peace to freedom-loving people'. (The story of
the neglected Dresden collection turned out to be a total fabrication: the
pictures had been taken to safety by their German curators and kept in
a dry tunnel, heated by electric stoves, their humidity and temperature
constantly monitored.) In 1957 the Dresden pictures were followed
home by the Pergamon altar, which went to East Berlin, and by one-
and-a-half million art objects and 500 boxes of archaeological material –
all, of course, to East Germany as well.

While these returns were being discussed, every Soviet institution
with looted art was instructed to draw up a list of what it held. It turned
out to be a formidable haul – over 200,000 objects in the Ministry of
Culture special depositories, and many hundreds of thousands more
scattered between stores held by the Academy of Science, the Ministry
of Defence, the Ministry of Finance and the Ministry of the Interior. In
the monastery at Zagorsk, turned into a hiding-place for looted Western
art in the late 1940s, were sculptures by Donatello, Verrocchio and
Pisanello, as well as nearly six thousand drawings. These lists, among
the papers found by Akinsha and Kozlov during their searches through
the state archives, showed, in greater detail, how the Hermitage in
Leningrad had 180 pictures from thirty-one known Western private
collections, among them the forty-four drawings by Goya from the
Gustenberg collection, and 547 others from unknown places; and that
the Pushkin Museum in Moscow had works by Manet, Goya, El Greco
and Daumier – none of them intended to be returned. A document
relating to all these items bore the words 'in temporary keeping in the
USSR'. 'Temporary', in this case, has turned out to be almost fifty years.

It might have been for ever, had Akinsha and Koglov not come across
all the incriminating documents casually consigned to the state archives,
thereby prompting a torrent of enquiries, which, in Yeltsin's Russia, can
no longer be ignored.

And what of the Trojan treasure?

Soon after the war ended, Wilhelm Unverzacht lost his job as director
of the Pre-and-Early History Museum because of his membership of
the Nazi Party. Just the same, he spent many months trying to recover
his missing collections. It was a slow and depressing task.

Concealed in their hiding-places, scattered around what had turned into different zones of occupation in 1945, many of Schliemann's second-category finds – the pottery that he set so much store by, as well as coins and bronzes – vanished and have never reappeared. However, not all.

From Lebus, the archaeological centre on the River Oder which was lost and retaken eight times by the Russians during the final push for Berlin, and which in 1945 lay almost totally in ruins, eventually came back a number of crates and boxes. These contained pottery and some bronze objects, so mixed up that it proved extremely hard to sort them out. Among the contents was material from Troy. Everything from Lebus subsequently went to the GDR, to the Academy of Sciences in East Berlin, though very little of this was known until the fall of the Berlin wall.

Apart from the Trojan vases recovered from Merkers in 1945, the fate of the art objects concealed in the salt mines of Thuringia has proved extremely difficult to disentangle. Of the crates believed to have been stored at Grasleben – and transferred between Berlin and the mine several times as bombing intensified – only a couple had inventories to say what they contained. Grasleben, originally taken by the Americans, was handed over to the British several months later, by which time it had been fairly comprehensively looted, both by soldiers and by passing refugees. The salt mine of Schönebeck, to which a number of objects from Troy had been taken by barge, passed from American, to British, then to Russian hands. While under British control, the most valuable things that came to light were sent to Celle Castle, a former Nazi administrative headquarters which had been turned by the Allies into a centre for displaced people. Its basements were made into a collecting point for retrieved art, but soon the staff began reporting break-ins and thefts from among the packing cases. Since there were no lists, and no indication of where anything had come from, no one knew what had been taken from here either. The chaos into which Germany sank in 1945, both political and economic, was not helpful to art in general, or to Schliemann's collection from Troy.

For years, as Berlin was gradually rebuilt, pieces of pottery kept turning up, some of it in the ashes of the old museum in Martin Gropius Bauer. Even today, odd pieces continue to dribble back, in ones and twos, as further discoveries are made in former East Germany, to the modern Pre-and-Early History Museum in the Charlottenburg Palace. For a long time no original records could be found; but Hitler, in 1943, had ordered all leading museums to record their collections on microfilm, and when Unverzacht died not long ago his widow discovered a copy of the missing microfilm from the Pre-and-Early History Museum among his papers. It has been estimated that half of Schliemann's pottery from Troy has now made its way back to Berlin, and since the reunification of Germany, more pieces are drifting back as the museums of the former GDR sort themselves out.

The gold and the silver, the jewellery and the beads, that formed Schliemann's most romantic Trojan find, and which were packed up and locked away in the Berlin Zoo flak-tower, went on a far longer and more complicated journey. Their very value, and the special property of gold, made them different. The acting chief curator of the Pushkin Museum in 1957 was a man called Eliasberg, and it was he who signed the papers demanded that year in the general stock-taking of stolen art – and which were among those found by Akinsha and Kozlov in the Moscow state archives. One of them reads : 'Exceptionally valuable and unique are archaeological complexes such as the so-called Great Trojan Treasure ("Priam's Treasure"), and other Trojan treasures excavated by H.Schliemann and formerly preserved in the Berlin Museum.' In 1957, therefore, King Priam's gold was safe, if hidden.

The present curator of the Pre-and-Early History Museum, Klaus Goldmann, has always refused to believe that the treasure really vanished. Since 1972, he has been putting together piece after piece of an immense jigsaw that has taken him to America, to the archives of countless collections and museums, led to the questioning of hundreds of former soldiers and to the acquiring and scrutinizing of many microfilms and diaries – and finally drawn him to Moscow, to gaze at but not explore the Pushkin Museum, the vast neo-classical temple built in 1912 on the site of the headquarters of Ivan the Terrible's secret police as a museum of fine arts, and now best known for its collection of French Impressionists.

For almost half a century, Schliemann's treasure has lain in the Pushkin Museum's vaults. Having already spent several millennia buried deep underground in a large silver vase, it proved simpler for its new Russian owners to bury the gold once more. To the dark it was therefore returned, locked up and as effectively lost as it was beneath the mound of Hissarlik.

It is due principally to the tenaciousness of Konstantin Akinsha and Grigorii Kozlov, and to their remarkable finds in the Russian ministry archives, that the treasure is once again in daylight, above ground. Reluctantly, alternately denying and agreeing that the collection had been looted by Soviet Trophy Brigades during the Second World War and kept hidden away in Moscow ever since, Russia finally announced in the late summer of 1994 that it would allow a number of international scholars into the Pushkin Museum to see what was there. For the archaeological world, it was an extraordinary moment.

Germany was invited first, as the country with the strongest claims to it; a Turkish delegation came next, and finally one British and one American scholar. Wearing white gloves to protect objects, the scholars were given a day and a half in which to examine and handle the treasure. They came away content. The boxes in the Pushkin vaults did indeed contain, as they had been promised, Priam's Gold – authentic, and, as far as they could tell, complete. The gold and silver were there, the flasks, the cups, the beads, the earrings, the gold diadem and the headdresses with their 4066 gold leaves. Many of them, according to Donald Easton, the British archaeologist who inspected the collection, still have the numbers they were given when catalogued by Hubert Schmidt in 1902. Some of the strings of gold bead were found to be fastened at each end with sealing wax – with the faint remains of an 'S'. That, he says, 'could have been either Schliemann or Schmidt'. Bits of dirt still sticking to some of the objects suggests that they had scarcely been touched, and certainly not cleaned, since Schliemann brought them out of the ground in 1873.

'What we saw in the Pushkin Museum agreed closely with our expectations,' says Donald Easton. 'The pieces had been weighed and inventoried sometime between 1945 and 1949 when the Soviets had a change of mind about their war booty. But they had been neither cleaned nor treated.' The Soviets, he believes, looked after the treasure well, having repacked it in a new box, which was then sealed and not opened at all until very recently.

The experts judged the gold in the jewellery to be surprisingly dull, but could not decide whether this was because the gold itself was of an inferior sort, or because it had not been cleaned. The famous sauceboat was seen to be shiny and very heavy, while the workmanship that had gone into the detailed appliqué rosettes and chainwork of the head-dresses – made memorable by the stern portrait of Sophia – was pronounced superb. Setting eyes at last on this most prized of Schliemann's finds, Donald Easton concluded that, as in Sophia's portrait, the head-dress could only have been worn on hair already piled high, or on some kind of turban, otherwise 'the pendent decoration would have hung down over the eyes'. The discovery of the treasure opens marvellous possibilities for fresh analysis and new research.

The scholars received a further surprise. The Hermitage in St Petersburg also turns out to have some of Priam's Treasure – 414 items, mainly bronzes and pots. Precisely how they got there, no one can say. Schliemann's Trojan finds, which started their modern travels in baskets whisked away from Hissarlik by night, are now as surely scattered, and over a far larger area, as they were in 1939, when Unverzacht combed Berlin for places of safe keeping. Some are still in Berlin, others in Moscow, St Petersburg, Istanbul, Athens – and where else? A number of pieces are still unaccounted for – will they come to light?

The future of Schliemann's treasure remains uncertain. As of February 1995, Turkey, Germany, Russia and even Greece are laying claim to it, while the international treaties and agreements invoked by one side or the other – the Hague Convention of 1954, the Unesco Convention of 1970, the 1990 Friendship treaty between Germany and Russia – seem to lead only to further disagreement. Most discussions between Russia and Germany – the main contender – are at a standstill, the dispute made trickier by the political confusions besetting Russia more generally, and the fact that day after day new masterpieces and art objects looted in the Second World War are coming to light buried away in Russian storehouses and basements, all of them needing identification, accounting for, returning to their owners or putting on display.

Meanwhile, the opening of frontiers throughout Eastern Europe has released a flow of Second World War stolen art not only on to the black market in Germany but into the auction houses of New York. Enterprising and unscrupulous art dealers are busy locating and selling every kind of looted art, from prints to sculpture, oil paintings to armour, manuscripts to coins, with very little regard for fine-sounding international laws. Restitution committees, set up to discuss both who holds what, and who is entitled to it, are at work in Belgium, the Netherlands, France, Italy, Hungary and Poland, while changes of borders and governments continue to further confuse all questions of ownership. Russia, pressed by all sides, will say only that it intends to put on a year long exhibition of the entire Schliemann collection, opening in Moscow in 1996.

In this free-for-all, of claims and counter claims, of objects identified and objects still missing, of the enduring bitterness of wartime memories, of diplomatic inertia and political deals, Schliemann's gold has become a talisman for both the looters and the looted. The treasure hunt is over; Priam's Gold is found. But the next step, deciding who it belongs to and where it is to go, is only just beginning. It promises to be as tantalising as Schliemann's long flirtation with the great museums of his day. Lost, found, fought over: history is repeating itself.

What would Schliemann himself have made of it all? It is hard to be sure just how this volatile and choleric man would have reacted to the artistic tug-of-war now taking place. The smuggler and adventurer in him might well have laughed. But the reverence he felt for his Trojan finds was such that he would surely have been anguished to see them so casually scattered. He might have thrown his weight behind one idea now gaining grounds among a number of scholars and archaeologists: that a museum be built at Troy itself, paid for by international money, to house his entire Trojan collection, a museum of the world, belonging to all.

Perhaps only then could the treasure he struggled so hard to find, fought so furiously to identify, and then loved so well, be said to be safe at last.

SELECTED BIBLIOGRAPHY

The most important sources for this book are the travel and excavation diaries kept by Schliemann throughout his life, as well as his letters. All these papers – which run to many hundreds of thousands of documents – are held by the Gennadius Library in Athens. Schliemann was not only an extremely prolific letter-writer, keeping copies himself of all the letters he wrote, but a hoarder of paper generally – his archive includes receipts for bills, business papers, plans, newspaper articles and even the exercise books in which he practised his foreign languages. While some of the diaries and letters are now known to have been lost – among them a number of important fieldwork diaries – new material continues to come to light from time to time, written in any one of the many languages in which Schliemann was fluent. A general description of the contents of the Gennadius collection has been drawn up by Donald Easton.

Schliemann wrote a fragment of autobiography, which he included in *Ilios : The City and the Country of the Trojans* (London : John Murray, 1880), and a short memoir by him appears in Shirley H. Weber's *Schliemann's First visit to America*, (Cambridge, Mass : Gennadion Monographs II, 1942).

Schliemann's own major works include: *La Chine et le Japon au temps présent* (Paris : Libraries Centrale, 1867) ; *Ithâque, Le Peloponnèse et Troie, recherches archéologiques* (Paris : C Reinwald, 1869) ; *Mycenae : A Narrative of Researches and Discoveries at Mycenae and Tiryns* (London : John Murray, 1877) ; *The Prehistoric Palaces of the Kings of Tiryns* (London : John Murray 1886) ; *Troja : Results of the Latest Researches and Discoveries on the Site of Homer's Troy* (London : John Murray, 1886) ; *Troy and its Remains* (London : John Murray, 1875).

Two collections of letters, both published, are important: 'Schliemann's Letters to Max Müller in Oxford' (*Journal of Hellenic Studies*, 82, 1962), and 'Heinrich Schliemann and the British Museum', ed. Lesley Fitton (British Museum occasional paper, no. 83).

From the 1870s on, Schliemann was the subject of countless reviews and articles in most of the major British, German, American and French academic and archaeological journals of the day. British publications, in particular, covered his work closely. The most important of these are *Archaeology, The Quarterly Review, The Illustrated London News, The Graphic, Life, St James's Gazette, The Times,* and *The Pall Mall Gazette.*

In recent years, Schliemann has been a source of great controversy among modern classical scholars and archaeologists who question the truthfulness of his reports. Two people, in particular, take a sceptical line : David A.Traill and W.M.Calder III. Papers by them and other critics appear in *Myth, Scandal and History : the Heinrich Schliemann Controversy,* ed. William M.Calder III and David A.Traill (Detroit : Wayne State University Press, 1986), and in *Greek, Roman and Byzantine Studies, The Classical Journal, Archaeology,* and other publications, as do the excellent and balanced papers on Troy and Schliemann by Donald Easton.

A number of biographies of Heinrich and Sophia Schliemann have been written this century. They include *Heinrich Schliemann : Kaufmann und Forscher* by Ernst Meyer (Göttingen : Musterschmidt Verlag, 1969) ; *Schliemann : The Story of a Gold-seeker* by Emil Ludwig (London : G.P.Putnam's Sons ; Boston : Little, Brown, 1931) ; *The Gold of Troy : The Story of Heinrich Schliemann and the Buried Cities of Ancient Greece* by Robert Payne (London : Robert Hale, 1958) ; *One Passion, Two Loves : The Story of Heinrich and Sophia Schliemann* by Lynn and Gray Poole (London : Gollancz, 1967) ; and *Schliemann's Excavations : An Archaeological and Historical Study* by Carl Schuchhardt (London : Macmillan, 1891). An extremely useful collection of Schliemann's writings, with a considerable amount of biographical information, has been put together by Leo Deuel as *Memoirs of Heinrich Schliemann : A Documentary Portrait Drawn from his Autobiographic Writings, Letters and Excavation Reports* (London : Hutchinson, 1978). And Ernst Meyer has edited three volumes of Schliemann's letters, concentrating less on Schliemann's private life than on the archaeology and purposefully avoiding, as he puts it, 'commonplace and all-too-human' matters : *Briefe von Heinrich Schliemann* (Berlin : Walter de Gruyter, 1936), *Heinrich Schliemann Briefwechsel,* vol. 1 ; 1842–75 ; vol. 11 ; 1876–90 (Berlin : Gebr. Mann, 1953–8).

For Homer, I have used the translations of *The Iliad* and *The Odyssey* by E.V.Rieu published in the Classics series by Penguin Books (Harmondsworth : 1951) ; for Pausanias's *Guide to Greece,* the translation by Peter Levi (Harmondsworth : Penguin Books, 1971).

CHAPTER 1

The material for this chapter comes from personal interviews conducted in Moscow in July 1993, and from conversations with Konstantin Akinsha and Grigorii Kozlov, the two museum curators who first investigated the wartime 'trophy brigades'. Over the last two years they have published a number of detailed articles about art-looting in *Art News*.

CHAPTER 2
The tale of Schliemann's childhood comes from his own autobiographical fragments, letters in the Gennadius Library, and Schliemann's correspondence with Schröder & Co.

CHAPTER 3
The portrait of Schliemann in America comes from Shirley H.Weber's edited *Schliemann's First Visit to America, 1850–1851*, and from his other travel diaries. A good account of sea travel in the middle of the nineteenth century is to be found in *The Sway of the Grand Saloon: A Social History of the North Atlantic* by John Malcolm Brinnin (London: Macmillan, 1972), and in *Travelling by Sea in the Nineteenth Century* by Basil Greenhill and Ann Giffard (London: A. & C.Black, 1972). Dickens, Henryk Sienkiewicz, William Chambers, Trollope and Benjamin Brown French (in *Witness to the Young Republic: A Yankee's Journal 1828–1870* ed. Donald Cole and John McDonough (University Press of New England) have all left accounts of casual meetings with the American President.

CHAPTERS 4 AND 5
Accounts of the Great Exhibition of 1851 are to be found in the Official Catalogue (1851) and in contemporary journals and newspapers, as well as in *The Great Exhibition* by C.H.Gibbs–Smith (London: HMSO, 1950).

CHAPTERS 6 AND 8
Hundreds of books have been written about the rise of archaeology in the eighteenth and nineteenth centuries, as well as about Homer and Homeric archaeology, and Mycenae and the Mycenaean world. They include: *Homer and the Homeric Age* by J.V.Luce (London: Thames & Hudson, 1975); *The World of Odysseus* by M.I.Finley (London: Chatto & Windus, 1956); *Schliemann's Troy: One Hundred Years After* by M.I.Finley (London: OUP, 1974); *Homer and his Critics* by Sir John Myers (London: Routledge & Kegan Paul, 1958); 'The Making of an Homeric Archaeologist: Schliemann's Diary of 1868' by Mark Lehrer and David Turner (Annual of the British School in Athens, vol. 84, 1989); *In Search of the Trojan War* by Michael Wood (London: BBC Books, 1985); *The Women of Homer* by Walter Copland Perry (London: Heineman, 1898); *Greece and its Myths* by Michael Senior (London: Gollancz, 1978); *The Legends of Troy in Art and History* by Margaret R.Scherer (Oxford: Phaidon Press, 1963); *The Deep Well* by Carl Nylander (London: Allen & Unwin, 1969); *Gods, Graves and Scholars* by C.W.Ceram (London: Gollancz,

1952); *Troy and the Trojans* by Carl Blegen (London: Thames & Hudson, 1963).

Accounts of Crete are to be found in *Time and Change* by Joan Evans (London: Longmans, Green & Co., 1947) and in *The Find of a Lifetime* by Sylvia L.Horwitz (London: Weidenfeld & Nicolson, 1981); *Troy, Mycenae, Tiryns, Orchomenos: The Hundredth Anniversary of Heinrich Schliemann's Death* (Athens: National Archaeological Museum, 1990); *A Hundred Years of Archaeology* by Glyn Daniel (London: Duckworth, 1950).

Oliver Dickinson is the author of a number of invaluable books and articles on the Aegean Bronze Age and Mycenae: 'Schliemann and the Shaft Graves (Greece and Rome' no. 23 1976), 'The Origins of Mycenaean Civilization', *Studies in Mediterranean Archaeology*, no. 49 (Göteborg: Paul Aströms Förlag, 1977), *The Aegean Bronze Age* (Cambridge: Cambridge University Press, 1994).

Two helpful museum publications are *Schliemann und die Schatze Alteuropas* (Staatliche Museen zu Berlin, 1993) and *Troia: Kaleidoskop aus der Antiken Welt* (January 1994).

CHAPTER 7
There are many accounts of the siege of Paris; *The Siege of Paris 1870–71: A Political and Social History* by Melvin Kranzberg (New York: Cornell University Press, 1950); *In France Amongst the Germans* by John Furley (London: Chapman & Hall, 1872); *With an Ambulance During the Franco-German War* by Charles E.Ryan (London: John Murray, 1896), all give good accounts. The story of Schliemann's search for a divorce comes in *Schliemann in Indianapolis* ed. Eli Lilly (Indianapolis: Indiana Historical Society, 1961).

CHAPTERS 8–14
Good portraits of Schliemann in his middle years are given by W.J.Stillman in *The Autobiography of a Journalist* (London: Grant Richards, 1890); Arthur de Gobineau in *Lettres d'un voyage en Russie, en Asie Mineure et en Grèce* ed. Janine Buenzod, (Etudes de Lettres) Series II, Tome IV, 1876); A.H.Sayce in *Reminiscences* (London: Macmillan, 1923); William Borlase in 'A Visit to Dr Schliemann's Troy' (*Fraser's Magazine*, 17 February 1878); and Flinders Petrie in *Seventy Years in Archaeology* (London: Sampson, Low, Marston, 1931). An account of Schliemann's relationship with Virchow comes in E.H.Ackerknecht's *Rudolf Virchow* (Madison: University of Wisconsin Press, 1953) and J.H.Ottaway's 'Rudolf Virchow: An Appreciation' (*Antiquity*, vol. 47, June 1973).

CHAPTERS 15 AND 16
The story of Europe's looted art, and of the Russian occupation of Berlin, is taken from papers in the Public Record Office in London and interviews with

historians of that period. There is of course an immense library on the subject, but the following books were particularly useful: *Nazi Contraband: American Policy on the Return of European Cultural Treasures 1945–55* by Michael Kurtz (London: Garland Publishing, 1985); *Berlin '45: The Grey City* by Richard Brett-Smith (London: Macmillan, 1966); *The Berlin Blockade* by Ann and John Tusa (London: Hodder & Stoughton, 1988); *The Protection of the Treasures of Art and History* by Lt.-Col. Sir Leonard Woolley (London: HMSO, 1947); *The International and National Protection of Movable Cultural Property: A Comparative Study* by Sharon A.Williams (Dobbs Ferry, NY: Oceana Publications, 1978); *Loot: The Heritage of Plunder* by Russell Chamberlin (London: Thames & Hudson, 1983); *Stalin: Triumph and Tragedy* by Dmitri Volkogonov (London: Weidenfeld & Nicolson, 1991); *Decision in Germany* by Lucius D.Clay (London: Heinemann, 1950); *Men and Monuments* by Janet Flanner (London: Hamish Hamilton, 1957); *Battlefield Berlin: Siege, Surrender and Occupation* by Peter Stowe and Richard Woods (London: Robert Hale, 1988); *Russia at War 1941–1945* by Alexander Werth (London: Barrie & Rockliff, 1964); *The Jackdaw of Linz: The Story of Hitler's Art Thefts* by David Roxan and Ken Wanstall (London: Cassell, 1964); *The Fall of Berlin* by Anthony Read and David Fisher (London: Hutchinson, 1992); *The World We Fought For* by Robert Kee (London: Hamish Hamilton, 1985); *The Russians and Berlin, 1945* by Erich Kuby (London: Heinemann, 1968); *Diplomat among Warriors* by Robert Murphy (London: Collins, 1964).

For accounts of Schliemann's treasure while in Berlin, I have relied on the help of Konstantin Akinsha and Grigori Kozlov, and on conversations with Klaus Goldmann, Director of the Pre-and-Early History Museum, and Mechthilde Unverzacht, the widow of the museum's wartime director, who has also written a long article about her husband's work in *Jahrbuch Preussischer Kulturbesitz*, XXV, 1988, Series 317.

INDEX